PENGUIN BOOKS

HISTORY IN OUR TIME

'It is Cannadine's ability to open up the big questions which distinguishes his approach. He is without fear, unawed alike by conventional disciplinary boundaries or established historical reputations' Peter Clarke, *London Review of Books*

'Acerbic, witty and incisive, Cannadine is a pleasure to read' *Good Book Guide*

'There is an exuberance about Cannadine's style. His work pullulates with ideas. His erudition is formidable ... One of the brightest historians of his age' Piers Brendon, *New Statesman*

'His outstanding characteristic is that he makes history so pleasurable' Hugh Brogan, *Observer*

'David Cannadine is an enterprising empirical historian who has dared to venture where social scientists fear to tread ... [he] writes with lucidity, wit and panache' Ben Pimlott, *Guardian*

'A witty historian of the highest quality' Angus Calder, *Scotland on Sunday*

'Cannadine ... is one of the foremost historians of modern Britain' *Kirkus Reviews*

D0995015

ABOUT THE AUTHOR

David Cannadine was born in Birmingham in 1950, and educated at the universities of Cambridge, Oxford and Princeton. From 1975 to 1988, he was a Fellow of Christ's College, Cambridge, and University Lecturer in History and has taught at Columbia University, New York. He is now Director at the Institute of Historical Research, University of London. He is the editor and author of many acclaimed books, including *The Decline and Fall of the British Aristocracy*, which won the Lionel Trilling Prize and the Governors' Award; *Aspects of Aristocracy*; *G. M. Trevelyan*; *The Pleasures of the Past*; and *Class in Britain*. He is a member of the Editorial Board of *Past and Present*, and he is General Editor of the *Penguin History of Britain* series. He writes regularly for newspapers and reviews in London and New York, and is a well-known broadcaster on radio and television.

Aspects of Aristocracy, *G. M. Trevelyan*, *The Pleasures of the Past* and *Class in Britain* are all published in Penguin.

DAVID CANNADINE

History In Our Time

PENGUIN BOOKS

PENGUIN BOOKS

Published by the Penguin Group
Penguin Books Ltd, 27 Wrights Lane, London w8 5TZ, England
Penguin Putnam Inc., 375 Hudson Street, New York, New York 10014, USA
Penguin Books Australia Ltd, Ringwood, Victoria, Australia
Penguin Books Canada Ltd, 10 Alcorn Avenue, Toronto, Ontario, Canada M4V 3B2
Penguin Books (NZ) Ltd, Private Bag 102902, NSMC, Auckland, New Zealand

Penguin Books Ltd, Registered Offices: Harmondsworth, Middlesex, England

This selection first published in the USA and Great Britain by Yale University Press 1998
Published in Penguin Books 2000
1 3 5 7 9 10 8 6 4 2

Printed in England by Clays Ltd, St Ives plc

FOR EVE

Contents

Part Three: Persons and Personalities

Preface

This is unavoidably and unapologetically a festive and high-spirited book – a celebration of the endless diversity and fascination of the past (even when mainly confined to the last two hundred years of British history), and of the insatiable curiosity which drives historians and biographers to want to know about it, to find out about it, to write about it, to tell us about it, and to make us think and argue about it. Inevitably, this means there is controversy and disagreement in plenty in these pages: writing history, and being reviewed by historians, are not now and have never been activities for the squeamish, the retiring, the faint-hearted or the thin-skinned. But there is also appreciation, admiration and applause in abundance, and not a little mirth and hilarity along the way. Those who prefer writing about the past to be dry-as-dust or damp-as-squib will not enjoy this book. It is about praising history and (with one or two necessary exceptions) praising historians, rather than burying it or burying them. These essays were great fun to write and, taken in moderation, I hope they will be no less entertaining to read.

They were composed in idle moments between 1988 and 1997, and the place of composition was almost evenly divided between Britain and America, as was the original place of publication. The years in question encompassed the retirement of Ronald Reagan, the eclipse of Margaret Thatcher, the short hello of George Bush, and the longer goodbye of John Major. The eras of Reagan–Bush and Thatcher–Major were lengthy enough to challenge and to change the way we looked, not only at the present, but also at the past, and the essays collected here are as much the product of these contemporary circumstances as they are comments on them. They are history in our time. The most recently written pieces, on Kitty Kelley and Princess Diana, were completed after the British government changed on 1 May 1997. It seems likely that New Labour will in its turn help to create a new approach to the historical landscape: but the outlines are not yet clear. It also seems possible that the post-Diana monarchy will open up new perspectives on the royal past: but here again, it is too soon to tell.

One of the most pronounced features of the Thatcher–Major years was the increasing destabilisation and discomfiture of the House of Windsor, and the growing output of writing (some good, some bad; some historically informed, most not) devoted to analysing it and explaining it (to say nothing of helping to bring this destabilisation and discomfiture about). Another was the widespread discussion, both in the United Kingdom and the United States, of Margaret Thatcher's espousal and definition of 'Victorian values': was this the use or the abuse of the past, and of what relevance were these (highly selective) nineteenth-century conventional wisdoms for the political rejuvenation of late twentieth-century Britain, and the moral rejuvenation of late twentieth-century America? Yet a third was the completion of two of the grandest official biographies of our time, those of Winston Churchill by Martin Gilbert, and of Harold Macmillan by Alistair Horne, both of which resonated powerfully with contemporary discussions about the meaning of Conservatism, and about the identity of Britain and its place in the world.

These are some of the issues which are addressed here, as a comment on, and contribution to, the unending dialogue between the living and the dead that is the essence and appeal of history. Most of the essays are reprinted as originally published, except for the restoration of some unavoidable editorial cuts, and the elimination of unnecessary overlaps and repetitions. Two of them ended with predictions, which I have let stand, although only one of them subsequently turned out to be right. Soon after the publication of Phillip Hall's book on the royal finances, the Queen undertook to pay tax on the income from her private fortune: given his evidence and his argument, she had little alternative. But the appearance of Hugo Young's biography of Margaret Thatcher was the prelude to her downfall rather than the triumph at the next election which I had mistakenly anticipated on her behalf. The essay on Diana, Princess of Wales is literally the most occasional piece, written in the extraordinary days between her death and funeral. This, too, seemed best left unaltered, as a reminder of and comment on the mood of the time.

These articles originally appeared in a variety of publications, and I am most grateful to the editors of *The American Scholar*, *The Guardian*, the *London Review of Books*, the *New Republic*, the *New York Review of Books*,

The New Yorker, *Past & Present*, *Prospect* and the *Times Literary Supplement*, not only for their kind permission to reproduce and reprint them here, but also for having given me so much space on their pages to air my views and parade my prose. During the last fifteen years, I have written more than sixty of these extended essays, which is surely enough for one authorial lifetime. Accordingly, this collection brings to an end my involvement with this sort of history writing. Once again, I am grateful to those friends and colleagues who have urged me to assemble these pieces between hard covers, to my agent, Mike Shaw, for his boundless enthusiasm and encouragement, to my editor, John Nicoll, for being the best publisher in the business, to Candida Brazil for her work on the text and to Joyce M. Horn for her help with the proofs, and to Linda Colley for making life more festive and high-spirited than it would otherwise be.

David Cannadine
New Haven and Norfolk
Thanksgiving
1997

PART ONE
Royals in Toils

I

Family Monarchy

'A *family* on the throne, observed Walter Bagehot, in one of those honeyed phrases which may mean more or less than they seem, 'is an interesting idea.' Indeed, it is. But during the past two hundred years of British royal history, it is an idea which has embodied itself in two very different human forms. The first version, which has generally been preponderant, has been the *happy* 'family on the throne'. Think of George III and Charlotte, with their large, playful, gurgling brood, immortalised in Zoffany's delightful conversation pieces. Think of Victoria and Albert, happily ensconced at Osborne, all *gemütlich* and Christmas trees, with Landseer and Winterhalter conveniently to hand with their paints and brushes. Think of George V and Queen Mary, an inseparably devoted couple, who did so much to uphold 'character' and 'family values' in the rackety era of the 'Bright Young Things'. Think of George VI, Elizabeth and the two young princesses, 'we four', as the King observed with characteristically mathematical precision, 'the royal family'. And think of Elizabeth and Philip, whose domestic felicity was proclaimed to the world in the BBC television documentary which was inevitably entitled 'Royal Family'.

At first glance, it might seem paradoxical for Britain's kings and queens, the inheritors of one of the most stable and magnificent thrones on earth, to project an image of monarchy which has often been deliberately bourgeois and literally non-majestic. But it has resonated successfully down the generations, and part of the reason for this success is that it has resonated at a variety of different levels. During the late eighteenth and nineteenth centuries, when homely, suburban, middle-class values were increasingly thought to be in the ascendant, it seemed altogether appropriate that the monarch should both reflect and embody them. At the same time, the crown was losing its traditional, public, masculine functions of warrior-king and law-giver, and one of the ways in which it resourcefully reinvented itself was by projecting an image of exemplary domesticity and marital fidelity which matched and mirrored its evolving constitutional impartiality. All this made it easy to elide the *royal* family into the *national* family: George III was regarded as the 'father of his people'; on Victoria's death it was noted that 'mother's come home'; and George V was known as 'Grandpapa England'. This, in turn, meant it was but a step to envisioning the whole of the British Empire as a great global family, with the monarch at its head – a sovereign who, from the 1930s, made this sense of family and of headship real by speaking to his subjects every Christmas on the wireless in their own front rooms, whether they lived in Cheltenham or Calcutta, Canberra or Cape Town, Calgary or Cairo.

But as Bagehot was perhaps hinting, interesting ideas do not need to be right or true, and the idea that the British monarchy has been for the best part of two centuries a long-running Balmorality play is at best inadequate, at worst plain misleading. Far from inhabiting some idealised form of middle-class suburbia, royal life is carried on in vast palaces, with scores of servants, which makes any sort of comfortable intimacy or confidential closeness virtually impossible, while allowing the quirks, oddities and indulgences of individual character to flourish and luxuriate like hot-house plants. Most monarchs and their consorts have been badly educated, have little if any historical understanding of themselves or their circumstances, are not used to thinking or talking about their feelings, tend to bottle them up and bury them deep, and occasionally give way to explosions of towering rage, in which hairbrushes are thrown and crockery is broken. Not surprisingly, royal relationships across the generations have often been strained and distant, rather than close and affectionate. When Victoria and Albert married off their children, it was with dynastic considerations in mind rather than their own emotional fulfilment or personal happiness. Most eldest sons, interminably waiting to become king, have not been on the best of terms with the sovereign to whose death they looked forward with a debilitating combination of guilt-ridden anxiety and eager anticipation. And younger sons (and daughters, too) have often found their lives empty of purpose: cut off by their royal status, but unable to find anything rewarding with which to fill the time.

Hence the second, alternative model of recent British royalty: not the happy, but the *dysfunctional* 'family on the throne'. This, too, is an interesting idea. Think, in this regard, of the sons of George III, and especially the Prince Regent who became George IV: they drank, gambled, ran up debts, fathered bastards, and as a result became the least esteemed royal generation in recent history. Think of the Prince of Wales who eventually became Edward VII: he, too, enjoyed the gaming tables, was a serial and incorrigible adulterer, and liked to surround himself with the fast set whose morals were as loose as his own. Think of the Prince of Wales who briefly succeeded (and failed) as Edward VIII: he specialised in affairs with married women, drank American cocktails and ate club sandwiches, and threw away his throne to marry a twice-divorced American adventuress, by whom he sired no progeny at all. And think of the children of Elizabeth and Philip: three of them have been divorced, and the fourth is reputedly living in sin – though the exact nature of the sin being committed remains much debated. Although Balmorality has generally prevailed, or at least has been believed to have prevailed, among British royalty during the last two hundred years, it has been interspersed with very different modes of behaviour at Brighton Pavilion, Sandringham, Fort Belvedere and Highgrove.

Thus understood, the morality of British royalty has swung back and forth across the generations, and it is only by chance that the happy family model has usually predominated over the dysfunctional. Consider these alternative possibilities, any one of which might easily have come to pass. If George III had died younger or gone mad sooner, his sons would have had much greater opportunities to enjoy and consolidate their debauched and self-indulgent idea of monarchy. If Victoria had succumbed to typhoid in 1861 instead of Albert, Edward VII might have reigned and rogered for fifty years, which would surely have tried the patience even of the long-suffering Queen Alexandra. If Edward VIII had not abdicated, but had instead renounced Mrs Simpson, he would probably have moved on to the next married woman who took his fancy, then the next one after that. And if the present queen had decided to call it a day at seventy, then King Charles III and his mistress would by now already be installed in Buckingham Palace. It is impossible to know whether the British monarchy would have survived developments such as these. But on balance, it probably would have done: few sovereigns in modern history have lost their crowns because they have been unfaithful to their wives – or to their husbands. All of which is simply to say that a family on the throne is an even more interesting idea than Bagehot may have recognised, and that the relationship between monarchy and morality in Britain is much more complex and contingent than is often allowed.

Such complexities and contingencies are completely lost on Kitty Kelley, whose concern is merely to expose the royal family's 'secrets of alcoholism, drug addiction, epilepsy, insanity, homosexuality, bisexuality, adultery, infidelity and illegitimacy' over the years since George V changed the House of Saxe-Coburg-Gotha into the House of Windsor in 1917.[1] Her method, already perfected in her unauthorised and unflattering biographies of Frank Sinatra and Nancy Reagan, is to write bestsellers that take what she describes as 'an unblinking look' at their subjects – which might, of course, mean that her eyes are permanently open or permanently closed. To this end, she has spent four years interviewing eight hundred people, ranging from footmen to courtiers, she has ransacked files of press cuttings on both sides of the Atlantic, and she has read most of the books published on the royal family, some of which are scholarly and reliable, many of which are not. The result is a work so bad that Britons cannot realise how fortunate they are in being unable to buy it: wholly lacking in historical perspective or context, saying little that is new or interesting, devoid of any coherent argument or overall interpretation, tediously prurient in its obsession with human weakness, and written in prose that makes tabloid journalism seem almost fastidious. The great mistake with this book is not that it has not been published in Britain, but that it has actually been published anywhere else.

For all her claim to begin her story in 1917, Kelley has virtually nothing to say until she reaches the wedding of the present queen thirty years later. The reign of George V is passed over in a few pages, and she seems unexpectedly uninterested in the strained relations between that monarch and his sons, about which the last word has certainly not yet been said. The abdication scarcely quickens her enthusiasm, and the Second World War gets similarly truncated treatment. Thereafter, she slows to take us through the standard episodes: the births of Charles and Anne; the death of King George VI; the coronation and the Townsend affair; the marriages and divorces of Princess Margaret, Princess Anne, the Prince of Wales and the Duke of York; the fire at Windsor Castle, the *annus horribilis* speech; and so on. In telling this story she parades a cast of cardboard characters: the Queen Mother with her gin bottle and liking for gambling; Princess Margaret, the house guest from hell; the Queen, who is better with horses and corgis than with people; Prince Philip, a boorish bloke, with a preference for quarter-deck language; Prince Charles, by turns opinionated and indecisive, defender of faith yet a faithless husband; the Duchess of York, part national laughing stock, part global embarrassment; and the Princess of Wales, spending a fortune on clothes and colonic irrigation. And she gives cameo parts to the royal entourage and its hangers on: Lord

Snowdon, Raine Spencer, Major Ronald Ferguson, Koo Stark, James Hewitt, Madam Vasso and the rest.

Thus described by Kelley, the House of Windsor is part Evelyn Waugh, part Tom Sharpe, wholly *Spitting Image*. It is not so much that she descends to personalities as that she is incapable of rising above them. But this is scarcely to say anything new: 'too little, too late' has been the general verdict in America. Few people today believe that members of the British royal family are paragons of virtue, setting the highest standards of behaviour. On the contrary, many now relish the fact that the House of Windsor, which was not so long ago thought to be so virtuous, turns out to be nothing of the kind. But so what? Most monarchs, like most mortals, have scarcely been individuals of unimpeachable character (King John? Henry VIII? James II?). Indeed, compared with many previous sovereigns, the failings of the Windsors which Kelley describes with such evident relish seem relatively harmless, and exactly what one might expect of any isolated, privileged, under-educated, self-indulgent royal clan. Nor, despite sanctimonious and hypocritical claims to the contrary, do such revelations make any contribution to the serious debate on the British monarchy, which has yet to take place. There are important arguments to be made about the relative merits of an hereditary or an elected head of state: but not at the level of the human frailties of particular monarchs or presidents. No one seriously contends that the American presidency should be abolished because Bill Clinton (perhaps Kelley's next victim?) is a self-confessed adulterer. So why should the abolition of the British monarchy be contemplated because the same is true of Prince Charles?

In any case, given the present public mood, and notwithstanding the accumulated scandals of the past fifteen years, there is no serious demand in Britain for the monarchy to be abolished. Whenever the latest royal misdemeanour is reported, journalists yet again inform us that the 'end of the House of Windsor' is imminent. But they never advance from this apocalyptic hyperbole to address the question implicit in such predictions: how in practice would the House of Windsor be ended? One means would be parliamentary legislation abolishing the monarchy: this is not a realistic possibility. Another is that the crowds rise up, storm Buckingham Palace, and bear its occupants off to the guillotine: even in the unhappy and feverish week between Princess Diana's death and her funeral, this was not remotely in prospect. Yet a third is that the royals throw in their collective hand, and that the Queen, Prince Charles and Prince William decide they have had enough: this seems highly unlikely. The fourth option which, until recent events, did seem to be gaining ground was the holding of a referendum when the present queen dies: but since everyone now wants Wills to succeed as posthumous vindication for his beatified mother, this, too, is now beyond the realm of practical or foreseeable politics.

Scandal, it bears repeating, undermines monarchies, but rarely ends them. It may be true that, according to a recent editorial in the *New York Times*, the British monarchy now exists primarily 'for our amusement'. But as long as people find it amusing, and want to be amused by it, they will be happy to see it undermined but uneager to kill it off. What, then, if anything, is the broader significance of these recent royal revelations, of which Kelley's book may best be regarded as an uninspired anthology? It seems clear that the last fifteen years have witnessed a significant swing of the moral pendulum, away from the happy family which the British monarchy was believed to be up until the 1970s, and towards the dysfunctional model which undeniably now prevails. There are many, familiar explanations for this development: the increasingly intrusive and undeferential media; the pioneering misdoings, mismatches and misdemeanours of Princess Margaret; the foolish, indiscreet, self-indulgent and irresponsible behaviour of the younger generation of royals; and the broader changes in contemporary attitudes in the West to sex, marriage, divorce and single-parenting. It is not yet possible to say whether this amounts to a temporary rejection of Balmorality, as has been the usual pattern in the past, or something more long-lasting. But since the royal pendulum always moves sooner or later, we should not be surprised at this change, and nor should we expect it to be permanent.

There is, however, another way of looking at these scandals, which suggests that they are not just the latest cyclical fluctuation in royal behaviour, but are part of more deeply rooted and fundamental changes, both in and to the British monarchy and the British nation, of which the House of Windsor itself (to say nothing of Kitty Kelley) seems only dimly aware. But in order to get a sense of what they are, we need to see the whole of the present queen's reign in a much longer historical perspective than it is generally set in by courtiers or by commentators. The royal regime which prevailed during the 1950s and 1960s, and which in many ways survives to this day, was still that which had evolved during the later part of the reign of Queen Victoria: it was rich, grand, popular, imperial, ceremonially splendid – and also (at least outwardly) a happy family. The creation of this new-old style of royalty was popularly (and excessively) attributed to Benjamin Disraeli; it was, quite appropriately, a great-power monarchy for the great-power nation Britain undeniably was at the time of Victoria's Diamond Jubilee in 1897; and with the abolition of the Russian, German and Austro–Hungarian thrones during and after the First World War, it became the *only* surviving great-power monarchy. It went on to survive Edward VIII and the Second World War, and Elizabeth II inherited it, virtually unaltered, in 1952.

Since then, a great deal has changed. Britain is no longer the great power, or the great Empire, it was one hundred or even fifty years ago. But in other ways, very little (too little) has changed: for Britain still has a great-power monarchy, with imperial pretensions, both in terms of the way the thing works, and the attitudes of the people who work it. Inevitably, this means that the dominant theme of the present queen's reign has been the growing credibility gap which has been opening up between the late Victorian monarchy Britain still has, and the post-Victorian nation Britain has been becoming. The recent controversies over the fire at Windsor Castle, the Queen's forced and belated decision to pay income tax, and the future replacement of the royal yacht may best be understood in this context, and as aspects and indicators of this problem, though they are all too rarely discussed as such. The same may be said about the scandals and delinquencies of the younger generation of royals. For in bringing to an end the happy family monarchy, they have done more than merely move the behavioural pendulum: they have also knocked away one of the principal props to the old imperial monarchy. From this perspective, such a change not only looks more irreversible than cyclical; it also draws attention to the many other ways in which the old imperial monarchy has not changed, or has not yet changed enough.

To say this is not to argue that the House of Windsor is at risk or that its future existence is in jeopardy. But what it is to say is that if the monarchy is to be repositioned and reinvented at the centre of the life of the nation, then the widening credibility gap between the great-power nation Britain no longer is, and the great-power monarchy Britain still has, urgently needs to be closed. And since Britain under Tony Blair finally seems to be settling down to the realities and opportunities of being a middle-ranking European power, emancipated from the Thatcherite thraldom of post-imperial nostalgia and regret, then the only way to close this crown-and-people gap is to tackle the problem from the side of the monarchy not the nation. In prospect, the present queen's accession seemed to hold out the hope of a new Elizabethan age of global greatness and mighty achievement. This was a euphoric but deluded aspiration. In retrospect, the more challenging task of her reign was the progressive de-Victorian-isation of the British monarchy to keep it in step and in touch with the progressive de-Victorianisation of the British nation. But as the public reaction to the death and funeral of the Princess of Wales abundantly demonstrated, the second of these processes is by now well advanced, while the first has scarcely yet been adequately recognised, let alone begun.

If this is right, then the Queen urgently needs to find a downsizing Disraeli who can de-imperialize the British monarchy, and get it out of the late-Victorian time warp in which it remains in so many ways trapped. Self-evidently, this is not a job for which Kitty Kelley should apply. Rumour has it that the Queen, the Prince of Wales, their relatives and their advisers are now giving this matter anxious (if belated) atten-tion. But how can they address this problem, when in so many ways they *are* the problem? And one of the ways in which they are the problem is that there are still too many royals around. In the days when Britain was a great power and a great empire, this did not seem incongruous or inappropriate. But if there is to be a downsized monarchy to match a downsized Britain, there must be a downsized royal family, restricted to a central stem consisting of the Queen Mother, the Queen, Prince Philip, the Prince of Wales and his two sons. As for the rest, it is not enough to have removed them from the civil list: the title of Royal Highness should be abolished, they should no longer be bowed or curtsied to, their names should be removed from the court circular, and they should be encour-aged to seek alternative accommodation and employment in private life. 'A family on the throne' is indeed 'an interesting idea': but in late twentieth-century, post-imperial Britain, it is an idea whose time ought finally to have passed.

(1997)

NOTE

1 Kitty Kelley, *The Royals* (New York, 1997).

2
Midas Monarchy

In 1871, when Queen Victoria was in the tenth year of her widowhood, and when even the great British public was becoming increasingly irritated by her continued seclusion at Windsor, Osborne and Balmoral, a young, clever, radical MP, named George Otto Trevelyan, published a pamphlet in which he had the effrontery to ask *What Does She Do with It?* Where, Trevelyan wanted to know, was all the money going which the Queen was paid by the government for the sole purpose of maintaining the duties and dignities of her position as head of state? Instead of being spent as it should have been, on court ceremonial, public appearances and regal display, he believed it was being improperly applied to the creation of a new, and essentially private royal fortune. Like everyone else, Trevelyan could only guess at the true extent of the Queen's recently accumulated wealth. 'In the absence of authentic information', he observed, 'it must not be a matter of wonder that statements which are probably great exaggerations should find belief.' But whatever its size, Trevelyan had no doubt that the amassing of great personal wealth by the monarch was 'unconstitutional and most objectionable'. As far as both the history and the extent of this royal nest-egg were concerned, he believed that 'the people of England have a right to be informed.'

More than a hundred years on, Trevelyan's arguments have lost none of their relevance, and none of their cogency. It is generally believed that the Queen is the wealthiest person in England, and very probably the fourth richest individual in the world. But no one, not even Her Majesty, seems to know the true extent of her fortune. (As Bunker Hunt, the one-time Texas billionaire, once observed, anyone who knows how much they are worth cannot be worth very much.) Estimates range from £100 million, which is scarcely serious riches at all, to more than £3,000 million, which is truly a mind-boggling accumulation. One reason for this uncertainty is that no one really knows what to include among the Queen's assets. Her shareholdings, and her houses and estates at Sandringham and Balmoral, are obviously her own, private possessions. But what of the crown jewels, the royal art collection, the royal yacht and the royal train, to say nothing of Buckingham Palace and Windsor Castle? And it is also the case, as Trevelyan had spotted, that the monarchy's determined refusal to allow any serious investigation into its wealth leaves the field wide open for journalistic speculation. The British people may feel they have a 'right to be informed': but that right has been consistently disregarded, and the 'authentic information' has been deliberately withheld.

Yet it is not only the lack of hard data about the extent of the royal fortune which is extraordinary: it is also – and here again Trevelyan was absolutely correct – the very existence of that fortune at all. Before 1800, British monarchs were without private financial status, and could not personally own land. When George III's children overspent, as they regularly did, it was Parliament which had to pay their debts. During the early years of Victoria's reign, the monarchy was looked down on by the richest and most venerable aristocrats in the country as impoverished and parvenu, and the Queen's marriage to a minor, hard-up German princeling did not improve matters. And when her eldest son, the Prince of Wales, resolved to live his social life among the fast set, it was feared by those in the know that he lacked the financial resources to do so. By the time Trevelyan wrote his pamphlet, things were clearly beginning to change. But not even he could have foreseen the apparently exponential growth in royal riches which has taken place during the last one hundred years, as the House of Windsor has evolved into a wealth-creating machine which even King Midas might have envied. It is to the unravelling of this extraordinary development that Phillip Hall has devoted the last ten years of his life, and, as a result, he has produced a fascinating, indeed sensational, book.[1]

Between the Glorious Revolution of 1688, and the death of Queen Victoria in 1901, Hall shows that royal finances were transformed in three significant ways. The first was by the creation of what is still known as the civil list. Before 1688, when the king's government had truly belonged to the king, royal finance and state finance were inextricably linked. But as a result of the spiralling costs of the wars against France, and because of Parliament's desire to keep a tight grip on the army, the control of military finance was taken over by the House of Commons, and from 1697 the new king, William III, was paid an annual sum by Parliament, to cover his own royal expenses and all civilian aspects of government expenditure. (Hence the name civil list.) During the reign of George III, the civil list (which had been fixed at £800,000 a year in 1760 when he acceded to the throne) proved insufficient to meet the growing expenses of civil government, and these were gradually taken over by Parliament. By 1830, when William IV became king, his much reduced civil list was allotted purely for 'the personal dignity' of the King and Queen. As head of state, the sovereign was paid by Parliament, and every time Victoria sought more money – as when she married Albert, or when one of her children left home – it was to Parliament that she applied for increased funds.

The second development, which was an unforeseen consequence of the creation of the civil list, was the gradual accumulation of a personal royal fortune, where none had hitherto existed. The passing of the Crown Private Estate Act in 1800 gave the monarch private financial status for the first time, and allowed him (or her) to own land individually, and to make a will to dispose of it. It was under these provisions that Victoria and Albert were able to acquire the estates at Balmoral and Osborne, soon after their marriage, as their own personal possessions. But where did they find the money? Some of it came from unexpected legacies. Some of it came from the Crown estates in the Duchies of Cornwall and Lancaster, which were deemed to be the monarch's personal possessions, and which were providing a significant income for the first time. And some of it may have come from the surplus which was beginning to appear on the civil list, thanks to Albert's managerial skills in cutting the costs of the royal establishment. During the remainder of the Queen's reign, her personal fortune continued to accumulate, largely because – as Trevelyan guessed – public money paid to her in the form of the civil list was being transferred to her own private funds.

It was partly because of this diversion of public monies for private uses that there developed a third characteristic of nineteenth-century royal finance, namely that the monarch became a taxpayer. In 1842, the then Tory Prime Minister, Sir Robert Peel, reintroduced income tax, which had previously been levied on a temporary basis during the Revolutionary and Napoleonic Wars. The Queen was determined – or advised?: the documentation is incomplete – that 'her own income should be subject to a similar burden', and this encompassed her civil list, her revenues from the Duchy of Lancaster, and any private income. For the remainder of her reign, the Queen paid income tax, and it never seems to have occurred to her that she should not. Her eldest son, however, had other ideas, and when he acceded to the throne as Edward VII in 1901, he immediately asked the Conservative government of Lord Salisbury whether he might be 'relieved' of the income tax he paid on the civil list. Much to the King's regret, the Cabinet refused to budge, arguing that he must continue to honour his mother's pledge to pay, and an announcement to this effect was formally made by the Chancellor of the Exchequer in the House of Commons.

By the early twentieth century, it thus appeared as though a new regime in royal finances had been satisfactorily established – satisfactorily, at least, to all except those radicals who resented the accumulation of a private fortune from public money, and to the new King who resented having to pay any tax whatsoever on his income. By the end of her reign, Queen Victoria had accumulated a considerable personal fortune, largely from her civil list surplus and the revenues of the Duchy of Lancaster, and it was no doubt as something of a quid pro quo that she had continued to pay income tax. But in 1894, she also acquired a major tax privilege, when the sovereign was declared exempt from the newly levied death duties. In the course of the next one hundred years, this immunity was to become of exceptional importance for Victoria's successors, and it is a pity that Hall does not devote more attention to it. For while many of the greatest aristocratic fortunes were cut down once a generation, the personal wealth of successive sovereigns kept on increasing, and this novel tax exemption was very much a portent of things to come. For during the twentieth century, while the taxes levied by the state rose inexorably, the advisers of successive monarchs negotiated a series of exemptions, which meant that by the Second World War, King George VI was paying almost no income tax at all.

How was it that the tax-paying conventions, established during the reign of Queen Victoria, and reaffirmed by the government shortly after her death, were gradually but inexorably overturned? If he had had his way, this would have begun in the reign of Edward VII. Although Queen Victoria was possessed of an ample fortune by the time of her death (though just how much is unclear, since sovereigns' wills are not published), she does not seem to have left much of it to her eldest son, beyond the estates at Balmoral and Osborne. From the age of twenty-one, Edward had been entitled to the income provided by the Duchy of Cornwall, but this had never been enough to support his extravagant lifestyle. When he came to the throne, he was much in debt: hence his request, vainly renewed in 1904, for the abolition of income tax on his civil list. But

thanks to the excellent advice he received from such men as Lord Rothschild and Sir Ernest Cassel, and thanks – Hall suggests – to some shady
but lucrative dealing in the market for peerages, Edward soon got himself
out of debt, and on his death probably left a personal fortune in the region
of £2 million, which made him rich by the standards of the time, but by
no means fabulously wealthy.

Surprisingly enough, it was during the reign of that most dull, dim and
dutiful of monarchs, King George V, that royal tax exemption really took
off. In 1910, when he was eager to conciliate the new sovereign at the time
of the constitutional crisis over the House of Lords, Lloyd George, the
then Chancellor of the Exchequer, agreed to relieve the civil list of income
tax. Between 1913 and 1922, the sums paid annually to Victoria's surviving children, to Queen Alexandra, and to George V's children, were also
made very largely tax-free, as was the Prince of Wales's income as Duke
of Cornwall. And to compensate for his voluntary reduction in the civil
list of £50,000 a year from 1931 to 1935, George V obtained exemption
from the tax on his income from the Duchy of Lancaster in 1933. Finally,
at some point during the reign of George VI, the monarch's income from
private investments was also declared to be free of tax. Very few of these
changes were reported in Parliament, let alone the press. But in 1952,
when the civil list of the present Queen was being negotiated, the then
Chancellor of the Exchequer, R.A. Butler, blandly announced in the Commons that she was 'naturally' free of tax. And so successful had the monarchy been in concealing these recent changes in its tax status, that there
was no one who could gainsay him: it was simply taken for granted that
these exemptions had always existed.

But it was not merely that the reduction of the monarchy's tax burden
ran contrary to the spirit of the times: it was also that this enabled Edward
VII, George V, Edward VIII when Prince of Wales and Duke of Cornwall, and George VI to channel unprecedented amounts of public money
into their own private fortunes, both from the civil list and from the
Duchy of Lancaster. As a result, when the present Queen acceded to the
throne, she was already a very wealthy woman, having inherited considerable sums from her father and, very probably, from her grandfather too.
During the course of her reign, the increased costs of royal administration,
and the proliferation of the royal family, have meant that she has not been
able to save money from the civil list in the way that her predecessors did,
even though it was substantially increased in 1975 and again in 1990. But
she enjoys a tax-free personal income of more than £2 million a year

from the Duchy of Lancaster, and assuming, as seems possible, that her stocks and shares were worth £20 million in 1971, then twenty years of tax-free income and reinvestment suggest that her holdings are today worth well in excess of £300 million.

Here, more than anywhere else, are the signs that the tax concessions won since 1910 have enabled the private royal fortune to grow at an unprecedented and unchecked rate during the twentieth century. Assuming her investments of £300 million yield an average return (and since she is well advised, this must be an underestimate), then the Queen's stock exchange earnings cannot be much short, Hall calculates, of £20 million a year. Because she does not pay tax at the standard rate of 40 per cent on this huge unearned income, the Queen enjoys a bonus of roughly £7 million a year, or £20,000 *a day*, which can be ploughed back, so as to increase her holdings – and her tax-free income – still further. As Hall admits, these figures are little more than inspired guesswork, for the true extent of the Queen's private investments has never been disclosed. The 1971 figure, based on the then Lord Chamberlain's evidence to an all-party Select Committee on the Civil List, may be too high, or – more probably – it may be too low. Nor is it possible to find out in which companies – or in which countries – the Queen's money is invested, because she is exempt from any legislation compelling the disclosure of her share ownership.

How, Hall rightly wishes to know, has this remarkable state of affairs been allowed to come about, and to persist into the last decade of the twentieth century? Part of the answer lies in the single-minded skill and determination with which generations of royal advisers have presented and defended the royal case. Although British monarchs this century have been extremely well off, this has never prevented their representatives from pleading poverty on their behalf, and asking for more money or more concessions. Despite the fact that the historical evidence is, Hall claims, at best dubious, they have persistently and successfully asserted the sovereign's rights to enjoy the incomes from the Duchies of Cornwall and Lancaster. Whenever it has been suggested that the sovereign should pay taxes, they have resorted to the vague concept of 'crown immunity', even though this clearly applies to the government rather than to the monarchy. Yet at the same time, they have also resisted attempts to inquire into the sovereign's personal finances on the grounds that this is an unwarranted invasion of privacy. And so whenever it has been suggested that the monarch's private wealth should be taken account of in calculating the civil list, the Palace has simply stonewalled and refused to co-operate.

Perhaps the financiers and courtiers who advise the sovereign can be forgiven for defending the monarchy so zealously and self-interestedly. Less excusable is the behaviour of the civil servants, especially Treasury grandees, whose job is supposedly to monitor public spending. But all too often, Hall claims, they have been only too eager to accommodate the sovereign's wishes. Least excusable of all has been the craven behaviour of successive Chancellors of the Exchequer, from Lloyd George, via Neville Chamberlain, to R.A Butler, who went out of their way to help the monarchy in its remorseless pursuit of tax exemptions, not least by coming up with ingenious arrangements which meant that very often there was no need to tell Parliament what was going on. As a result, it has been quite impossible for backbench MPs to keep a proper, constitutional check on this inexorable accumulation of financial privileges and private wealth. Most MPs did not know what was going on, and even those few who had their suspicions were simply not well enough informed to ask the appropriate questions in the House. As a sustained display of dissimulation and deception, the winning of royal immunity from taxation during the twentieth century, and the consequent creation of a vast family fortune out of public moneys, is an astonishing story.

Put the other way round, this means that as a work of historical detection, *Royal Fortune* is a remarkable achievement, not least because its author was naturally given no assistance from the Palace. The Royal Archives were closed to him, as they are to most people who wish to look at recent material, or 'sensitive' matters, and some essential documents from the Treasury files in the Public Record Office had unaccountably disappeared. But by following up hints and suggestions in *Hansard*, by looking at the private papers of many of the figures most closely involved, such as Lloyd George and Ramsay MacDonald, and by combing the available official documents, Hall has managed to put together the first serious financial history of the monarchy in the modern period. Inevitably, there are parts of his account which are sketchy and speculative, his broader grasp of the historical context seems rather weak, there are some important collections, such as Lord Esher's papers, which he does not seem to have consulted, and his prose rarely rises above the level of the pedestrian. But for all that, the book is a major contribution to the current discussions about the royal family, and the blurb writer does not exaggerate in claiming that 'debates about the monarchy will never be the same again'.

It was one of the most unattractive and avaricious of Britain's twentieth-century monarchs, King Edward VIII, who once observed, albeit in rather a different context, that 'Something must be done.' And something certainly, and urgently, needs to be done about the royal fortune. But what, exactly? To begin with, Parliament should sponsor a fully comprehensive history of the monarchy's finances during the last two hundred years, which should be written by a reputable scholar, who must be given full access to all the relevant royal material. At the same time, there should be set up a Royal Commission on the Organisation and Finances of the Monarchy, which should establish the truth about the current scale of royal wealth, both public and private, and provide that 'authentic information' which Trevelyan rightly demanded more than one hundred years ago. This should then make it possible to set up a new Department of the Crown, under the auspices of the government, which would be responsible for the administration and financing of all the public aspects of the monarchy, and which should be headed by a permanent secretary, who might also double as the Queen's private secretary, and who should be recruited from the civil service rather than from the grouse moors. Most important of all, the Queen should be compelled by Parliament to declare her private wealth, and her private income, and to pay her taxes, as her great-great-grandmother and her great-grandfather did before her. Like so much else about the twentieth-century British monarchy, royal tax avoidance is nothing more than a recently invented tradition. But in this case, the sooner it is disinvented, the better.

(1992)

NOTE

1 Phillip Hall, *Royal Fortune: Tax, Money and the Monarchy* (London, 1992).

3
Constitutional Monarchy

Of all the memorable phrases that have been minted and mobilised to describe modern British royalty, 'constitutional monarchy' is virtually the only one which seems to have been neither anticipated nor invented by Walter Bagehot. According to Vernon Bogdanor, it was first popularised by Macaulay in his *History of England*, which was published more than a decade before *The English Constitution* appeared between hard covers.[1] But with this (admittedly important) exception, it is Bagehot's silken aphorisms and honeyed sentences which have shimmered and glistened down the decades, and such has been their evocative power they have both defined and inhibited the terms in which the monarchy has been understood and discussed by later generations. For it was he who first drew the distinction between the 'efficient' and the 'dignified' parts of the constitution; he who opined that 'the crown' had become 'the head of our morality'; he who insisted that 'a princely marriage is the brilliant edition of a universal fact, and as such it rivets mankind'; and he who warned that the monarchy's 'mystery is its life. We must not let in daylight upon magic.' Small wonder that Bagehot was studied in their formative years by George V, George VI, Queen Elizabeth II and the Prince of Wales. He brought the constitution alive, rendered royalty readable, and far from letting in demystifying daylight, made monarchy magical again.

Whether he ever got royalty right is a rather different matter. His work may have become the canonical text and essential handbook for twentieth-century constitutional monarchs, but no one would have predicted such an exalted and authoritative future when it first appeared. In its day, *The English Constitution* was no more than a piece of sassy, flashy, ephemeral journalism, which was neither as well informed as it was well written, nor as consistent in its opinions as has often been subsequently supposed. On close reading, Bagehot's remarks about the British monarchy are so confused and

contradictory that it is difficult to believe that any apprentice monarch could
derive much practical wisdom or prescriptive guidance from them. At different times, Bagehot seems to be implying that the monarchy is very
important, very much liked, and very splendid. But then on other occasions,
he seems to be maintaining exactly the contrary position. Nor should this
come as any surprise. For when he was writing, in the 1860s, it was hard
for anyone beyond the narrowest confines of government to know exactly
what was going on at Windsor, Osborne or Balmoral. Albert was dead, the
Queen was in seclusion, and the monarchy's power, popularity and
pageantry were all problematic. Inevitably, most commentators had trouble
making sense of all this, and despite his matchless style, much that Bagehot
wrote merely reflected and refined this confused contemporary discussion.

Consider his famous observation that 'it is only during the period of the
present reign that in England the duties of a constitutional sovereign have
ever been well performed'. This sounds definitive and authoritative. Yet it
is difficult to believe that Peel would have endorsed this view of royal
behaviour in the aftermath of the Bedchamber crisis, or Palmerston following his dismissal from the Home Office in 1851, or Gladstone when he was
vainly trying to carry Home Rule. In each case, the monarch asserted herself with a vigorous and successful partiality which also made a mockery of
Bagehot's oft-quoted claim that a constitutional sovereign had only three
rights: 'the right to be consulted, the right to encourage, [and] the right to
warn'. So far as is known, Bagehot simply made these 'rights' up, and
neither Victoria nor Albert ever recognised or accepted such a passive and
restricted definition of the royal prerogative. He believed that the crown had
a duty to 'watch and control' ministers, while she absolutely refused to be
'the queen of a democratic monarchy'. Indeed, in other parts of his own discussion, Bagehot apparently endorsed these much more aggressive royal
views concerning the sovereign's powers, and he recognised that the Queen
and the Prince had played an active and generally beneficent part in the politics of the 1840s and 1850s. 'The Crown', he concluded, in a characteristically knowing but enigmatic way, 'does more than it seems.'

Has the British monarchy subsequently ceased to do so, and if that is now
the position, then how, when and why did this change occur? Or does it
still continue to do more than most people suppose, in which case, what
does it (and could it) do, and is it right that it does what it does (and that
it could do what it might do)? These are some of the questions which Vernon Bogdanor raises (but does not always answer) in his wide-ranging,

important and provocative survey. He provides a history of constitutional monarchy which, after a rapid romp from Magna Carta to Queen Victoria, slows down when it reaches the twentieth century. He describes the functions and powers of constitutional monarchy (both actual and latent), the unwritten rules and conventions under which it operates, and the important part played by successive private secretaries to the sovereign. He mounts a vigorous and considered defence of constitutional monarchy as the best sort of head of state it is possible for any nation to possess. And he concludes by suggesting how the House of Windsor might (and must?) develop, adapt and reform in the future. As such, Bogdanor's is the most complete account of the crown and the constitution yet to appear, and it fills a big gap. For the author's words on royal finances apply to his subject more broadly: 'there are probably few members of the public who understand either the arrangements or their rationale. This cannot be to the advantage of the monarchy in a democratic age.'

As Bogdanor reminds us, the essence of constitutional (i.e. post-Victorian) monarchy is that the king (or queen) must act on the advice of the government, and must be publicly neutral in expressing political opinions. But there have also been occasions when the sovereign has intervened, sometimes at the very boundaries of Bagehot's three rights. In some cases, the crown has acted as referee and conciliator, seeking to bring politicians together in times of excessive partisanship or national emergency: in the crisis following the House of Lords' rejection of the 'People's Budget'; in the highly charged confrontation between Ulster Unionists and Irish Home Rulers four years later; and in the formation of the National Government in 1931, which Bogdanor thinks was probably the least 'constitutional' of these royal initiatives. In other instances, the monarch has exercised the power to select the prime minister in those unusual circumstances when neither the electorate nor a parliamentary party could make the choice: King George V in 1916 (Lloyd George) and 1923 (Baldwin); King George VI in 1940 (Churchill); and Queen Elizabeth II in 1957 (Macmillan) and 1963 (Douglas-Home). All these episodes were (and are) complex and controversial. But Bogdanor argues that in each case, the sovereign did the right and the proper thing.

Self-evidently, to give such a history of modern constitutional monarchy is to go some way towards providing an account of what it does. We all know that the sovereign appoints the prime minister (though usually this is little more than a formality) and dissolves Parliament (of which essentially the same may be said). There are also the weekly prime ministerial audiences, the contents of which seem destined to remain confidential, though it is a fair inference that this is the time when Bagehot's three royal rights come most regularly into play. But as Bagehot sometimes observed in his time, and as Bogdanor insists today, there was and is more to the royal prerogative than that. The monarch's latent powers still go far beyond warning, encouraging and being consulted, and may yet include the right to dismiss a prime minister, the right to withhold or compel a dissolution, and even, in a dire national emergency, the right to veto legislation. None of this seems in the realm of practical politics. But if proportional representation is adopted in this country, the sovereign will have more to do, not less. As continental experience shows, one party is unlikely to have an overall parliamentary majority under PR, the choice of prime minister and the formation of a government will be much more difficult and contentious matters than they have been for most of this century, and this means that the monarch will inevitably be drawn into the horse-trading of coalition-making.

If these developments come to pass (and Bogdanor seems rather eager that they should), then the crown will not only have more to do: it might be criticised in certain quarters for increased and excessive interference. The author is clearly worried by this prospect, and hopes the politicians will do all they can to 'protect' the sovereign, should it arise; for he is strongly on the side of constitutional monarchy. Citing the additional examples of Scandinavia and the Low Countries, he insists that it provides the most secure and stable support for democratic government that has yet been devised. Moreover, the crown furnishes a sense of continuity with the past, and embodies the identity of the nation as a whole, in ways that an elected president never can. The monarch may only reign by the consent of Parliament (as the 'Glorious Revolution' and the abdication both made plain), and it may be further fettered by being financially dependent on the Commons. But in the last resort, it is the sovereign and not the politicians who is the guardian of the constitution. Nor, Bogdanor insists, is it the monarchy which holds back reform and perpetuates class distinctions: as the examples of Japan and the Netherlands emphatically show, it is perfectly possible to modernise a country under a royal regime. If Britain today is excessively conservative and class conscious, it is not Buckingham Palace which is to blame: it is the weak-willed politicians down the road at Westminster.

Nevertheless, Bogdanor also thinks that the royal establishment needs to change – and that it is going to change. The rules of succession should be altered so they no longer discriminate against women. The Prince of Wales ought to get divorced, but remarriage would present more of a problem. The Royal Marriages Act should be repealed, the sovereign should no longer be compelled to be a Protestant, and it would probably be no bad thing if the Church of England were disestablished. The Queen does a good and important job as head of the Commonwealth, but there is no guarantee that it will outlast her reign, and in any case, a greater effort ought to be made to reorient the throne towards Europe. All of which is simply to say that the old magical monarchy has gone, and that a new, more practical monarchy needs to be developed which will be better attuned to the non-deferential spirit of the times. These can scarcely be called novel or surprising suggestions. Rather less expected is the ardour with which the author urges us to be more proud of the monarchy, and more pleased by it, than we generally tend these days to be.

As this summary should serve to show, Bogdanor's account is written as much in the shadow of Edmund Burke as it is of Walter Bagehot. He stresses the organic development of the British constitution, prefers evolution to revolution, and thinks stability is better than strife. He reminds us that it is only in this century that European monarchies have collapsed on a large scale, and that they have usually done so in the aftermath of war and defeat. He contends that countries that have lost their crowns, and have made the bumpy transitions to republics, are much less fortunate than those which have been able to keep their kings and queens. And he comes out strongly in favour of the importance and viability of the Commonwealth, and of the sovereign as its head. For those who have been awaiting a cogent defence of the British monarchy since the *annus horribilis*, this tough, unsentimental and well-informed polemic will come as very comforting news. And even those who do not accept these arguments would be well advised to agree with the author that it is going to be extremely difficult to get rid of the House of Windsor by peaceful means. As Bogdanor rightly insists, the most pressing practical question is not whether the monarchy is going to survive but, rather, what kind of monarchy have we got, and what kind of monarchy do we want?

This is certainly the most serious contribution that has yet been made to the current 'debate' [sic] on the British monarchy. But it cannot be, and should not be, the last word on the subject. Much that Bogdanor says about the secrecy surrounding the sovereign, and the uncertainty about the Queen's reserve powers, will merely confirm the views of those who believe that there can be no true democracy until the crown ceases to be able to do 'more than it seems'. It may be true that the monarchy is not directly to blame for the limited reforms that have taken place in twentieth-century Britain, but the conservative opinions of successive sovereigns merit more attention than they receive here. It is comforting to describe Britain as a democracy sustained and supported by the sovereign, but it might be more accurate to argue that the crown, the House of Lords and the secret world of Whitehall combine to thwart the people's will, rather than to give effect to it. And while the monarchy may be more a symptom than the cause of Britain's present malaise, this does not mean, *pace* Bogdanor, that it should be immune from investigation and reform. For if, as seems increasingly likely, proportional representation is introduced, the hereditary element in the House of Lords is diminished or abolished, and the Church of England is disestablished, then the monarchy will inevitably be significantly changed. To argue, as Bogdanor seems to be doing, that we should basically leave it alone, is thus patently unrealistic.

The real problem with this account is that the twentieth-century constitution provides too shallow and too short a foundation on which to construct a comprehensive discussion of the crown today. From a more ample and extended viewpoint, the best prospect for the future of the British throne lies in serious, self-conscious and long-overdue de-Victorianisation: stripping the monarchy of much of its ostentation, reining in the scale of its ceremonial, abolishing its established religious associations, reducing its dependence on the aristocracy and the House of Lords, and lessening its imperial and international pretensions, thereby narrowing the large, growing and damaging credibility gap which exists between the little England where we now are, and the great-power monarchy under which we still live. But to conceive and to carry out such changes require more historical understanding than is displayed here (or, one suspects, at the Palace), and a greater effort to see the monarchy in the context of British society as a whole than is displayed here (or, one suspects, at the Palace). As Bogdanor himself rather coyly admits, monarchy is not just about the niceties and secrecies and hypotheticals of constitutional behaviour: it is, or it ought to be, at least as much about imagination. Bagehot apart, this is not a quality for which commentators (or courtiers, or kings, or queens) have been generally renowned.

(1995)

NOTE

1 Vernon Bogdanor, *The Monarchy and the Constitution* (Oxford, 1995).

4

Welfare Monarchy

The second chapter of the Gospel according to St Matthew records the most celebrated example of royal charity in human history, as the three kings, atop their camels, and guided by the star in the east, bear their gold, frankincense and myrrh to Bethlehem. As this story makes plain, monarchs are customarily supposed to be vastly richer than ordinary mortals, and to give with truly regal generosity to those many unfortunates huddled at the opposite end of the wealth, power and status spectrum. But there was more to this mangered and magical moment than supererogatory royal beneficence. Even in the cosy, impromptu confines of the Christmas stable, the gift relationship was more subtle, complex and ambiguous than that. For there was also in it an implicit challenge, and a reciprocal presumption, that such exceptional presents, which were hardly of immediate relevance or practical utility, would eventually be matched by exceptional behaviour on the part of the recipient. And while those who offered these gifts were themselves only reputedly royal, the infant to whom they were given was unquestionably so, being none other than the future King of Kings himself. Monarchs, this story reminds us, not only make benefactions, they also receive them – which adds a suggestively majestic connotation to the otherwise plebeian notion of 'give and take'.

Despite this early example of right royal generosity, British sovereigns have until relatively recently been much more concerned with taking than with giving. Like most pre-modern monarchs, they were remorselessly acquisitive, seeking lands, booty and wives to enhance their riches, might and prestige. When they gave things away, it was with similar considerations in mind, which explains why they were more likely to grant estates and titles to close relatives or loyal servants than to hand out alms to the deserving poor. And when they spent, it was on themselves or their immediate family rather than on ordinary people: on castles, palaces, pictures, high living and conspicuous display – the essential accoutrements of confident, splendid, semi-divine sovereignty. At least until the late seventeenth century, this is what the British monarchy was: kings ruled as well as reigned, they dispensed justice, led their troops into battle, patronised painters and builders, governed the country, and made and modified its laws. By contrast, they spent little of their time, and less of their resources, on doing good works. From Edward II until William and Mary, they presented Maundy money to a handful of deserving indigents once each year; and from the Normans until the early Georges, largesse was distributed to the poor at royal pageants and progresses. Even adding occasional personal gifts, and the sporadic exercise of the royal touch, this was scarcely significant: on the whole, they preferred to leave charity to the church and the Poor Law.

Such a lack of royal interest in philanthropic activity and social amelioration should not come as any surprise: in a world where the sovereign's authority was divinely ordained and generally accepted by the majority of the population, and where poverty was the ineradicable condition which most people endured uncomplainingly, gifts to the poor were neither politically imperative nor socially worthwhile. But as the eighteenth century merged into the nineteenth, all this began to change. Many of the traditional royal tasks fell away, as monarchs ceased to rule, to make laws, to build magnificent palaces, to patronise great artists, or to lead the troops into battle. The easy assurance of the crown's authority was threatened by exceptional population increases, urban and industrial expansion, widespread popular unrest, the extension of the franchise, the growth of an intrusive state, new ideas about democracy, political revolutions abroad, and even occasional mutterings in favour of republicanism at home. And as wealth was created in unprecedented abundance, which was distributed more widely down the social scale than ever before, poverty was no longer regarded as a condition which had to be stoically borne, but was redefined as a problem which should certainly be alleviated, and might even be eradicated completely – perhaps by the agency of the state, but more likely by the massively proliferated voluntary societies which were devoted to philanthropic endeavour.

According to Frank Prochaska, it was in these changed and challenging circumstances that British monarchs first turned their attention to the sort of deliberate, large-scale charitable activity that their forbears had disdained, but with which we are now all so familiar.[1] Some did so out of a genuine sense of noblesse oblige. Others did so without pausing to try to fathom their motives. But in retrospect, this amounts to a momentous and very successful change in the direction of sovereign endeavour. It gave members of the royal family something new and necessary to do. It enabled them to reinvent themselves as anxious, concerned, generous, philanthropic, benevolent and public-spirited. And it held out the prospect that if they treated their subjects with such unprecedented consideration and condescension, then their subjects might continue to remain loyal and deferential to them in return. In short, this book describes how the royal family, by a mixture of lucky accident and conscious design, came to exploit the reciprocal potentialities in the gift relationship as part of their strategy for survival in an increasingly uncertain world. More precisely, it describes how the traditionally acquisitive monarchy was replaced by a new give-and-take monarchy, and how the familiar cast of royal warriors, law-makers, art patrons and demi-gods was swollen and superseded by a new and very different breed of royal social workers, hospital visitors, behind-the-scenes lobbyists and champions of voluntary activity outside the state.

Although there had been signs and portents of these developments during the reigns of Queen Anne and the early Hanoverians, the British monarchy first seriously embraced good works during the time of King George III, who in this as in much else was the father and founder of modern royalty. He allowed his name to be associated with many new philanthropic ventures, especially London hospitals, and personally gave £14,000 a year to good causes, which makes him, in relative terms, the most bountiful sovereign that this nation has ever known. Even his sons, who enjoyed a bad press in their days, may have escaped complete derision because they were more involved with charitable associations and voluntary societies than posterity has generally recognised. Predictably, George IV was less generous to others than his father had been, while being much more generous to himself. By contrast, William IV's erratic giving apparently helped redeem his generally deserved reputation as a reactionary buffoon, as did the conduct of his wife, Queen Adelaide, who on average was probably giving away some £40,000 a year. This not only made her, by a considerable margin, the most benevolent royal benefactress ever: it also prefigured those close connections between matriarchy, domesticity, kindness and charity which have been so marked a feature of the British monarchy from Queen Victoria, via Queen Alexandra, Queen Mary and the Queen Mother, to Queen Elizabeth II and the Princess of Wales.

These early royal philanthropists probably gave more in terms of money than they did in terms of time. But with Victoria and Albert, this state of affairs was reversed, and the familiar pattern was established whereby the main royal contributions to charity were sympathy, patronage, moral support and personal appearances rather than substantial regular subscriptions or occasional major benefactions. She concentrated on organisations concerned with women and children; he was more interested in educational schemes and the problems of poverty. Together, they spent a great deal of time on these good causes: perhaps more, Prochaska suggests, than on any other single activity. Gladstone was unimpressed, and regarded philanthropic work as an inadequate training in royal statecraft for their eldest son, the young and wayward Prince of Wales. But since Victoria would not let him read state papers, or go to Ireland as Viceroy, doing good was just about the only thing left for him – apart from doing bad. And like Queen Adelaide, but in a significantly different way, he turned out to be unexpectedly accomplished. As Prince of Wales, and even more so as King Edward VII, he was extremely successful in persuading his rich, parvenu, socially ambitious friends like Cassell, Rothschild and Speyer to give seriously large sums to the Royal Hospital Fund. Here was the role that his successors have also made very much their own: urging others to part with their money for charitable purposes, rather than parting with it themselves.

During the First World War, these philanthropic endeavours moved into an even higher gear, as King George V and Queen Mary started making regular, morale-boosting visits to factories and hospitals throughout the country. The demise of the Russian, German and Austrian monarchies, combined with fears for the future of the British throne, meant that these efforts were redoubled during the 1920s and 1930s. The Duke and (especially) the Duchess of York were dutiful, hard-working and good with ordinary people. But the Prince of Wales was much less enthusiastic, and as King Edward VIII he did not improve. When he observed in South Wales that 'something must be done', he clearly had not the slightest intention of doing anything himself. The Second World War was an intensified and more highly profiled repeat of the First, as King George VI and Queen Elizabeth regularly visited the bombed-out East End and blitzed provincial cities. But in 1945, with a Labour government hostile to voluntarism and enamoured of centralised planning, the whole world of royal-related charities suddenly looked at risk. In particular, the welfare state seemed to portend the end of those many London and local hospitals with which the royal connection was so strong and had been for so long. Not surprisingly, the King looked on these developments, which seemed to threaten one of his family's most valuable public functions, with considerable unease.

But these gloomy forebodings were not borne out. Even in the heyday of the welfare state, widespread voluntary activity continued, and there was still plenty for the Queen Mother, the Queen, Prince Philip and Princess Margaret to do. And as the welfare state entered both a political and an economic crisis from the late 1970s, the cult of voluntarism came back into its own, as a central tenet of Mrs Thatcher's 'Victorian values'. With a few conspicuous exceptions such as the disastrous 'It's a Royal Knockout', a new generation of Windsors has taken over where their for-bears left off. Prince Charles devotes himself to rather idiosyncratic and unfocused inner city initiatives, Princess Anne has transformed her pub-lic image by her work for the Save the Children Fund, and for a time it seemed as though the Princess of Wales was going to revive the legendary royal touch in her close, tactile encounters with AIDS victims. Today, most members of the royal family work harder at charitable activities than they do at anything else, and most voluntary organisations are clear that in terms of good publicity and enlarged public subscriptions, the benefits are real. As the author mordantly concludes, the British monarchy will not be in serious trouble until the begging letters stop arriving at Buckingham Palace. Notwithstanding the *annus horribilis*, there seems no serious likeli-hood of this happening in the foreseeable future.

Such is Prochaska's account of the apparently inexorable rise of the wel-fare monarchy, and he deserves high praise for the meticulous detail and scholarly originality which his book displays. Unlike much writing on the subject, he treats the crown seriously rather than sensationally, historically rather than biographically, critically rather than deferentially, analytically rather than anecdotally. As a result, he opens up a whole world of royal endeavour which has been neglected by contemporary commentators such as Walter Bagehot (for whom charitable activity was neither 'dignified' nor 'efficient') and by countless recent royal biographers (from Harold Nicol-son and Elizabeth Longford to Philip Ziegler and Kenneth Rose). But if we add this philanthropic monarchy to the ceremonial monarchy, the fam-ily monarchy, and the imperial monarchy, then we can better discern the varied and interconnected means whereby the British throne has survived and adapted: bread and circuses, home and away. And of these new activities, changed identities and invented justifications, this charitable crown has so successfully and so completely intruded itself into the remotest recesses of British life that no one has previously thought to ask just when this began to happen, why and how it did so, or what are the consequences of this relatively recent, but by now very deep, royal entrenchment in our civil society.

This, in turn, means it is easy to see why, during the last two hundred years, successive royal generations have taken so enthusiastically to what had once been an all but off-limits activity. There have for so long been so many charitable associations clamouring for royal patronage that they have to be shared around the whole extended tribe, and this has meant that all of them, however remotely related to the sovereign, can claim to be fulfilling some useful and important public purpose. Moreover, the values which pervade philanthropic voluntarism are comfortingly similar to those of the monarchical mind-set: amateur and unintellectual, sceptical of professionals and experts, distrustful of politicians and state activity, more concerned with 'character' than with circumstance, and more at ease with individual case histories than with deeper social, economic or cultural forces. And in exchange for patronage, moral support, public appearances and limited benefactions, even the least admirable members of the royal family have been able to win the respect and support of many thousands of people, of all social levels, and in all walks of life, actively engaged in voluntary work. Thus regarded, charitable activity has become the place where the royal culture of hierarchical condescension, and the popular culture of social aspiration, have completely and successfully merged. From Guinness to Geldof, outsiders have been recognised and rewarded for doing good deeds. The fact that voluntary associations, royal involvement and the honours system, have all expanded together is, Prochaska rightly insists, more than mere coincidence.

As is the fact that the phrase 'welfare monarchy' can mean one of two things: either royal bounty – or royal benefits. Ever since the civil list was instituted during the later seventeenth century, the royal family has been on welfare, enjoying state subsidies funded by the taxpayer. Perhaps this is why their charitable activity began, albeit in a tentative sort of way, under Queen Anne, who may have sensed the need for some reciprocal gestures. By the early nineteenth century, George III's children were deeply in debt: they were getting far more money from the government and from their father than they themselves ever raised or gave away. In *The Black Book*, the radical John Wade opined that the crown was the premier beneficiary of the nation's benevolence – a view, Prochaska notes, 'which had much to recommend it'. Throughout her reign, Queen Victoria received many legacies as well as intestate estates in the Duchy of Lancaster, and she accumulated a considerable private fortune out of her savings from the civil list. And during the first three decades of the twentieth century, as royal tax exemptions grew, so did royal charitable work – the latter, unsurprisingly, obtaining far more publicity than the former. With the modern British monarchy (as with the three kings), there are close and important connections between royal giving and royal taking, and it is a pity Prochaska does not explore them.

The key to royal bounty, it seems clear, is mutual benefits and public relations. Only a small proportion of royal income goes to charity; and only a small proportion of charitable income is derived from royalty. But it is helpful for charities to have royal connections, and it is essential for royals to have charitable connections. Consider the forlorn counter-example provided by the Duke of Windsor. If, after his abdication, he had shown the slightest interest in helping anyone else, apart from himself and his wife, he would surely have enjoyed a much better press than he did. But as Prince of Wales and King, he had never grasped the importance of being seen to give as well as take and, thereafter, he was incapable of learning new tricks. By contrast, the labours of the Princess Royal have not only helped save many children: they have also helped save Princess Anne herself. Unlike her sad and separated siblings, this has enabled her to weather divorce and to remarry, while actually gaining in public esteem. Here is a classic example of the way in which charitable endeavour exalts the prestige and the status of the giver. This may sound unduly cynical. But as with all philanthropic activity, it is not easy to unravel the mutually reinforcing motives of selflessness and self-interest, and Prochaska does not try to do so. All that can safely be said is that most members of the royal family have difficulty distinguishing between concern about society, concern about the social order and concern about what best to do so they can remain at the top of it.

Royal motivation is habitually unfathomable: as are the processes whereby the throne changes and adapts. To be sure there are some important moments in the evolution of the charitable monarchy which can be pinpointed, especially the decisions taken by George III, by Victoria and Albert, and by George V after the First World War. And there were also important non-royals whose intervention was sometimes crucial: among them Sir Henry Burdett and the ubiquitous Viscount Esher, who successfully persuaded Edward VII to pressure his plutocratic friends into philanthropic gestures. But very often, the agents of change cannot be found or named, and Prochaska is reduced to invoking that well-known abstraction 'the Palace'. To make things more complex, there is the in-house royal view, memorably put by the Queen Mother, recalling her labours in the Second World War: 'everybody just did their best.' All this makes it extremely difficult to decide whether the evolution of the charitable crown has been the result of deliberate calculation, or a gradual, piecemeal, unselfconscious development, or the outcome of a constantly changing interaction between the two. Prochaska is no more sure about this than he is about royal motivation, preferring instead to shelter behind an epigraph chosen from, of all people, Oliver Cromwell: 'A man never rises so high as when he does not know where he is going.' This can hardly be described as appropriate or helpful or incisive.

Nevertheless, it bears repeating that this book tells us more about the functioning of the modern British monarchy than any previous account has yet done. As the author rightly points out, if we seriously want to debate the costs, utility, and future of the royal throne (and, by the way, do we?, have we?, are we?, can we?: in all cases the answer so far seems in practice to have been 'no'), then the best place to begin is surely to try to be better informed as to what it actually does in terms of both activity and accomplishment. Thanks to Prochaska, we are much better informed about some of these things than we were. But despite his excellent, pioneering account, the inner dynamics and essential workings of this most tenacious and adaptable of national institutions remain in some ways as obscure and elusive as ever. The magic may have faded in recent years but, *pace* Walter Bagehot, the daylight which has replaced it is by and large pale, feeble, sporadic, un-serious, ill-informed, and wholly inadequate. The British monarchy may neither want nor deserve better; the British people do. Or at least, they ought to.

(1995)

NOTE

1 F. Prochaska, *Royal Bounty: The Making of a Welfare Monarchy* (New Haven and London, 1995).

5
Mrs Jordan

The task of rescuing women from the chauvinistic condescension of male posterity has thus far been unevenly undertaken and incompletely accomplished. Writers and actresses, suffragettes and nuns, servants and prostitutes have fared relatively well. But upper-class women – Clio's own sisters, cousins and aunts – have received much less attention. Studies of aristocratic ladies are few and far between; feminist biographies of queens and princesses are in conspicuously short supply; and royal mistresses have rarely been emancipated from the boudoired and bodiced banalities of Georgette Heyer and Barbara Cartland. Yet from the Restoration in 1660 to the early twentieth century, the only English monarch who was both male and monogamous was probably King George III. Put the other way, this means that from Nell Gwynn to Mrs Keppel (and beyond), the courtesan was an integral part of royal history. But while much is known about such women as the Duchess of Portsmouth, Elizabeth Villiers, Henrietta Howard and the Countess of Warwick, no serious attempt has yet been made to write that alternative version of royal history which their lives and loves collectively constitute.

In any such account, the life and love of Dora Jordan would occupy a place both ample and ambiguous. It would be ample because for more than twenty years she was the consort of the Duke of Clarence, the future King William IV, bore him ten children, and lived with him in a state of domestic happiness and connubial bliss. But it would also be ambiguous because before, during and after this well-known, much-publicised and highly controversial royal liaison, she was a self-made career woman and a self-supporting working mother. For Mrs Jordan was the greatest comic actress of her day – adored by theatre-goers in London and the provinces; acclaimed by Hazlitt, Byron and Coleridge; cartooned by Gillray, Cruickshank, Rowlandson and Dent; and portrayed by Romney, Beechey, Hoppner, Matthew

Peters and John Russell. Nor has she been entirely forgotten by posterity. To be sure, she was not even mentioned by name in Percy Fitzgerald's two-volume life of King William IV, published in 1884. But she merited an entry in the *Dictionary of National Biography*, there were two early twentieth-century lives, her correspondence with the Duke of Clarence was edited and published by Arthur Aspinall, and in 1965 Brian Fothergill produced a lengthy and appreciative study of Mrs Jordan as an actress.

Why, then, has Claire Tomalin, a biographer who excels in the recovery of the forgotten lives of lost women, sought to tell again a story which has already been more than thrice told?[1] One clear reason is that, notwithstanding the more tolerant attitude of the twentieth century, she still regrets the way in which some prudish, moralising, hypocritical Victorians sought to pretend that Dora Jordan had never existed, by trying to make her into a non-person. Another is that she is thoroughly dissatisfied with the unsympathetic attitude towards her heroine adopted by such right-royal writers of an earlier generation as Roger Fulford. And she is no less critical of the condescending tone which characterised Aspinall's highly selective edition of Mrs Jordan's letters, which also unduly influenced subsequent writers (notably Brian Fothergill) who depended on them. Above all, Tomalin wishes to bring alive, as no one else has yet done, a remarkable female personality, with a strong and distinctive voice, whose life was more dramatic than any of the parts she played, whether on the stage or off it, and which still possesses the power to captivate, to move, to shock and to anger.

Like her near-contemporaries Sarah Siddons and Elizabeth Farren, Dora Jordan was born (in 1761) in humble circumstances, but with strong theatrical connections. Her parents, who were unmarried, were Grace Phillips and Francis Bland, and her mother was herself an actress. When Dora was thirteen, her father disappeared, and not long after, she made her first appearance on the stage in Dublin. She was soon taken up by Richard Daly, an unscrupulous theatre-manager, who seduced her on the casting couch, and by whom she bore her first child. By then, she had left for England and was working for Tate Wilkinson's Yorkshire theatre company, which travelled the northern circuit. Between 1782 and 1785, she established herself as a provincial actress of rare natural ability – tireless, quick to learn, brilliant at comedy, and with a remarkable capacity to establish a close rapport with her audience. It was only a matter of time before London beckoned, in the shape of Sheridan's theatre at Drury Lane. Long before the decade was out, Mrs Jordan had become to comedy what Mrs Siddons was to tragedy. She was well paid, and the talk and the toast of metropolitan Whig society. But she also encountered the second villain of her life, one Richard Ford, by whom she had three more illegitimate children. Then, sometime in 1789, she met Prince William, Duke of Clarence, the third of George III's seven surviving sons.

This generation of royal males was notoriously described by the Duke of Wellington as being 'the damnedest millstones about the necks of any government that can be imagined'. Their father wanted them brought up to adorn the royal line, and to serve their country faithfully, and to that end he sent most of them abroad into the armed services. But in reaction to the King's devoted and decorous domestic life, they drank, gambled, womanised and piled up mountainous debts, which Parliament was regularly called upon to pay. To make matters worse, they were obliged by the Royal Marriage Act of 1772 to obtain their father's consent when selecting a bride. The theory was that this would prevent them from contracting inappropriate unions; but in practice, it had precisely the reverse effect. Some, like the Prince of Wales and the Duke of Sussex, married clandestinely, with embarrassing and disastrous consequences. Others, like the Duke of Clarence and the Duke of Kent, took long-term mistresses – not, as was usually the case among royal men, in addition to the wives they had tired of, but rather because it was too difficult to find an acceptable wife at all. So, from 1791 until 1811, this was the surrogate role which Mrs Jordan played for (and with) the Duke of Clarence.

At first glance, it was an odd union. She was shrewd, successful, self-supporting and widely acclaimed. He was dull, boorish, a failure in his career in the Royal Navy and shared fully in his brothers' general unpopularity. She had three surviving children by previous liaisons; he had none. For most of their time together, it was Dora who went out to work (a quite unprecedented thing for a royal mistress to do), while the Duke stayed at home. And while he gave her an annual allowance, she also helped to pay off some of his perpetually increasing debts. So this was hardly a relationship based on the conventional gender roles of strong, assertive, public husband, and weak, submissive, domestic wife. Instead, she provided the loving, experienced, resourceful mother figure which so many of George III's sons, starved of maternal affection, seem to have sought (she was four years older than he was); while he offered her a position in society which, though not unimpeachable, was certainly better than anything she could have established for herself. And so they settled down to two decades of domestic harmony, largely spent at Bushey Park near

Hampton Court, during which time she bore the Duke ten children, the FitzClarences.

But in 1811, this *gemütlich* existence came abruptly to an end. For reasons (or non-reasons) which remain not fully clear, the Duke decided he had had enough of Mrs Jordan, and turned his attentions to a young heiress named Catherine Tynley Long, in part no doubt because he hoped her fortune might help pay off his debts. She refused him, but by then Clarence had formally separated from Dora. He made financial provision for her and also for the children he had fathered by her. But he never wrote to her or met her again, and although she had ample reason to feel herself 'a most injured woman', the need to provide for the offspring of her two earlier liaisons obliged her to continue to work on the stage. Her popularity remained undimmed, and she could still earn a handsome living. But the profligacy of her first-born children and of their in-laws meant she soon found herself unexpectedly and heavily in debt. Fearful of arrest, with her energy flagging and her health failing, she fled the country in August 1815, and went into exile in France. Ill, impoverished and friendless, she was dead within less than a year. The Duke of Clarence seems not to have mentioned this to anybody, and in July 1818, he married Adelaide of Saxe-Meiningen.

The details of Mrs Jordan's life have been well known for a long time: but Tomalin triumphantly succeeds in saying – and in seeing – much that is new and worthwhile. In part she does so by her mastery of the context, brilliantly recreating Dora's milieu – sometimes out of *Tom Jones*, sometimes from *Vanity Fair* – in which royalty and politicians mixed with actors and actresses, in a *fin de siècle* atmosphere heavy with assignation, infidelity, betrayal and revolution. In part she does so by her characteristically skilled control of the narrative – constantly keeping Dora in the foreground, but always ensuring that the other figures, especially the Duke of Clarence, receive the attention they deserve. Above all, she takes Dora seriously as a woman in ways that previous royal writers (all, incidentally, men) never did: a woman who in her early days on the stage was vulnerable to predatory theatre managers; a woman who in later years had to bring up her children while at the same time continuing her stage career; a woman who was eventually cast aside and left to die without a single gesture of 'love, friendship, imagination and simple decency' from the man whose life she had enriched and whose children she had borne.

Whether Tomalin fully succeeds in bringing Mrs Jordan herself to life is somewhat less clear. One difficulty is that the documentation is so tantalisingly inadequate. There are no letters from Dora before she began her liaison with the Duke, and thereafter we only have her side of the correspondence. The result is that her formative years can only be viewed from the outside, while the relationship with Clarence never fully catches fire. Another problem is that, like many actresses but more than most, Dora assumed and projected such an array of varied identities that it is not clear who, if anybody, she herself actually was. She was a great comedienne whose life ended in tragedy. Her theatrical repertoire ranged from Lady Teazle in *The School for Scandal* to Rosalind in *As You Like It*. She played women, breeches-part men, and women dressed up as men – and all of these even when heavily and visibly pregnant. She was portrayed by Hoppner as 'The Comic Muse', by Romney as 'The Country Girl', and by Sir William Beechey as a patrician lady of great estate. And at different times, she was known as Dorothy Bland, Miss Francis, Mrs Jordan, Mrs Ford, Nell of Clarence, Mrs James and Dorothée Bland. Amidst such a plethora of diverse images, her 'real' identity remains unavoidably elusive.

Indeed, as the long-term partner of the unmarried Duke of Clarence, and one who continued to earn her own living for most of the time they lived together, it is not clear that she was a royal mistress in the conventional sense of that word at all. Despite the fact that they were both actresses, Dora Jordan was no latter-day Nell Gwyn. Time and again, in Tomalin's account, she resolutely refuses to be so conveniently and customarily categorised. Perhaps this was a way of protecting herself, but if so, it was not a defence which was available to her FitzClarence children. Her daughters did not need it: they married successfully into the traditionally governing classes, losing any lingering taint of bastardy by taking their husbands' rank and titles. But inevitably, in the prevailingly patriarchal world of the time, her sons were neither so lucky nor so happy. For them, the stain of illegitimacy lingered ineradicably, and William's eventual and unexpected accession to the throne in 1830 only made matters worse. They importuned their father for peerages and for pensions, but with very limited success. The eldest son, George FitzClarence, was eventually created Earl of Munster. It was not enough, and in 1842, he killed himself.

Dora's sons and Dora's daughters thus lived very different lives, and as these very varied biographies suggest, gender and identity, legitimacy and illegitimacy matter more in the recent history of the British monarchy than is usually recognised. But that, in turn, is merely an oblique way of saying that this book, slightly surprisingly, tells us much more about royalty than it does about actresses. Put more positively, this means that it is not without a certain chilling contemporary resonance. Now, as then, the thing that matters above all else in the royal family's domestic quarrels, internal feuds and marital breakdowns is whether you are on the inside or on the outside. 'Any fight', Tomalin notes, when Dora was cast out by Clarence, 'was going to be conducted on such unequal terms that she was bound to lose.' More than a century later, the Duke of Windsor found himself in exactly the same position, and was obliged to spend the whole of his embittered post-abdication exile coming to terms with precisely the same treatment. The Princess of Wales should take note. So should the Duchess of York.

(1994)

NOTE

1 Claire Tomalin, *Mrs Jordan's Profession: The Story of a Great Actress and a Future King* (London, 1994).

6

Queen Victoria

Ever since Disraeli made Queen Victoria Empress of India in 1876, the Conservative Party has been one of the lion-supporters of the British crown, and to this day, the monstrous regiment of Tory women, and the Blimpish cohorts of retired colonels, are among the most loyal and devoted of Her Majesty's subjects. But for all that, the true-blue-rinse Thatcher years have not been a happy or an easy time for the House of Windsor. In public, the Prime Minister professes respect and admiration for her sovereign lady and the whole royal family. But it is difficult to believe that in private she offers the same unstinted 'devotion' that Disraeli lavished so fulsomely (and so calculatingly) on his 'faery queen'. As the visible embodiment of stultifying tradition, obscurantist snobbery, unearned riches, hereditary privilege, vested interests, paternalistic decency and patrician wetness, the crown and its court exemplify many of the attitudes which Mrs Thatcher most vehemently detests. And as the successful leader of the nation in arms (remember the Falklands?), and the most long-serving occupant of 10 Downing Street this century, the Prime Minister has in many quarters displaced the monarchy as the most potent symbol of national identity. 'No wonder', she once reputedly remarked of the Windsors, 'they stand on ceremony: what else have they got?'

Nor has the younger generation of royals exactly endeared itself to the national headmistress. Prince Edward has never recovered from the fiasco of 'It's a Royal Knockout', Fergie's foray into fiction was equally ill-advised, and if Marina Ogilvy had not existed, the tabloids would probably have invented her (which to some extent they undoubtedly did). Even the Prince of Wales seems more than a little accident-prone. Like his predecessors, he is effectively without a job until the throne becomes vacant – which may not be until well into the next century. Meanwhile, there is no longer an empire to provide him with the appropriate apprenticeship of a proconsular posting, and he is understandably eager to do more than accompany his wife on her shopping trips. But while his comments on modern architecture and urban planning may be sincerely meant, it is right royal naiveté to suppose that Britain's social and environmental problems can best be solved by turning the whole country into a Canaletto-like theme park. And his concern for the underprivileged and disadvantaged has not exactly endeared him to the Conservative Central Office. As Norman Tebbit replied, in words reminiscent of Walter Bagehot, it is not surprising that the Prince is so sympathetic towards the unemployed: he is by way of being one of them himself.

All this is indicative of a deeper change in perceptions of royalty that has taken place during the last decade or so. The puppets of *Spitting Image*, and the trivialities of the tabloids, make it increasingly difficult to maintain the illusion of reverential seriousness so essential to the survival of royal mystique. Such rigid organs of weekend Toryism as the *Sunday Times* and the *Sunday Telegraph* regularly carry articles which zealously criticise an institution once thought by them to be beyond censure and above reproach, and a clutch of recent biographies has toppled several notable icons from their pedestals. Kenneth Rose depicted George V as an ogre so boorish and philistine that in retrospect he appears almost pathetically comical. In his books on Edward VIII, Michael Bloch has washed a great deal of the abdication dirty linen in public, and much of the mud has stuck to the Duke of Windsor himself, to say nothing of the Duchess. Sarah Bradford's biography of George VI portrayed him as the ultimate sacrificial sovereign, overwhelmed and destroyed by events he could neither control nor comprehend. And Philip Ziegler's official life of Lord Mountbatten suggested that the royal family's 'beloved Uncle Dickie' was in fact an interfering manipulator of unscrupulous methods, and a shameless adventurer of colossal and inordinate vanity.

With so much daylight now being let in, it is hardly surprising that the old royal magic is not quite what it once was. By its very nature, monarchy can be either revered or discussed: it can rarely be both at the same time, and in Thatcher's Britain the trend has been emphatically away from reverence and towards discussion. But in this increasingly critical reappraisal, professional historians have thus far played very little part. Most recent royal lives have still been penned by genteel amateurs, and there is no book on the modern British monarchy comparable in scholarly stature to Dennis Mack Smith on the kings of Italy. Dorothy Thompson's study of Queen Victoria is thus the more to be welcomed, for she is a writer in a very different tradition from such conventional courtly biographers as Elizabeth Longford, Cecil Woodham-Smith and Georgina Battiscombe.[1] She lectures in history at Birmingham University, she specialises in the study of early nineteenth-century popular protest, and her published work on the Chartist movement has, she admits, been 'written in general sympathy with it'. As a socialist, she sides with 'ordinary people' against the 'constant erosion of the democratic process', and 'the authoritarianism of the rich and powerful'. And as a feminist, she believes that 'the opinions and feelings of women, as workers, as thinkers, as carers and nurturers of the young and old, must be heard.'

No one has ever written seriously about Queen Victoria before from such an emancipated and non-establishment perspective, and the resulting book is a fascinating essay in royal revisionism and queenly consciousness-raising. Despite the wealth of material available, and the abundance of questions that could (and should) be posed, feminist historians have almost entirely ignored the modern British monarchy. Yet Queen Victoria was a woman before she was a sovereign or an icon, and this statement of the obvious is justified by the fact that it has in most serious ways been ignored by every previous biographer. Of course, she has been regularly depicted as the heiress presumptive, the virgin queen, the wife-and-mother, the grieving widow and the apotheosised matriarch. But in earlier accounts, these ostensibly gender-specific descriptions have been employed cosmetically, as chronological markers, rather than analytically, as investigative categories. And no previous biographer has made any attempt to look at Queen Victoria in the broader, and in many ways very different context, of nineteenth-century womanhood as a whole. Thompson's aim, by contrast, is to 'explore some of the moments when the fact that a woman was on the throne seems to be of particular significance during a century in which women were increasingly discouraged from taking part in the public life of the country'. The result is a valuable retelling of a familiar story, which seeks for the first time to do full justice to the Queen in terms of her gender and her sex.

When Victoria began her reign in 1837, she followed a line of Hanoverian men, who had occupied the throne since Anne, the last queen regnant, had died in 1714. By the early decades of the nineteenth century, the younger generation of royal males had largely forfeited public sympathy. George IV, William IV, the Duke of Kent (who was Victoria's father) and the Duke of Cumberland were 'bigamists, adulterers, squanderers of public funds', whose behaviour was 'repulsive to civilised taste'. Not surprisingly, it was the royal women who captured the public's imagination, especially George IV's daughter, Princess Charlotte (who died in childbirth in 1817), and his wife, Queen Caroline (whose determination to fight for her royal rights in 1820 meant she briefly became the darling of the London mob). So when Victoria came to the throne, there was still a fund of residual sympathy on which she could draw as a royal woman; and her youth and her purity were further novel advantages. But there was a downside to all this. She had spent most of her early life in the secluded, domestic company of her mother, her governess and her half-sister, and she had been educated as a woman rather than as a future sovereign. She was forbidden by the Salic Law from inheriting the Kingdom of Hanover, which now passed to her uncle, the Duke of Cumberland, and there were some who thought that she should not be allowed to inherit the English throne, either.

But it was not just that Victoria was an untrained woman obliged to do what was still regarded in many quarters as essentially a man's job: she was an unmarried woman at that, and the man who eventually became her husband was much better fitted for the task of rulership than she was. For Prince Albert was very well educated, was fascinated by statecraft, and was determined to play a full part in the political life of his adopted country. As the husband of a regnant queen, his position was, uniquely, both legally and constitutionally subordinate: he could be Prince Consort, but not King Consort. But Albert's zeal for work and power of mind, combined with Victoria's frequent pregnancies, meant that he soon took effective charge of royal affairs. He often dealt with politicians directly, was always present when the Queen saw her ministers, drafted most of Victoria's letters and memoranda, guided her in the formulation of all of her opinions, and became in fact, though not in law, the real power behind the throne. Increasingly, in the 1840s and 1850s, it was Albert who bore the public and professional burdens of monarchy, while the Queen preferred the domestic privacy of Osborne and Balmoral. As she once remarked, with only slight exaggeration, she 'had always disliked politics, and did not consider them a woman's province'.

But then Albert died. Like many a Victorian woman, the Queen wanted to withdraw into the self-enclosed seclusion of private grief and gloom, and, for over a decade, that is precisely what she tried to do. But although she was now a widow, she was also still the queen, and during the 1860s and early 1870s, she found it exceptionally difficult to reconcile her personal inclinations and her regal duties. 'Public and private', she once lamented, 'it [both] now falls upon me!' Without Albert's assistance, her grip on political business inevitably relaxed (though it never did so completely). She refused to perform the ceremonial duties associated with monarchy, and virtually absented herself from London altogether. She found consolation and companionship in the arms of John Brown, and Thompson suggests that there was more to Victoria's involvement with her Highland servant than it has been usual to suppose. Inevitably, there was widespread and growing dissatisfaction at the Queen's non-performance of her public duties. Dowager queens consort were relatively commonplace in English history, but bereaved queens regnant were much more unusual. Some argued that since she was effectively a full-time widow, Victoria should abdicate in favour of her eldest son, the Prince of Wales. Others contended that since the monarchy had effectively disappeared from sight already, it should now be closed down altogether, and a republic instituted instead.

Not surprisingly, the politicians tried hard to get the Queen to put public appearances before private grief. Gladstone treated her like an institution, and met with little success. Disraeli treated her like a women, and fared much better. Hence Victoria's re-emergence, during the last decades of her reign, as a public icon, a national symbol, and an imperial totem. But once again, her gender mattered. In Britain itself (though not, significantly, in much of Ireland), she became a national mother-figure, 'who stood in a kind of moral holy ground above the coarse realities of day-to-day politics'; internationally, she re-emerged as an imperial matriarch, presiding with maternal devotion over the greater British family spread around the globe. But even at her two jubilees, she insisted on donning her widow's weeds, and she obstinately refused to wear a crown, preferring a bonnet instead. Once more, the boundaries between the private and the public were blurred over and confused. And what had so often been true of the Queen in life remained so at her death. The popular reaction was that her passing was a personal tragedy: the nation had lost the head of the family – 'Mother's come home.' But it was the Queen herself who had insisted that she should be given a public and military funeral.

Although the details of Victoria's life are well and widely known, and although Thompson rightly describes her book as a work of reinterpretation rather than of original research, it abounds in valuable suggestions and shrewd insights. She will not allow us to forget one of the central paradoxes of Victorian Britain, namely that while the highest office in the country was held by a woman, political life was almost exclusively a male preserve. She reminds us that Victoria was brought up in a domestic, female-dominated environment, but that after 1837 she was obliged to deal publicly with men, who were also very much better educated than the Queen was. She points out that the John Brown affair shows that even the sovereign of England was forced to defer to the rules of the double standard: a widowed king could have taken a lover, and no one would have minded (or even noticed), but a widowed queen could not. And she shows again and again how Victoria was constantly torn between the competing claims (and attractions) of private, female domesticity, and public, masculine, kingship, claims which she never fully understood or reconciled. Thanks to Thompson's work, no future study of the Queen will be able to ignore this central theme.

But for all its valuable and original insights, the book as a whole is curiously uneven in its coverage and uncertain in its viewpoint. Despite the volume's subtitle, there is no real discussion of power at all: indeed, for someone who has so frequently and so passionately proclaimed her sympathy for the suffering and downtrodden masses, Thompson treats the Queen and the monarchy in a manner which is often disappointingly deferential and conventionally bland. One-quarter of the book is devoted to a discussion of republicanism; but it fails to do adequate justice to the widespread examination of the role of the monarchy which was carried on in the press and in Parliament between 1837 and the Golden Jubilee, and in any case, it has little to do with the central theme of the book. A further twenty-five pages are spent on inconclusive speculation about the Queen and John Brown; but the exact nature of their relationship still remains unclear, and while Thompson may wish that Victoria had publicly struck a blow against the tyranny of the double standard, the fact remains that she didn't. And the treatment of her last two decades is cursory in the extreme: the apotheosis of the Queen is dealt with in scarcely a dozen pages, and there are some rather fanciful speculations about Liberal and Fabian courtiers which seem decidedly wide of the mark. Even in a book as brief as this, such proportioning seems a touch eccentric.

More generally, Thompson fails to explore those 'moments when a woman was on the throne' in the detail that they require if they are to yield serious and substantial insights. It is surely significant that the first two crises of Victoria's reign – the Lady Flora Hastings scandal and the Bedchamber affair – began as essentially domestic difficulties, which later spilled over into the public arena. As such, they might usefully be seen in the context of Victoria's abrupt and unsure transition from cosseted daughter to public figure. But no such analysis is attempted here. It is also clear that it took Albert and Victoria some years to work out the personal and functional aspects of their royal relationship. But while there is ample documentary material on this subject, it is almost completely neglected. In the same way, Victoria's letters to her eldest daughter provide a mass of information on her attitude to marriage, to child-rearing, and to the role of women in public life. But they go virtually undiscussed. And more attention should have been given to the fundamental transformation which took place during the Queen's reign, from ruling sovereign to constitutional monarch. Again, gender mattered. If Albert had lived, it seems clear that he would have resisted that development much more tenaciously, while the gradual emasculation (and *feminization*) of monarchy was probably more easily accomplished when a woman was on the throne.

Nor are these the only ways in which the Queen's gender was politically and historically significant. Her easy relations with Melbourne, Disraeli and Rosebery, and her loathing of Gladstone, deserve more detailed analysis than they receive here. It would also have been helpful if Thompson had turned this problem inside out, and investigated how the politicians, who were only used to conducting public business with other men, went about conducting public business with their sovereign who was also a woman. How far, for instance, was the widespread anxiety and bewilderment that was felt about her in the aftermath of Albert's death not just because she was widowed, or even because of John Brown, but (to use a word that was taboo then for very different reasons than it is taboo today) because she was *menopausal*? At the same time, we need to know more about the Queen's awareness (and deliberate exploitation) of her own gender. One of the reasons why she clung so fervently to her reclusive widowhood may have been that (in the manner of Florence Nightingale and her post-Crimea 'illnesses') it gave her extra leverage and control in dealing with the politicians, who were so much better educated than she was and who, in the absence of her beloved and expert Albert, genuinely threatened and intimidated her.

In the same way, Thompson also makes heavy weather of trying to understand the Queen in the broader context of nineteenth-century womanhood, where she seems incapable of making up her mind what she thinks. On the one hand, she would clearly like to depict Victoria as a champion and supporter of women's rights. She informs us that in the late

1830s, 'the fact that the monarch was a woman may well have encouraged the incipient feminism' of the time. Perhaps so: but little evidence is advanced in support of this claim. She tells us that Victoria's court 'was one in which the equality of the sexes was recognised to a degree', with the result that 'a positive contribution was made towards the achievement of equal status for women.' But this novel view is asserted rather than demonstrated. She claims that 'a modern feminist, indeed, perhaps almost any modern woman' would approve of the fact that the widowed Queen took John Brown as her lover. Maybe: but so what? And she feels sure that the Queen herself deserves some of the credit for the improvements in the position of women which took place during the last quarter of the nineteenth century: 'her presence and status must on occasion have helped the legal processes forward.' It's a nice idea. But how, exactly, did this happen?

Not surprisingly, Thompson finds the argument that Victoria was some sort of regal proto-feminist extremely difficult to sustain, and it is easy to see why a book originally commissioned for inclusion in the Virago Pioneers series has in the end been published separately. For the fact is, as Thompson elsewhere recognises, that Victoria did not view the world in the late twentieth-century terms of the existence or the advancement of women's rights (or, come to that, of *men*'s rights, either). On the contrary, the improvement of the lot of ordinary women was a subject about which she thought little and cared less. As Thompson admits, Victoria was resolutely opposed to women taking up careers in the great professions. She was not interested in establishing 'a clear female right to an active presence in conventional politics', and by the end of her reign, when she projected 'a domestic, familial and passive image of a woman', there was 'little help in the image of the female monarch' to those campaigning for women's rights. From the standpoint of nineteenth-century British feminists, the fact that a woman was on the throne was at best irrelevantly coincidental, and at worst was positively unhelpful.

Yet Thompson remains convinced that the presence of a female sovereign really did matter in the broader perspective of nineteenth-century history. Once again, this is much easier to assert than it is to prove. She suggests that republican and revolutionary movements found it more difficult to take root in England because it would have been unchivalrous to get rid of the Queen. But as the examples of Mary Queen of Scots and Marie Antoinette imply, womanhood is no guarantee of immunity when the knives are out. She argues that Victoria's gender 'provided the basis for her re-emergence as a national symbol' at the end of her reign. But a very similar transformation was simultaneously taking place in the German, Russian and Austrian monarchies, and in every case, the sovereign who became the cynosure of national attention was male. And she even goes so far as to argue that 'there must have been many ways in which the presence of a woman at the head of the state worked at a deeper level to weaken prejudice and make change more possible.' But this could hardly be said of Russia under Catherine the Great, China under the Empress Dowager – or even Britain under Margaret Thatcher. Of course, it is easy to produce counter-examples to generalisations such as these, and they do not necessarily invalidate Thompson's arguments. But they do suggest her case must be made with more evidential cogency and expositional subtlety than she displays.

The real problem with understanding Victoria from the perspective that Thompson employs is that the Queen belongs to that growing band of past figures that feminist historians feel understandably uneasy with, and incline on the whole to neglect. *For she was an exceptional woman*: exceptional in her temperament, exceptional in her background, exceptional in her occupation, exceptional in her longevity, exceptional in her historical significance, and exceptional in the documentation she has left behind. In trying to understand her, it is important to be reminded so insistently and so forcefully that she was a woman trying to do a man's job as well as her own. But that is only part of the story. For Victoria was also a much more complex historical personality than is implied in this analysis of her as a woman at large and adrift in a man's world, and the rediscovery of that complex royal totality is still very much in its infancy. Thanks (among other things) to Mrs Thatcher, the British monarchy is now more problematic than it has been at any time since the third quarter of the nineteenth century. But that problematic has still to be fully addressed or understood in serious historical terms.

(1990)

NOTE

1 Dorothy Thompson, *Queen Victoria: Gender and Power* (London, 1990).

7
King Edward VIII

He was, in his time, the most famous and most controversial member of Britain's royal family. As a young man, he seemed extravagantly blessed with charm, good looks and charisma, and the fondest hopes were entertained of his prospects by his many friends and admirers. When the supreme opportunity of his life eventually presented itself, he began his great task with considerable popular support, and it seemed at first as though he must carry all before him. But within a year, his splendid position was completely forfeit, and he was obliged to leave the country, defeated and disgraced. Thereafter, he was deserted by most of his friends, and was condemned to wander the world as an unhappy and embittered exile. For despite the romantic legends which gathered around him as 'the prince over the water', he was a sad and forlorn figure. He brooded resentfully on his banishment, raged and fulminated ineffectually against his enemies, grew more paranoid and more pitiful with each passing year, and sired no male heir. Yet at his death, it was impossible not to feel an overwhelming sense of talents wasted, of promise unfulfilled, and of opportunities thrown away.

This was the melancholy fate which befell Charles Edward Stuart, otherwise known as 'Bonnie Prince Charlie', or 'The Young Pretender'. In 1745, he led a rising of Highland clans, invaded England, and reached as far south as Derby. His objective was to overturn the House of Hanover and restore the deposed Stuart dynasty, but this abortive coup collapsed in bloody disarray at the Battle of Culloden, which effectively ended the Jacobite challenge to the British throne. Two hundred years later, royal history came dangerously close to repeating itself in the tragic tale of King Edward VIII, previously Prince of Wales, and subsequently Duke of Windsor. For his life may be described in precisely the same words that have been used here to summarise the hapless career of the Young Pretender. But as is implied by that unusual phrase '*subsequently* Duke of Windsor', there was one significant difference in the misfortunes of these two similarly sad men. For whereas Bonnie Prince Charlie failed to obtain the throne he so ardently coveted, Edward VIII voluntarily gave his up after a reign which lasted less than the calendar year 1936.

Yet as he brooded on his abdication in his long and lonely years of exile, the Duke of Windsor later came to believe that he had been compelled to relinquish his crown. As heir to the throne, so this self-justifying argument ran, he had been a noticeably forward-looking and reformist Prince of Wales, who sought to modernise the royal family and bring what remained an essentially Victorian institution into belated contact with the twentieth century. And as King of England, he had hoped to shake up the staid and stuffy ruling establishment, epitomised by such (to him) antediluvian figures as Stanley Baldwin, the Prime Minister, and Cosmo Gordon Lang, the Archbishop of Canterbury. But, so the argument continued, in falling in love with Mrs Wallis Simpson, a divorced American, King Edward played straight into his enemies' hands, by giving them the perfect pretext to force him out. Compelled by them to chose between his crown and his happiness, he unhesitatingly decided on the second. He gave up the throne, married Wallis and remained completely devoted to her until the day he died. Thus was born the twentieth century's greatest romance: the story of a prince charming who became king-emperor, and then renounced the most illustrious position in the world for the sake of the woman he loved.

According to Frances Donaldson, whose brilliant biography, *Edward VIII*, was published in 1974, only two years after the Duke's death, the reality was far less glamorous and much more prosaic. Her book was not an authorised life, and she did not have access to the ex-King's archives. But by talking to the still very considerable number of people who had known him, she succeeded in producing what seemed to be a wholly convincing portrait. She depicted his unhappy upbringing, his desperate need for a mother-substitute, and his lengthy love affair with the already married Freda Dudley Ward. She showed how the fair-haired idol of the Empire and the media gradually declined into an inconsiderate and self-absorbed neurotic. She vividly conveyed his abject infatuation with Wallis Simpson, and his total inability, throughout the abdication crisis, to take in any viewpoint but his own. She noted his pro-German sympathies and described the Nazi plot to capture him in the Iberian Peninsula during the spring of 1940. And she recounted his wartime activities as the accident-prone governor of the Bahamas, and the long period of unhappy and unbroken exile which followed. From this distinctly unflattering account, it seemed possible to draw only one conclusion: in the broader perspective of British history, Edward's abdication was just about the best thing that could have happened – both to the monarchy and to the country.

Thus provoked, the widowed Duchess's French attorney, Maître Suzanne Blum, appointed a young English lawyer-historian, Michael Bloch, to present the case for the defence, and gave him full and exclusive access to the late Duke's papers. In a series of fiercely partisan volumes, he argued that the Duke was a far more admirable and honourable man than his enemies ever allowed, and that after the abdication, he was shoddily and shabbily treated by his relatives. In *Wallis and Edward: Letters 1931–1937* (1986), he let the lovers speak for themselves, by publishing their intimate correspondence, from their first meeting until the time of their marriage. In *Operation Willi: The Plot to Kidnap the Duke of Windsor, July 1940* (1984), he insisted that the Duke was far more the victim than the instigator of the Nazi intrigues which sprang up around him at that time. In *The Duke of Windsor's War* (1982), he analysed his years as Governor of the Bahamas, and claimed that the Duke did a much better job than was generally admitted, while the British establishment continued its vendetta against him, almost to the ends of the earth. And in *The Secret File on the Duke of Windsor* (1988), he showed how, from 1937 until 1955, the royal family set out to ensure that he should never return to his native land. No one, Bloch concluded, could read this account of right royal vindictiveness without a 'sense of shame and shock'.

Either way, it is clear that King Edward VIII left skeletons a-plenty rattling in the royal closet, and it is in this contentious context – unique in the history or historiography of any recent British monarch – that Philip Ziegler's life of Edward VIII must be read and understood.[1] For this is the official biography, commissioned by the present Queen, and as such it takes its place somewhat uneasily alongside those earlier works of grave and courtly commemoration: *King George V* by Sir Harold Nicolson, *Queen Mary* by James Pope-Hennessy, and *King George VI* by Sir John Wheeler-Bennett. These weighty, tactful and deferential volumes contained much material from the Royal Archives which had never been published before. They established authoritative interpretations of personality and achievements which it has proved extremely difficult to challenge. They said little about the private lives of their subjects, and even less about their health, or their finances. And it was taken for granted that they were dealing with royal paragons, who were admiringly portrayed as virtuous individuals, the very embodiment of duty and honour, who adorned and enhanced the British throne, which they so selflessly and steadfastly served.

Given the very different nature of his subject, Ziegler could hardly have been expected to adhere to this well-tried, courtly formula in the case of Edward VIII. Much that he has to say merely retraces the ground so impressively covered before in Frances Donaldson's earlier study, and a great deal of the most important (and sensational) documentation has already been published by Michael Bloch. Although it is generally agreed that the Duke was a sad and unfortunate man, seriously conflicting interpretations exist concerning his character, his reign and his abdication, and the part played by other members of the royal family in ensuring his subsequent exile. Nor would it have been appropriate or convincing to produce a tactful public life of a man whose tactless private life was both his obsession and his undoing. And far from being a royal paragon, the Duke is still widely regarded as having been the black sheep in the regal flock, the man who selfishly turned his back on the very institution of monarchy which commissioned lives of sovereigns are customarily intended to celebrate. But as the author of the much-acclaimed official biography of another twentieth-century royal maverick, Lord Mountbatten, it should come as no surprise to learn that Ziegler has produced another shrewdly judged, highly polished and totally riveting book.

The man who was briefly to reign as Edward VIII was born in 1894 and, as the future king of England, was brought up in a bizarre royal environment which was in many ways more deprived than privileged. His father, who in 1910 acceded to the throne as King George V, was a boorish, philistine and bad-tempered man, and his mother, Queen Mary, though more cultivated, was shy and distant. The young Prince Edward grew up to be quick, bright and eager to please, but his social horizons were severely limited, and his early education – initially at the hands of an uninspired private tutor and later at the Royal Naval College at Osborne – was wholly inadequate. In 1911, he was invested as Prince of Wales at a specially invented ceremony staged at Caernarvon Castle, and after a spell at Oxford University, which was too brief and too belated to remedy the defects in his education, the Prince was soon caught up in the gruesome drama of the First World War. Like most men of his class and generation, he was eager to get to the Western Front. But his life could not be risked, and he became increasingly annoyed that he was kept back from the trenches. This early and unhappy experience of the shackles and constraints of royalty led to the Prince's first serious disagreements with his father, and may even have caused him to wonder whether he wanted to be king at all.

In the years immediately after the war he established a unique reputation as a glamorous celebrity, partly because he seemed to be a thoroughly 'modern' man, partly by his visits to provincial towns, where his charm and compassion almost invariably impressed, and partly by his sensationally successful tours to the Empire and the United States. Almost everywhere he went, he was rapturously received: nothing like this had ever happened before in the entire history of the British royal family, and there has been nothing quite like it since. But the schedules were gruelling, and they clearly took their toll of his highly strung temperament. 'Have you ever seen a Post Captain cry?', he once asked Lord Louis Mountbatten. 'Well, you'd better get used to it, you may see it again.' At home, he sought solace in the arms (and the bed) of the already married Freda Dudley Ward; but while she was admirably discreet, and the relationship brought him much comfort, it was clearly a dangerous liaison. As long as the Prince remained in love with her, there was no prospect of his finding a suitable wife, and this affair only heightened the tension which now existed almost permanently between father and son. In private, the Prince was thus a deeply unhappy man, and this inevitably took its toll on his public duties, to which he was becoming increasingly inattentive.

Then, in January 1931, he met Mrs Simpson, and was almost at once bewitched and besotted by her. The exact nature of the hold she exercised over him will always remain unknowable, but there can be no doubting his abject constancy and unquestioning devotion. His long-standing friendship with Freda Dudley Ward was abruptly terminated, and Lady Furness, his current paramour, was also summarily dismissed. By 1935, the Prince was so helplessly and hopelessly in love that it was even rumoured (or hoped) that he was seriously considering renouncing his rights of succession, so that he could marry Wallis as soon as she obtained her second divorce. But within a year, his father was dead, and it was as King Edward VIII, rather than as Prince of Wales, that he now had to resolve the matter. Throughout his brief reign, this was his one constant preoccupation, to the exclusion of virtually everything else. He read state papers cursorily if at all, and was increasingly offhand in carrying out his public duties. He did nothing to 'modernise' the monarchy, as some had hoped, and others had feared. He urged that 'something must be done' to help the millions of unemployed, but he himself did nothing. And while he spoke indiscreetly (and unconstitutionally) of taking control of Britain's foreign affairs, and was undoubtedly in favour of closer ties with Nazi Germany, he was on the whole content to let his government pursue its own policy of appeasement.

For the only matter that seriously concerned him was securing Wallis as his bride. He had always been determined that his private life should be his own affair, and even as king, he stubbornly and naively persisted in thinking that he could make (and break) the rules governing his behaviour with impunity. But in believing that personal inclination mattered as much as – or even more than – public duty, he was setting himself against everything decent and decorous that the monarchy had come to stand for in British life. For Wallis was a divorced woman, and in the 1930s, divorce was contrary to the teachings of the Church of England. Yet it was that very church whose faith and doctrine the King was obliged by Parliament to uphold and defend, and whose prelates should soon be crowning – and anointing – him sovereign. Under these circumstances, it was just not possible for Wallis to become queen, and for the guardians of traditional values, it was clear what the King must do. The Prime Minister, the Archbishop of Canterbury and the King's two private secretaries, Alec Hardinge and Alan Lascelles, had no doubt that their sovereign should put his public duty before his romantic inclinations, and this view was shared by Queen Mary, by her second son, the increasingly anxious Duke of York, and by his wife Elizabeth. But the King insisted that his personal happiness must come first, and gave up his throne that he might marry his love, which he duly did in France in June 1937.

The post-abdication settlement only widened this rift still further. From the very outset, relations between the new King George VI (as the Duke of York had become) and the exiled Duke of Windsor (as the ex-king was now styled) were poisoned by disagreements over money. The Duke foolishly claimed he was short of funds, and demanded a generous annual allowance. But the King's advisers soon discovered that Windsor had lied about the true extent of his very considerable fortune, and the two brothers never really trusted one another again. The treatment meted out to the Duchess of Windsor only made matters worse. She was explicitly denied the title 'Her Royal Highness', and until she stayed in Buckingham Palace in 1972 at the time of her husband's funeral, no member of the royal family would receive her in their house. To the Duke, who had blithely supposed that by abdicating, all would be forgiven and forgotten, these were calculated insults which he resented for the rest of his life. But to his family, they were the inevitable – and regrettable – consequence of his own ill-judged actions. If the divorced Wallis was not fit to be queen, then it automatically followed that she was not fit to be a member of the royal family in any other, less exalted, station. The impasse was total, and was never bridged.

Thus cast adrift, the Windsors were effectively left to their own devices. But having been excessively privileged and protected as Prince of Wales and as King (when he had very much resented it), the Duke did not find it easy to adjust to the harsh realities of the real world. The Windsors settled – temporarily, they hoped – in France, and began to live what already seemed to be something of a shadow-life. Their visit to Germany, ostensibly to study working-class housing conditions, was a public relations disaster, and a second projected trip to the United States was abruptly cancelled. On the outbreak of war, the Duke made his defeatist sentiments amply and tactlessly plain, served for a brief period with the British Military Mission in France, and when the Germany army broke through Holland and Belgium, fled to Spain with the Duchess. There an unseemly wrangle took place with the British government about arrangements for their evacuation, and German intelligence hatched a plot to kidnap the Duke, with a view to installing him as a puppet monarch in the event of England's surrender. Ziegler insists that the Duke of Windsor knew little about this, and would never have been a Nazi collaborator. But this can be no more than surmise.

Eventually, Churchill persuaded the Duke to become Governor of the Bahamas, where, for the duration of the war, he discharged his proconsular duties with a grudging competence, mingled with occasional imaginative touches. But he was still defeatist about Britain's military prospects, constantly complained that he had been banished to a backwater, and committed several major errors of judgement, most notably in the aftermath of the murder of Sir Harry Oakes. Time and again, he pestered his brother to recognise and receive the Duchess, and the Prime Minister to find him a better job. But in neither endeavour was he successful. The King, his wife and his mother would not be moved, and although Churchill was personally sympathetic, there was nothing he could, or would, do about it. Nor, after Labour's victory in the general election of 1945, was the new Prime Minister, Clement Attlee, any more favourably disposed. Predictably, the Duke's relations with the royal family deteriorated still further. In the early 1950s, he twice returned to England – in each case without the Duchess – to attend the funerals of King George VI and Queen Mary. Outwardly, he was affable and composed. But inwardly, he seethed with bitterness and resentment. 'What a smug stinking lot my relations are,' he exploded almost incoherently in a letter to the Duchess, 'and you've never seen such a seedy worn-out bunch of old hags most of them have become.'

With no prospect of an official position, and with no hope, even though there was a new sovereign, that his wife would ever be received at court, there was nothing left for the Duke but to make the best of what he reluctantly recognised must be a life of permanent exile. The Windsors settled in France, entertained lavishly, and spent much time travelling, especially in the United States. The Duke watched his investments with care, pottered for hours in his garden, and wrote (with much assistance) his memoirs, *A King's Story*. But for a man as lacking in inner resources as he, it was a lonely and empty life. His political views, which had never been liberal even in his youth, became increasingly reactionary. He feared Communism everywhere, even in England and the United States, and became an ardent admirer of Senator Barry Goldwater. Very gradually, there was a thawing in the relations between the Windsors and the royal family. In 1967, the Duke – and the Duchess – were invited to attend the dedication of a plaque outside Marlborough House in memory of Queen Mary. Five years after, by which time the Duke was stricken with inoperable cancer, the Queen paid a timely call on her uncle while visiting Paris. Nine days later, he was dead.

Because so much has already been written about the Windsors, the broad outlines, and much of the detail, of Ziegler's biography are already thoroughly familiar. But having enjoyed full and unrestricted access to the Royal Archives, to the cabinet minutes in the Public Record Office, and to the private papers of all the significant actors in this drama, he naturally has much to add to the earlier and more narrowly based accounts of Donaldson and Bloch. His discovery of the two thousand-odd letters which the Prince of Wales wrote to Freda Dudley Ward during the 1920s has enabled him to fill out what had previously been a significant blank in our knowledge of the Prince's life, and also to demonstrate the full extent of his psychological dependence on her. In the same way, his careful study of cabinet minutes, and of the papers of such crucial political figures as Neville Chamberlain and Winston Churchill, shows just how much time successive governments were obliged to lavish on the Duke's affairs, often

– as in 1936 and 1940 – when there were more important things to be doing. And the fact that Ziegler has been able to consult the papers of the King's private secretaries, and other members of the royal family, enables him to set the Duke's complaints about the way he was treated after 1936 in a broader perspective. We now know, for the first time, the full story of the post-abdication financial settlement, and the controversy to which it gave rise, and can better understand why the royal family took, and maintained, what seemed to the Duke to be so vindictive and uncompromising an attitude towards the Duchess.

Compared with previous official royal biographies this book thus seems positively breathtaking in its candour. But how does Ziegler fare in reconciling the conflicting accounts offered by Frances Donaldson and Michael Bloch? In general, he agrees with the interpretation of Edward VIII's life and character put forward by Donaldson: a gifted and glamorous youth, who somehow, somewhere, went sadly and tragically wrong. At the same time, he follows Bloch in doing full justice to the Duke's abiding sense of bitterness and betrayal, and in suggesting that King George VI was strongly encouraged by Queen Mary and Queen Elizabeth, by Alec Hardinge and Alan Lascelles, to take a harsher line with his errant elder brother than he might have chosen to do, if left to himself. But in addition – and this was something Donaldson was not concerned to do, and Bloch had no intention of doing – Ziegler makes out a strong case for the inexorable rightness of his relatives' actions. Given the iron logic of the rules governing admission to the royal family in the 1930s, the only attitude which they could adopt to the Duchess in the aftermath of the abdication was one of complete public ostracism, and having taken up that position, there was no real prospect that it would ever be – or could ever be – abandoned.

It is impossible not to be impressed by the consummate skill which the author continually displays in reconciling these discrepant accounts, interpretational contradictions and conflicting viewpoints. Although this is the official biography of a maverick monarch, whose own official life was short, sensational and suspect, the author writes with an even-tempered mellifluousness which would have done credit to Nicolson, or Pope-Hennessy or Wheeler-Bennett. Everyone's faults are readily admitted, everyone's feelings are invariably respected, and everyone is sooner or later given the benefit of the doubt. Family quarrels, thwarted love, bitter jealousy, long-harboured resentment, insurmountable estrangement, deep personal sadness: all these searing domestic unhappinesses, which were the very essence of the Duke's unenviable existence, are soothed and smoothed aside by Ziegler's urbane, detached, emollient and well-ordered prose. Here, above all, the book visibly betrays its identity as a royal commission. And it suffers as a result. For while it pushes the boundaries of official biography to their limits, it fails to do justice to the personal tragedy which was the Duke of Windsor's life and fate. On every page, this book impresses; but at a deeper level, it fails to move.

Perhaps it was deliberately written in this mandarin mode in the hope of ending the controversy that clung to Edward VIII for so much of his adult life, and has continued to haunt and embarrass the royal family far beyond his grave. But it leaves too many unanswered questions for such an expectation to be realised. Many of them centre on the King's character and psychology. As a boy, his sense of his own worth was inadequately developed. As Prince of Wales, he was highly strung, drank too much, and ate and slept too little. As King, he was lonely, frightened and inclined to see conspiracies all around him. And as Duke of Windsor, his long exile only fed his paranoia still further. At his best, he could dazzle by his charm and his humanity; but at his worst, he was inconsiderate and self-absorbed. He was loyal yet ruthless, mean but generous. He was a solitary individual, yet the crowds adored him. No wonder Ziegler abandons the attempt to make sense of all of this, and wearily concludes that the Duke was 'a kaleidoscope of conflicting elements'. But while that may be a judicious summing-up, it hardly abounds in imaginative insight. After six hundred pages, the subject of this biography remains irritatingly elusive.

Nor has Ziegler resolved the deeper contradiction which underlies the life and career of Edward VIII. Was he, as his courtly critics averred, a genetic freak, a rotten apple, a randomly unfortunate aberration from the decent and dutiful family norm? Or was he, as might be more subversively argued, a man who in many ways ran recognisably true to the royal type, but just somehow got out of control? In many ways, he was indeed a textbook product of his dynasty and profession. His upbringing was no different from that of his three younger brothers, and his lack of intellectual curiosity or aesthetic refinement was a characteristic he shared with both King George V and George VI. As Prince of Wales, he disagreed with his father, but that had been a common feature of royal family life since the eighteenth century. He disliked party politicians, but so had every English king from the time of William III. Like most British monarchs, his political views were generally reactionary, and as he grew older, he took an obsessive delight in medals and uniforms, precedence and protocol.

And like any member of his royal caste, his knowledge of the real world was lamentably limited, and he was almost pathetically dependent on servants and secretaries for his day-to-day existence.

In all these ways, the Duke of Windsor ran true to type. But in other respects, he stubbornly (and inexplicably) refused to conform. He rebelled against the dutiful ethos his parents sought to instill in him, wanted his private life and loves to be his own business, and took against the courtiers, prelates and aristocrats who had furnished his father's kingly entourage. If needs be, he was prepared to renounce his heritage and his destiny, on the grounds that no throne was worth the price he was required to pay for it. He wilfully refused to understand his constitutional role as king, never realised the magnitude of his action in abdicating, and was no more successful in grasping his position as Duke of Windsor. Therein, perhaps, lay the essence of his tragedy. For reasons which will probably never be fully known, he was determined to rebel against a system which he only dimly understood, and rebellions as ill-founded as that stand little chance of success. He may have been the one that got away, but having made his escape, he found, like Bonnie Prince Charlie before him, that he had nowhere left to go.

(1991)

NOTE

1 Philip Ziegler, *King Edward VIII: The Official Biography* (London, 1990).

8
King George VI

The reign of King George VI lasted for little more than fifteen years, yet his death, in February 1952, was greeted with shocked surprise, genuine sorrow, and widespread grief, feelings which were much more than a Pavlovian reaction to the passing of just another monarch. In England, he was sincerely mourned as 'George the Good', 'George the Faithful', even 'George Well-Beloved', and Winston Churchill caught the public sense of personal loss in a vibrantly emotional eulogy which even he had never surpassed. The French Ambassador, René Massigli, reported to his Foreign Secretary that 'George VI was a great King, and perhaps a very great King.' In the United States, the House of Representatives passed a resolution of sympathy, while the *Los Angeles Times* affirmed that 'Great Britain's sorrow will find an echo all over the civilized world'. So, indeed, it did. India's Parliament adjourned for two days as a mark of respect to its last king-emperor, and one Australian MP declared, with bereaved and homely directness, 'We have lost a great bloke.' As Richard Dimbleby put it, describing the King's lying-in-state at Westminster Hall with measured and stately phrases that only in retrospect seem implausibly hyperbolic: 'The sunset of his death tinged the whole world's sky.'

Yet when George VI had acceded to the British throne, in December 1936, no one would have dared predict that his reign would turn out half so well. For it began at the end of the unprecedented 'Year of Three Kings', as the death of George V in January had been followed by the sensational abdication of his eldest son, Edward VIII. As a result, it was widely believed that the monarchy had been severely damaged, and it was not at all clear that the new king was the man to restore its prestige. Lamentably ill-educated, blighted by poor health, devoid of presence or glamour, and further hampered by overwhelming shyness and a debilitating stammer, George VI was initially greeted with muted enthusiasm verging on resentful disappointment. It was variously rumoured that he would die before the Coronation, that he would not be able to survive such a gruelling and protracted ceremony, that he was simply not up to the job. In his darkest moments, there can be no doubt that this last anxiety was one that the unhappy and reluctant king himself fully shared. How was it, then, that a reign which began so tentatively ended so triumphantly? What exactly was King George VI's contribution to the modern British monarchy? And what, if anything, was his broader contribution to modern British history?

Until very recently, only one book has even indirectly addressed these questions: the official biography of George VI by Sir John Wheeler-Bennett, published in 1958. The author admitted to being a 'staunch and romantic monarchist', and in the course of his work became 'a sincere admirer' of the late king. Indeed, he once likened royal biography to matrimony – an enterprise 'not to be entered into inadvisedly or lightly; but reverently, discreetly, advisedly, soberly, and in the fear of God'. Predictably, he produced a work that was massive in bulk but unrevealing in content. Apart from some heartfelt remarks on the King's speech impediment (Wheeler-Bennett was himself a fellow-sufferer, and had even been to the same therapist), his book was the history of an icon rather than of an individual. Its tone was courtly and obsequious, while the prose was purple and ponderous to the point of prolixity. How, indeed, could it have been otherwise? George VI had scarcely been dead five years, his elder brother was still very much alive, and the abdication remained a subject of controversy, embarrassment and annoyance to the royal family. Most of the official papers were as yet unavailable, and men like Harold Macmillan, Dwight D. Eisenhower and Jawaharlal Nehru, with whom the King had corresponded and had dealings, were still active public figures.

Inevitably, the result was a biography which did not probe very deeply into the King's private life, into the workings of the monarchy as an institution, or into the sovereign's place in the history of his country and empire. In so far as Wheeler-Bennett made any attempt at analysis, he did so almost entirely in terms of that vague yet vital concept, so beloved of the British upper classes: 'character'. The key to understanding the life and reign of George VI, he insisted, was that the monarch was a decent, dignified and dutiful man. His virtues were the unostentatious qualities of the English country gentleman: high-minded in his morals, paternal in his outlook, pious in his Christianity, quiet in his courage. Although not brought up in the expectation of inheriting the throne, he was thus well equipped to shoulder this burden when it unexpectedly fell upon him. His robust common sense, his devotion to duty, his unquestioned patriotism and his irreproachable family life enabled him to repair the damage wrought by the abdication, to restore the traditional lustre to the monarchy and to leave to his daughter a throne more securely established in the hearts and minds of his subjects than it had ever been before. If George VI's reign showed anything, it was that 'character' mattered most – a quality which, by implication, the King's elder brother had conspicuously lacked.

More than a generation on, it is high time that George VI was exhumed from this sanitised sarcophagus, and instead treated seriously as a three-dimensional historical figure, which is precisely what Sarah Bradford seeks to do in her fascinating new biography.[1] Her objective is simple and straightforward: 'to provide a reappraisal in the light of our vastly increased knowledge of the period of his life and reign.' To this end, she has encouraged many of the King's surviving contemporaries to talk much more candidly than they were prepared to do to Wheeler-Bennett. She has examined the official archives which have become open, not just of the British government, but also of the French, the Germans and the Americans. She has ransacked over fifty collections of private papers in England and overseas, and she has worked her way through the mass of relevant memoirs and monographs that have appeared during the last three decades. And she has enjoyed one further benefit which only the passing of time could bestow: with one conspicuous exception (of whom more later) most of the central figures of the abdication crisis and King's reign are now dead. The result is that Bradford is able to provide the most candid and convincing account yet of the private life and public ordeal of this sad, successful – and ultimately sacrificial – sovereign.

In its essential outlines, the story she has to tell is already familiar enough. He was born in 1895, on what for the royal family was the most inappropriate day of the year: the fourteenth of December being the anniversary of Prince Albert's death. His great-grandmother, Queen Victoria, still had six years to reign, and as if to console her for the child's unfortunate date of arrival, he was christened Albert Frederick Arthur George. His parents, who in 1910 became King George V and Queen Mary, were shy and reserved with each other, and were quite incapable of showing their children any warmth or affection. Prince Bertie (as he was known in the family) was the second son, and was from the outset overshadowed by his elder brother, the Prince of Wales, partly because he was heir to the throne, and partly because he exuded charm and charisma from an early age. In addition, Bertie was knock-kneed, left-handed, highly strung, spoke with a stammer and was not over-bright. His formal education by Henry Hansell, an uninspired tutor, was distinctly limited, and he never developed an interest in the arts or the life of the mind. In 1913 he became a naval cadet, and during the First World War was present at the Battle of Jutland. But by then, he was in almost constant pain from an undiagnosed duodenal ulcer, and he was eventually invalided out of the Navy.

By the end of the war, Bertie had little to show except an uninterrupted record of failure and defeat, and an understandable sense of inferiority and unworthiness. But during the 1920s and 1930s, he gradually began to carve a small niche for himself. His father created him Duke of York, and bestowed upon him the Order of the Garter. He took to visiting factories and industrial areas, something which no other member of the royal family would deign to do. He established an annual camp, attended by upper- and lower-class boys, designed to alleviate social tensions. He brought his stammer under control, thanks to the ministrations of Lionel Logue, and undertook an unexpectedly successful tour to Australia in 1927. By then, he was no longer fighting his battles alone, for in 1923 he had married Lady Elizabeth Bowes-Lyon. In a life not distinguished for good luck or sound judgement, his choice of wife was a stroke of genius. She possessed many of the gifts her husband conspicuously lacked, being beautiful, charming, cultivated, and brilliant at public relations, and she brought him the comfort, security and understanding which his mother had never been able to provide. She bore him two daughters, Princess Elizabeth and Princess Margaret, and by the early 1930s his life at last seemed set: with his devoted wife and happy family, he could look forward to a peaceful and secure future of private tranquillity and unostentatious public service.

All this was brutally and irrevocably shattered by the death of George V and the trauma of the Abdication. From their prim and proper perspective, the Duke and Duchess of York regarded the new regime of Edward VIII as the negation of everything the monarchy stood for. The King was lax in his religious observances, cavalier in his conduct of public duties, and far from assiduous (or responsible) in his attention to state papers. Even worse, he was infatuated with Wallis Simpson, an American who had already divorced her first husband, and was soon to part with her second. Like Queen Mary, the Yorks dismissed her as an adventuress, felt that her association with the King was damaging to the prestige of the monarchy, and regarded her as totally unfitted to be a member of the royal family. As if this was not bad enough, it suddenly emerged, in late November, that the King had decided to abdicate his throne so that he could marry her. For the Duke of York, this was a prospect almost too terrible to contemplate. It was not just that he feared the abdication would do untold harm to the standing of the monarchy. It would also oblige him, as the next brother in line, to take over as sovereign and to live the rest of his life under the remorseless gaze of the public eye. No wonder he sobbed for an hour on Queen Mary's knee when he learned what his fate would be.

In fact, the new reign began more promisingly than many had dared to hope, and the Coronation was something of a personal triumph. King Edward VIII (now the exiled and married Duke of Windsor) was soon forgotten, and by taking the name George, the new king deliberately emphasised that there would be a return to the traditional standards of his father's day. Thanks to the dresses of Norman Hartnell, and the photographs of Cecil Beaton, the new queen was successfully packaged and presented as a crinolined, romantic figure, straight out of a Winterhalter painting. And the royal visits to France, and to North America, received unprecedented media attention, and did wonders for the King's morale. But both in public and in private, there was a darker side to all of this. In Europe, Hitler was already on the rampage. The King was a strong supporter of Neville Chamberlain and his policy of appeasement, and at the time of Munich even offered to make a personal appeal to Hitler 'as one ex-serviceman to another', a gesture which was as ill-judged as it was well-intentioned. And there were endless squabbles with the Duke of Windsor: over the purchase of the private estates at Sandringham and Balmoral, over the pension which the ex-king was to receive, and over the granting of the title 'Royal Highness' to him, but not to his wife.

Then came the war. As in peacetime, the King worked hard at his job – probably too hard. He refused to consider leaving the country, and although he spent his nights at Windsor, he travelled to London each day to share the anxieties of the blitz with his subjects. As the Queen remarked, when Buckingham Palace received a direct hit, it meant they could look the East End squarely in the face. He journeyed far and wide across his kingdom, consoling those many people who had been bombed out of their homes, and doing his best to keep their morale high. He provided a haven of refuge for those continental royalties who had been driven from their realms: King Haakon of Norway, Queen Wilhelmina of the Netherlands and King George of Greece. And although he had been distinctly unenthusiastic about Churchill when he first became his prime minister, the King gave him loyal and increasingly admiring support throughout the war. But for all his earnest endeavours, George VI was never really at the centre of events. Although head of state and commander-in-chief, he played no significant part in the formulation of strategy or policy, and as the symbol of the nation's resolve to defy Hitler, he was inevitably outclassed and upstaged by Churchill himself.

Not surprisingly, the King regarded the peace with scarcely concealed apprehension: it seemed like 1918 all over again. In Romania, Yugoslavia and Italy, his fellow-sovereigns were sent into exile. He thought the British people 'ungrateful' to have rejected Churchill in his hour of triumph. He was concerned about the radical policies of the new Labour government, and ministers like Gaitskell thought him 'fairly reactionary'. The royal tour to South Africa neither restored his health nor cemented the British connection, and he much regretted the independence of India and the loss of his imperial title. The Duke of Windsor continued to plague him with demands that he be given employment and that his wife be accorded royal rank, and the wedding of Princess Elizabeth to Philip Mountbatten in 1947 only made things worse. The King was much upset by the break-up of his family circle, and while this young, radiant couple seemed to hold out the hope of a brighter future, George VI increasingly seemed a forlorn figure from the past. As he admitted, only a year later, 'Everything is going now. Before long, I also shall have to go.' By then he was suffering from advanced arteriosclerosis, and in 1951, lung cancer was diagnosed (about which the King himself was never told). Appropriately enough, this most domestic of sovereigns died in his sleep from a coronary thrombosis.

Such is Bradford's accomplished account: does it also provide the more fundamental 'reappraisal' that she promises in her introduction? Beyond any doubt, the monarch and his reign come alive far more convincingly than they did in the pious and pompous pages of Wheeler-Bennett's book. To begin with, Bradford vividly conveys the extraordinary nature of royal existence and of kingly attitudes. The austerities of war and of peacetime reconstruction meant that courtly ritual was much less elaborate than it had been in his father's day. But even so, George VI lived a life of cosseted privilege which seems scarcely believable to lesser mortals. Despite his much publicised knowledge of the factory floor (for which, incidentally, Bradford advances very little evidence), he knew next to nothing about how most of his subjects lived, and his prescriptions for promoting industrial peace and ending the class war were naive in the extreme. Like most monarchs, George VI was obsessed with medals and decorations, clothes and uniforms, precedent and protocol. He rebuked General Montgomery, the victor of Alamein, for wearing a beret rather than a peaked cap, and one of the greatest solaces of his declining years was that he personally designed a new style of trousers to wear with the Order of the Garter. And he was surrounded by courtiers and equerries whose world-views were, if anything, even more blinkered and reactionary than his own. Indeed, his two private secretaries, Alec Hardinge and Alan Lascelles were snobbish, narrow-minded, obscurantist and completely lacking in flexibility or imagination.

At the same time, Bradford also paints a much more convincing portrait of the man and the monarch. We learn the true extent of the King's limited intellect: his religious beliefs were childlike in their simplicity; he rarely read a book and delighted in schoolboy jokes and risqué stories; and he was insensitive to art, although surrounded by one of the greatest private picture collections in the world. We are told much more about the courageous efforts he made to discharge his kingly duties: how he strove to overcome his deep sense of inferiority; how he forced himself to deliver speeches and give radio broadcasts; and how he fretted endlessly over affairs of state over which he had no effective control. ('I am very worried about ...' was one of the most recurrent entries in his diary.) And we are given a vivid picture of his declining years which is poignant in the extreme: as Churchill aptly put it, 'the King walked with death, as if death were a companion, an acquaintance, whom he recognised and did not fear.' The end result may merely be to embroider the familiar picture of dull and decent dutifulness: but the individual who emerges is a more human and sympathetic figure than before.

Put more positively, this means that George VI was in many ways the ideal man to take on the emasculated job of being a constitutional monarch in twentieth-century Britain. He was only residually a law-maker, but that was fine by him, since unlike his elder brother, he harboured no desire to assert himself in matters of high policy. He was commander-in-chief in name but not in substance, and this, too, was just as well, since his own military career had been neither glorious nor successful. And he seems to have been understandably (but excessively) dependent on three women: his mother, Queen Mary, who stood by him throughout the abdication crisis; his wife, Queen Elizabeth, whom he regarded as 'the most wonderful woman in the world'; and his elder daughter, whose departure from the family circle at the time of her marriage he so much regretted. Supported and sustained by three generations of firm and formidable Windsor women, George VI seems to have been the ultimate castrated male. In the British royal family, kings reigned, but matriarchy ruled. Just how far this was really true, we are not likely to know until at least the new century. For the King's widow, Queen Elizabeth the Queen Mother, is still very much alive, though in her ninetieth year, and as long as she remains on the scene, the full story of her husband's reign can never be told – even in a book as well researched as this.

But George VI was more than just a castrated male: his even crueller fate was to be monarchy's sacrificial victim, 'the proverbial sheep being led to the slaughter', as he once described himself. For it seems likely that had he not been obliged to step into his elder brother's shoes in the aftermath of the abdication, he might well have lived much longer. As a substitute sovereign, he drove himself too hard, in his efforts to prove that he was up to the job, and in his desire to discharge his obligations as he understood them. And the resulting stresses and strains of kingship meant that he smoked more heavily than ever, an activity which undoubtedly brought on the lung cancer which hastened his passing. At the time of his death, it was widely believed that the King had given his life for his country, and in this analysis there was more than a grain of truth. Yet in the broader perspective of history, he was not the only victim of the events of 1936. For in addition to destroying George VI, the abdication also destroyed Edward VIII. In George's case, it was because the job he felt compelled to take on drove him to an early grave. But as far as Windsor was concerned, he was condemned to the living death of perpetual and pointless exile, wearily wandering the world, getting more paranoid and more pathetic, more tanned and more tired. If either of the two brothers had been formed on more heroic lines, the abdication might have assumed the dimensions of a Greek tragedy.

But since neither of them was, it never rose above the undignified level of an increasingly bitter family quarrel, and much of the interest of Bradford's book lies in her treatment of this episode. In recent years, the case for the Duke of Windsor (such as it is) has been put with great force (but rather less conviction) in the many writings of Michael Bloch. This book is the first to put the other side in any detail, and the argument is very cogently made. According to the conventions prevailing in the 1930s (when the Church of England did not recognise divorce), Wallis Simpson was simply unacceptable, not just as the wife of the King but as a member of the royal family. Yet Edward not only persisted in this ill-judged venture: he also kept his younger brother inexcusably in the dark once he had resolved to abdicate. And while *he* was determined to put personal preference before public duty, this left the Duke of York with no alternative but to order his priorities in exactly the opposite way. Nor did he behave any better once he had abdicated. Although his financial settlement was more than generous, he was constantly haggling for more money. He kept telephoning his brother, presuming to tell him how to do the job he himself had voluntarily relinquished, and he made no attempt to understand why his wife would not be given the title 'Her Royal Highness', or received at court. In short, he never grasped the magnitude – or the consequences – of what he had done.

Although Bradford devotes a sixty-page chapter to the abdication, it is significant that the Duke of York himself hardly appears in it at all. For even though the eventual outcome was that he took over the starring role, he was essentially a minor character during most of the unfolding drama, and that, in essence, remained the dominant theme throughout his subsequent reign. As King, he was at the centre of the public stage, but as a constitutional monarch, he was by definition on the edge of events, which means it is very difficult to assess his place in history with a steady and sure eye. Indeed, the only real criticism of this book is that it makes no attempt whatsoever to do so. But it is easy to see why. For all the goodness of his character and the dutifulness of his reign, the best that can be said of George VI is that he had a sort of greatness thrust upon him, beneath the weight of which he eventually collapsed – which is why, as Richard Dimbleby's words tacitly acknowledged, the impact of his death was in many ways much greater than the impact of his life. At no stage in his career did he ever seriously make history. Instead, it was history that happened to him. And that is just about the hardest kind of history to write – or to live.

(1990)

NOTE

1 Sarah Bradford, *King George VI* (London, 1989).

9

The Prince of Wales

The Prince of Wales was in his mid-forties, with his youth long since behind him, and his throne still many distant, tantalising years away. His childhood and schooldays had been lonely and unhappy, and they were made harder to bear by his distant mother, his disappointed father and his more robust and much-preferred sister. He had married a woman renowned for her beauty rather than her brains, largely because he had been told it was his duty to do so. By her he had promptly fathered two healthy sons, after which he soon sought comfort, consolation and companionship elsewhere. There was criticism in the press of his wayward and unfocused life, but the idea that he should be given serious employment such as a proconsular posting did not secure the necessary approval. At his country house and in London, the Prince set up what was virtually an alternative court in waiting. The trouble was that his mother remained in excellent health, with every prospect of celebrating both her golden and her diamond jubilees. The most the Prince could realistically look forward to was that he would inherit the throne as an old man, and reign for a few tired, belated, sunset years. But there were some who feared, and others who hoped, that the Queen might outlive her eldest son, so that he would never become king at all.

Such might have been the gloomy mid-career appraisal of His Royal Highness Prince Albert Edward, later (and briefly) King Edward VII, and it is not coincidental that many of the same things are now being said about His Royal Highness Prince Charles Philip Arthur George. For while, in some ways, the British monarchy is constantly developing and evolving, in other respects it is remarkably consistent and unchanging, and one of its most unvarying features during the last three hundred years has been the miserable lot of successive Princes of Wales. To Edward VII and Prince Charles may be added the names of every long-suffering heir since the Hanoverians took over: George II, George IV and Edward VIII, not forgetting poor Prince Frederick, the son of George II and father of George III, who did not survive to reign at all. Whatever their differences of character and temperament, all of them had to confront the same simple yet daunting structural problem, which some could not even comprehend, and none successfully solved: how to keep busy, avoid trouble, stay happy and remain hopeful, while fretting away the best years of their lives waiting for the monarch to die.

Thus regarded, Prince Charles's present predicament is no exception to this general royal rule. On the contrary, it is predictably familiar. For all its privileges of rank and wealth, being heir to the British throne is one the most wretched and frustrating non-jobs around, as salad days merge inexorably and imperceptibly into locust years. To make matters worse, it is not even clear that those who have waited most patiently and been trained most assiduously for the throne make the best incumbents when they finally get there. Cruel and paradoxical though it undoubtedly is, the record shows that the most successful twentieth-century monarchs have been those who were not actually born to succeed. King George V was twenty-seven before the death of his elder brother, the Duke of Clarence, put him directly in line to the throne; King George VI was forty-one when the abdication of Edward VIII propelled him suddenly and unexpectedly to take up the crown; and Queen Elizabeth II spent her first decade with no inkling that she herself might one day have to reign. Taken together, these examples suggest that the best preparation for the job of sovereign is not to be prepared for it at all, or not to be too well prepared for it, or for too long.

There is no evidence in Jonathan Dimbleby's interim (and interminable) biography that Prince Charles is reflective or mature or self-aware enough to have grasped this sad, simple and vital truth.[1] To be sure, we are repeatedly informed that he is drawn to history, nostalgia, heritage and tradition. But the first of these is not easily reconciled with the rest. Despite having read history at Cambridge, the Prince's sense of the past is, like that of most royals, romantic, escapist and superficial. He seems to have little understanding of the way in which the British monarchy has changed (and not changed) across the centuries. He shows no inclination to think about his own situation in the context of the Princes of Wales who have gone before him. His view of the military is suffused by regret for the vanished days when the Royal Navy really ruled the waves. And he seems to dislike almost everything that has happened in Britain as a result of the industrial revolution, the massive growth of towns and cities and the liberating decade of the 1960s. But here again, it is the Prince's typicality and trueness to type that stand out: like most twentieth-century British royals, he is visibly ill at ease in his own time, and vainly seeks to put the clock back to an earlier – though invariably unspecified – golden age.

Not surprisingly, then, his understanding of the world in which he finds himself is also conventionally princely, which means that it is blinkered, limited and naive. He does not like politicians, whom he regards as too much concerned with short-term objectives, and more interested in partisan success than with the good of the country as a whole. Nor does he approve of experts and professionals, who are the very antithesis of his ideal of amateurish gentility, and who have, in his opinion, done the nation a great deal of harm. He has no awareness of the sheer complexity of contemporary society, of deep-rooted, long-term economic and social changes, or of the workings of market forces, and he thinks that the best solution to any current problem is to encourage everybody to pull together for the good of the country. Above all, he feels that what is generally needed is a little more deference and a little more character, thereby ensuring the stability of the social fabric, and the preservation of that vital continuity between past and present. Such are the views of Prince Charles in (and about) the last decade of the twentieth century - views which George V, and even George III, would wholeheartedly have endorsed.

They would have been equally sympathetic to his plans and prescriptions for confronting (or, more usually, escaping) the future. Like so many heirs to the throne before him, Prince Charles wants a different style monarchy when he finally becomes king – and like so many of his forbears again, it is not at all clear that he will (or should) be allowed to get his way. But as any historian could tell him, such a desire for change is itself extremely traditional, and it is tradition which suffuses all of his pet projects and favourite schemes. Modern architecture is intrinsically suspect, whereas the classical style is by definition superior – an absurd opinion, which in a society less diseased by deference than Britain would long ago have been laughed off the stage. Ordinary people should be housed in model villages like Poundbury - but this merely amounts to saying that the best solution to the country's current housing shortage is to build more estate cottages for the agricultural labourers. As for London, the only hope is to return to the eighteenth century, and recreate the capital that Canaletto celebrated – a view which is not only unrealistic and unrealisable, but which betrays a complete ignorance of the many ways in which life was, for the majority of Londoners, so much worse then than it is now.

Like many of his predecessors, the present Prince of Wales is unable to come to terms with the limitations (and the privileges) of his own position, and for all its well-disposed intentions, Dimbleby's biography fails to provide the essential historical perspective which might have helped him to do so. He makes no attempt to write about what it means to be heir to the throne in the light of those who have gone before, and his knowledge of the British monarchy before the reign of King George VI is either very limited or coyly and mistakenly concealed. The result is that throughout the book, he is far too close to his subject, which means that all sense of proportion is lost. At more than six hundred pages, the biography is much longer than Prince Charles's very limited accomplishments thus far merit. There is no need for lengthy accounts of such esoteric and ephemeral episodes as the mass in the Vatican that never was, or the dinner in Palm Beach with Armand Hammer that finally did happen. The Prince's many charities and trusts are no doubt worthy ventures: but they are described in a detail which is altogether excessive. And the lengthy sections devoted to his spiritual journeys of self-discovery, and his explorations of eastern religions, are embarrassing rather than enlightening.

The idea behind this book was that the more we were told about the Prince of Wales, the more we would come to admire him as a character of decency and distinction. But as Dimbleby candidly admits, this is a very high-risk strategy. To be sure, Charles emerges from this account as a man who genuinely cares about the arts, the environment and education; who worries about the homeless and the hopeless in our inner cities; who found Thatcher's brand of conservatism to be lacking in compassion and humanity; who writes letters which on occasion show real insight and depth of feeling; and who works hard and assiduously in the discharge of his public duties. Thus described, he is probably the most civilised and sympathetic member of the royal family since Prince Albert. 'All I want to do', Dimbleby quotes Charles as remarking plaintively on one occasion, 'is to help other people.' But as Albert unhappily discovered, and as Charles has also found out to his dismay, there is a considerable difference between being good and doing good. Royalty is not now, and never has been, primarily about helping other people, and any prince who thinks it is is doomed to disappointment and frustration.

This means that there is a great deal of disappointment and frustration in the course of Dimbleby's pages. Perhaps as a result, there is also a surfeit of self-pity. 'What are you supposed to do', Prince Charles complained on learning that there was not unanimous support for the proposal that he might be made Governor-General of Australia, 'when you are prepared to do something to help and are told you are not wanted?' There are several serious answers to that ignorant, pathetic and self-indulgent question. One is that in the aftermath of the Whitlam–Kerr imbroglio, it is probably just as well that he was not made Governor–General. Another is that it is entirely reasonable, with the growth of republican sentiment in Australia, that many people did not want a royal proconsul. A third is that the Prince should long ago have learned to distinguish between his person and his position, and should not have regarded this prudent and essentially political decision as a personal rebuff. And finally, it might be observed that this response vividly illustrates the vanity, wimpishness, petulance, arrogance and self-centredness which are unattractively in evidence throughout Dimbleby's book. In one guise, Charles may be Prince Charming; in another he is the whinger of Windsor.

Despite the author's sympathetic intentions, it is thus not clear that this biography will succeed in rehabilitating Prince Charles in the eyes of the British public. For all his undoubted decency and dutifulness, he emerges as a curiously unwinning and unintegrated character. He likes good manners, but can be abominably rude. He does not eat meat, yet he enjoys hunting, shooting and fishing. He complains endlessly about his lot, but seems ungrateful for the privileges of his position. He champions the Queen's English, yet his unscripted remarks are embarrassingly incoherent, contorted and ungrammatical. He resents intrusions into his privacy, but divulges the most intimate details of his own life and of his family life to his biographer. He is drawn to Henry V's soliloquy before the Battle of Agincourt, yet does not seem to realise that Shakespeare was parading both the vanity and the vainglory of kingship. He seems to think, in his more arrogant moments, that he can walk on water, but he also possesses a remarkable capacity for shooting himself in the foot. And in marrying Lady Diana Spencer, he thought he had chosen the ideal bride, yet it turned out that he had made the most terrible mistake of his life.

The most important thing that a Prince of Wales has to do is to choose the right wife. Neither George IV nor Edward VIII managed it, and Charles is understandably haunted and harassed by his own failure, and by the sustained and adverse publicity to which he has been subjected as a result. So much so, indeed, that the prime purpose of this book is not just rehabilitation, but retaliation: an attempt to regain the initiative for the Prince of Wales in the unedifying and long-drawn-out battle with his estranged wife for popular opinion and public support. To some degree, at least, this enterprise deserves success. It is clear from Dimbleby's account that Charles is the more substantial and serious figure, less prone than Diana to fritter away his time working out, lunching out, shopping out, crying out and passing out. It also seems clear that, having proposed, he was sincerely resolved to be faithful to her, and to make the marriage work. During the early stages of their life together, he showed genuine concern about her depression, bulimia and cries for help. And he was (and is) a more affectionate and attentive father than the most spiteful and sensationalist tabloid revelations would claim.

But this is only part of the picture. For it also emerges that the Prince of Wales was wholly mistaken to embark upon this marriage in the first place. By the time he reached his early thirties, he was clearly getting desperate, and as he became more anxious, he also became more indecisive. He set much store by Lord Mountbatten's advice – 'choose a suitable and sweet-charactered girl before she meets anyone else she might fall for' – but it was hopelessly out of date. The more explicit presumption among many courtiers that his bride's virginity was of greater importance than her maturity was no less unworldly and ill-founded. And although the age gap of thirteen years was not insuperable, the fact that Charles and Diana had few interests, fewer experiences and no friends in common did not bode well. Two of the Prince's friends – Lord Romsey and Nicholas Soames – were aware of this, and wisely but vainly tried to dissuade him. Despite Jonathan Dimbleby's subsequent disclaimers, it really does seem that Charles was bullied into proposing marriage by his father, and that while he knew Diana was in love with him, he was emphatically not then in love with her.

To make matters worse, it emerges that no one – and least of all Charles himself – had thought what the marriage would involve, either for him or for her. He was already set in his ways, and seems never to have realised that his comfortable, self-sufficient bachelor life would have to be reordered, rearranged and renegotiated to take account of his wife's existence. And although the courtiers had been worrying about the need for a Princess of Wales for more than a decade, they seem to have given very little serious attention to the question of how she should be treated when she finally materialised. One result of this was that Charles and Diana never seem to have established a relationship which went beyond sex and superficiality, which meant that the marriage was in serious trouble almost from the beginning. Another was that she seems to have had precious little help and support from the palace bureaucracy as she adjusted to her new role. And it never seems to have occurred to anyone that as she grew up, she would become the most spectacular royal celebrity and media star there has ever been, or that she might acquire opinions and develop a character of her own, and resent being treated as a docile, decorous, dutiful trophy wife.

Self-evidently, the faults were not all on one side, and Dimbleby makes as strong a case for Charles as he can. But when it came to vanity, petulance and self-centredness, the Prince soon – and quite unexpectedly – met his match in the Princess, as the virgin bride became the mouse that roared. He also came to resent the fact that she was so much more popular and glamorous than he was, and possessed a far more deft touch than he did in handling and manipulating the media. As their marriage deteriorated, and as Charles took up again with Camilla Parker Bowles, it is as easy to understand why the Princess encouraged her friends to talk to Andrew Morton as it is to understand that the Prince was horrified and humiliated when *Diana: Her True Story* appeared. For someone as lonely, insecure and unhappy as Charles, it proved impossible to maintain a dignified silence, and the temptation to reply has eventually become irresistible. Hence this book. But whether this right royal riposte will succeed in rehabilitating the Prince is far from certain. For while Dimbleby claims that the Prince of Wales is 'an individual of singular distinction and virtue', there is too much contrary evidence in his biography to make this conclusion credible.

In any case, the Prince's virtues and distinctions (or lack of them) are not the fundamental issue, and only someone as self-absorbed as Charles could seriously suppose that they are. The real problem is the failed marriage, and this is compounded by the still-considerable popularity of the Princess of Wales. If their separation continues indefinitely, the Prince risks becoming an even more risible figure than he already is to many people. Yet if he initiates divorce proceedings, he may sink still lower in public estimation. And whatever he decides to do, Diana will not go away. In earlier times, she could have been beheaded, incarcerated, or exiled. But these are not acceptable options today. Whether she wants revenge or not, she will probably remain a thorn in Charles's side for the rest of his life. She has powerful friends in high places, she can always upstage him in the media when she so decides, and she can be confident that at some future date she will finally triumph when she sees her son crowned as King William V. If Charles was an authentically noble or heroic figure, it might be possible to agree with him that he is trapped in a Greek tragedy. As it is, the spectacle of these two sad, spoiled, solipsistic individuals slugging it out in public via their proxy authors is merely nauseating, pathetic, contemptible and demeaning.

To firm and fervent monarchists, it is also highly – perhaps self-destructively – irresponsible. It may be true, as the so-called (and often self-appointed) 'constitutional experts' tell us, that Charles's rights of succession are unaffected by all of this. But there can be no doubt that the much-publicised collapse of the Waleses' marriage and their own competing complicity in the media coverage, are doing the House of Windsor a great deal of damage. When Paul Johnson appears to be talking sense on a contemporary issue, and when the defence of the monarchy is left to such comic-opera characters as Lords Rees-Mogg and St John of Fawsley, then things are clearly getting rather desperate. For the Prince and his advisers, the last redoubt of hope must be that in ten, twenty or thirty years' time, this will all have blown over and been forgotten. Like most Princes of Wales, only more so, Charles has to go on waiting as patiently as he can for as long as he has to.

The difficulty is that at present, it is impossible to know whether this strategy will actually work. As benefits a man of pessimistic inclinations, the Prince himself clearly has his doubts. For instead of accepting his lot as heir to the throne, and whiling away the time until the crown inevitably and inexorably becomes his, Charles constantly gives the impression that he is running for office. And perhaps, in the end, he will be and should be, though whether he fully understands this is not clear. Consider the remarks he made on his visit to Australia earlier this year. They were interesting, apparently his own and, as is so often the case, had clearly not been fully thought through by or at the Palace. It is the sign, Charles observed, of a mature nation that such issues as whether the monarchy should be kept or abolished can be discussed openly and candidly, and be subjected to a referendum. This was something, he went on, about which only the Australian people themselves had the right to decide. Quite so. But if the Australians are to be allowed to exercise this right, then for how much longer can – or should – the inhabitants of Britain be denied it?

(1994)

NOTE

1 Jonathan Dimbleby, *The Prince of Wales: A Biography* (London, 1994).

10

Diana, Princess of Wales

A FUNERAL ANTICIPATED

The death of Diana, Princess of Wales, from a road accident at the relatively tender age of thirty-six, has left unmoved and untouched only the hardest of hearts and the meanest of spirits. During a period of mourning the like of which Britain has never witnessed before, this has been overwhelmingly the general verdict. She died too young, with what should have been the greater part of her life stretching out before her. She died suddenly and without warning, at a time when she seemed healthier and happier than she had ever been. And she died horribly, brutally and violently – a death which was literally heart-piercing for her, as it was metaphorically heart-piercing for everyone else. Thus did the fairy story which had begun so romantically in July 1981, with a horse-drawn carriage outside St Paul's Cathedral in London, come to a shocking end sixteen years later, with a drunken driver and a wrecked car in a Paris underpass. Almost a week after her death, it is still not possible to write these words without a shudder.

Even so, the depth and intensity of the reaction to her death during the last six days have taken many people by surprise. From around the globe, world leaders have paid their tributes: among them the Prime Ministers of Australia and New Zealand, the President of France, the Secretary-General of the United Nations, and Nelson Mandela. In the United States, what would otherwise have been a long and uneventful Labor Day weekend was transformed into a non-stop news bulletin, as journalists were called back from the beach to file their copy, and top television presenters were sent to London to cover the story first-hand. But inevitably, it is in Britain that the response has been most pronounced. Flags have been flying at half mast, normal television schedules have been abandoned, the

Prime Minister spoke emotionally about 'the people's princess', and today there takes place the full-scale ceremonial funeral in Westminster Abbey, which has rightly been described as 'a unique tribute to a unique person'.

These official reactions have been far surpassed by those of the ordinary people whose princess Tony Blair proclaimed Diana to have been. In the Boston hotel where I was staying the weekend that she died, I was offered condolences by porters, waiters and fellow guests. It was the same in New York later in the week, where I only had to open my mouth and speak in an English accent for expressions of sympathy to come rolling in from complete strangers. As for Britain: it seems as though Diana in death has finally slain the stiff upper lip with which she had been so uncomfortable in life. On scores of radio and television interviews, men and women have wept openly and unashamedly. Thousands have queued, by day and by night, to sign the books of condolence at St James's Palace, where her coffin reposed. There, at Kensington Palace, and outside Buckingham Palace itself, the gateways and lawns have been knee-deep in flowers, many with touching inscriptions from those who had never known Diana personally, but who regarded her as a true and real and close friend.

Inevitably, commentators have been searching for comparable deaths and comparable reactions, and just as inevitably, they have found them. Not since the demise of Princess Grace of Monaco in 1982 has a royal car accident had such tragic consequences. Not since John Lennon was shot in 1980 has the death of a Briton evoked such a world-wide response. Not since Lord Mountbatten was murdered by the IRA in 1979 has a member of the royal family come to such a violent end. Not since Winston Churchill died in 1965 have so many Britons mourned one of their own so deeply and so sorrowingly. Not since the assassination of John F. Kennedy in 1963 have youth and hope and good looks and charm been so cruelly and devastatingly snuffed out. And not since their grieving forbears laid their wreaths at the Cenotaph in Whitehall in July 1919 have so many ordinary Britons paid such spontaneous homage in our capital city.

There is something to be said for each of these comparisons: but not, in truth, very much. In each case, they mislead more than they illuminate. Unlike Princess Grace, Diana was not a celebrity in her own right before she married, with an accomplished career in film already to her credit. Unlike John Lennon, she was not a creative figure who helped transform the popular culture of an entire generation. Unlike Lord Mountbatten, she had not held a succession of high-ranking military and proconsular posts. Unlike Winston Churchill, she was not the saviour of her country in its darkest and finest hour. Unlike John F. Kennedy, she had been neither President of the United States, nor (albeit only briefly) the hero of the world's hopes. And while her death was beyond doubt a waste and a tragedy, there had been three-quarters of a million such wasted, tragic British deaths during the course of the First World War.

The fact that comparisons such as these have been regularly and repeatedly made during the last week suggests a lack of proportion remarkable even by contemporary journalistic standards. Indeed, at one level it has been the media which has inflated this personal tragedy into the worldwide story it has since become. In the era of global communications, the news of Diana's death was instantly available everywhere: many people on the east coast of the United States knew about it before they went to bed late last Saturday night, while those in Britain only woke up to it on Sunday morning. And the need to keep the story running for the whole week separating Diana's death from her funeral has given it a cumulative, self-reinforcing momentum, as every possible angle has been explored by every possible commentator and reporter, with the result that it is difficult to think of any previous death which has received such sustained, intense, blanket coverage as this.

Yet while the reaction to Diana's death has been to some extent media driven, that is clearly not the whole truth. Her death, even more than her life, seems to have caught and intensified a certain popular mood. Many of those who have been most upset by it seem to be among the marginalised in society, the outcasts and rejects of Thatcherite Britain, those with whom she herself came most recently and most publicly to identify: the poor of the inner cities, sufferers from AIDS, immigrants feeling the sting of racism, members of the gay community, battered women, deserted wives. To them, Diana seems to have offered some sort of hope – even if it was only the general reassurance that she cared for them, and felt their pain. A cynic would say she was no more than the self-appointed high priestess of the contemporary cult of victimhood. A more generous verdict would be that these were the very people of whose hearts she was the undoubted queen.

This suggests a more plausible historical comparison than those which have generally been drawn during this last week. In some ways, the figure she most closely resembles is Princess Caroline, the unhappy wife of the Prince of Wales who eventually, in 1820, became King George IV. Like Diana, Caroline was drawn into an arranged marriage with an unfaithful husband, which went rapidly and publicly wrong. Like Diana, she was cast out from the royal court and obliged to make her own life in her own way.

Like Diana, she was determined to go down fighting, and she certainly did not go quietly. And like Diana again, she was seen by many as the victim of a harsh, overbearing establishment, which won her great popular support from the marginalised and disaffected, especially wronged women and those who resented the long period of Tory dominance which had lasted since 1809. In her own day, Caroline was every bit as much the 'people's princess' as Diana has been in ours.

But as with Caroline, this picture of Diana as an ordinary woman, as being 'one of us' and 'on our side', was not entirely plausible. She was the daughter of a rich aristocrat, married the eldest son of one of the wealthiest women in the world, and her divorce settlement was reckoned in millions of pounds. The Spencer earldom dates back to the mid-eighteenth century, by comparison with which the House of Windsor seems distinctly upstart and parvenu. Her last hours were spent at the Ritz hotel in Paris and in a Mercedes, in the company of a man whose father is a billionaire. These are not the circumstances of ordinary people. On the contrary, Diana lived a jet-set life, of private planes, hired helicopters, speedboats and fast cars. This was a high-risk existence, and others before her had also been destroyed by it, notably Prince William of Gloucester in a flying accident in 1972, and the second husband of Princess Caroline of Monaco, who was killed when his speedboat capsized.

Yet for all her wealth, privilege and connections, Diana *did* seem to many to be an authentically anti-establishment figure, and this was not only on account of her identification with those at the bottom of society. For her youthful, spontaneous, warm-hearted, media-wise style made the rest of the royal family, and thus the whole institution of monarchy, seem by comparison unacceptably Victorian, middle-aged and unglamorous: out of touch with contemporary life; stiff, aloof and inhibited; obsessed with protocol, precedence and procedure; cold, uncaring and unsympathetic; male chauvinist, hypocritical and addicted to blood sports. Indeed, it has been this view of the monarchy – the Diana view – which has been most widely rehearsed this week. It is, no doubt, at best a partial picture. But for the time being it also seems the most plausible picture, which the predictably constipated and unimaginative behaviour of the royal family during most of this week has scarcely been calculated to dispel.

Here again, another comparison suggests itself: with the Prince of Wales who later became Edward VIII, abdicated to marry Wallis Simpson, and eventually became the sad, exiled and embittered Duke of Windsor. Like Diana, he had once been a young, glamorous figure, who in his heyday was the focus of much popularity and media attention. Like Diana, he seemed to promise a new-style, new generation monarchy, more modern and approachable, and more in tune with the lives and expectations of ordinary people. Like Diana, he was disapproved of by crusty and reactionary courtiers, who thought him frivolous, self-indulgent and irresponsible. Like Diana, he regarded personal happiness as being at least as important as royal duty. Like Diana, he was eventually frozen out, condemned to live the sort of semi-detached royal life which might eventually have been her lot. And like Diana again, it was only in death that the royal family rushed to reclaim him as one of their own.

What conclusions might we draw from these comparisons, as they relate to the debate about the future of the British monarchy, which has inevitably been reignited in the aftermath of Diana's death? This week, two views seem to have been emerging. The first, and the more popular, contends that if the royal family is to survive the loss of its most loved member, it will have to learn the lessons she taught, and become less remote and more accessible: Diana may be dead, but the Diana monarchy is the only plausible future model. Alternatively, it has been suggested – rather daringly, considering the general mood – that by popularising a new candid and confessional royal style, part Oprah Winfrey, part Susie Orbach, Diana actually did the monarchy untold damage, and that the best thing now would be to draw a line under this regrettable aberration, and return to the traditional, more restrained way of doing things which has served the institution so well for most of this century.

At first glance, and in opposition to this week's conventional wisdom, the examples of Queen Caroline and Edward VIII suggest that the second of these routes is more likely to be taken than the first. In their day, Caroline and Edward both made a great stir and enjoyed widespread public affection and support. But their long-term effect on the British monarchy was minimal. It survived; it always survives. But they did not. Caroline died in 1821, and soon became a forgotten figure, while Edward VIII was followed by George VI, who did everything he could to stress continuity with the much more formal royal regime of his father, George V. From this perspective, it may well be that Diana will be remembered as no more than a colourful but ephemeral celebrity, part Cinderella, part Marilyn Monroe, part Mother Teresa, part Eva Peron: an ever-changing amalgam of shifting, postmodern identities, which were as much the projection of our fantasies on to her as they were an expression of her own uncertainties and contradictions.

But there is one significant way in which these comparisons – like the many comparisons which have been made this past week – mislead. The Duke of Windsor sired no progeny, and Caroline's only child, Princess Charlotte, predeceased her in 1817. One of the reasons why Edward and Caroline exerted so little influence beyond the grave was that they left behind them no descendants through whom they might exert it. But Diana leaves behind two sons, one of whom is destined one day to be King of England. He may or may not adopt his mother's style. (The betting at the moment, predictably, is that he will.) But whether he does or whether he doesn't, he will always remain visibly her son, and for years to come there will be many people who will find it impossible to contemplate his slim, long-legged body, his thatch of red-fair hair, and his bashful, downcast, through-the-eyelashes look, without seeing in them the image of his mother. In a very real sense, she will live on in him.

Nor is this all. More than a generation ago, the death and funeral of John Kennedy (and here that comparison *is* apt) marked the beginning of the Camelot myth which endured intact almost down to our own times – a partial version of the truth, but one which for years carried almost everything before it. And who can doubt that the events of this week have marked the beginning of the myth of Diana as saint and martyr, of which essentially the same ought to be said? From this perspective, her funeral will conclude and consolidate a public relations triumph far surpassing anything she achieved in life: we shall always remember the day she died and the day she was buried, her grave will soon become a place of national and international pilgrimage, the vacant plinth at the north-west corner of Trafalgar Square need no longer lack a statue, and biographies will cascade from the presses with haunting, bitter-sweet pictures. Diana, Princess of Wales, is dead; but Diana, Queen of Hearts, yet lives.

A FUNERAL OBSERVED

On Saturday, 6 September 1997, the largest audience in history looked upon what was surely the ultimate royal funeral. More than one billion people watched it world-wide, on small or large screens; more than thirty million Britons were tearfully glued to their televisions; and one million more people lined the streets and filled the parks of London. The procession took two hours to make its sorrowing way from Kensington Palace, arriving outside Westminster Abbey with near-miraculous punctuality, at just the moment when Big Ben began to strike eleven o'clock. The service lasted exactly one hour, and there was scarcely a dry eye by the end of the first hymn, 'I vow to thee my country', which had also been sung at Diana's wedding. And as the solitary hearse drew away at the end, beginning its long journey to Althorp, it was inundated with flowers, thrown in its path, on its bonnet and on its roof, from thousands of well-wishers paying their very final respects.

Yet for all the meticulousness of the planning and the magnificence of the execution, this was in many ways a very unroyal and untraditional occasion. Unlike the funerals of Churchill and Mountbatten, there were no massed military bands, no orders, stars and decorations, no ceremonial swords or plumed hats, no sailors pulling the gun carriage. In the year of the Hong Kong handover, and the fiftieth anniversary of Indian independence, this was, appropriately, Britain's first post-imperial public funeral. Instead, the international celebrities came to mourn one of their own: Luciano Pavarotti, Henry Kissinger, Steven Spielberg, Diana Ross, Tom Hanks. And there were charity workers from the causes with which Diana had been most recently associated, who had been invited with the same end in view: ordinary men and women and children, some on crutches, others in wheelchairs. In its novel and unmartial amalgam of showbiz and inclusivity, this was very much a new generation, New Labour occasion.

Indeed, the funeral marked the end of a very good week for Tony Blair. His description of Diana as 'the people's princess' caught a mood which intensified as the days drew on. He seems to have played a substantial and well-judged part in nudging (or nagging) Buckingham Palace towards a more generous and large-scale approach to the funeral. He read the lesson at the service ('Faith, hope and love' from Corinthians) with an intelligent eloquence and compassionate authority that John Major could never have equalled. And for the whole of the week, the Tory Party, and Labour's midsummer problems, had virtually ceased to exist. William Hague all but vanished from sight, and the controversies surrounding relief for Monserrat, the millennium dome project and Scottish and Welsh devolution have been temporarily forgotten. Such are the benefits that the saddest of national events can bring an incumbent administration.

By contrast, the British monarchy fared noticeably less well. As she arrived at what will surely be the last great royal funeral before her own, the Queen Mother must have reflected that for all her seventy years of dutiful and reticent service to the throne, her send-off, which it had been hoped would bring the monarchy a new surge of popular support, will never equal Diana's in depth of feeling or spontaneity of emotion. The

Queen's broadcast to the nation, on the eve of the funeral, clawed back some of the ground that the royal family had lost by its silent, week-long, self-imposed incarceration in Balmoral, but it was a predictably wooden performance. As for Prince Charles: in the month before Diana died, she had been falling in public esteem, while he was gaining ground, as was the idea that he might one day hope to marry Mrs Parker Bowles. But that is surely now an impossible prospect, and many people will find it hard to forgive him for what they see as his part in Diana's tragedy.

Much of this, of course, is monstrously unfair, especially in regard to the Prince of Wales. There seems no reason to think that he was any more unfaithful a husband than Diana was a wife; by his own lights he is at least as caring and concerned a father as she was a mother; and his post-divorce liaison with Mrs Parker Bowles has been carried on with much more judgement and discretion than Diana's much-flaunted and much-vaunted relationship with Dodi Fayed. It is also the case that over the years, Charles must have done a great deal more for charity than Diana, that he has never courted publicity in the way she incorrigibly did, and that, for all his naivety, petulance, vanity and self-centredness, he is by all accounts the most decent, sensitive, civilised, well-educated heir to the British throne there has been in many a generation. But in the present climate, all this avails him nothing. Charles could never compete with Diana for public sympathy and support while she was alive, and now she is beatified, the contest becomes even more unequal.

From her grave to his, Diana is going to haunt Charles in death even more than she came to haunt him in life. This must be for him a terrible, nightmarish prospect. Indeed, his position has now been so suddenly and so shatteringly weakened that it is not clear what he can do to retrieve it. Bullied by a boorish father, kept at arm's length by a distant mother, and completely upstaged by a superstar wife: his has indeed been an unenviable lot, and it is a lot which is now more unenviable than ever. With few exceptions, the twentieth century has been an unprecedentedly constraining time for British royal men, even as it has provided unprecedented opportunities for British royal women, and Charles and Diana exemplify both of these trends in their most exaggerated form. No wonder Charles looks so bewildered and bemused – and now so bereaved. He may still be the heir to the throne, and he may still succeed to it: but there is already a sense that history has passed him by.

Significantly, it was Diana's blood relations who dominated her funeral, while her royal ex-relatives were banished to the sidelines, and Charles in particular. Earl Spencer walked directly behind the coffin, with Prince William on his right and Prince Harry on his left, relegating the Duke of Edinburgh and the Prince of Wales to the furthest distance away. Both Diana's sisters read poems during the service; it was at their request that Elton John sang 'Candle in the Wind'; and in his eulogy of his sister, Lord Spencer paid off his sister's accumulated scores against the royal establishment. He referred to the decision to deprive Diana of the title 'Her Royal Highness' at the time of the divorce: a decision which many thought petty then, and which now seems unconscionably mean-spirited. He alluded to the cold, unfeeling treatment which his sister had received at the hands of the royal court. And he vowed that her children would be brought up in the open, loving, relaxed style that she would have wished.

Public ceremonials are often as much about the sublimation of conflict as they are about the articulation of consensus, and at Diana's funeral, the House of Spencer, strongly supported on this occasion by the British (and global) public, won its sublimated conflict with the House of Windsor game, set and match. In earlier times, it was the prerogative of the aristocracy to chastise and rebuke the monarchy as and when it was deemed necessary, and that prerogative was today called triumphantly out of abeyance by Diana's brother. So it was that the three moments of loudest applause (something, incidentally, which would itself have seemed inconceivable at any previous royal funeral) were when, in response to public pressure, the Union Jack was raised to half-mast above Buckingham Palace on the Queen's departure for the Abbey; when Elton John finished his song, specially rewritten for the occasion; and when Earl Spencer concluded his fighting eulogy.

Those who felt that Diana had been 'one of them' while alive turned out in their hundreds of thousands to be 'on her side' now she was dead. For all its magnificent pageantry and celebrity aura, this was in many ways a genuinely populist funeral, symbolising some sort of victory of the people whose princess she was over the Palace whose princess she wasn't. It is not yet apparent what sort of victory this was, nor how important it was. And it is too early to know whether this is a one-off success, or the portent of a more general, more actively critical attitude to the post-Diana British monarchy. It is unlikely that the majority of people who turned up to mourn their queen of hearts were rabid republicans – or that they will become so. But it is also far from clear that they will accept her funeral as an adequate apology for the many wrongs which they believe Diana suffered at the hands of the royal establishment.

One further imaginative gesture which the Queen might consider making is abolishing the title 'Royal Highness' for all except those in direct line of succession to the throne. This would go some way towards atoning for the slight which Diana was obliged to endure, and it would get rid of some of the old regime flummery with which the monarchy is still excessively encrusted. (There is nothing royal or high about Princess Michael of Kent – except the level of her debts.) It would also reflect and acknowledge the general mood of the country under New Labour, where there is – or there ought to be – precious little sympathy for the perpetuation of anachronistic, titular privileges such as this, and the bowing, curtsying and demeaningly deferential behaviour which accompany them. Indeed, if the Queen herself is not prepared to contemplate or propose such a change, perhaps Tony Blair might formally advise her to do so.

As for the longer term, it is too soon to know what the consequences of Diana's death will be for the royal family or the monarchy. But this much, at least, can be reckoned upon. Some time ahead, Diana's eldest son is going to become king, and he will go to his coronation in Westminster Abbey. On that future day, some future Dimbleby will utter these words, or their close equivalent: 'And so the crown of England is placed upon King William's head, in whose face we see once again the face of his mother. How proud she would have been to be here in the Abbey today.' It will be a moment of total, show-stopping, heartstring-tugging emotion, and once the shock of Diana's death has passed, there will be many of her generation who will begin living for that day: Diana's final victory. Until then, the Queen Mother, the Queen and Prince Charles will seem for many little more than an outmoded holding operation. Diana has not finished with the British monarchy yet. The future still very much belongs to her.

(1997)

PART TWO
Hindsight's Insights

I I

Patriotism

No Prime Minister this century, not even Lloyd George or Winston Churchill, has played what is termed the patriotic card with such sustained and self-conscious success as Mrs Thatcher. For ten triumphant years, she has been waving the flag, blowing the bugle, sending the gunboats, rallying the troops, leading the charge. Abroad, she has trounced the Argentinians, restored the special relationship with the United States, reasserted Britain's voice in the Commonwealth, and disregarded the continental jabberings of the all-too-Common Marketeers. At home, she has vanquished the trade unions, beaten inflation, rolled back the welfare state, and set the people free. Like George III, she glories in the name of Briton and, like Queen Victoria, she is not interested in the possibilities of defeat, because they simply do not exist. To her admirers (and to her cartoonists) she has become the very embodiment of national identity, national regeneration and national purpose – a conquering heroine, a blue-rinse Boudicca, a pearls-and-twinset Britannia. Not since Palmerston's day has a British premier been so pugnaciously populist or so publicly patriotic.

Inevitably, the losers in this poker game of tub-thumping – and there are many – view Mrs Thatcher's remarkable blend of matriarchal machismo and female chauvinism in rather a different light. She may be the Prime Minister of the Home Counties, but among the Welsh and the Scots, the poor and the sick, the unemployed and the immigrant communities, her writ hardly runs. She celebrates private gain and individual self-help, but she has deliberately subverted that public spirit of disinterested endeavour which was once the glory of the civil service, the universities and the BBC. She claims to stand for national economic recovery, but she has turned the City into a paradise for international speculators and insider dealers, she has allowed British industry to be sold off to the highest overseas bidder (remember Rowntrees?), and she has wilfully countenanced a catastrophic contraction in the country's manufacturing base. And while she aspires to cut an influential figure on the world stage, her hooliganish handling of Britain's foreign policy has left the country dangerously isolated – disliked by most of the Third World, virtually friendless in the Commonwealth, widely distrusted in Europe, and excessively and humiliatingly dependent on American goodwill.

From Hampstead to Brixton, Oxford University to the late-lamented GLC, Lambeth Palace to Highgrove House, Mrs Thatcher's claims to divine the national will, to represent the national interest, and to promote the national well-being have been questioned, contested and rejected. She, in turn, dismisses her opponents as Tory-wet appeasers, fellow-travelling intellectuals, self-seeking Socialists, or fanatical Marxist subversives, whose patriotic protestations are no more than treason's traitorous disguises. *They* respond by asserting – in a manner reminiscent of the opposition to Sir Robert Walpole – that it is the dissidents, not the government, who are the true patriots, who possess the more comprehensive and the more honourable sense of the common weal. In electoral terms, this has not amounted to very much: the Prime Minister's opponents are (thus far) too diverse, too divided and too dispirited to have caught the public imagination or to have captured the rhetorical initiative. Nevertheless, their very existence underscores one of the most significant developments of the Thatcher years. Instead of being an unspoken assumption or a consensual concept, patriotism is now high on the agenda of public discussion and public disagreement.

It was in response (and reaction) to these developments that Raphael Samuel and his co-labourers in the History Workshop organised a conference on patriotism which was held at Oxford in the spring of 1984, just two years after the Falklands War, and less than twelve months after the Tory landslide at the polls.[1] 'Organised' may, perhaps, be putting it too strongly: the conference itself was higher on enthusiasm than on efficiency, and it has taken five years to get the augmented proceedings into print. Ironically, then, it is to Mrs Thatcher herself that the workshoppers should feel most indebted: without her continued and unprecedented pre-eminence, the three major issues which these books address might long since have lost their topicality. Predictably, their prime concern is to place patriotism as emphatically on the agenda of historical inquiry as it is on the agenda of political discussion. More particularly, they seek to analyse – and to discredit – the patriotism of the right which remains, for them, so regrettably in the ascendant. And their final aim is to reclaim patriotism for the left, partly by uncovering the historical antecedents of oppositional loyalty, and partly by trying to mobilise the many disparate victims of Tory misrule into 'an anti-Thatcher majority. Instead of being the last refuge of the scoundrel, patriotism in the 1980s has thus become the first priority of the socialist.

The essays collected in volume 1 promise to 'demystify the prevailing conception of nationality', by exposing it as a mistaken historical construct and a one-sided political view. In its conventional guise, we are told, British history is no more than a dark record of evil and oppression: the true patriotic tradition is that of popular resistance to tyranny, most notably found in the mid-seventeenth century, when for one brief shining moment, ordinary people actually took charge of their own history. But since then, it has been downhill all the way. For much of the eighteenth century, to be patriotic still meant to be in opposition: but by the later part of Queen Victoria's reign, the Tories had successfully established their claim to be the one true national, imperial and patriotic party. Thereafter, the left has always been at a disadvantage, and its twentieth-century experience has largely been one of defeat and disappointment. Even the ending of empire has not lead to the abandonment of jingoistic excesses. As Anthony Barnett notes, in a particularly sceptical and sensible contribution, there can be no future for the patriotism of the left unless it comes to terms with the success – and the sincerity – of the patriotism of the right.

The best essays in this volume offer a useful – if largely familiar – guide to the changing contours of national feeling in Britain from the eighteenth century to the present day. But this is hardly a path-breaking investigation into the history and politics of British patriotism, or into the making and unmaking of British national identity. Many of the papers are so narrow in their focus that they fail to address (or to establish) the broader themes which should have been identified. There is no discussion of the state, of the deeper meanings of national identity, or of the differences between nationalism, patriotism, jingoism and imperialism. Most of the essays are pervaded by a tone of Little England parochialism, and ignore 'abroad' completely. Yet as Richard Gott points out, 'Nationalism and patriotism do not exist in a vacuum. They occur as a by-product of a country's relationship with the outside world.' But no such perspective is offered here. Even more disturbing is the determined refusal to address what must surely be the fundamental question: why it is that certain forms of patriotism, associated with certain economic interests, certain social groups and certain political opinions, have acquired (and lost) a national resonance, while other forms have not?

For the second volume, the focus shifts from 'national identity' to 'separate societies', to alternative and more personal forms of belonging. A series of autobiographical essays vividly recaptures the narrowness and diversity of children's worlds: a Folkestone boyhood, a Catholic education, a secondary school on Tyneside, the chapel community in Bicester. There are studies of women – as nurses in the Crimea, as factory workers at Woolwich Arsenal, and as non-combatants during the Second World War – which remind us that for many of them, the public world of power, politics and patriotism almost entirely passed them by. There are essays on the non-English parts of Britain: Christopher Harvie subtly contextualises Sir Walter Scott; Tim Williams explains why the Welsh language almost died out during the nineteenth century; and Raphael Samuel looks at the importance of Catholicism for Irish immigrants. And there are studies of minority communities which mainly concern the consciousness-raising experiences of blacks and homosexuals. Best of all, however, is David Feldman's account of the sudden Jewish influx into the East End from the 1880s, which vividly depicts the resulting tensions between the assimilationist elite, and the newcomers who were more eager to retain their autonomous identity.

Thus described, as an inchoate amalgam of separate communities, it seems as if the British nation has never really existed at all – a conclusion which sits somewhat awkwardly with the chauvinistic concerns of the first volume. Put less glibly, this means that too many of the essays in *Minorities and Outsiders* merely replicate the very parochialism they should be trying to understand in a broader perspective. There is no discussion of civic pride, of the county community, of the love-hate relationship between the metropolis and the provinces, or of how these local loyalties connect (or compete) with a larger sense of national identity. The essays on Scott, on the Welsh language and on Irish immigrants seem strangely ignorant of recent work that has been done on 'British' as distinct from 'English' history. As in the first volume, the international perspective is also inexcusably lacking. We are constantly told that Britain was (and is) a racist society, much less tolerant of minorities than it is comfortably fashionable to suppose. No doubt there is some truth in this. But compared with the ante-bellum United States, Nazi Germany or Soviet Russia (to say nothing of Nigeria or South Africa), Britain's treatment of outsiders has not been as totally deplorable as is repeatedly insisted upon here.

In the third volume, the workshoppers turn to what they call 'national fictions': to the ideas and images, the myths and traditions which form the imaginative constructs of national character and national identity. An essay on John Bull reminds us that at the time of the Napoleonic Wars, his symbolic significance was much more ambiguous than it later became. In the same way, it was only towards the end of the nineteenth century that Britannia became the upper middle-class lady so beloved of *Punch* cartoons. Even the cult of the countryside turns out, on closer inspection, to have been much more contested than the all-pervasive *Country Life* aesthetic of our own time might imply: Vaughan Williams's music now seems for many the essence of pastoral cosiness, but he himself was a lifelong socialist. And many writers whose patriotic attitudes are generally supposed to be clear-cut were in fact much more equivocal: Conrad and Kipling were both out of sympathy with much that was happening in early twentieth-century Britain; Orwell's patriotism did not encompass the working class or left-wing intellectuals; and Le Carré turns out to be little more than Ian Fleming, thinly disguised.

Some of these essays are both suggestive and substantial, and as such they are among the most valuable in the entire collection. But once again, the volume as a whole is conspicuous in its limitations: there is nothing here on the Union Jack or the national anthem, on St George or Nelson, on Elgar or Arthur Bryant. Of course, it is instructive to be reminded that many of today's most unifying national symbols were once much more contested in their meaning and appeal, and that popular imaginative writing about Britain contains more layers of significance than a superficial reading suggests. But in historical terms, these repeated exercises in ambiguous contextualisation and multifaceted analysis do not get us very far. Sooner or later, most symbols, most icons, become invested with one particular set of national values, while most composers, most writers, become associated with one specific interpretation of England. For the historian, the important task is to find out how, why and when this happened. Alternatively, we need to know why national myths in Britain centre round John Bull, Britannia and the monarchy, rather than – say – Oliver Cromwell and the Tolpuddle Martyrs. But questions such as these go largely unexplored here.

Taken together, these volumes exemplify the strengths and the weaknesses of the history workshoppers' approach to the past, and both by now are very familiar. There is enthusiasm and idealism in admirable abundance, and a readiness to confront important issues which many professional his-

torians simply refuse to address; there is a welcome candour about the ideological presuppositions and political objectives which underlay this value-
laden historical enterprise; and Raphael Samuel's many contributions are
quite unrivalled displays of free-associational virtuosity. But this neither
justifies nor excuses the unacceptably uneven quality of the finished product. Despite the editor's best efforts, all three volumes are lacking in thematic coherence. Much of the writing is too antiquarian, too anecdotal,
too self-indulgent, and is virtually devoid of conceptual sophistication or
explanatory force. Some of these essays have been published before; some
should not have been published here; some should not have been published anywhere. Like many such collections, the whole is no greater than
the sum of its parts and, inevitably, this means the three central objectives
of this enterprise are less fully achieved than they might have been.

To begin with, the workshoppers are neither very happy nor very successful in dealing with the patriotism of the right. By definition, most conservatives feel no need to explain or to investigate something which is so
obviously congenial to their instincts (and interests). On the other hand,
many socialists can neither understand nor empathise with a belief system
which is as alien to their own way of thinking as Marx is to the Prime
Minister or pornography is to Mrs Whitehouse. It is easy for them to
expose the fallacies and the false assumptions which on occasions underlay the right's more extravagant patriotic claims. But this only makes it
harder for them to address patriotism as the important historical phenomenon which it undoubtedly is. One thousand pages, fifty contributors
and three volumes on, we still do not know how or why 'the nation' was
roused in 1588 or 1940, or why so many men rushed to the colours in
1914. To say that 'the country had gone mad' at the time of the Falklands
War merely demonstrates the workshoppers' inability to understand the
very thing they seek to explain. Concerned incomprehension and enraged
disapproval are not the most helpful feelings with which to undertake
serious historical inquiry.

To some extent, at least, they fare rather better in their attempts to
establish a valid, alternative patriotism of the left. In these confrontational
days when virtually anyone who dares disagree with the government is
branded a Marxist or a traitor, it is heartening to be reminded that in the
past (as in the present) there have been people who have clashed with the
authorities whose motives and conduct have been entirely patriotic. It
should not need saying – but in the 1980s, alas, it does – that the interests of the nation are not always, and not necessarily, best served by

abjectly agreeing with the prime minister of the day. But in other ways, the position (and prospects) of the patriotic left seem rather less promising, since another strand in radical thought is so entirely opposed to this way of proceeding. For many socialists, including some of the contributors to this volume, loyalty to class, to gender, to ideology and to internationalism, transcends, condemns and subverts what they see as the petty parochialism, the jingoistic excesses and the transient claims of the bourgeois nation state. Quite simply, they do not like patriotism in any guise at all. Ironically, but inevitably, these volumes thus expose the weaknesses and divisions of the left much more damagingly than they analyse or subvert the shortcomings of the right.

As for patriotism in general, the conclusions are at best blandly portentous and at worst disappointingly unexceptionable: it is, we learn, 'never self-contained'. Many different people, in many different places, at many different times, and for many different reasons, have experienced patriotic feelings welling up within them. But these sentiments may be conformist or subversive, governmental or oppositional, selfless or selfish, national or local, socialist or capitalist, proletarian or bourgeois, pacifist or militarist, Catholic or Protestant, an instrument of social control from above or of determined resistance from below. The most that can be said is that patriotism is ideologically ambiguous, politically contentious, morally uncertain and historically unspecific – a battle zone, a contested territory, an arena of disputation, where the combatants, the engagement and the outcome change according to circumstance. Thus described, patriotism is the ultimate floating signifier – something at once so protean and so pervasive as to be devoid of any conceptual rigour, analytical purchase or explanatory power. As Edith Cavell once remarked (and she had good cause to know), patriotism alone is not enough.

(1989)

NOTE

1 Raphael Samuel (ed.), *Patriotism: The Making and Unmaking of British National Identity*, vol. 1: *History and Politics*; vol. 2: *Minorities and Outsiders*; vol. 3: *National Fictions* (London, 1989).

12
Privacy

'I think very few people are completely normal really, deep down in their private lives.' These frivolously dispiriting words are spoken by Amanda, to her new husband, Victor, early in Act I of Noel Coward's play of that name. But they might also serve as the damning epigraph for this book of that name.[1] It is the latest instalment in the five-volume series, originally conceived by Georges Duby and the late Philippe Ariès, which was first published in France in the mid-1980s, and is now appearing in translation, the idea of which was to provide a wide-ranging survey of western private life from the Roman Empire to the present day. As the editors candidly, if rather theatrically, admitted, their enterprise was 'fraught with peril'. By definition, much of the inwardness of private life remains unknowable, and the further back in time the historian probes, the more this is bound to be so. Indeed, until the nineteenth century, the very idea of private life as something separated off from the public realm would have been incomprehensible to most European men and women. Undismayed by the vaulting nature of their ambition, and by the unavoidable anachronism inherent in its realisation, Duby and Ariès brought together a team of (mainly French) historians, and charged them to 'put their eyes to keyholes', and 'to spy out what happens in other people's houses, and tell the neighbours about it'.

For the first two books in the series, this worked reasonably well. Volume 1 ranged across the length and breadth of the Roman Empire, and even-handedly surveyed the early Middle Ages in the West, and Byzantium in the tenth and eleventh centuries. It also dealt with many subjects commonsensically encompassed by the term 'private life': individuals and groups, work and leisure, homes and households, the body and the inner self, religion and belief. The second volume, covering the period from AD 1000 to the early sixteenth century, made imaginative use of contemporary literary sources, and showed how notions of privacy and intimacy evolved even in a society dominated by noble households and great abbeys. But there was a regrettable contraction of geographical range, and this was narrowed still further in the third volume, which was almost entirely restricted to France. The timescale was also more limited, being confined essentially to the early modern period, and most of the essays were evocative rather than analytical. Ironically enough, this latest volume, which deals with the very period when the idea of a fully developed private life first truly flowered, is much the weakest so far. It is confined to the 'long' nineteenth century (1789 to 1914), and it displays a narrowness of sympathy by comparison with which Amanda's disenchanted comment on the human condition seems positively benevolent and up-beat.

It is also, apart from a brief, token, unassimilated chapter on early nineteenth-century England, exclusively concerned with the French. Of course, the rich diversity of private life in nineteenth-century France is an entirely legitimate subject of historical study. But it is certainly not the same thing as the history of private life in the western world *tout court*, which is what this series was intended to be about. It tells us nothing of Germany, the Low Countries, the Iberian Peninsula, or European communities overseas. Nor is any helpful guidance offered in this volume as to the representativeness – or otherwise – of the French experience. At one point, we learn that English society influenced France 'in a hundred different ways'. Then, at another, we are informed that British pre-eminence was superseded by Germany and the United States. But later on we are told that 'private life in the nineteenth century cannot easily be separated from the national cultures within which it flourished', and that 'France seems to constitute a separate case in the history of western individualism.' It is impossible for the reader to make anything of these contradictory signals.

In addition to being flawed by these unjustified (and unjustifiable) limitations in geographical scope, the book is further harmed by its prose, which often fluctuates wildly between the pretentious and the banal, as is well illustrated in Michelle Perrot's sometimes bizarre introduction. 'Today's worker', we are told, 'looks upon his or her home as an ever more personalised refuge from the boss's surveillance and the discipline of the factory.' He (or she) does? 'Ideology, rhetoric and practice', she goes on to say, 'in the spheres of economics, politics and ethics were re-cast in the early twentieth century to embrace "the masses".' They were? 'Processes of sectorization, dissociation, and dissemination', we are further informed, 'are at work everywhere.' They are? Not surprisingly, the editor has little time for traditional brands of more rigorous historical investigation. 'The standard approaches of economic and social history' are grandly dismissed as being 'insufficient'. Historical demography 'offers only a crude framework' of inquiry. Perhaps so. But whatever its shortcomings, it is certainly not as crude as the framework that is on offer here.

After these pretentious platitudes, it is a welcome relief to turn to Lynn Hunt's essay on 'The Unstable Boundaries of the French Revolution', which explores with characteristic insight and authority the changing and contested borders between the private and the public during the years 1789–94. Among many other things, the initial aim of the Revolutionaries was to reassert the classical view that the public realm was much more important than the private domain, and should, indeed, have full control over it. As a result, the state became unprecedentedly intrusive in the private affairs of individuals: the regulations concerning marriage were secularised and reformed; the time of day and the monthly calendar were both restructured; and even individual names and patterns of dress became politicised. But as the institutional structure of the *ancien régime* was swept away, especially the nobility, the church, and the corporations, this also provided new – and unintended – opportunities for individuals to shape their private lives, especially in such matters as religion and marriage. In short, while the initial aim of the Revolution was to diminish the realm of personal privacy, Hunt suggests that its unintended consequence was to provide new space and opportunities for people to live their personal lives.

This is a stimulating and salutary chapter, and it is a pity that its approach is so little emulated in the pages which follow. For what Hunt rightly insists upon is the need to de-ghettoise the study of the private, and to reintegrate it with the study of the public. She will not allow us to forget that most people lived (and still live) lives that were partly private, partly public, and that it is essential to study the relationship between them. Yet in the remainder of the book, the public realm is effectively ignored, on the grounds that the nineteenth century was obsessed with privacy, as more and more people fled from the world and lived their lives behind closed doors. But was private life in France ever this cosy, this comfortable, this detached from public affairs? The 1800s saw unprecedented mobilisation for the Napoleonic Wars. There was subsequent invasion and defeat; wives were widowed; children were orphaned. In

1830, there was one political revolution and, seventeen years later, there was another. In 1870, there was the Paris Commune, and the humiliation of the Franco–Prussian War, and at the turn of the century, the country was all but rent asunder over the Dreyfus Affair. Once in every generation, the personal lives of French men and women were violently intruded upon by public events, the effects of which must surely have been profound and long lasting. But in the pages which follow, this essential matter goes unexplored.

Except, that is, in the only essay to step beyond the bounds of France: Catherine Hall's chapter on 'The Sweet Delights of Home', as evolved by the British middle class during the early decades of the nineteenth century. She begins with an examination of the 'Queen Caroline Affair' of 1820, which arose because of the determination of George IV, the new monarch, to put his wife on public trial for adultery. Beyond any doubt, Caroline had been an unfaithful wife. But the King had been at least as unfaithful a husband. The result was a massive upsurge of popular opinion, in support of the wronged Queen, and in defence of new notions of virtuous domesticity which, it was widely believed, King George IV had blatantly transgressed. The remainder of Hall's essay attempts to show precisely how these new – and essentially middle-class – notions came into being. Part of the answer, Hall suggests, lies in the growth of Evangelical religion, and part lies in the increased separation of home from workplace. The result was the rise of middle-class suburbia, the confining of women into the private sphere of home, and the monopolising by men of the public sphere of affairs. And very gradually, this new arrangement of separate spheres spread in Britain to the aristocracy above and the working class beneath.

Readers of Hall's earlier, collaborative work will already be familiar with the outlines of her argument, and she has little to add that is new. The belief that the royal family should embody domestic virtue long antedated the accession of George IV: as witnessed by the popular appeal of his own father during the 1780s and 1790s. The claim that there was a 'moral majority' in support of Queen Caroline is both quantitatively unverifiable and terminologically anachronistic. And it is not at all clear that middle-class Victorian women were as exclusively confined to the home as Hall would have us believe. In genteel suburbs like Birmingham's Edgbaston, there was much vigorous, non-home-based local activity, centred on churches, assembly rooms, charitable institutions and voluntary societies. Nor does Hall convincingly show that women were forced out of nineteenth-century British public life. This view has been so often repeated in feminist historiography that it has attained the status of a self-evident, unchallengeable truth. But it has yet to be verified, and the existence of such public women as Harriet Martineau, Frances Burdett Coutts, Florence Nightingale and Queen Victoria suggests that such verification may prove rather difficult.

Michelle Perrot then returns to write about 'The Family Triumphant' and 'Roles and Characters'. But there is nothing celebratory in these chapters. On the contrary, she regards the middle-class family as a repressive and suffocating institution, which 'took the place of God', and 'sought to regulate its members' activities'. The paterfamilias was possessed of 'absolute superiority' according to the Civil Code: he could read his wife's private correspondence, and could order the arrest of his children. Inevitably, the family seethed with inner tensions and conflicts, which occasionally erupted into terrible violence. Husbands quarrelled with wives over the household budget. Recalcitrant children were despatched to reform schools or lunatic asylums. Sons longed for their fathers' deaths, and then argued bitterly over their inheritance. Adolescents rebelled against the 'heightened surveillance' of their parents. Many bourgeois marriages were 'dictated by family and company interests'. There was constant fear of scandal, especially madness, illegitimacy, bankruptcy or the birth of an abnormal child. Perrot's conclusion is as sombre as it is cumbersome: 'a source of existential anxiety, nineteenth-century family totalitarianism was in many ways profoundly neurotic.'

By contrast, Anne Martin-Fugier's essay on 'Bourgeois Rituals' seems much better balanced. For her, the family was a place 'for sentimentality, tenderness and joy', and she provides ample evidence of the way in which the ceremonials of private life generated and reinforced these feelings. She explores the carefully structured schedule of a family day, and notes how much time and attention were given over to conversation and entertainments inside the home, and to the maintenance of social relations outside. She examines the annual calendar, and gives appropriate weight to Christmas and to the summer holidays, as essential elements in the rituals of family life. And she investigates the most significant rites of passage: baptism, First Communion, engagement, marriage, old age, death and mourning. Her treatment is more evocative than analytical, she makes no attempt to explore the different levels of meaning that must have been attached to such a sacred-yet-secular festival as Christmas, and she has little to say about the emotions associated with marriage or mourning. But as a celebration of the warmth and comfort of family life, this chapter is a welcome antidote to Perrot's morbid and unsympathetic musings. 'The family', Martin-Fugier rightly and imaginatively concludes, 'shared common emotions, and rejoiced in its own existence.'

Unfortunately, there seems to be no one else in this volume who shares this perspective: certainly not Roger-Henri Guerrand, in his essay on 'Private Spaces'. He begins with a view of social relations which can hardly be called subtle: 'throughout the nineteenth century, the dominant class displayed contempt for proletarians.' He provides a useful survey of bourgeois apartments and town houses, as well as the chateaux built by the old and new nobility during and after the Second Empire, and his description of urban and rural slums vividly evokes the squalor and deprivation of working-class life. (It also suggests that homes and workplaces continued to be mixed up together, at least among the French working class, for a great deal longer than Hall's argument would allow.) But Guerrand's main purpose, in a chapter which becomes increasingly unbalanced as it proceeds, is to expose the provision of single-family company housing as an elaborate conspiracy on the part of the entrepreneurial middle class to 'trap' their employees in domesticity, so as to make them more docile and pliant workers. Only when 'the subversive winds of socialism and social art' began to blow, and architects began to react against the idea of 'confinement in the single-family home' by designing apartment buildings, was it possible for members of the working class to emancipate themselves from the thraldom and tyranny of the bourgeoisie. This seems a rather simplistic view of architectural history no less than of social history.

According to Alain Perron, in another wayward chapter entitled 'The Secret of the Individual', the most significant trend during the nineteenth century was the growth in personal identity, by which he means the increased awareness people had of themselves and their subjective experience. This seems an unexceptionable opinion, and there is considerable evidence that can be cited in its support, from the development of the photograph to improved sanitary facilities which, Perron insists, resulted in increased 'communing with the self'. But much of this essay consists of increasingly wild generalisations which are at best unverifiable and at worst almost meaningless. Thus we are informed that as the nineteenth century advanced, 'introspection became commonplace', fetishism and masturbation were on the increase, and 'the body became an obsession'. But none of this can be historically proven. We are further told that 'the formulation of individual ambitions' caused 'family structures to disintegrate', and that there are 'innumerable signs of growing disregard for family members, and of the evaporation of family feeling'. But what is the evidence for this? And when we learn that 'dolls encouraged daughters to think about their relations to their own mothers', and that, by 1914, 'animals were on the verge of becoming sovereign masters of domestic space', we have reached the realms of pure fantasy.

Corbin's next chapter, on 'Intimate Relations', seems no less confused. He tells us that many middle-class adolescent males 'abhorred the commonplace, and believed themselves called to do great things'. They did? We learn that many brides were subjected to brutal sexual initiation 'because many husbands concealed their true nature until the wedding night'. How can we know this? He informs us that 'sexuality, a central part of every modern marriage, in the nineteenth century was merely a backdrop to married life.' But it is difficult to believe that either part of this generalisation can be verified. And we are told that the wider use of contraceptives, the rise of sexology, the increase in divorce rates, and the growth in the amount of adultery meant that the traditional, bourgeois notion of romantic love was 'on the wane' during the last quarter of the nineteenth century. Of course, these were new developments which, in the long run (i.e. after 1945) were to have the greatest impact on sexual relations and family life. But as Corbin coyly admits elsewhere, divorce and adultery were very much the exception in the late nineteenth century, and 'criticism of matrimony was only heard from the emancipated few'.

Only those who like their books to have sad endings will find this volume to be essential reading, since it closes with a chapter entitled 'Cries and Whispers', which presents a morbid cavalcade of the disaffected, the despairing and the unhappy, who are misleadingly presented as if they stood for French humanity as a whole. 'Individual feelings of malaise', we are portentously informed, 'assumed considerable historical importance at this time.' There were widespread fears about the degeneration of the species and of the family. The urban working class aroused feelings of 'revulsion, terror and fascination'. Women became increasingly hysterical, 'to draw the attention of those around them to their private suffering'. In both the country and the town, there was a massive increase in alcoholism. The suicide rate rose rapidly and alarmingly: men preferred the rope, women opted for drowning. There was a predictable growth in the medical profession, in hospitals and in asylums. Not surprisingly, 'neurasthenia and psychasthenia' became 'common diagnoses'. In short, the inhabitants of *fin de siècle* France seem to have been struck down by irresistible collective neurosis: and those few who did not succumb to this all-pervasive depression were merely demonstrating 'obligatory happiness'.

The most that can be said for this quite extraordinary book is that it is beautifully produced, that the profuse illustrations are a constant delight, and that the essays by Hunt, Hall and Martin-Fugier will well repay a second reading. But the volume as a whole is not at all satisfactory. It claims to be treating a subject of continental – perhaps global – significance, yet is only concerned with one country. Much of the writing consists of wild and pretentious generalisations, which range from the unverifiable to the meaningless. And many of the contributors are more eager to indict, to prosecute and to convict the middle-class family than they are to understand it, to explain it, or even to imagine it. How devastatingly has Georges Duby's metaphor about historians spying through the keyholes of the past redounded in this volume! For the view taken through the keyhole by most of the contributors is at best limited, at worst plain misleading. They have zealously sought out the most disagreeable elements in nineteenth-century private and family life, but in so doing, they have missed – indeed wilfully missed – the totality of the picture. And as a result, they have unintentionally cast the very gravest doubts on the type of history which they practise.

It should by now be clear why Amanda's words furnish so appropriate a summary, and so damning a criticism, of this book: for it dwells almost exclusively on the darker side of human nature with morbid relish bordering on the obsessional. Wherever possible the family life of the nineteenth-century bourgeoisie is given an unambiguously pathological interpretation. Husbands and wives retreated into domesticity because they were unable to 'connect with others'. Their upholstered furniture and heavy wall hangings were 'a sign of unconscious fear of the masses'. The developing craze for collecting and for keeping diaries were 'forms of self-destruction'. The growing affection for animals betokened 'a veritable collective neurosis'. Piano playing was a form of masturbation. The obsession with 'drapery, slip covers, casing and upholstery' showed 'the extraordinary hypertrophy' of the bourgeois erotic imagination. And 'the fascination that the lesbian exerted on the male imagination' was 'yet another symptom of the morbid character of male desire in the nineteenth century'. The best that can be said of such remarks, like many other statements in this book, is that they are tendentious generalisations which are quite incapable of historical proof.

Equally one-sidedly, the majority of the contributors condemn the nineteenth-century bourgeois family as a 'totalitarian unit', a 'nest of vipers', a 'place seething with internal conflict', between men and women over power in the home, and between the generations over money and freedom. They see the family as a life-denying institution, founded on patriarchal tyranny and the oppression of women and children, which was mainly concerned with the transmission of wealth and property. Victor Hugo is regularly brought on to do duty as the typical domineering patriarch, 'who sat like a god in the tabernacle of his home', and locked away his demented daughter, Adèle, for the sake of the good name of the family. And there is a cameo part for Pierre Rivere, the 'red-eyed parricide', who killed not only his mother, but also his sister and brother for good measure. Appropriately enough, Michelle Perrot quotes André Gide: 'Families, I hate you', and that view seems to be shared by many of the contributors. Apart from Anne Martin-Fugier, none of the authors seems willing to admit that the nineteenth-century family might have been a place of warmth, tenderness, security, comfort, fulfilment and hope. The cosy world of domestic happiness recently and vividly evoked by Simon Schama and Peter Gay finds no answering echo here.

The book is also insufficiently nuanced in its treatment of privacy as it was experienced (or not experienced) by different social levels. We are told, quite correctly, that in the country and in the town, the working classes were often so poor, so crowded together and housed so close to their work that they were obliged to live 'a different style of private life' from their betters. But put more bluntly, this means that many of them had no real private lives at all. Even the middle classes, apparently safe and *gemütlich* behind their closed doors and lace curtains, were usually obliged to share their houses with servants. But the extent to which this must have limited their privacy, their intimacy and their freedom is never seriously considered. (Indeed, the very fact that most middle-class people today do not have live-in servants must mean that contemporary private life is fundamentally different from what it was only a hundred years ago.) Nor can the very rich have enjoyed anything closely resembling what we would call private life. Their houses, both in the town and the country, were not domestic residences as we would understand that term. On the contrary, they provided theatrical settings, for entertaining, for politicking, for the informal conduct of public business. As Michelet observed, 'the rich ... have no privacy, no secrecy, no home.' But this remark, though quoted, goes unexplored.

It is also unclear precisely what role French women played in public affairs during the period covered by this book. The prevailing view put forward here is that during 'the nineteenth century, women were restricted to the private sphere more than ever before'. But if this was indeed the case, we need to know why. Perhaps it was because of the country's essentially conservative Catholic culture, which might, in turn, explain why women did not get the vote until 1945. But as in the case of England, this view that women were forced out of public life and back into the home has been asserted more than it has been proved. Indeed, Olwen Hufton has recently suggested that there is no convincing evidence that nineteenth-century French women were more homebound than their *ancien régime* forbears. At the top of the scale, they continued to play their traditional parts as social and political hostesses; while poorer women took part in bread riots in 1812 and 1816, were among the demonstrators in 1830, and were to be found on the barricades in 1848. And in between times, many of them were actually working. During the second half of the nineteenth century, French women provided between one-quarter and one-third of their country's workforce, which was a higher proportion than in England. In the light of these figures, the argument advanced here, that most Frenchwomen between, say, 1820 and 1914 spent their lives imprisoned in the home, stands in need of serious re-examination.

Nor is this book any more convincing in describing the relations between the sexes. Two models are provided: both of them are the merest carica-tures, and in addition, they are mutually exclusive. The first stresses the brute force of male dominance, and 'feminine passivity and docility'. According to this interpretation, men made 'ever more strenuous efforts' during the nineteenth century to control women, who were increasingly 'oppressed' by 'their experience of the male world'. But this picture, of the physically masterful man, and the pathetically passive woman, is on both counts the crudest form of sexual stereotyping. And so is the second model, which simply reverses these propositions. Men, so this argument runs, were 'convinced of their sexual inferiority', and so were 'obsessed by fear' of the 'terrifying, castrating female'. While women were smouldering volcanoes of devouring sexual passion, their menfolk were pitiful, proto-typical wimps, racked with anxiety, worried about their virility and no bet-ter at maintaining their jobs than keeping up their erections. To sustain two interpretations of the relations between men and women which are so crude, so condescending and so contradictory, is indeed an extraordinary accomplishment. How is it possible to take a book on family life and private life seriously which deals with the relations between the sexes in so simplistic a fashion?

The final problem with this book is that it is distorted by the very limited historical perspective which the contributors often display. On the one hand, many aspects of life and thought which are deemed to have originated during the nineteenth century – the keeping of private diaries, the cult of friendship, the concern for bodily modesty, the desire for separate spaces, the craving for individuality – had their origins in earlier centuries, and are, indeed, dealt with in the preceding volume in the series. On the other, the book gives altogether disproportionate space to those late nineteenth-century minorities who desired to bring the repressive, patriarchal family to an end: 'playwrights, left-wing politicians, bourgeois feminists, neo-Malthusian propagandists, advocates of free love, and the scientists who invented the discipline of sexology'. It is with these people – the forerunners of contemporary progressive opinion – that the authors' sympathies primarily lie, and it is easy to see why. For this enables them to berate the nineteenth-century family from the ahistorical standpoint of the 1980s. How ironic that the very period when the concept of private life first becomes non-anachronistic should find itself treated here in this unacceptably anachronistic way.

To these specific objections should be added some that are more deeply rooted, and more wide-ranging in their implications. For it seems clear that most of the contributors to this book know very little economic or social history, and are at least a generation out of date in what they do know. Many of them implicitly accept what might be called a vulgarised version of the arguments put forward nearly thirty years ago by E.P. Thompson in his *The Making of the English Working Class*. In that seminal book, Thompson suggested an eighteenth-century golden age of freedom and rights; depicted the Industrial Revolution as a disaster which took away those rights, and subjugated and enslaved the people; and implied that since then, their unfinished struggle had been to regain those lost rights. If women are substituted for workers, this provides the basic trajectory for much recent feminist history: an eighteenth century in which women played a conspicuous part in the public sphere; a nineteenth century in which they were driven into the home; and a twentieth century in which they have sought to re-emerge. This is a comforting and reassuring teleology. But a generation of historical research has largely overturned this view of the history of men, and there is no necessary reason to suppose that it is any more valid for the history of women.

The second historical model which this book – like much other feminist writing – implicitly accepts is equally out of date. Following on from Thompson once more, the key to British history during the modern period is taken to be class conflict. During the Industrial Revolution, so this argument goes, the middle classes triumphed, in the shape of the new entrepreneurial bourgeoisie, and they gradually imposed their values on the classes above, and even more on the classes below, by means of 'social control'. Again, if this account is suitably adjusted, it provides the essential underpinning of much women's history, which is preoccupied with the middle classes, and with the manufacturing middle classes at that. But again, the interpretation has been largely discredited in its original form: the rise of the entrepreneur looks much less majestic than it once did; class conflict no longer looms so large in histories of Victorian society; and the concept of 'social control' has very largely been abandoned. Yet these interpretations all too often remain self-evident truths for feminist historians.

Relying heavily on these two essentially outmoded historical models, the main contribution of feminist historians has been to graft on to them the distinction between the private and the public. As a result, they argue, of the Industrial Revolution, women were increasingly confined to the private sphere, while men took full control of the public. And it is that argument which forms the central organising principle of this book: 'the greatest debt of all', the editor writes, 'is to recent feminist reflection on the public and the private, the formation of distinct spheres of life.' But it is no longer clear that there were these two distinct spheres. In the nineteenth century, women spent time inside the home, and time outside. Some of them worked, and others took part in public life. And some men, like Mr Pooter, were more interested in domestic arrangements than in their job; some preferred the life of clubs and hotels to the hurly-burly of business; some restricted their activities to their professional endeavours; others went into politics. Under these extremely varied circumstances, which are not restricted to either gender, it becomes increasingly difficult to maintain that there were two separately demarcated realms: the public, inhabited by dominant men; and the private, inhabited by downtrodden women.

Two general conclusions follow from this. The first is that there is an urgent need to end the widespread segregation of women's history and women's studies from what, for want of a better phrase, might be termed mainstream historical inquiry. In many ways, the most significant, and regrettable, separate sphere is not the domestic confinement of women in the past, but the isolated position of women's studies departments in universities in the present. For it is high time that the work undertaken there was reintegrated with more recent developments in historical scholarship: not just for the benefit of women's studies, but for the general well-being and enhancement of history as a whole. The second lesson to be drawn from this book is that, like those many binary distinctions of which historians have recently been so enamoured – conflict and consensus, class and community, continuity and change, high politics and low politics, elite culture and popular culture – the contrast between public and private lives has by now long since outlived its usefulness. Although this book may be faulted for many reasons, it does accomplish at least one worthwhile objective, albeit unintended: for it unanswerably subverts the very subject that it seeks to illuminate. As it is written about here, it gives private life the kiss of death.

(1991)

NOTE

1 *A History of Private Life*, vol. 4: *From the Fires of Revolution to the Great War*, ed. Michelle Perrot, trans. Arthur Goldhammer (Cambridge, Mass., 1991).

13
Divorce

'Those whom God hath joined together,' proclaims the English *Book of Common Prayer*, in solemn and binding exhortation, 'let no man put asunder.' And, until relatively recently, it was God, rather than man, who had his way in regulating matrimonial matters. For most of the last five hundred years, marriage in England has been regarded as a sacred and indissoluble contract, and the overwhelming majority of such unions have been terminated only by the death of one of the partners. Even if the husband was the king, the combined weight of religious teaching and popular morality was such that divorce was an extremely rare and hazardous enterprise. In 1529, Henry VIII sought to rid himself of his first wife, Catherine of Aragon, but he was only able to do so by unleashing on his country a political, social and religious revolution understatedly described as the Reformation. In 1820, George IV tried to divorce his wife, Queen Caroline, but a sudden, massive upsurge of hostile public opinion made it impossible for him to obtain the necessary parliamentary legislation. And in 1936, King Edward VIII failed in his attempt to keep his throne and marry Mrs Wallis Simpson, not because she was his mistress, nor because she was an American, but because she was divorced, and it was widely believed that neither the British public, nor the British Empire, would stand for that.

Since the Second World War, however, there has been a dramatic increase in the number of divorces in England, and, once again, the royal family's experience vividly illustrates this sudden and remarkable change in attitudes and practices. In the mid-1950s, Princess Margaret publicly terminated her romance with the divorced Peter Townsend, on the grounds that marrying him would have been contrary to the teaching of the Church of England. But in 1978, her own marriage to Lord Snowdon was dissolved, and since then, matrimonial breakdown has become almost as commonplace in royal circles as motoring fines for exceeding the speed limit. The parents of the Princess of Wales have been divorced, as have the parents of the Duchess of York. The younger brother of the Duke of Kent (Prince Michael), and his eldest son (the Earl of St Andrews) both married wives whose previous husbands were alive. And although it has not yet been formally dissolved, the marriage between Princess Anne and Captain Mark Phillips has irretrievably broken down. In the early 1860s, at the time of the wedding of the then Prince of Wales, Walter Bagehot observed that 'a royal marriage is a princely edition of a universal fact, and as such it rivets mankind.' But today, the word 'divorce' could be readily substituted, and the remark would still be almost equally appropriate.

In the Britain of the 1990s, it is widely reported that one-third of all marriages now being entered into will be terminated by divorce. (The figure in the United States, incidentally, is even higher: at least one-half.) Even Mrs Thatcher, for all her pious talk of reviving and restoring what she calls 'Victorian values', is not untainted by these developments. Her own husband, Denis, has himself been married and divorced once before. Three of the most prominent members of her Cabinets – Douglas Hurd (the Foreign Secretary), Nigel Lawson (previously Chancellor of the Exchequer), and Nicholas Ridley (former Secretary of State for Trade and Industry) – have seen their first marriages collapse. Her once blue-eyed boy, Cecil Parkinson, now Minister of Transport, is a self-confessed adulterer, who has fathered an illegitimate child. And these famous examples are but the most conspicuous signs of a profound and pervasive revolution in social attitudes and matrimonial arrangements. Instead of being a scandalous rarity, marital breakdown is now a morally neutral commonplace. In late twentieth-century Britain – to borrow, but necessarily adapt, William Hogarth's famous phrase – it is not only marriage, but also divorce, which is very much 'à la mode'.

Self-evidently, this divorce explosion is a subject of great contemporary concern, not just in Britain, but throughout the western world. Will the rates raise even higher? Is the social fabric disintegrating? Should governments intervene to make divorce more difficult? But as with many current social problems, these questions need to be posed and answered in a proper historical perspective. What happened if a marriage broke down in the days when, for the majority of people, divorce was virtually impossible? How was it that a privileged minority were, nevertheless, able to obtain separation or dissolution? And how can we explain the dramatic shift from widespread non-divorce before 1940, to the position today, where divorce is essentially an administrative convenience? It is to answering these questions that Lawrence Stone has devoted his most recent book.[1] As in his previous works, he tackles a large subject, raises important issues, and settles them briskly and provocatively. He ventures with ease and authority across half a millennium of English legal, demographic, familial, religious, sexual and cultural history. And he provides an unforgettable picture of one of the most tragic of all human experiences: the irreparable breakdown of intimate and affective relations between men and women.

As Stone rightly points out, it is impossible to understand divorce in England without first understanding marriage, and judged by the practices which prevailed in contemporary Europe, marriage in England during the early modern period was distinctly unusual. In part, this was because neither the church nor the state was as fully in control of proceedings as was the case in many continental countries. Of course, many couples married according to the rules and rituals of the Church of England, and had their union recorded in the parish register. But a remarkably large number (exactly how many is uncertain) did not. Some settled for a 'contract marriage', which merely involved the verbal exchange of promises before two witnesses, and thus offered ample opportunity for misunderstanding, deceit and later denial. Others preferred 'clandestine marriage', which was essentially a contract marriage topped off by an irregular religious service, illicitly performed by a clergyman, and in breach of ecclesiastical law. Not until 1753, with the passing of Lord Chancellor Hardwicke's Marriage Act, were contract and clandestine marriages outlawed; and only in 1836, with the establishment of civil registration of births, marriages and deaths, did secular marriage become legally possible.

But it was not just that marriage in early modern England took a variety of forms, and was chaotically administered. It was further distinguished from continental practices because the husband enjoyed near-absolute control and authority over his wife. Especially after 1688, England's all-male governing elite believed that they lived in the freest country in the world. But their wives might have been forgiven for taking rather a different view. For in legal terms, they were totally subordinate: their person, their possessions, their income and their children were all part of their husband's property; in the eyes of the law, wives possessed no separate, autonomous existence of their own. One reason for this was the prevailing ideology of patriarchalism, which placed the husband on top in every sense. But it was also because of the patrilineal system of inheritance, whereby property almost invariably passed in the direct male line. Hence the widely accepted justification for the double sexual standard: husbands could be adulterous with relative impunity; but if a wife slept with another man, she might produce an illegitimate son, which would threaten the direct transference of property in the family from one generation to the next.

Inevitably, both the manner in which marriages were made, and the grossly inequitable distribution of power within them left their mark on the ways in which marriages were broken. Strictly speaking, divorce in England was illegal from the Reformation until 1857. Other Protestant nations established their own divorce laws, but for largely accidental reasons, the medieval church's absolute ban on divorce remained intact and unchanged in England. The result was that from the sixteenth to the nineteenth centuries, England simultaneously possessed the laxest marriage laws, and the strictest divorce laws, in Europe. They were administered – if that is the correct word – by three separate legal systems, ecclesiastical law, equity law and common law, and each had its separate courts, judges, lawyers, procedures and rules of evidence. Only the rich, the determined and the well connected could entrust their affairs to such bodies with any hope of success. Yet not surprisingly, marriages did fail in modern England. How did people use, twist and defy the law to deal with marital breakdown? And what were their chances of obtaining a full, legal divorce, with permission to remarry?

Among those at the lower end of the social scale, who were ill-educated and possessed little or no property, there were probably thousands of unreported desertions and elopements. Wives were driven out by poverty, brutality, alcohol or adultery; husbands just left home, and often established a new relationship, or even a bigamous marriage. Inevitably, it was the abandoned wives who suffered the most in terms of poverty, degradation and despair, especially if they were left with the children to support. An alternative method was to authenticate plebeian separation by making it public: hence the extraordinary custom known as 'wife-sale', a transfer of property closely imitating the ritual of a cattle or sheep market. If a husband wished to be rid of his wife, and provided there was another man who wanted her, the woman was put up for sale in the local market-place, with a halter round her neck, and was sold for a price to the other man, thereby breaking the previous marriage in the most public possible way. Between 1780 and 1850, there were three hundred recorded cases of such 'wife sales', but the legal basis of such ceremonial transactions was highly suspect.

Among the property-owning middle classes and their social superiors, the most popular way to end an unhappy marriage was by informal deed of private separation, a practice which developed during the late seventeenth century, and had become widely used by the time of the Napoleonic Wars. Its advantage was that it enabled a growing number of incompatible but non-adulterous couples to break free from an insupportable cohabitation. Like 'wife-sale', it was a collusive means of self-divorce, but since it was an essentially private arrangement, with deeds drawn up by attorneys, it avoided public embarrassment and expensive litigation, and it usually resulted in terms which were satisfactory to both parties. The personal, legal and economic safeguards were spelled out in detail for the wife, and even the custody and maintenance of the children were subject to negotiation. As such, it showed how an officially non-divorcing society could devise its own quasi-legal instruments to cope with the reality of marital discord. But for all its widespread use, the legal status of the private separation deed was highly dubious, the wife's property was always liable to be seized by her husband, and the only options available after separation were loneliness (which was usually the lot of the wife), or adultery or bigamy (which were frequently the choice of the husband).

Judicial separation was a more serious matter than private separation, since this involved expensive and extensive litigation in the ecclesiastical courts, and there was still no possibility of obtaining permission to remarry. It could only be granted on two grounds, adultery and/or life-threatening behaviour, and suits were much more frequently brought by men than by women. If a husband could prove that his wife had been adulterous, he could obtain separation from her without having to pay any form of maintenance. But the hearing could take anything up to two years, and the rules of evidence were particularly idiosyncratic. Neither the husband, nor his wife, nor her lover could give evidence; all testimonies had to be in writing; and there had to be two witnesses to every act. Almost invariably, it was the servants who provided (or made up) the evidence and, as the foremost historian of the English aristocracy, Stone is at his best in describing the ambiguous relationship between those below and above stairs. Servants came and went with bewildering rapidity, even in the greatest of houses. In accordance with the conventional wisdom of the double standard, they were more likely to inform a master of his wife's adultery than vice versa. And they testified in court for a variety of motives: duty, loyalty, affection, spite, revenge, greed or even just plain curiosity.

The next step was a successful action at common law for what was quaintly referred to as 'criminal conversation'. Since a wife was legally her husband's property, her seduction by another man was deemed to amount to the ultimate act of trespass. In an earlier time, the cuckolded husband might have sought redress by challenging his wife's seducer to a duel; but by the seventeenth century, it became more common to sue him instead for substantial damages. These actions for criminal conversation reached their peak between the 1790s and the 1820s. Extensive damages were awarded, and detailed court reporting lead to widespread publicity of the most sensational and salacious kind. But at the very same time, they were beginning to incur widespread criticism. In no other European country was it possible to trade honour for cash in this sordid way. The proceedings were grossly unjust to the wife, who could not appear in court, and could not defend herself, and many plaintiffs refused to accept what they regarded as tainted money as damages. Indeed, for most men, the only incentive to instigate an action for criminal conversation was that, by the late eighteenth century, a successful outcome was the essential precondition for the ultimate form of marital separation: full divorce by private Act of Parliament.

In the aftermath of the Reformation, divorce and remarriage were simply not available in Protestant England. But in 1700, the Duke of Norfolk succeeded in dissolving his marriage by petitioning Parliament for a private Act, and thereafter, this became the only accepted legal means whereby men of great rank and wealth could divorce their wives and remarry – provided they had already obtained a judicial separation in the ecclesiastical court, and won an action for criminal conversation at common law. During the first half of the eighteenth century, the overwhelming majority of petitioners were rich, titled landowners. But thereafter, and as the numbers increased, they were drawn from a wider – though still necessarily prosperous – social background. As with actions for criminal conversation, parliamentary divorce markedly discriminated against the wife: it was her adultery which provided the only grounds for such a measure; she herself could not bring an action for divorce against her husband; and in common law, it was the husband who had sole right to the custody of the children. Not surprisingly, many divorced wives were lonely and unhappy, and often found it difficult to re-establish themselves in polite society.

Three conclusions emerge from Stone's comprehensive survey of separation and divorce in early modern England. The first is that the whole business was overwhelmingly weighted in favour of men, and against women: many wives were subjected to beating, starving, locking up, expulsion from the marital bed, imprisonment in madhouses, and infection with venereal diseases; the double standard enabled husbands to commit adultery with relative impunity, whereas for a wife it almost invariably spelled the end of her marriage; and the legal procedures for separation and divorce were emphatically biased towards the husband. The second conclusion is that the system was equally prejudiced in favour of the rich, the well-born and the powerful, and against the poor, the lowly and the ill-connected. Litigation in the ecclesiastical courts or at common law was time-consuming and expensive, and a parliamentary divorce cost at least £5,000. For those without substantial means, these options were simply unavailable. And the third is that only the very tiniest minority actually resorted to law, or to Parliament, to resolve their marital difficulties. In the early nineteenth century, a mere one marriage in three thousand ended up in court, and between 1700 and 1857, the total number of parliamentary divorce Acts obtained scarcely exceeded three hundred.

How was it that this uniquely restrictive and repressive system was eventually reformed, so that divorce in England eventually became as easily obtainable as anywhere else in the western world? As Stone reminds us, arguments were advanced that marriages should be dissolved on the grounds of irreconcilable incompatibility and mutual hatred from the time of Milton onwards. But it was only during the early nineteenth century, as attitudes towards women and the family became less patriarchally authoritarian and more governed by feelings of mutual affection, that demands for reform gained momentum. In part, this was because the old system had become largely discredited: judicial separation via the ecclesiastical courts was effectively an incitement to adultery; actions for criminal conversation discriminated against women in a way that seemed increasingly unacceptable; and parliamentary divorce was little more than a lottery unjustly reserved for the rich. Put more positively, there was a growing desire to bring divorce under the comprehensive secular control of the state; to overhaul the antiquated and inefficient legal system and to create a single integrated judicial structure; and to free women from the worst excesses of legal subordination and the double standard.

As these proposals suggest, the demand for reform came from lawyers, politicians and well-connected upper-class women, rather than from crusading feminists, and they scored their first great success with the Divorce Reform Act of 1857, which after extended debate was finally forced through Parliament by the Prime Minister, Lord Palmerston. It abolished ecclesiastical courts, the action for criminal conversation, and parliamentary divorce, and concentrated all matrimonial litigation in a new secular High Court in London. It enabled wives to sue their husbands for divorce, made provision for awarding the custody of children to either parent, and protected the property and earnings of separated wives from seizure by their husbands. But it did not do away entirely with the double standard, and it made no attempt to make divorce more readily available to the poorer classes of society. In 1912 a Royal Commission recommended complete equality of access to the divorce courts on the part of men and women, and in 1923 this duly became the law of the land. But it was only in 1937 that the Royal Commission's other major proposal – recognising desertion, cruelty, habitual drunkenness and incurable insanity as valid grounds for divorce, in addition to adultery – was embodied in the Divorce Reform Act, which was skilfully piloted through Parliament by A.P. Herbert, an independent back-bench MP.

From the long-term perspective of the four hundred years in which there had been no liberalisation of the English divorce laws whatsoever, these extensive reforms seem long overdue. Yet in practice, none of the legislation passed between 1857 and 1937 ushered in a divorce revolution. By 1914, there were only eight hundred divorces a year, in a country with over six million married couples, and most of these were probably explained by a shift in categories, as husbands and wives who had previously separated, either privately or judicially, now took advantage of the changes in the law, and got divorced instead. The First World War led to a temporary tripling of divorce rates, partly because lonely wives entered into adulterous liaisons while their husbands were at the front, and partly because there was a sudden upsurge in hasty, juvenile marriages. But by the 1930s, the annual divorce rate had settled down to four thousand a year, and much of this apparent increase was probably another statistical illusion, as members of the lower middle classes with failed marriages gained access to the courts for the first time, thanks to the establishment of legal aid. For in sentiment and in practice, interwar Britain remained overwhelmingly a non-divorcing – indeed, and an anti-divorcing – society, as King Edward VIII and Mrs Simpson learned, to their cost.

In the immediate aftermath of the Second World War, the divorce rate shot up to an unprecedented 60,000 a year – partly because the events of 1939–45 had destabilised many marriages, and partly because legal aid was now freely available under a Labour government, which meant that poor people were able to obtain divorces for the first time in large numbers. But in the 1950s, the divorce rate levelled off at less than 25,000 a year, and it was only in the very changed social, moral, cultural and political climate of the 1960s that the figures rose dramatically, from 24,000 at the beginning of the decade to 54,000 at the end. In 1966, two independent working parties, one made up of lawyers, the other of clergymen, recommended radical changes in the divorce laws. They urged that divorce should no longer be seen as something that was religiously or morally objectionable: instead, it should be available on demand, as a legal remedy for irretrievable matrimonial breakdown. This revolutionary proposal was embodied in the Divorce Reform Act of 1969, which was guided through Parliament by another backbench MP, Leo Abse. The result of this legislation is that rich and poor, men and women, royalty and cabinet ministers, can divorce with equal ease and relative speed. And that is precisely what has happened: in 1985, 160,000 divorces took place in England and Wales.

How is this 'divorce revolution', correctly described by Stone as 'the most profound and far-reaching change to have occurred in the last five hundred years', to be explained? Clearly, it will no longer suffice to write it off as a statistical mirage: since the 1960s, the massive increase in the number of divorces suggests a correspondingly unprecedented increase in the number of marital breakdowns. But as Stone rightly points out, this is very much a global phenomenon, and can only be explained in the most nebulous and general terms. The changes in moral values and sexual attitudes mean that the traditional constraints of religion and public opinion are no longer as powerful as they were. The legal, sexual and financial emancipation of women has also clearly been of the greatest significance. And the pervasive culture of instant personal gratification has largely subverted the traditional idea of marriage as a long-term relationship based on duties, sacrifices and responsibilities. But whatever may be the benefits arising from easier divorce, and whatever may be the explanations for this change, Stone is not entirely convinced that the results have been for the better. More children than ever are suffering because of the break-up of their parents' marriages, and divorce which is too easy to obtain may be at least as damaging to individuals and to society as divorce that is too difficult.

This is a remarkable story and, for all its immense legal and technical complexity, it is handled by Stone with his customary assurance and panache. As such, it is bound to give rise to controversy, and the author would doubtless be extremely disappointed if it did not. As in all his work, he is much more forthcoming on the elite than on the majority of the population, and on men than on women. Some readers may be offended by the brisk, detached and matter-of-fact tone, which does not always seem appropriate to the tragic and traumatic subject with which it deals. (Although, in fairness to Stone, it should be mentioned that two further volumes of case studies – *Uncertain Unions* and *Broken Lives* – will follow shortly.) Despite the analysis of atypical separations and infrequent divorces, there is much about the causes and incidence of marital breakdown in the early modern period about which we still remain in ignorance, and the rather odd proportioning of the book is more a reflection of Stone's sources and expertise than of the substantive historical issues themselves. Most of his research is based on ecclesiastical court records, from 1660 to 1857, which means he gives a great deal more space to the early modern period, when divorce was exceptionally rare, than to the last hundred years, when it became commonplace.

But this broad perspective yields one final historical irony, which Stone understandably relishes. The contemporary practice of easy, almost relaxed, divorce, may seem a far cry from the rigid and unforgiving world of our Victorian forbears. But in the longer term, this apparently novel and uncertain revolution is not so unprecedented as it may at first sight appear. Today in England, many couples live together before (or without) marrying, make only private commitments to each other, and beget and bring up their children out of wedlock. And one-third of all the marriages that *are* legally entered into end abruptly and in an untimely way. But all this was also true in the early modern period. The only significant difference is that then it was death which undermined the family; now it is divorce. In this perspective, the dramatic and unprecedented rise in the divorce rate during the last one hundred years is merely a compensatory mechanism for the contemporaneous decline in adult mortality. This leads to a further irony, which even Stone fails to notice. Mrs Thatcher may wish to restore the stern and unbending attitudes of the nineteenth century. But in the case of the family, history has long since passed her by. As far as the rules governing the making and breaking of marriage in England today are concerned, it is *pre*-Victorian practices which are once again firmly in the ascendant.

(1990)

NOTE

1 Lawrence Stone, *Road to Divorce: England, 1530–1987* (Oxford, 1990).

14
Suicide

Only during the twentieth century have most people in the West (but not, alas, elsewhere) begun to die in old age and from natural causes, with the result that any death which does not conform to this comforting and conventional image now seems more than usually shocking. Since 1945, those who die young or in middle age, from incurable illness or by accidental violence, are deemed to have drawn the short straw in the lottery of life. Even more atypical is that small minority of people who do away with themselves. Suicide, self-destruction, auto-annihilation: these are not pretty words. But then, the deed they describe is not pretty either. On the contrary, the wilful (or irresponsible) act of entering what Shakespeare so vividly called 'the secret house of death' is something to which that overused word 'tragedy' may quite correctly be applied, since it arouses feelings of both pity and terror among those many people for whom life is an infinitely precious thing.

Yet although committing suicide is a highly atypical way to die in the modern West, there are in fact many different reasons why people choose to terminate their existence. Some people kill themselves as a political act, to thwart their enemies, as did Hitler and Goebbels. Some take their own lives to avoid exposure, humiliation and blackmail, as was reputedly the case with Lord Castlereagh and Tchaikovsky. Some choose to end it all because of professional anxieties and personal unhappiness or despair, like Thomas Chatterton and Marilyn Monroe. Some decide to exit because it seems the most rational thing to do in the face of illness or old age, as happened with Arthur Koestler. Some do away with themselves in complex states of mind that are still far from being clearly understood, as with Van Gogh and Virginia Woolf. And – especially in the realms of fiction – many women destroy themselves because of the intolerable burdens of romantic involvement: witness Tosca, Madam Butterfly, Anna Karenina and Mrs Tanqueray.

Famous fatalities like these seem so varied in motive, so diverse in meaning, and so eclectic in method that they defy reduction to a simplistic formula or monocausal explanation. It can be argued that in some cases, these successful suicides had ultimately found the pace of life in the fast lane too much to bear, and that it was this broader circumstantial pressure, at least as much as their personal decisions, that actually forced them into killing themselves. Indeed, this same explanatory tension between individual impulse and general context may also be seen lower down the social scale. During the nineteenth century, one favourite suicidal stereotype was the wicked man of business (like Ralph Nickleby) whose self-inflicted death seemed appropriate punishment for his misdeeds. Another was the fallen woman, seduced, dishonoured and abandoned (like Martha in *David Copperfield*), for whom there seemed no other way out. In both cases, the ultimate end may perhaps be explained in terms of individual temperament and personal decisions. But it can also be put down to the intolerable pressures and adverse conditions of modern existence: entrepreneurial stress, urban poverty and big-city living.

As such, these famous examples of suicidal behaviour, and these varied explanations of suicidal activity, merely echo the long-running academic debate in the literature on suicide between those who favour a psychological explanation and those who prefer a sociological one. Where does an individual's responsibility for self-destruction end, and where does society's responsibility begin? Among sociologists, it was Durkheim who most influentially argued that while suicide might appear to be the result of many private, unconnected, individual acts, it should be better understood as a collective phenomenon, the outcome of deeply rooted social forces. Indeed, he regarded official suicide statistics as the best measure of the health (or sickness) of society: the higher the figures, the weaker were the ties that held the community together. Accordingly, he was much alarmed by the rise which they appeared to show in many western nations during the nineteenth century. Judged by this criterion, contemporary Europe was a society in decay and disintegration. Under the destabilising impact of industrial development and urban growth, traditional bonds of social cohesion had dissolved, leaving many people alienated, lonely, insecure and afraid. And this, he insisted, was the real reason why they took – and were taking – their own lives in ever-increasing numbers.

For Durkheim and the sociologists, the correct way to understand suicide was thus to measure and analyse national data. But for Freud and the psychoanalysts, it was – predictably – the collection of individual case studies which seemed the more appropriate method. In negative terms, they argued that Durkheim accepted official statistics too uncritically, and that he never really explored (or explained) how these broad social trends became actual in individual instances. More positively, they suggested that suicidal tendencies were most common among those of a certain depressive temperament, and that the urge to self-destruction thus lay deeply rooted, not in society in general, but in a person's particular psychology. Thus joined, the debate between the sociological and the psychoanalytical approaches to suicide has stumbled on for over half a century. By now, it seems generally agreed that both the environment and the individual must be taken into account, since the social isolation which so often accompanies suicide may be either the cause or the consequence of depression and loneliness. But beyond reaching that measured yet bland conclusion, the massive outpouring of suicidological writing since the Second World War has often seemed to outsiders to be inaccessible, unrewarding – and completely ahistorical.

Like childhood and adolescence, sexuality and homosexuality, madness and old age, suicide is undeniably one of the central moral and medical issues in our society today. But, like them again, it is also as much an historical as a contemporary phenomenon. Yet compared with these other subjects, very little attempt has been made to understand suicide in time or over time. We are all vaguely aware that ancient Greece, imperial Rome, feudal Japan, Christian Europe and pre-modern India had their own customs and cultures of self-destruction. But almost nothing is known about the history of suicide even in the post-Enlightenment West. Olive Anderson's book is thus much to be welcomed, as the first major historical study of this central human problem.[1] Because it is – like death more generally – so protean a subject, she has adopted a variety of approaches to nineteenth-century suicide which display an unusual range of scholarly accomplishments. Her first section is an exercise in quantitative history, which examines and interprets the official data. The second is a piece of people's history, which recovers the individual experiences of those who actually ended their lives. The third is an essay in the history of *mentalités*, which explores the general social attitudes which prevailed at the time. And the final section is an example of history from above, as she turns to consider the efforts at punishment and prevention by those in authority.

As Anderson is at pains to point out, the main reason why suicide in Britain has been so little studied by historians is that the official figures are so suspect that they have been dismissed in some quarters as totally unreliable. In any society, the narrow line between accident and suicide, and the widespread practice of concealment, mean that the full extent of deliberate human self-destruction must inevitably remain uncertain. Moreover, in nineteenth-century England, the systematic compilation of government statistics only began in the 1850s, which was much later than in many European countries; the procedures whereby verdicts were returned and registered were subject to considerable local and temporal variation; and so the aggregate official figures can only be regarded at best as very – and varyingly – approximate. But Anderson is not deterred by this. As she rightly insists, all government statistics – even for the twentieth century – need very careful handling. But that is no reason for dismissing them. On the contrary, she argues that the suicide figures can be sensibly and rewardingly interpreted; that they do provide a reliable guide to overall national changes; and that they can be supplemented with more precise data to yield further important insights about the significance of place and time, of age and gender, of work and occupation.

Inevitably, this means that her early chapters are dense with tables and calculations. But they do yield some remarkably original conclusions. Both gender and age counted a great deal in suicide. Men preferred to use the razor or the rope, while most women preferred drowning or poison, and it was men, much more than women, who chose suicide rather than endure the burdens of enfeebled old age. In the same way, location was also very important. Contrary to widespread assumptions – both at the time and since – there seems no evidence to support the view that more people were driven to self-destruction by the pressures of urbanisation and industrialisation. The most that can be said is that suicide rates were higher in the south-east and the east Midlands (in counties like Sussex and Northampton), and lower in the south-west and the north-east (in such counties as Devon and Durham). But they actually rose in some rural areas (like Cornwall and North Wales), and were at their highest in historic county towns (like Worcester or Exeter) and in residential centres (like Bath or Croydon). In small and medium-sized industrial centres (like Dudley or Huddersfield), the suicide rate was relatively low, and it actually fell among young people in big towns and cities, most noticeably in London itself. Nor should this be a great surprise. For occupation mattered, too. Suicide was most common among soldiers, lawyers, doctors, publicans and domestic servants, yet was rarest among miners and industrial workers. In short, in Victorian England, self-destruction was relatively infrequent in the Coketown of Dickens or the London of Mayhew, and was more typical of Trollope's Barset or the Hardy country.

But what did suicide actually mean in personal terms? What were the commonest paths to self-destruction, and what were the thoughts and feelings of those who took this course? By examining the case histories kept by three London coroners for the early 1860s, Anderson shows that even in the great metropolis, patterns of suicide varied very considerably, from Southwark to the City to Westminster to central-north London. This is partly to be explained by the different economic and occupational structures of neighbouring areas, and partly by the presence (or absence) of railway stations and the river (where suicide could be most easily attempted) and hospitals (where attempted suicides could be treated). Nevertheless, some generalisations do emerge. Most of the victims – both men and women – were middle aged, and were neither very rich, nor very poor. They rarely did away with themselves because of poverty, loneliness, family tensions, emotional distress, sexual misadventure or business failure. On the contrary, in the vast majority of cases, it was alcoholism which seemed to be the overriding explanation – not only for their eventual suicide, but also for the form it actually took. In their last moments, many were so confused that they rarely knew exactly what they were doing. More often than not, Anderson insists, their deaths were squalid and almost casual.

But elsewhere, at this time, the suicide experience was very different. In rural east Sussex, as in London, it was rarely the very poor who took their own lives, and among those who did destroy themselves, drink played virtually no part. On the contrary, in most cases, suicide was resorted to by the elderly as a means of deliverance from ill-health, failing powers and – less often – a loss of neighbourly self-esteem. As a result, it tended to be more sturdy and deliberate, direct and resolute than in mid-Victorian London. By the end of the century, however, the pattern of metropolitan suicide had itself changed dramatically. Alcoholism, once of overwhelming importance, had all but disappeared. The number of men who killed themselves was now greatly in excess of the number of women. And it was among professionals and businessmen that self-destruction had become most widespread. Above all, the growth in commuting meant that suicide increasingly took place at work rather than at home or out of doors. The coroners reports suggest that suicide in Edwardian London was increasingly an introspective agony over private fears and feelings, a solution to worry, depression and disappointment. Suicide notes were far more common, and a slow and painful death from poison was more likely than the sudden jerk of the rope.

Of course, these individual experiences took place within the context of a general suicide culture, and it is with the ways of thinking and feeling about self-destruction which these people had subconsciously absorbed since childhood that Anderson next concerns herself. As revealed in the ballads, stories, plays, visual images and newspaper reports, suicide in early Victorian London was one of the basic facts of life: it was neither a taboo subject, nor did it evoke primitive feelings of folkloric horror. There were essentially four suicidal stereotypes: the wicked man (classically exemplified in Dickens's Jonas Chuzzlewit), the sad woman (as in *Suicide of the Drunkard's Daughter*, drawn by Cruickshank), the romantic victim (such as the woman depicted in Lord Gerald Fitzgerald's etching *The Bridge of Sighs*) and the comic (so well evoked in the street ballad 'The Rat-Catcher's Daughter'). Suicide was regularly the stuff of sentimental moralising, and was also frequently joked about. But it was never seen as glamorous and heroic, and was only rarely viewed as terrifying or disgusting. On the contrary, Anderson insists, the majority of Londoners commonly regarded it as abnormal behaviour in extenuating circumstances, as a sad ending deserving sympathy and forgiveness, and only very occasionally as something bizarre or criminal. So, when they sat on juries, they were most inclined to return verdicts of 'state of mind unknown' or 'mind unsound'. Sympathy was only forfeit – and a verdict of *felo de se* returned – if there was damning evidence of deliberate suicide in cold blood.

But attitudes, like experiences, varied greatly in place and time. In the rural areas of Sussex, old folkloric beliefs about suicide – that it was the work of the Devil, and that a suicide's corpse was unlucky – apparently lingered on. Yet they coexisted with attitudes which were more harsh and less sympathetic than those which prevailed among Londoners during the early 1860s. On the whole, the coroners, juries and magistrates seem to have been readier than the metropolitan authorities to reach unsympathetic verdicts, and to foist responsibility on to the surviving relatives. But in early twentieth-century London, attitudes had changed again, although they represented the adaptation, rather than the abandonment, of mid-Victorian conventional wisdoms. The fashionable *fin de siècle* romanticisation of suicide, associated with figures like Beardsley, seems to have made no impact on popular attitudes, and most people continued to believe that ordinary well-balanced folk did not do away with themselves. Nevertheless, there was one major change, in that suicide was gradually removed from the agenda of everyday experience, as the official procedures connected with it became increasingly arcane and remote. Coroners were by now full-time professional appointees, increasingly divorced from the community, rather than part-time holders of an office elected on a mass franchise. And purpose-built courtrooms and mortuaries superseded pubs and other makeshift buildings as the setting for official inquiries. As a result, suicide increasingly became an unfamiliar and embarrassing subject, a social disgrace of which suburban dwellers in particular became ever more frightened and ashamed.

What was actually done to punish or to prevent suicide by those in power and authority? Since suicide was both a sin and a crime, the sanctions of the civil, criminal and ecclesiastical law were in theory very great. But in practice they were weak – and getting weaker. In the case of successful suicides, juries rarely returned verdicts which brought the matter within the jurisdiction of state law, and the Church of England's intransigent position on burials was gradually modified by a combination of ecclesiastical reform and the loss of its monopoly on cemeteries. The advent of the police force meant that arrests for attempted suicide became more common. But the constabulary were mainly interested in preserving public order, few of those apprehended were sent for trial, convictions were rare and sentences were light. Suicide prevention was thus mainly left in the hands of charitable organisations and urban missionaries, who displayed great zeal and resourcefulness. But their religious preoccupations meant that their appeal and their impact were necessarily limited. Only in 1907 did the Salvation Army set up its Anti-Suicide Bureau. It was open to anyone seeking help, it provided advice, comfort and a ready ear, it took an essentially secular view of the problem, and as such was the direct forerunner of modern therapy, counselling and Samaritan-style treatment.

Other experts, such as William Farr, saw the will to suicide, not as the by-product of poverty or sin, but as the outcome of a defective environment. In the realm of social medicine, some attempts were made to lessen the temptations to self-destruction by pressing successive governments to restrict the availability of firearms and poisons. But although they met with some success, these measures were soon rendered irrelevant by the widespread proliferation of the railway train and the gas oven. More significant were the efforts at prevention by medical men. General practitioners were probably the least important, because most lacked the knowledge or the opportunity to treat attempted suicides, and their usual response was to commit such people to an asylum. Medical officers in large remand prisons examined those who had been convicted of attempted suicide, but since they were rarely detained for longer than one week, little could be achieved. The greatest contribution to suicide prevention thus came from the asylum doctors. They were able to monitor attempted suicides who had been admitted to their care, they seem to have been generally successful in stopping further attempts, and their labours apparently resulted in a high rate of discharge.

As this summary should make plain, and as the author herself robustly insists, this is unapologetically an historian's book. In part, this is because Anderson ranges with such impressive authority across a broad spectrum of social, religious, medical, urban, cultural, legal and administrative history. In part, it is because her prime aim is to throw more light on the history of Victorian and Edwardian England. But it is also because the research strategy and expositional structure have been determined by the requirements of historical methodology rather than by past or present suicidological debate. On the other hand, the fourfold historical approach she has adopted – official statistics, individual case studies, cultural backgrounds, prevention techniques and crisis intervention – approximates very closely to the most widespread research strategies used by suicidologists today. As a result, this book enables us to address and to answer two sets of questions, one historical, the other contemporary. First: what light does it throw on our general perception of Victorian and Edwardian England, and on the suicide stereotypes of that era? Second: what contribution does this historical approach make to the suicidologists' debates as they have evolved since the time of Durkheim and Freud?

Anderson's vision of nineteenth-century England might best be labelled as both atomistic and optimistic. Repeatedly, her book stresses the differences between early and late Victorian England, between the country and the town, between one part of London and another. Despite the aggregate national suicide statistics, there was in fact no such thing as a 'national' – or even a 'Victorian' – suicide experience. But while her insistence on the diversity of Victorian civilisation is a familiar feature of modern scholarship, her essentially up-beat and Whiggish interpretation is rather less fashionable – and thus all the more welcome. There is no nostalgia in her pages for the old world that was being lost, and little condemnation of the new which was replacing it. For those who were young, and who lived in its expanding towns and cities, Victorian England was, she insists, a good place to be. Only for those who were becalmed and marooned in the small-town world of the countryside, or who suffered the infirmities of extreme old age, was it especially unappealing. At the same time, the sanctions of the civil and ecclesiastical law were applied sparingly and humanely, the juries were generally compassionate and the big-city coroners were efficient, and the growing efforts at suicide prevention were characterised by zeal and a real measure of success.

As the author readily admits, hers is both a pioneering and a partial picture. There are many gaps which still need to be filled in. Her evidence is overwhelmingly drawn from London and the south-east: there is little detailed material from the north or the great industrial cities, Wales gets only the briefest discussion, Scotland an occasional mention, and Ireland not even that. There is no attempt to address elite suicide, except in the context of the discussion about the reliability of the data, from which it emerges – predictably – that many upper-class cases simply went unrecorded. There is no consideration of the wide gulf that seems to have existed between the popular contemporary suicide stereotypes, and the very different and diverse realities. And there are real difficulties in discussing alcoholism as a 'cause' of suicide, since self-evidently, many such people never even tried – or try – to kill themselves. Above all, we need to know much more about suicide during the first half of the nineteenth century, when social and economic circumstances do seem to have been much more unsettled, and when elite suicide also seems to have been unusually widespread. It may be that this was a period of soaring suicide rates brought about by industrialisation and urban growth, and that the improvement from the 1850s was thus not so much part of a long-term trend, as a dramatic downturn after an earlier period of real distress.

This book should find an equally appreciative and responsive audience among the suicidologists. Within its own terms of reference, it emphatically undermines the Durkheimian view that rising suicide rates were the product of the unstable nineteenth-century environment created by industrial growth and urban expansion. Moreover, it casts the greatest possible doubts on the whole notion of national suicide statistics and national suicide experiences. In the same way, it eloquently illustrates the limitations of the Freudian approach: the endless accumulation of one-off case-studies based on a specific and narrow set of psychoanalytic assumptions, but devoid of any of the broader perspectives of time, place, age, gender and occupation. More positively, Anderson does show, in support of

Durkheim, that the official figures can be made to yield findings of real importance, provided that they are carefully and correctly interpreted. And, in support of Freud, she does demonstrate the advent of a new, more depressive mode of suicidal behaviour in late nineteenth-century London. In short, her book may be read as offering partial historical validation for the current consensus among writers on suicide that the individual and the social milieu interact, and that the one cannot be studied without paying attention to the other.

But in fact, her fundamental message to the professionals is far less reassuring. Again and again, she reminds us that 'dying by suicide was an experience deeply affected by its specific historical context.' Ultimately, the ahistorical theories of the sociologists, and the free-floating case-studies of the psychoanalysts, are both equally suspect to her, since they never get beyond what she regards as 'a superficial level of understanding'. 'Only at a level of generalisation so broad as to be almost meaningless', she insists, 'is it right to portray as unchanging or universal either the experience of suicide or the circumstances which precipitated it.' The people who took their lives, the paths which led them to that end, and the experience of dying in this way were deeply influenced by specific historical circumstances. Like sex, poverty and power, suicide may always be with us. But like them again, the actual form it takes is essentially time-specific and culture-bound, not only in the past but – and this is Anderson's clear and significant implication – in the present, too. As Goethe once put it, 'suicide is an incident in human life which, however much disputed and discussed, demands the sympathy of every man, and in every age must be dealt with anew.' But we cannot hope to address the problem comprehensively today unless we know a great deal more about how past societies went about it. Only by making a greater effort at historical understanding can this most secret house of death be made to yield up more of its confidences.

(1988)

NOTE

1 Olive Anderson, *Suicide in Victorian and Edwardian England* (Oxford, 1988).

15
Victorians

To an altogether exceptional degree, Britain's twentieth-century history is still haunted by its nineteenth-century past. The physical products of the Victorian world are everywhere in evidence, not just as cosy period pieces, like Liberty fabrics, or Doulton vases, or William Morris wallpapers, but as an integral and functioning part of our contemporary civilisation. Take away such buildings as St Pancras Station, Leeds Town Hall, the Victoria and Albert Museum, the Clifton suspension bridge, and the Houses of Parliament, and the texture and tone of British life would be significantly altered. In the same way, many apparently venerable English traditions, which now seem as timeless and immutable as the Tower of London itself, only date back in their present guise to the late nineteenth century: royal pageantry, the old school tie, cricket and tennis, Gilbert and Sullivan, Marks and Spencer, bacon and eggs, fish and chips. And the governing elite of Britain remained essentially Victorian in upbringing and outlook until well into the second half of the twentieth century. It was only in 1963 that the first prime minister took office who had not been born when the Queen-Empress was still on the throne, and even today, the British electorate is constantly being reminded that Mrs Thatcher's much-revered father was an exemplary product of the late Victorian era.

The intimidating abundance of this Victorian inheritance has provoked mixed reactions among most twentieth-century Britons who have been obliged to live with it. On the left of the political spectrum, the usual response has varied between guilt and anger – at the poverty and inequality, the hypocrisy and humbug, the snobbery and exploitation, the Philistine materialism and heartless laissez-faire, and the imperial hubris and racial arrogance which they believe characterised Britain in what was to them only ostensibly its national heyday. But to those on the right, the Victorian age was a time when Britain was truly at its zenith, when the country was the workshop of the world, when the pound was a sterling currency, when God was an Englishman and Englishmen were godly, when Britannia ruled the waves, and when the sun never set on the Empire's broad and majestic dominions. For those who reject it, the Victorian experience is something to feel embarrassed about, to apologise for, to escape from, and never to repeat. But to those who remain enthralled, it is a fabulous story of outstanding success and splendid achievement, by comparison with which Britain's twentieth-century record seems at best unimpressive, and often distinctly lack-lustre.

Inevitably, the balance between disapproval and admiration has varied across the years. The interwar period began with a strident rejection of nineteenth-century stuffiness, exemplified by the brittle glitter of the 'Bright Young Things' and the barbed insouciance of Lytton Strachey's *Eminent Victorians* (1918). But this soon led to a reaction against these indulgent and ironical excesses: in the later volumes of *The Forsyte Saga*, John Galsworthy transformed the eponymous Soames from a Victorian ogre into a venerable paragon; and in 1936, G.M. Young published his famous *Portrait of an Age*, which remains the most brilliant and beguiling evocation of nineteenth-century England. After the Second World War, the revolt began anew: the Victorian Empire was dismantled, the slums and centres of Victorian cities were razed to the ground, and the 'permissive' legislation of the 1960s was deliberately designed to mitigate the harshness of the Victorian moral code. But this again provoked its own reaction – in part conservationist and aesthetic, as evidenced by the successful establishment of the Victorian Society, in part scholarly and academic, as a new generation of historians began to uncover the complex realities which often belied the crude stereotypes so commonly associated with the nineteenth century.

Since the early 1980s, the mood has changed again, for Britain is now ruled by a prime minister who regards the Victorian achievement as something neither to be demolished nor embalmed but to be celebrated, emulated and even *recreated*. Although she heads a government which has been called the most radical and iconoclastic of the twentieth century, Mrs Thatcher self-consciously presents herself as a moral crusader who is passionately attached to the politics of nostalgia. For her aim is to revive and to re-establish those wholesome Victorian values of hard work, self-help, thrift, sobriety and respectability which she learned at her father's knee, which she feels certain made Britain great in the past, and which she believes, with equal conviction, are now making Britain great again.

Throughout the twentieth century, the Victorian age has always been much more than past history: but now, for the first time, it has become the touchstone for national recovery and moral regeneration. It is in this perspective that these three important studies of Britain's recent past need to be seen and set. How, in the light of this renewed – and highly politicised – interest in the Victorians, should they be interpreted? And what do they tell us about Mrs Thatcher's real understanding, not only of Britain's nineteenth-century history, but also, by implication, of its present circumstances and future prospects?

Asa Brigg's *Victorian Things* completes a trilogy which was arrestingly begun with *Victorian People* (1954), and brilliantly continued with *Victorian Cities* (1963).[1] Although he has been a prodigiously productive scholar, moving easily and expertly across the social, political, urban, economic and cultural history of modern Britain, it is chiefly on these three books that Briggs's reputation rests as the foremost interpreter of the Victorian age since G.M. Young himself. *Victorian People* sought to uncover the particular characteristics of the 1850s and 1860s by exploring the personalities and preoccupations of such individuals as J.A. Roebuck and the Crimean War, Thomas Hughes and the public schools, and Benjamin Disraeli and the passing of the Second Reform Act. *Victorian Cities*, by contrast, ranged across the whole of the nineteenth century, beginning with Manchester, the 'shock city' of the 1830s and 1840s, and ending with late Victorian London, the 'world metropolis'. Both books were characterised by a determination to break down the traditional barriers between different historical sub-specialisms, by an enviable capacity to make suggestive connections between apparently unrelated subjects, and by an exceptionally acute feel for the tone and timbre of the times.

In *Victorian Things*, Briggs presents another series of linked case-studies, this time designed to illuminate nineteenth-century material culture. He is not just concerned with how certain objects were made and how they were used: by looking at the written records which place them in their social context, he also aims to recreate what he calls 'the intelligible universe' of the Victorians themselves. He begins with an account of the most famous display of nineteenth-century things, the Great Exhibition of 1851, which so vividly conveyed the Victorians' sense of wonder at their own material progress, and their delight in collecting and in classification. For many of them, seeing was indeed believing, and Briggs goes on to show how developments in the making of spectacles and in photography meant that the Victorians observed and recorded themselves with a precision and a fascination that no civilisation had displayed before. Hence, too, their many and varied 'images of fame'. On jugs, plates, chamberpots, matchboxes and biscuit-tin lids, it was not only British monarchs and statesmen who were commemorated, but also such foreign worthies as Garibaldi and Lincoln, and such sportsmen as the cricketer W.G. Grace, and Captain Webb, the first man to swim the English Channel.

Briggs then turns to consider some 'common things', whose meanings were more varied and ambiguous. Steel pens were first mass-produced in the 1830s: they were indispensable for the compulsory elementary education which came later in the century, and they made the fortune of the Midlands industrialist Josiah Mason, which he used to found what later became Birmingham University. Nearby, the town of Redditch was almost entirely given over to the manufacture of needles: in one guise, they were the very essence of domesticity, but they were also used by workers in the sweated trades, where exploitation, rather than homeliness, was the dominant theme. Of course, the very idea of 'Home, sweet home' was itself a Victorian creation, and Briggs devotes a chapter to analysing the many manuals of housekeeping, of which Mrs Beeton's *Book of Household Management* was only the most famous, and to a discussion of the development of furnishings and decoration. But it is in his study of the making and wearing of clothes that he ranges most widely, describing not only the changes in fashions and the evolution of the garment industry, but also the significance of different styles of headwear. For her Diamond Jubilee celebrations, Queen Victoria preferred a bonnet to a crown. All Victorian men, even beggars, wore hats; and it was, after all, the cloth cap which became the most famous symbol of the Labour Party.

In his last three chapters, Briggs moves on to energy, machinery, technology and communications. There is a splendid discussion of 'carboniferous capitalism' (the phrase is Lewis Mumford's), which vividly conveys the magic and wonder of coal. It was the source of heat, light and power in unprecedented abundance; it was the only raw material which Britain exported in large quantities; and it became for many people the ultimate symbol of industrial greatness. The postage stamp was another quintessentially Victorian thing. Sir Rowland Hill, who invented the penny post, soon became a national hero who ranked with James Watt. By the 1870s, stamp collecting was well established, both as a hobby and as an industry, and by the end of the century, the whole empire was bound together in an imperial postal system. But in many ways, Briggs insists in his con-

cluding chapter, the 1890s were as much the beginning of a new age of
things as they were the culmination of the old. The gas light and elec-
tricity portended the decline and fall of coal as the main source of power.
The phonograph and the cinema promised a transformation in entertainment, as did the typewriter and the wireless in communications, and the
bicycle, the tram and the internal combustion engine were soon to revo-
lutionise transport.

Admirers of the two earlier instalments of this trilogy will immediately
recognise the same robust and imaginative approach in this final volume.
As always, Briggs is very sensitive to the diversity of the Victorian
experience, and to the important differences between the early, the mid
and the late Victorian eras. He places in historical perspective a mass of
recent antiquarian writings on such varied subjects as pottery, furniture,
textiles and photography. He vividly depicts Victorian England as a
society which took an almost childlike delight in the goods and objects that
it created and manufactured for itself, and he shows how extensive and
elaborate were the connections which linked such artefacts to the Victorian world. So, when he discusses the manufacture of matches, he not only
tells us how they were actually made, and about the industrial diseases to
which the production process gave rise; he also describes the abortive
attempt to tax matches in 1871, and the famous strike of Bryant and May
employees in 1888. There was, he rightly insists, no one single universe
of Victorian things for those who made them or used them. As W.S.
Gilbert put it in *H.M.S. Pinafore*, in one of the few apposite remarks
which Briggs does not quote, 'Things are seldom what they seem.'

But for all its originality and fascination, *Victorian Things* is in some
ways the least satisfactory volume of this remarkable trilogy. Like its two
predecessors, it conveys a great deal of fascinating information; but unlike
them, it lacks the necessary framework of ideas to give structure and
coherence to what is on occasions an excess of miscellaneous detail.
Although the book is concerned with goods and chattels, the underlying
theme of Victorian consumerism is never directly addressed. There are
occasional, rather coy comments on bedrooms, bathrooms and underwear,
but no attempt is made to explore such closely related issues as gender
and sexuality. The final chapter makes plain that by the late nineteenth
century, the Germans and the Americans had become much better than
the British at inventing, producing and marketing new things: yet there is
no effort to explain why this was so. The dust-jacket informs us that the
book 'raises important theoretical issues concerning the meaning of

objects, cultural anthropology, and the developments of taste'. But this is not so: most of the recent work on material culture – studying through artefacts the beliefs, values, ideas, attitudes and assumptions of a particular society at a given time – is all but ignored. Like the Paris Exposition of 1900, *Victorian Things* does 'not leave a clear impression. It abounds in interesting details, but it lacks great lines.'

By contrast, F.M.L. Thompson's *Rise of Respectable Society* is a remarkable display of mandarin iconoclasm and opinionated synthesis, which may most usefully be seen as a development and extension of his earlier work.[2] His first book was a pioneering study of aristocratic survival and decline in modern England, which a quarter of a century on remains unsurpassed. He has written the official history of the chartered surveyors, one of the most reputable professions of Victorian England, and his account of the building of nineteenth-century Hampstead is the classic study of the making of middle-class suburbia. In short, Thompson's work has been as much concerned with the countryside as the town, and has constantly stressed the close links between them. He has been most interested in the aristocracy and the bourgeoisie, and especially in the way these groups shaded imperceptibly one into the other, and he has been more at home with the professional and the entrepreneurial middle classes than with the labouring proletariat. He has also been distinctly unimpressed by such fashionable but imprecise ideas as 'social control', and he has taken great delight in pointing out that, while Victorian England may have witnessed the triumph of the steam engine, it remained in many ways a 'horse-drawn society'.

In this most recent book, Thompson sets out to provide 'a seriously argued revision of Victorian social history', and from the very first page, the revisionism never lets up. Victorian England may have been the first industrial nation, which witnessed 'the age of great cities'; but until the last quarter of the nineteenth century, the towns and the factories were the exception rather than the rule. At the time of the passing of the Great Reform Act, it was workers in such traditional occupations as agriculture who formed the backbone of the popular agitation, and even in mid-Victorian England, it was Barset, rather than Coketown, which was still – if diminishingly – in the ascendant. Since industrialisation advanced so slowly and unevenly, Thompson argues, there was ample time for working-class families to adapt to it. Even in the cotton mills, very few married mothers worked, and the numbers of child labourers fell throughout the century. Family loyalties, neighbourhood ties, and inherited cultures were much more resilient than many middle-class observers believed. A significant proportion of proletarian women even married into the petty bourgeoisie, and by the late nineteenth century, family limitation had become an integral feature of working-class life.

Indeed, for most proletarian children, Thompson insists, the family provided an orderly and secure environment, at once disciplined and affectionate. A significant proportion of boys and girls were sent to school by their parents well before elementary education was made compulsory by the state, and the street life which they enjoyed in their neighbourhood was on the whole neither violent nor criminal, but warm and friendly. By twentieth-century standards, working-class housing was certainly not lavish: but it was usually clean, decent and respectable. The sordid, teeming slums and the anonymous, overcrowded ghettos were very much in the minority, as was the unwashed, dishonest, immoral, impoverished residuum which inhabited them. Most members of the working class, Thompson argues, were fiercely independent and self-reliant. They were thrifty, joined friendly societies, and made adequate provision for accident and misfortune. They worked hard, and got on well with their employers: strikes were the exception rather than the rule, and the unrest of the 1830s and 1840s was an aberration which was soon forgotten. Even the miners, who in the twentieth century have often been seen as the shock-troops of the class struggle, were generally deferential, co-operative and well behaved.

Within this generally congenial environment, Thompson contends, the working classes evolved their own popular culture which was increasingly self-contained and apolitical. As the amount of leisure available increased, they took to the seaside, tended their allotments, and played soccer and rugby. Their drinking habits were relatively restrained, and public houses were as much places of business as they were centres of conviviality. The music halls were more concerned with romance, fantasy and escape than they were with putting out crude Tory propaganda. Attempts to regulate working-class gambling were not on the whole successful, and policemen were much resented as intrusive agents of middle-class morality. Most people in poverty were too proud to accept poor relief, and were determined to keep out of the workhouse: indeed, Thompson suggests, the cult of respectable independence may well have arisen in response to the Poor Law of 1834, which the working classes viewed with such suspicion and abhorrence. At best, most workers regarded the state as irrelevant; at worst, they resented its legislation and its agents as interfering nuisances. By the late nineteenth century, they were not much interested in politics, showed little enthusiasm for the nascent Labour Party, and were mainly concerned with getting on with their own lives.

Even when summarised thus briefly, it should be clear that Thompson's book is indeed revisionism with a vengeance. The Industrial Revolution is brutally dismissed from the centre of the historical stage. The notion that Victorian society was divided into three classes, perpetually at war with each other, is condemned as 'little more than a rhetorical device'. The belief that the working class acquired a heightened degree of self-consciousness, either in the 1830s or the 1890s, is emphatically rejected, and the theory of the 'labour aristocracy' is consigned to oblivion. The nineteenth-century 'middle-class moralists and reformers', who regarded the workers with such ignorant and meddlesome condescension, and whose biased reports and erroneous observations have so misled Marxist social historians, are repeatedly rebuked and ridiculed. Throughout the Victorian era, Thompson insists, the social fabric of England held together as a seamless web, with each occupational group or status stratum merging imperceptibly into another. Above all, the working classes were very much in charge of their own lives. They did not ape the values and morals of their superiors, and nor were they the supine victims of government legislation or propaganda. On the contrary, in such matters as education and birth control, 'they worked out their own standards and values for themselves', and Thompson thinks they did it rather well.

As a piece of iconoclastic synthesis, *The Rise of Respectable Society* is undoubtedly a tour de force. But it is not quite clear that Thompson carries everything before him. Having rejected the analysis of contemporary liberal and interventionist reformers, he has embraced instead the very different, but no less partial, views of the robustly unconcerned aristocracy and the comfortable suburban middle classes, the very groups with whom he has always felt most at home. As a result, the social and political tensions which characterised the first and final years of the queen's reign are dismissed too easily. The fact that it was government legislation which was largely responsible for improving factory conditions, regulating working-class housing, and making possible public holidays is only grudgingly admitted. And behind the consensual, improving, up-beat picture which Thompson paints so vividly and so vigorously, the darker side of the Victorian world can still occasionally be glimpsed. As he himself admits, infant mortality remained 'shockingly high', schooling was not 'a pleasant or happy experience', working-class houses were 'drab, cheerless, cramped and unimaginative', and when Seebohm Rowntree made his survey of York, in the 1890s, one-third of the town's inhabitants were still poverty-stricken. Even if Victorian England was not on the brink of starvation, turmoil and chaos, it was hardly a society in the full flower of personal freedom or material abundance.

Like *Victorian Things*, Harold Perkin's study of *The Rise of Professional Society* completes a large-scale project of great originality and distinction.[3] For it is the sequel to *The Origins of Modern English Society, 1780–1880*, first published in 1963, which offered a bold and vigorous account of Britain's social development in the aftermath of the Industrial Revolution. During the early nineteenth century, Perkin argued, three new classes, and one old order, competed for power and wealth – a proletarianised working class, a middle class divided between manufacturers and professionals, and a tenacious but embattled aristocracy. By the 1830s and 1840s, these disputes had been subsumed into struggles between different class ideals: the aristocratic, which was hierarchical, leisured and paternal; the professional, which stressed expertise and reward by merit; the entrepreneurial, which valued industrial capital and private profit; and the working-class, which was more concerned with survival, self-help and co-operation. By the mid-Victorian years, Perkin concluded, this conflict had been resolved in favour of the entrepreneurial middle class, and so Britain became the first 'viable class society' in the world. It was class conscious, but not divided by class conflict, and it was dominated by the laissez-faire ideology of the manufacturers and businessmen.

In his latest book, Perkin begins by describing the years from 1880 to 1914 as witnessing 'the zenith of class society'. Segregation by income, status, appearance, health, education and employment was at its greatest extent, and politics also became more class based than ever before. Most landowners and businessmen, frightened by the prospect of Home Rule for Ireland, and worried by economic depression, threw in their lot with the Conservatives, while the massive increase in trade union membership and the founding of the Labour Party portended a new militancy among many working men. The result was a bitter and protracted battle between capital and labour, beginning with the strikes of the late 1880s, much intensified in the industrial disputes of the early 1910s, and only resolved after the General Strike of 1926, which for Perkin constituted 'the crisis of class society'. At the same time, the professional middle classes were also growing both in numbers and in confidence. They took up such radical causes as land reform and municipal socialism. They joined the Fabian Society and captured the leadership of the Edwardian Liberal Party. And many of them, like the young William Beveridge, were strongly in favour of the welfare reforms which were enacted by the government between 1905 and 1914.

In fact, Perkin argues, the crisis of the old class society was successfully surmounted, and in that process, the new professional society itself effectively came into being. This was partly because of the First World War, which greatly increased the power of the state, and thus the power of the administrators. But it was also because, by the late 1920s, the old-style class war had very largely been given up, as businessmen, trade union leaders and government representatives tacitly agreed to co-operate in running the country on the basis of their increasingly shared ideals of professional disinterest. In politics, the old aristocratic elite was in irrevocable decline, and the middle classes had emphatically taken over, as evidenced by the dominance of such non-patrician Tory prime ministers as Stanley Baldwin and Neville Chamberlain. In business, the rise of the corporate economy meant the disappearance of the traditional owner-capitalist, and the advent of a new breed of salaried manager. Even among the working class, the trade union leaders tended to resemble their new-style employers in attitudes and outlook. Most of these men came from comfortable backgrounds, neither very rich nor very poor, and had been educated at public school. The only real difference between them was that the professionals in one group were essentially the servants of the state, while the others operated in the private sector.

According to Perkin, the thirty years after the Second World War witnessed the zenith of this professional society. As the creators and also the beneficiaries of the welfare state, the public sector professionals proliferated in unprecedented abundance – civil servants, local government officials, doctors and nurses, social workers, teachers and academics. Moreover, as long as the mixed economy continued to grow, with full employment and low inflation, the private sector professionals – the salaried managers in industry, finance and the service sector – were equally contented. But during the mid-1970s, this professional society began to fall apart. The energy crisis, stagflation and growing unemployment undermined the financial basis of the welfare state, while the arrogant assumptions of superiority which characterised the public sector employees eventually provoked a backlash in the private sector. And this has been intensified by Mrs Thatcher, with her celebration of entrepreneurial virtues, her passionate commitment to the free market, and her hostility to such state-funded institutions as the universities, the civil service and the BBC. How, exactly, this crisis in professional society will be resolved is unclear.

As with Perkin's previous volume, this long-awaited sequel is an audacious and exciting piece of synthesis. He ranges across the most crowded and contested terrain of British history with felicitous ease and astonishing erudition. His mastery of political, economic, social and urban history is intimidating in its completeness. Time and again, he presents old and familiar subjects in a new context, and thus a new light: the late nineteenth-century land question, the so-called 'strange death of Liberal England', the General Strike of 1926, the politics of Churchill's wartime coalition, and so on. His argument that the anti-industrial ethos inculcated by the public schools was professional rather than aristocratic in its origins is both novel and suggestive. But above all, this book is a genuine example of that all-too-rare genre: social history so total that it is truly the history of society. It encompasses plutocrats and paupers as well as peers and professionals. It provides vivid set-piece descriptions of English society at different moments – in the 1890s, the 1920s and the 1960s. It shows how social structures and social classes evolved and decayed over time. And it deliberately explains these social developments in essentially social terms, by describing how the professional classes themselves became the great motor of historical change.

Inevitably, any book as brave and bold as this is bound to have its problems. As Thompson's work reminds us, it is no longer enough to depict late Victorian England in simplistic terms as a class society, and the notion of class ideals seems no more convincing in this volume than it did in its predecessor. On several occasions, we are informed that the professional ideal 'took steps', 'organised assaults', and 'selected social problems'. But this is anthropomorphic metaphor implausibly masquerading as historical explanation. Above all, the central thesis concerning the rise of professionalism can only be sustained by extending the concept so broadly as to rob it of any real explanatory power. At different times, we are told that Lord Beaverbrook and Ernest Bevin were professionals, and that women's liberation and the new morality of the 1960s were products of 'the professional ideal of rational discourse'. Moreover, as Perkin coyly admits, it is not clear that the old class society did break down between 1910 and 1926, since 'it is exceptionally difficult to discern the emerging threads of professional interest through the remnants of declining class.' In short, what Perkin has really given us in this book is a detailed and informative study of the professions, unconvincingly inflated into a history of British society as a whole.

How much historical validation do these three fascinating books lend to the idea of 'Victorian values', as adumbrated by the Prime Minister? At first glance, it seems that Thompson has produced a supremely Thatcherite view of the Victorian age, stressing thrift, self-help, sobriety, respectability and independence, attaching little importance to the influence of the state or the interference of middle-class intellectuals, and resoundingly proclaiming that Victorian England was indeed a success story. But he is far too accomplished and ironic a scholar to provide such unsubtle propaganda for Conservative Central Office. As he subversively notes, those beliefs most commonly described today as 'Victorian values' were essentially the product of the nineteenth-century working class – one of the social groups (along with the aristocracy and the intelligentsia) which the Prime Minister herself most actively dislikes. And if Britain's nineteenth-century experience is any guide, the attempt by any middle-class ideologue to impose his – or her – own values on society via gov- ernment legislation or incessant propaganda is very unlikely to succeed. Above all, the society which Thompson describes is in so many ways so utterly different from our own – in material circumstances, in economic and social structures, and in the part played by the state – that it is diffi- cult to believe it can offer any relevant lessons for the Britain of the 1980s.

As a firm believer in the merits and mores of the welfare state, Lord Briggs is more direct in his refutation of the Thatcherite view of the nine- teenth century. For the Victorian Britain he so vividly depicts was neither as abstemious, as laissez-faire or as economically triumphant as the Prime Minister would have us believe. At all levels of society, there were many who loved spending, consumption, extravagance and display: how else, indeed, could all those Victorian things have been called into existence in the first place? Most Victorians also believed that certain essential services (such as the post and the telegraph) should be controlled by the state in the interests of the public, and not be left to private enterprise. Moreover, by the 1880s and 1890s, the British economy was already in conspicuous decline: there was little sign of that flourishing enterprise capitalism which Mrs Thatcher so admires. And so, while the artefacts which Victorian England produced may have survived in unprecedented abundance, it is clear that the 'intelligible universes' of attitudes and beliefs to which they originally belonged were quite exceptionally varied, and often totally different from those conventional wisdoms which prevail in late twentieth-century Britain.

But as Perkin's book makes abundantly plain, it is not just that Mrs Thatcher misunderstands 'Victorian values' in terms of the nineteenth century: it is also that the recent resurgence of the free market ideology, which is so fundamental a part of her political programme, actually has very little to do with the world of small-business capitalism and working-class self-help with which that notion is most readily and rightly associated. It is not yet clear that Perkin's sociological analysis of Thatcherism – the backlash of the private sector professionals against the public service ethos – is correct. But he is certainly right to point out that in a country where a mere one hundred firms produce one-half of the manufacturing output, where a handful of companies dominate each separate industry, and where individual capitalists and traditional entrepreneurs are but a small sector of the economy, exhortations to individual thrift, self-help and respectability are of very questionable relevance indeed. The brand of free enterprise that is in the ascendant in Thatcherite Britain is thus a very different version of capitalism from that which prevailed in the country's nineteenth-century heyday as 'the workshop of the world'.

To conclude from reading these three books that the values, beliefs and attitudes of the Victorians were more varied, subtle, complex and inconsistent than Mrs Thatcher would have us believe is neither very novel nor very surprising. After all, she trained as a chemist and a lawyer, has been a professional politician for nearly forty years, and has never claimed to be much of an historian. But this is not the most important point at issue. For if past experience is any guide, the most significant lesson to be drawn from the Prime Minister's ritualistic invocation of the regenerative power of 'Victorian values' is that it is but one further indication of the very national decline she seeks so ardently to prevent and to reverse. In civilisations as diverse as the later Roman Empire, medieval Islam and seventeenth-century Spain, the call to return to the stricter morals, the homelier virtues and the less corrupt beliefs of an earlier, greater and purer age was the stock-in-trade of many leaders valiantly, but vainly, presiding over nations and empires in decline. This is something of which Mrs Thatcher seems to be unaware. But it is far from clear that Britain under her stewardship is going to prove an exception to this general historical rule.

Of course, it is still too soon to know. But this much, at least, seems certain. However admirable such values as thrift, sobriety, self-help, respectability and independence may be, it is abundantly clear that the relationship between ideology, government, social class and economic structure is far more complex and problematic than Mrs Thatcher seems to think. It is also clear that the quite exceptional economic and imperial pre-eminence which Britain enjoyed during most of the nineteenth century was as much the result of sheer good luck as it was the product of 'Victorian values', and that it is idle to suppose that it can ever be recovered or repeated. Quite understandably, the Victorians evolved a variety of beliefs which helped them come to terms with the burdens and opportunities of global greatness, and with the benefits and dangers of an industrial economy. But the tasks which face Britain today – adjustment to a diminished position in the world, the reordering of its relations with Europe, and the management of an economy dominated not by small domestic producers but by multinational corporations – are of a very different order, and require the creation and acceptance of a correspondingly different set of values if they are to be successfully accomplished.

Pace Mrs Thatcher, it is neither desirable nor possible for late twentieth-century Britain to return to the nostalgic never-never land of Victorian values and Victorian pre-eminence. On the contrary, the best way for the country to come to terms with contemporary circumstances, which only seem much diminished when judged by the altogether exceptional yardstick of the Victorian era, is to step out of the shadow of the nineteenth century, and into the light of common day.

(1990)

NOTES

1 Asa Briggs, *Victorian Things* (London, 1988).
2 F.M.L. Thompson, *The Rise of Respectable Society: A Social History of Victorian Britain, 1830–1900* (London, 1988).
3 Harold Perkin, *The Rise of Professional Society: Britain since 1880* (London, 1989).

16
Empire

In 1921, a year which is well within the recollection of many people still alive today, the ultimate responsibility for the government of more than one-quarter of the land and peoples of the globe resided in London. The British Empire was at its apogee, and on its far-flung dominions beyond the seas, the sun did not always shine, but never dared to set. It had been growing from Tudor times, and most rapidly since the loss of the thirteen American colonies after 1776. The Napoleonic Wars had seen the conquest and subjugation of large swathes of India. The mid-Victorian years witnessed substantial emigration to Canada, New Zealand, South Africa and Australia. The last quarter of the nineteenth century brought the 'Scramble for Africa', from which the British emerged with what they thought was, appropriately, the lion's share of the spoils. And after the First World War, the break-up of the Turkish Empire meant new imperial responsibilities in the Middle East, as Iraq, Jordan and Palestine were administered by Britain on behalf of the fledgling League of Nations. The result of these successive phases of acquisitiveness was that scarcely seventy years ago, the British were the proud possessors of the largest territorial empire that has ever existed in human history.

How did it happen? For what reasons, and by what processes, did the inhabitants of a small group of islands off the coast of Europe, with a population less than that of France, and a military tradition much weaker than that of Germany, come to exercise dominion for so long over a wholly disproportionate area of the globe? According to Sir John Seeley, lecturing in 1882, before the last great expansionist impulses had seriously begun, the British seemed to have 'conquered and peopled half [sic] the world' in what he called a 'fit of absence of mind'. They had, he implied, never consciously sought to make themselves the supreme imperial power: they just woke up one morning and found that they had sleep-walked their way to dominion over palm and pine. In noting that his fellow-countrymen were in some ways strangely indifferent to their empire, Seeley was not entirely mistaken. But in seeming to depict it as the product of such British characteristics as muddling through and understatement, he failed to do justice to the Empire (or, indeed, to the British). For expansion on a scale so vigorous, so ample and so unrivalled must surely have had causes that were themselves correspondingly substantial, deeply rooted and wide-ranging.

Such has been the generally held belief, with the result that since Seeley's time, many more elaborate explanations of the drive to empire have been advanced, by politicians, by contemporary commentators and by professional historians. Some have been economic: for J.A. Hobson and for Lenin (developing Marx), imperialism was the highest stage of capitalism, the inevitable by-product of late nineteenth-century developments in industry, business, trade and finance. Some have been sociological: for Joseph Schumpeter, overseas expansion was undertaken by those traditional, pre-modern aristocratic classes, whose status and security were threatened at home by industry, urbanisation and democracy, and who sought consolation in military glory and knightly conquests on the imperial frontier. Some have been political, diplomatic and strategic: for Ronald Robinson and J.A. Gallagher, the British Empire in Africa came about principally because successive governments sought to safeguard the essential sea routes to India, one via the Cape of Good Hope, the other through the Suez Canal. And some have been more concerned to stress the primacy of events on the periphery rather than the expansionist impulses in the imperial metropolis: for John S. Galbraith and D.K. Fieldhouse, empire happened because the unexpected breakdown of indigenous regimes in Asia and Africa obliged the British to step in to restore order, and, once involved, they found it extremely difficult to disengage themselves.

These theories are considerably more sophisticated than those attributed to Seeley, yet they have also been much criticised in their turn. Individually, each one is monocausal: but it is difficult to believe that a phenomenon so complex and long-lasting as imperialism can have had only one single, all-encompassing explanation. Put the other way, this means that they are also mutually exclusive: empire is depicted as having been either capitalist-modern or aristocratic-atavistic, while the forces making for expansion were located either in Europe or in the world beyond. This is plainly unsatisfactory. Moreover, each of these four interpretations explains much less than their proponents have claimed. The economic argument falls down because large parts of Africa which were annexed by the British failed to provide markets, or raw materials, or investment opportunities. The sociological argument is difficult to sustain because the British aristocracy played no more than a subordinate and subsidiary part in the creation of the British Empire. The political-diplomatic-strategic argument is inadequate because the routes to India were as much concerned with trade as they were with troops. And the peripheral argument does scant justice to the powerful drives to dominion which undoubtedly did exist in England for much of the 'long' nineteenth century.

At the British end of things, there are further difficulties. To begin with, the three interpretations that are preoccupied with the imperial metropolis are severely weakened by their inadequate treatment of the expansionist impulses supposedly emanating from Britain itself. The economic interpretation bandies about phrases such as 'the industrial revolution' and 'finance capitalism' without ever describing or explaining them; the sociological interpretation betrays a dismaying ignorance of the social structure and social history of nineteenth-century Britain; and the political-diplomatic-strategic interpretation sidesteps the whole problem of who the policy-makers were and what they were doing, by subsuming all of them under the arresting yet meaningless heading of the 'official mind'. It is also important to remember that during the nineteenth century, Britain was not the only European power with imperial aspirations: France, Italy, Germany and Belgium also sought to claim their 'place in the sun'. But all too often, the British drive to empire has been studied in isolation, which means that the essential connections between overseas expansion, foreign policy, international relations and great-power rivalries have received less attention than they should have.

If the perspective is shifted from Britain to its empire, the explanatory difficulties multiply still further. For it clearly will not do to characterise the whole imperial domain by the portmanteau term 'periphery'. Throughout its history, the British Empire was an astonishingly diverse dominion, 'a rag-bag of territorial bits and pieces', created and governed in a correspondingly disorganised and unsystematic way. There were the surviving colonies from the pre-1776 empire, in Canada and the West Indies. There were the 'empty' lands of settlement, in Australia, New Zealand and South Africa. There was the Raj in India, a unique amalgam of direct and indirect rule. There was a string of naval bases, which encircled the world: Gibraltar, Malta, Cyprus, Aden, Singapore and Hong Kong. There was the African empire running from Cairo to the Cape, with offshoots to the west, which was mostly acquired in the 1880s and 1890s. There were areas that were never officially annexed, but which were under varying degrees of 'informal' British influence, especially in South America. And there were the League of Nations Mandates, not only in the Middle East, but also the former German colonies in east and south-west Africa. To suppose that an empire so vast and so varied could have come into being for one single or simple reason is clearly absurd.

These were some of the contradictory and indecisive conclusions that were reached by imperial historians, as they researched, debated and disagreed during the 1950s, 1960s and 1970s. To add to the confusion, the very period when they were trying to understand how the British Empire had come into being was also the time when the Empire itself was moving rapidly towards dissolution and oblivion. In the thirty years following Indian independence in 1947, the greatest empire the world had ever known came to an end with unprecedented speed, as one colony after another was given its freedom. Perhaps it was not altogether surprising that during the same period, imperial history began to fragment and to disintegrate, like the very subject it had been attempting to define, describe and analyse. General explanations and global theories went out of fashion, while 'area studies' and the histories of individual regions became much more popular. As Third World nations increasingly asserted their independence, the history of the British Empire was rewritten as a brief (and usually regrettable) intrusion into the affairs of Africa and Asia. Indeed, as the sun set, and as the Empire passed away, there were some scholars who went so far as to wonder whether it had ever really existed at all. Considering the general lack of interest shown in the British Empire by historians of Britain itself, it was not an altogether absurd question to ask.

It is in this context – of which the authors are both aware and appreciative – that this new account of British imperialism must be set and understood.[1] Cain and Hopkins have been a long time at their labours, and have already stated their aims and set out their arguments in a series of important preliminary articles, which have themselves been much discussed. Those essays were inevitably schematic and speculative, but in these two massively erudite volumes they make their case with impressive and intimidating thoroughness. In terms of methodology, their concerns are to reunify a subject which has been collapsing under the weight of its own erudition; to write a history of British imperialism which gives equal attention to the metropolis and to the colonies, and establishes a systematic connection between them; and to break down the barriers which customarily exist between historians of the eighteenth, nineteenth and twentieth centuries. And in terms of interpretation, they seek to reinstate, but also to refashion, the traditional arguments that the chief impulses to empire were more metropolitan than peripheral, and that they were economic rather than sociological or political-diplomatic-strategic.

The pattern of British overseas expansion was set, they believe, during the 'long' eighteenth century. The 'Glorious Revolution' of 1688 ushered in a new political regime, controlled by an oligarchic landowning elite with a well-developed taste for commercial enterprise. At the same time, the Revolution also brought into being a new class of merchants, financiers and businessmen, who established themselves as junior partners to the ruling aristocracy. They ran the Bank of England, invested in the national debt, financed the great overseas trading companies and dominated the new insurance houses. Together, these patricians and plutocrats formed a new breed, to whom Cain and Hopkins give the name 'gentlemanly capitalists', and it was this alliance between land and money which created Britain's eighteenth-century Empire. The years from the 1780s to the 1820s may have witnessed the first, classical phase of the Industrial Revolution: but its impact was very restricted, both domestically and internationally, and provincial manufacturers were limited in wealth, lowly in status and lacking in influence. It was the 'gentlemanly capitalists' who created an empire appropriately based on credit and commerce, who settled and governed the thirteen American colonies, who sought vainly to keep hold of them after 1776, and who then turned their attentions to acquiring new dominions in India.

During the nineteenth century, the 'gentlemanly capitalists' continued to be in charge. Industrialists remained isolated from London, inferior in social status, and ineffective politically, as evidenced by Joseph Chamberlain's failure to carry his 'Tariff Reform' campaign in the 1900s. But there were significant changes in the governing classes of Britain and its empire. The aristocracy gradually lost its pre-eminent position, while the rapidly expanding service sector gave increased opportunities to those who worked in the City of London. At the same time, the public schools began to turn out a new-style gentry, who believed in the traditional virtues of public service and Christian duty, and who came to dominate the rapidly expanding professions. They were primarily drawn from the south of England, they shared the values and attitudes of the political and financial elite, and they moved in essentially the same social worlds. According to Cain and

Hopkins, it was the export of this composite, remodelled version of 'gentlemanly capitalism' which effectively created the Empire of Kipling, Elgar and Queen Victoria. Between 1850 and 1914, British investments overseas were far greater than in domestic industry, increasing spectacularly from £200 million to £4,000 million, and where British capital led, British gentlemen were not far behind.

By 1900, London was the financial centre of the world, and the fact that it was also the capital of the greatest empire in the world was not at all coincidence. The settler colonies of Canada, New Zealand and Australia may have gained a certain degree of constitutional freedom with responsible government: but their heavy borrowing on the London money market, to finance nation-building infrastructural investment, meant that enhanced political autonomy was accompanied by increasing economic subordination. In South America, and especially in Argentina, Brazil and Chile, similar loans to fund similar undertakings made these ostensibly independent nations an integral part of Britain's 'informal empire'. In India, the prime concern of the Raj was not with promoting the sales of Manchester cotton goods, but with ensuring that there was sufficient revenue to service the country's vast foreign debts, most of which were held in London. In Africa, Britain's chief interests were again financial – government loans and the Suez Canal in Egypt, and the Rand gold mines in the Transvaal – and the imperial impulse was strongest in these two areas. By contrast, the City was reluctant to invest as extensively in China or the Ottoman Empire, and this lower British profile may help explain why partition did not take place before 1914.

Thus described, the history of the British Empire during the classical era of 'High Imperialism' appears in a new and provocative light. To be sure, by the late nineteenth century, Britain's industrial pre-eminence was slipping, and there was justified fear of economic competition from the United States and Germany. But Cain and Hopkins reject the view that the massive extension of both the formal and the informal Empire was an essentially defensive measure, by a 'weary titan' which was losing its industrial hegemony. On the contrary, they argue that in financial terms, Britain's supremacy was actually increasing, and that the unprecedented expansion of the Empire from the 1880s was the direct result of the unprecedented exports of capital which bound the developing world ever more tightly and dependently to the imperial metropolis. Moreover, they suggest that it was this very British success which contributed to the intensification of Anglo-German antagonisms. After 1870, Germany was a nation with a booming economy and an invincible army, which was also determined to acquire colonies and build a navy. Sooner or later, the authors argue, conflict between these two powers was inevitable. From their perspective, the First World War was – as Lenin always insisted – primarily an imperial war.

In their second volume, Cain and Hopkins offer an interpretation of the twentieth-century Empire which is no less original. Britain was not an imperial power 'in decline' before 1914: and nor was it before 1945. Once Lloyd George and his wartime government of buccaneers and business-men had been seen off, the 'gentlemanly capitalists' reasserted their control. Like their nineteenth-century predecessors, they were largely indifferent to the claims of captains of industry, and their overriding aim was to restore Britain's position as the world's greatest financial and impe-rial power. There were many obstacles to such a course: Britain was heav-ily in debt to the United States, it could no longer afford to export almost unlimited supplies of capital, and the attempt to restore the Gold Stan-dard in 1925 had to be abandoned six years later. Nevertheless, the impe-rial mission was taken up with renewed vigour, commitment and determination. The mandates that the British accepted under the League of Nations suggested a continued appetite for territorial expansion, while the creation of the sterling area and the establishment of preferential tariffs during the 1930s bound the Empire even more tightly together.

As in the nineteenth century, the interwar Empire was still very much dominated by the mother country, which continued to hold (and to pull) the purse-strings. The dominions may have gained recognition of their autonomy with the passing of the Statute of Westminster in 1931, but their high levels of accumulated indebtedness to the London money mar-ket meant that Britain's economic control long outlived its political con-trol. In South America, the British were determined to retain their pre-eminent position in Argentina and Brazil, and despite challenges from the United States during the 1920s, and from Nazi Germany in the late 1930s, they generally succeeded. In India, the political reforms of 1919 and 1935 were designed to strengthen British rule, not weaken it: how else could the credit-worthiness of the Raj be preserved, and the remittance payments back to the metropolis be guaranteed? In tropical Africa, author-ity and finance were no less closely linked, but in a different way: the City would not invest, there was insufficient capital, and the challenge to inter-war imperial statecraft was to devise ways of increasing it, or of finding substitutes for it. And in China, despite the revolution of 1911, Britain remained the most significant foreign investor, successfully maintaining its influence there until the Sino-Japanese War broke out in 1937.

Accordingly, Cain and Hopkins insist that it is profoundly mistaken to see the history of the British Empire from 1914 to 1939 as being one of slow but irreversible decline. The Second World War was fought as much to safeguard the Empire as it was to defend Britain from Nazi tyranny, and in 1945, the surviving 'gentlemanly capitalists' were more concerned to develop than to dissolve their dominions. From this perspective, the end of Empire came rapidly and unexpectedly. But finance was the key to its fall no less than to its rise: for the changing patterns of Britain's post-war overseas investments meant that the Empire was no longer needed to protect them. As a result of the Second World War, India ceased to be Britain's debtor and became one of its creditors, which meant that there seemed little need to keep the Raj going. The huge holdings in South America were liquidated during the late 1940s, while those in China were nationalised by the Communists. The United States succeeded Britain as the prime investor in Canada and Australia. Africa had never mattered all that much. When the British began to invest overseas again, they did so in the United States and in Europe, and the City of London reinvented itself as an international financial centre. By then, the Empire had long since served its turn, and all that remained was for the latter-day 'gentlemanly capitalists' to dismantle it as rapidly and as honourably as possible.

Such is Cain and Hopkins's account of the rise and fall of the British Empire, and no praise can be too high for the skill with which it is unfolded and sustained across more than eight hundred pages of text. They seem to have read everything that is germane to the subject; they are as well informed about Britain as they are about the Empire; and they have mastered the specialist literature on Canada, Australia, New Zealand and India, as well as that on China, Africa, Latin America and the Middle East. Only Ireland, the West Indies and South-East Asia have escaped their attention. Moreover, they write with uncommon grace and style; they are never overwhelmed by the mass of material; and the organisation is admirable throughout. In a subject where detailed knowledge has increased at the cost of diminishing general comprehension, this prodigious labour of scholarship and learning, synthesis and argument is a landmark in its breadth of vision and its boldness of spirit. It will be essential reading for anyone interested in the history of Britain, of the British Empire, or of any of the separate nations which were once part of it. We may live in a post-colonial world, but thanks to Cain and Hopkins, the British Empire has struck back with a vengeance.

But have they got it right? Any argument which covers so long a span of time, and ventures over so broad a geographical area is going to provoke dissent. One problem which runs right through these volumes is the inadequate treatment of Britain's manufacturing economy. The authors seem convinced that many imperial historians argued that the Industrial Revolution made the British Empire both necessary and possible. Yet they can cite very few reputable scholars who have ever maintained such a crude and simplistic view. Moreover, their own argument that the Industrial Revolution was a very limited, piecemeal affair draws heavily on the findings of a particularly myopic phase in the historiography of that subject which now seems to be coming to an end. It is also not clear that the industrial sector of the economy can be separated from the financial-service sector as conveniently, completely or convincingly as their analysis requires. After all, much of the banking, the shipping and the insurance which formed a substantial part of Britain's so-called 'invisible' earnings existed to facilitate international trade in British manufactured goods, and in the raw materials which were imported to make their production possible. Domestic industry and overseas finance were complementary not competing.

Put another way, this also means that there are real difficulties with the idea of 'gentlemanly capitalism', a concept so vague that it is in danger of losing any real explanatory power. Assuredly, there may never have been a coherent, monolithic industrial interest in Britain. But nor did the financial service sector speak with one single voice. 'The City' was never the unified lobby that the authors' argument requires it to have been: it was a bewilderingly diverse place, in which the few great dynasties like the Rothschilds and Barings were quite untypical of the whole. Nor is it clear that there were close and constant connections between financiers and government in the formulation of imperial policy: they may all have been to the same public schools, and have been members of the same clubs, but as the authors coyly admit on more than one occasion, the City was 'in many ways above politics'. And we are never told what it was that drove these 'gentlemanly capitalists' abroad to begin with: the authors briefly mention that greater profits were to be made, but they do not develop the idea. In short, the concept of 'gentlemanly capitalism' suffers from the same problems as that of the 'official mind': it is an arresting phrase which does not stand up well to sceptical scrutiny.

There is also the question, which the authors do not choose to explore, of how it was that *English* gentlemen made the *British* Empire. This is more than a matter of mere pedantry: for there never has been such a thing as a 'British' gentleman, nor such an institution as the 'English' Empire. The reason that the Empire was British was that many of the people who made it and governed it were not English at all, but came from Wales, Ireland and Scotland. Cardiff exported its coals (and its miners) all over the world. The Scottish were especially important in the affairs of Canada and India. And so were (and are) the Irish in Australia: ask Paul Keating. Such figures, many of whom can hardly be described, incidentally, as 'gentlemanly capitalists', do not fit easily into the Cain–Hopkins scheme of things. In the same way, different parts of England forged close ties with the Empire, that were independent of London – especially Lancashire, Tyneside and Birmingham. Viewed from the south-east, the Empire may seem like the creation of 'gentlemanly capitalist' insiders. But if the perspective is shifted to northern England or the rest of the British Isles, the creators of the Empire assume very different national (and social) identities. Many of them were outsiders, who saw the Empire as a means of self-advancement, and they made it British – not English – in the process.

To these conceptual difficulties must be added problems of chronology. Their account (and explanation) of the different phases of imperial expansion is insufficiently nuanced. The years from 1688 to 1850 are treated very schematically, and occupy scarcely fifty pages of text. For much of this period, Britain was indeed a pre-industrial nation, and the authors might have strengthened their case considerably if they had explored the drive to Empire more fully in the seventy-odd years following the 'Glorious Revolution'. Nor does their interpretation of the period after 1776 entirely convince. For it seems clear that there was a real change in the nature of the imperial dynamic at this time, partly in response to the loss of the American colonies, partly because of the Industrial Revolution, and partly because of the increased rivalry between the British and the French. As a result, the conquest of large tracts of India during the 1790s and 1800s seems to have occurred for a variety of reasons which were very different from those which had led to expansion earlier in the Empire's history. And we never learn how it was that the British became entangled in the affairs of New Zealand, Canada or South Africa at around this time, or why people (surely not 'gentlemanly capitalists'?) began to emigrate there.

In fact, the book only really gets going when it reaches the last quarter of the nineteenth century, the era of the so-called 'New Imperialism', the 'Scramble for Africa', and the massive expansion in Britain's overseas investments. But here, too, there are difficulties with an interpretation which treats empire as little more than the by-product of metropolitan financial expansion. It is easy to see why the British were involved in Egypt and South Africa, but what of the vast tracts of the continent they annexed in-between? In the same way, the British government seems to have been much more interested in the affairs of the Ottoman and Chinese empires than were British investors, which hardly conforms to the authors' general thesis. Perhaps it was because of the growing rivalries among the great powers of Europe, a subject to which Cain and Hopkins give insufficient attention. Moreover, they are far too eager to write off the consequences of Britain's perceived (and undoubted) late nineteenth-century industrial retardation. For all the pomp and circumstance of Queen Victoria's Diamond Jubilee of 1897, British policy-makers were genuinely worried that the country was being overtaken. And it was, after all, that former manufacturer turned politician, Joseph Chamberlain, a man who was the very antithesis of a 'gentlemanly capitalist', who believed passionately that industrial leadership, imperial connection and great-power status were, for Britain, inextricably interlinked.

It is also not clear how far the survival of the British Empire during the interwar years, and its disappearance soon after, can – or should – be explained in terms which must be consistent with the account offered by Cain and Hopkins about how it came into existence in the first place. The continuing importance, during the 1920s and 1930s, of British investment and of colonial indebtedness seems clear: but was this all that was holding the Empire together at this time? And when it comes to explaining the end of Empire, the authors admit that economic change has to take its place alongside other forces: the decline of British power, the rising costs of imperial administration and defence, the loss of the imperial will and sense of mission, the irresistible force of colonial nationalism, and the pressures of international opinion, including in the United States. This is an impressive and salutary list. But it does prompt this subversive thought: if a multicausal explanation seems to fit for imperial decline, why should it be inappropriate for imperial expansion?

Despite the prodigious labours that have gone into the making of these two remarkable volumes, their essential argument can be reduced to one simple sentence: namely that 'finance' was the 'governor of the imperial engine'. This has, of course, been said before, by J. A. Hobson, and it is surely no coincidence that P.J. Cain has for some years been actively engaged in seeking to rehabilitate Hobson as the pre-eminent theorist of imperialism. For it was Hobson who first drew attention to the difference between the 'industrial' north of England, and the more dominant 'financial' south; it was Hobson who was convinced that the occupation of Egypt and the waging of the Boer War were undertaken to safeguard British assets overseas; and it was Hobson who argued, much more subtly than Lenin, that overseas investment was the key to empire. For a long time Hobson was, along with Lenin, one of the whipping-boys of those who sought to dismiss the economic theory of imperialism. Ninety years after Hobson wrote his book, he has now received, at the hands of Cain and Hopkins, a sort of posthumous vindication. For it is difficult to believe that a more comprehensive and compelling study of the economic dynamics to empire will ever be produced.

Yet the very magnitude of their accomplishment only serves to underline the limitations intrinsic to such an enterprise. Like Hobson, these volumes are too preoccupied with the age of 'High Imperialism' from the 1870s to the First World War, and give insufficient attention to what went before. Like Hobson, the analysis is excessively monocausal, and gives inadequate weight to the many other explanations for empire – not just political-diplomatic-strategic, but also religious, humanitarian, ideological and cultural. Like Hobson, the approach is too much concerned with the imperial metropolis, and the authors do not convince when they seek to dismiss approaches to their subject which stress the autonomous impulses emanating from the periphery. Like Hobson, Cain and Hopkins fail to recognise the extent to which the Empire was always an imaginative construct, existing as much (or more) inside the minds of men and women as it existed on the ground and on the map. In short, this work demonstrates not only the strengths, but also the weaknesses, of adopting an approach to the history of British overseas expansion which, for all its unrivalled mastery of recent scholarship, is in many ways extremely traditional. The Empire has struck back, not once, but twice.

(1995)

NOTE

1 P.J. Cain and A.G. Hopkins, *British Imperialism*, vol. 1: *Innovation and Expansion, 1688–1914*; vol. 2: *Crisis and Deconstruction, 1914–1990* (London, 1993).

17
Britons

In June 1955, a dinner took place in Christ's College, Cambridge, to mark
the presentation of a festschrift to G.M. Trevelyan. The assembled company included J.H. Plumb, C.V. Wedgwood, A.L. Rowse, H.J. Habakkuk,
G. Kitson Clark and Noel Annan. They consumed venison provided by
the Marquess of Cholmondeley, and no doubt the wine was also of the
very highest quality. In his after-dinner speech, Trevelyan observed that
with the decline of the traditional landowning class, it was up to the universities to provide a new aristocracy, with time to think and freedom to
write. And the essays which his admirers had contributed were appropriately patrician in their tone and substance, including such subjects as the
houses and estates of the second Earl of Nottingham, the contrasting
careers of Sir Robert Walpole and his father, and the rise and ramifica-
tions of the modern British intellectual aristocracy. Only in the light of
subsequent developments, and from the proletarian perspective of such an
organisation as History Workshop, does it seem mildly odd that these
illustrious scholars should have thought of themselves as social historians,
and that their festschrift, so laden with aristocratic subject-matter, should
have been entitled *Studies in Social History*.

At the time, however, it paid appropriate homage to the author of the
most famous and successful social history of England ever written.
Trevelyan's characterisation of this genre as 'the history of the people with
the politics left out' has been much quoted, more often derided, and
almost invariably misunderstood. He actually said that social history *might*
be described that way, and he himself only adopted that essentially working definition with some reluctance, at the behest of his publisher, Robert
Longman, who wanted a book that would complement, but not overlap
with, Trevelyan's earlier *History of England*, in which the politics had
understandably predominated. In the preface to his *Social History*,

Trevelyan was careful to insist on the close links between economic, social and political change, and he took pains to delineate his subject in catholic and comprehensive terms. It should encompass, he suggested, the human as well as the economic relations of different classes, the character of family and household life, the conditions of labour and leisure, the attitude of man towards nature, and the cumulative influence of all these subjects on culture, including religion, architecture, literature, music, learning and thought.

Nevertheless, when social history took off in the later 1950s and the 1960s, it was self-consciously in revolt against everything Trevelyan was thought to have stood for. It was much influenced by the mood of the time – decolonisation, student protest and active campaigns against the Vietnam War – and was inspired by Marxist passion rather than Whiggish condescension. It concentrated on the Industrial Revolution and its aftermath, and was concerned with the labouring masses rather than their social superiors. It stressed deprivation, struggle and violence, rather than consensual decency and national character. And it resulted in some of the most outstanding, influential and controversial history-writing in postwar Britain: Edward Thompson's *The Making of the English Working Class* (1963), Eric Hobsbawm's *Labouring Men* (1964), and John Foster's *Class Struggle and the Industrial Revolution* (1974). To the extent that the findings of this generation of scholarship were ever synthesised, it was in an audaciously ambitious book by Harold Perkin, *The Origins of Modern English Society, 1780–1880* (1969). Although very anxious to proclaim that he himself was not a Marxist, Perkin's work shared the preoccupations, and accepted the basic interpretive framework, of the Thompson–Hobsbawm–Foster approach.

For the central concern of all these writers was *class*. The overall trajectory of modern British history was presented in terms of social dynamics: a declining aristocracy, a rising bourgeoisie, and an evolving proletariat. At various times during the early part of the nineteenth century, class conflict – over the distribution of income and of power – was endemic throughout British society. The material conditions of the labouring masses were terrible, but despite their deprivation and exploitation, they managed to forge the richest and most vital proletarian culture that England has ever known. As a result of the conflicts in the workplace, they came to feel a sense of community and identity among themselves, over and against their middle-class employers. Inevitably, and inexorably,

their bitter experience of class conflict led to the rise of class consciousness, and to the radical politics that were its expression, with the result
that during the 1800s, and again in the early 1830s, England may have
come close to revolution. But in the mid-Victorian period, these subversive impulses were effectively repressed and overwhelmed, and it was only
in the late nineteenth century that working-class consciousness emerged
again in the form of the 'new' unionism and the Labour Party.

Twenty years on, it is easier to criticise the limitations of this work than
to remember the excitement with which it was originally (and rightly)
greeted. Despite their hostility to Trevelyan's approach, these Marxists in
fact shared with him a deeply rooted dislike of industrial production,
urban life and factory employment – not surprisingly since, like him, they
were much indebted to the older tradition of working-class historiography
associated with Toynbee and the Hammonds. Because Marx had said so,
they took it for granted that class existed, that it could be found, and that
it was the major explanatory variable, regardless of whether this was actually the case or not. They placed too much stress on radical political
activism, and ignored what Geoffrey Best once described as the 'flag-salut-
ing, peer-respecting, foreigner-hating' side of the plebeian mind. They
paid little attention to women, to religion, to the role of the state, or to
the structure of authority. They too easily assumed that it was at work,
rather than at home, that class consciousness originated. And they were
insufficiently sensitive to the geographical and territorial dimensions of the
working-class experience. Class feeling might exist in Oldham, in the
1830s and 1840s, but what did that imply about class feeling nationally, or
anywhere else? Much of their writing implicitly and mistakenly presumed
that the experience of factory workers in industrial Lancashire or Yorkshire was the national norm.

Most of the social history which has been written during the last decade
and a half has been in conscious reaction to these early heroic adventures
– partly because the dynamics of the scholarly process invariably work like
that, and partly because the Marxist input into British scholarship has significantly declined in confidence, vigour and importance during the
Thatcher years. The debates initiated in the 1960s – on the standard of
living, the existence of class, and the labour aristocracy – have become
increasingly sterile, introverted and unproductive. Detailed studies of
localities suggest that class conflict and class consciousness were far less
widespread or significant than was previously believed. The recent re-
evaluation of the Industrial Revolution, which stresses its gradual nature

and localised impact, has further undermined the old certainties about class formation and class identity. In so far as the working class was made or remade during the late nineteenth century, this had more to do with conservative culture than with radical politics. And these findings, combined with recent work demonstrating the close links between the bourgeoisie and the aristocracy, suggest that the simple tripartite model of Britain's social evolution since the mid-eighteenth century needs to be substantially revised.

Put more positively, this means that the even greater expansion of social history during the last fifteen years has been more concerned with the rediscovery of experience than with the search for class. Many of the subjects that Trevelyan enumerated – family and household life, the conditions of labour and leisure, the attitude of man towards nature – have been extensively investigated by the self-styled 'new' social historians, and they have been joined by historians of population, of crime, of medicine, of education, of sex, of childhood, of marriage, of women, of cities, of housing and of gardens. The result is that articles, dissertations and monographs have proliferated on a bewildering variety of subjects, and in seemingly exponential abundance. There are specialist societies, journals and conferences for each of these subdisciplines; almost every reputable publisher now has a new social history of England in progress; and all British universities offer social history courses at undergraduate and postgraduate level. Indeed, in his recent inaugural lecture as Regius Professor of Modern History at Cambridge University, Patrick Collinson felt moved to remark (and to warn?) that social history had now become 'a hard-hat area which seems to threaten us with the kind of intolerant hegemony once exercised by political and constitutional history'.

But as these remarks imply, the 'new' social history has not been without its critics. Some condemn it for being essentially antiquarian, for all too often celebrating experience but eschewing interpretation, analysis or explanation. Some see it as no more than a mindless extension of Trevelyan's original laundry list, an inchoate amalgam of fashionable fads, trivial inanities and prurient sensationalism, which it is neither possible nor worthwhile to synthesise satisfactorily. Some condemn it for having lost all connection with power or with public life – and this at a time when political historians are becoming increasingly interested in the state and structures of authority: not for nothing was Collinson's inaugural lecture subtitled 'History with the Politics Put Back'. And some, harking back to the criticisms originally levelled at Trevelyan, see it as a subject devoid of methodological coherence. Political history is about the distribution of power, and economic history is about the allocation of scarce resources. But what is social history about? 'Class' now seems discredited as an organising principle, and 'experience' is even less robust. In terms of its popular appeal, social history may now be a hard-hat enterprise; but in terms of its intellectual rigour, it is decidedly soft-centred.

It is against this historiographical background, at once shifting, challenging and uncertain, that these three substantial volumes, which offer a collective survey of Britain's social history from the mid-eighteenth century to the mid-twentieth, must be located and evaluated.[1] In upbringing and training, the social historians who write here are a very different breed from the men and women who did homage to Trevelyan over the venison and the port. At the same time, they largely leave aside the approaches pioneered by the Marxist writers of the fifties and sixties: these volumes are most emphatically *not* organised around the categories of class, and they do not address head-on such once-fashionable notions as the labour aristocracy or social control. And they deliberately desist from offering any prepackaged synthesis of more recent work: instead, a team of experts write separate essays, loosely but plausibly grouped together in what the editor terms 'three broad thematic clusters': regional communities, social environment and social institutions. The result is the most comprehensive social history of modern Britain ever attempted, and the whole venture stands as a worthy monument to the enlightened patronage of Cambridge University Press, the inspired direction of the editor, and the outstandingly high level of most individual contributions.

The first volume vividly demonstrates the historical diversity of British life, by looking at the social histories of different regions. The editor begins with a splendidly synoptic account of urban development, pointing out the essentially rural matrix in which towns evolved during the eighteenth century, and suggesting that it was the lower middle classes, rather than businessmen in the Chamberlain mould, who were the dominant voice in the management of most Victorian cities. W.A. Armstrong looks at the countryside, and argues that broad interpretations of social change may more usefully be cast in terms of agrarian conditions, the impact of industrialisation, and associated demographic developments, than in terms of class. Two essays on Scotland (by Rosalind Mitchison and T.C. Smout) and Wales (by D.W. Howell and C. Baber) impressively link economic, social and political changes, in describing the rise and fall of Clydeside and of the Glamorgan coalfield. J.K. Walton performs the same service for the north-west, again reminding us just how varied were both the economy and society of Lancashire and Cheshire. D.J. Rowe writes about Northumberland and Durham, a region which industrialised late and unevenly, and never succeeded in overcoming the disadvantages of distance and remoteness. And P.L. Garside looks at the varied efforts made to cope with London's government, housing and transport, and at the impact the great metropolis made on the surrounding region.

As the editor himself admits, the geographical coverage of this volume is inevitably uneven. It is a welcome antidote to English parochialism to begin with Wales and Scotland, and to leave London until last, and each of these essays conveys a sense of place and locality with a vividness and a conviction that Trevelyan himself would certainly have applauded. But it is a pity that there is no essay on Ulster, that the chapter on the north-east excludes Yorkshire, that Birmingham and the Midlands go effectively undiscussed, and that there is no sustained treatment of any primarily agricultural area, such as East Anglia or the West Country. Moreover, by concentrating so much on those northern and Celtic regions which were the homes of the great staple industries, this means that insufficient attention is given to those areas in the Midlands and the south where interwar conditions were noticeably less depressed. Nor does Garside's essay on 'London and the Home Counties' repair this omission: there is much fascinating material on the growth and government of the metropolis itself, but the diverse economic life of the city, and the expansion of new towns like Slough in the twenties and thirties, barely rate a mention.

In volume 2, the focus shifts to an exploration of the living and the working environment. Michael Anderson discusses the social implications of demographic change, and points out, among other things, that limited life expectancy meant that one-parent families were more the norm in Victorian England than they are today. Leonore Davidoff summarises her earlier work on the family, and seeks to flesh out the reality of home life often hinted at in Anderson's tables. In his essay on work, Patrick Joyce goes to great lengths to tell us that the uneven development of the Victorian economy meant that the factory hand was not the only kind of labourer in nineteenth-century England. M.J. Daunton looks at housing from two very different perspectives: the building of homes as physical artefacts, and the social life they contained (and influenced); and the changing patterns of house ownership, management and occupation. D.J. Oddy writes about food, drink and nutrition, and reminds us just how badly nourished most people were in Britain before the twentieth century. And Hugh Cunningham surveys changing patterns of recreation, both in terms of the growing amount of time that many people had for such activities, and also the different and changing ways in which their leisure was spent.

Like the first volume, this is something of a mixed bag. Michael Anderson handles his graphs and tables with customary assurance and insight, but Leonore Davidoff's essay seems curiously arid and lifeless, devoid of any real sense of people or place. And Patrick Joyce not only ignores the middle class entirely in his discussion of work: he also writes with such self-indulgent incomprehensibility that it is often not at all clear what – if anything – he actually means. By contrast, Daunton's essay is a model of well-organised lucidity, Oddy does full justice to local variations in diet, while never losing sight of the broader, national picture, and Cunningham's chapter abounds with suggestive insights, as when he argues that the study of leisure pursuits is one of the best ways of analysing the changing relationship between local identity and national consciousness. There is much here that is of value, and it is easy to see why these topics were chosen. But there is, perhaps unavoidably, a nuts and bolts feeling about this volume as a whole. Compare some of the imaginative chapter headings to be found in Theodore Zeldin's magisterially irritating history of France from 1848 to 1945: 'Good and Bad Taste', 'Newspapers and Corruption', 'Worry, Boredom and Hysteria', and 'The Ambitions of Ordinary Men'. Such an approach can be easily dismissed as an amalgam of Gallic chic and pointillist obsession. But what would one give for a social history of modern Britain written from such a refreshing and imaginative perspective!

The final volume moves on to consider those institutions which have most impinged on people's lives, some as agencies of state control and coercion, some as voluntary organisations of self-help and self-improvement, some an uneasy amalgam of the two. Pat Thane describes the minimalist notion of government which prevailed from Lord Liverpool to Gladstone, and Jose Harris provides a masterly account of the changing relations between society and the state in twentieth-century Britain. Gillian Sutherland's survey of education reminds us how limited was government provision, not just before Forster's Act of 1870, but even down to R.A. Butler's legislation of 1944, and Virginia Berridge points out that much the same was true in the realm of health and medicine. In the most impassioned piece in the entire collection, V.A.C. Gatrell depicts modern Britain as a 'policeman-state', in which the working classes have been the victims of an ever more powerful and disingenuous centralising authority. James Obelkevich sketches out the contours of religious revival and decline, F.K. Prochaska describes the many faces of philanthropy, voluntarism and self-help, and R.J. Morris performs the same service for clubs, societies and associations.

Almost without exception, these essays are well handled, by acknowledged experts in their field. But it is regrettable that there is no single chapter devoted to trade unions. Undeniably, their power today is not what it once was. Yet for much of the nineteenth and twentieth centuries, they were the most important agency of working-class self-betterment and self-advancement, of unrivalled importance in improving not only the wages, but also the conditions, of labouring men. It is also extremely difficult to reconcile the pictures of the British state as painted by Thane and Gatrell. The one sees it as being of little significance in the lives of most ordinary people, rarely impinging on daily lives before the close of the nineteenth century. The other sees it as essentially intrusive, coercive, predatory and malevolent – at least as far as the poor and disadvantaged were concerned. Of course, it would be absurd and unreasonable to expect complete unanimity in a volume so diverse and so distinguished. But this fundamental discrepancy does raise important questions about the nature of the modern British state, and thus about the nature of modern British working-class life.

As individual essays, these twenty-one chapters offer the most valuable survey yet provided of the social history of modern Britain. But do they, collectively, add up to anything more than that? In what sense, if at all, is the whole greater than the sum of its parts? In his coyly mandarin introduction, Professor Thompson disclaims any ambition to offer an overall synthesis or general interpretation. 'Raising an overarching superstructure over the individual contributions in these volumes', he argues, 'would come close to courting a disaster akin to those which customarily visit university buildings designed in committee.' Perhaps so. But it is worth remarking that one such single-handed (and far from disastrous) synthesis already exists, and that it has been appropriately provided by Professor Thompson himself, in his recent survey, *The Rise of Respectable Society: A Social History of Victorian Britain, 1830–1900.* For the picture he paints there of nineteenth-century British society bears a close and recognisable resemblance to that presented here by his assembled team: a slow and uneven transformation of the economy and of society; a social fabric in which different layers and levels dissolved imperceptibly into each other, largely devoid of class antagonisms; and a working class which was very much in control of its own destiny, regardless of the vainly intrusive ambitions of law-makers and administrators.

This summary (albeit at one editorial remove) of the general interpretation advanced in these three volumes should make it plain that this is very much (and very properly) social history in its contemporary mode. How does it look in the longer perspective of social history, as it has been carried on in Britain over the half-century since Trevelyan penned his elegiac books? In terms of contemporary practice, the sheer bulk of these volumes is the most eloquent testimony to the vigour and variety of the subject as it has flourished during the 1970s and 1980s. But the fact that twenty-one authors can fill 1,400 pages, yet neither exhaust nor encompass the whole field, is also the most emphatic sign that social history is in real danger of imminent and unrestrainable fragmentation. And for all the gain in knowledge to which these detailed essays on particular topics bear emphatic and erudite witness, they inevitably mean that the broader contours and implications of social development somehow get lost sight of. In almost every essay, there is a vague, general, underlying sense that massive social and economic change coexisted with quite remarkable political stability. Yet this central issue never gets explicitly addressed. In the same way, many of these contributors believe that the most significant trend that can be discerned is a shift, in both regional identity and social behaviour, from distinctiveness to uniformity. But once again, this important question is never confronted head-on.

Viewed from the rather different perspective of the social history of the fifties and sixties, this suggests that the earlier approach, which looked at the broader issues of class formation and social evolution, had rather more to recommend it than it is often now fashionable to suppose. The essays on Scotland, Wales and the north-west seem constantly to teeter on the brink of class analysis, and both Gillian Sutherland and Hugh Cunningham make it plain that neither education nor leisure can be properly understood except in terms of class. But what, exactly, those classes were, are, and ought to be, these volumes do not help us to find out. At the same time, the picture revealed here of many working-class lives – nasty, mean, brutish and short, and lacking in adequate housing, education or nutrition – suggests that some of the outraged passion of Edward Thompson (and of the Hammonds before him) was not entirely misplaced. Above all, these volumes conspicuously fail to provide any general guide to the evolving social landscape of Britain's history during the last two hundred years – changes which, for all the problems of definition and methodology, can only be described and understood in essentially class terms.

But it is not just that these books suggest that the approaches and concerns of the 1950s and 1960s have in recent times been discarded too zealously: they also remind us of something much more profound that has been lost to social history in the years since Trevelyan put down his pen, and that is something which can only be described as a human sense of fellow-feeling. For all their graphs and their tables, their painstaking researches and their unquestionable expertise, none of these writers show much sign of being *moved* – by life, by people, by the very humanity which they are supposed to be describing. Look at the faces of the nineteenth-century slum children which peer out from the covers of these books: vulnerable but unafraid, ardent and anxious, innocent yet worldly. But once inside these volumes, there is scarcely a sentence which touches these human qualities, or conveys with any imaginative conviction what it must have been like for millions of ordinary British people to grow up, love and hate, worry and hope, age and die. At the most fundamental level, these essays lack that deeper insight into human nature and human life which is the authentic cadence of great history. Trevelyan really possessed that voice, and it is high time that today's social historians began to listen to it again.

(1990)

NOTE

1 F.M.L. Thompson (ed.), *The Cambridge Social History of Britain, 1750–1950*, vol. 1: *Regions and Communities*; vol. 2: *People and their Environment*; vol. 3: *Social Agencies and Institutions* (Cambridge, 1990).

18
Intellectuals

In some ways, the fiftieth anniversary reunions at American universities are just like all the others that have gone before. The alumni fly in from far and near, and once again exchange news and gossip in an atmosphere of nostalgic good will. There is another class book, which provides the most up-to-date account of the lives and doings of peers and contemporaries, and there is another class president, who is elected, like his predecessors, on the presumption that he embodies the collective identity and corporate distinction of the year as a whole. But for all the comforting familiarity of these rituals, the fiftieth anniversary reunion is an unprecedentedly poignant occasion – the gathering of a class which, for the first time, has passed its allotted span of three score years and ten. Inevitably, there are more absent friends and obituary notices than ever before. Most who do attend have recently retired, and are living off their pensions – and off their memories. And all are wondering who will have died – or whether they themselves will have died – before the next reunion takes place. Half a century on, intimations of mortality are inescapable, and the survivors are forced to recognise that their bright day is drawing to a close, and that their class will soon be heading for the dark.

The best way to approach Noel Annan's *Our Age* is to think of the author as the class president, not just of a year, but of an entire British generation, which has recently celebrated its fiftieth reunion, has taken its final curtain call, and is now in the process of quitting the public stage.[1] 'Our age' was the phrase used by Sir Maurice Bowra, the most famous Oxford wit of his time, to describe those he regarded as his contemporaries, and Lord Annan takes it to encompass those who grew up between the end of the First World War and the late 1940s, many of whom became part of the British Establishment between the late 1950s and the early 1980s. They were predominantly from upper middle-class backgrounds, were mostly educated at public school, and attended Oxford or Cambridge Universities or the London School of Economics. They were academics, writers, journalists, poets, pundits, politicians – and spies. They were the men (and they were nearly all men) who formed public opinion and made public policy. They included George Orwell and Kenneth Clark, Graham Greene and C.P. Snow, Eric Hobsbawm and F.R. Leavis, Michael Oakeshott and Roy Jenkins, Anthony Blunt and Harold Wilson. Harold Macmillan was a touch too old to be a member (he was born in 1894 and went up to Oxford in 1912), but Mrs Thatcher just squeezes in (she was born in 1925, and went up to Oxford in 1943).

As the class president of this generation, Noel Annan is self-appointed rather than elected. But his qualifications for the post are undeniable. For his whole career has been bound up with the arts, education, public service and public affairs. He was born in 1916, and educated at Stowe (one of the few progressive public schools of the time), and at King's College Cambridge (where he was elected to the university's most exclusive society known as the Apostles). During the Second World War, he worked in military intelligence, and was later involved in the administration of the British Zone of occupied Germany. He then returned to Cambridge, became a Fellow of his college and a University Lecturer in Politics, and was elected Provost of King's at the astonishingly early age of thirty-nine. Ten years later he left Cambridge for London, where he became head of University College, and in 1978 he was elected the first full-time Vice-Chancellor of London University. By then, he was also a trustee of the National Gallery and of the British Museum, and a director of the Royal Opera House at Covent Garden. In 1965, he was made a life peer, and in 1977 he published the Annan Report on the future of broadcasting in Britain.

Thus described, Lord Annan belongs to a select group of people known in Britain as 'the great and the good', men and women of high intelligence and unassailable prestige, who dutifully serve on government committees and the boards of public bodies, and who bring to the conduct of business a disinterested tone of superior wisdom and high-minded worldliness. But unlike many educational administrators and professional committee men, Lord Annan has continued to be interested in the life of the mind, and in the history of ideas. His first book, published in 1951, was a sympathetic and authoritative biography of Leslie Stephen, the late Victorian thinker and agnostic. His most famous piece of writing is an essay on 'The Intellectual Aristocracy', which appeared in 1956 in the festschrift for G.M. Trevelyan, and explored the close interconnections between leading middle-class families, like the Darwins, the Keyneses, the Huxleys and the Wedgwoods, who were pre-eminent in British academic life between the 1880s and the 1930s. And for the last twenty years, Annan has been a regular contributor to the *New York Review of Books*, where he has written widely and discerningly on the history, politics, literature and culture of modern Britain.

Our Age is a natural extension of these interests and concerns. It explores the generation which both merged with, and took over from, the traditional, dynastic intellectual aristocracy. It is concerned to investigate their beliefs and assumptions, their achievements and their failures, in the realms of morality, politics and intellectual endeavour, and it has been put together from the extensive corpus of Annan's recent journalistic writing. This makes for an uneven and inadequately structured book, which cannot be easily characterised or categorised. It is neither history, nor biography, nor personal memoir, although it contains elements of all three. It is about politicians more than civil servants, humanists rather than scientists, and secular concerns loom much larger than religious preoccupations. It has little to say about the influence of American intellectuals on British life, or about the impact of Jewish scholars, fleeing from Nazi persecution, and it is much stronger on Cambridge and London than on Oxford. As Annan himself admits, his book merely sets down 'the impression I as an individual have formed of the part of my times that I know something about'. But for all its limitations, the result is a work which should be essential reading for anyone interested in twentieth-century Britain, or twentieth-century ideas.

Like every young generation, that to which Noel Annan belonged was in conscious and deliberate revolt against its immediate predecessor. In this case, however, the sense of rebellion was sharpened by the great divide of the First World War, which meant that the young men of the twenties and thirties held very different attitudes from the old men of the Edwardian era. They had little time for the ideal of the English gentleman, as celebrated by Kipling, Buchan and Sapper, they regarded the military as Blimpish bunglers, and they did not like the regimented barbarism of the public schools. (Esmond Romilly ran away from Wellington, and Cyril Connolly wrote a devastating indictment of Eton in *Enemies of Promise*.) Instead, they believed in individual freedom and the good life, and they made homosexuality a cult, thereby repudiating their forbears' beliefs in the most emphatic way. By the 1960s, the most creative figures in the arts in Britain were all known to be homosexuals: Wystan Auden, the poet; Benjamin Britten, the composer; Frederick Ashton, the choreographer; and Francis Bacon, the painter. Not surprisingly, this was the decade in which Annan's generation set about reforming the laws relating to obscenity, censorship, divorce, homosexuality, and corporal punishment in schools. To its critics, this was 'permissive' legislation; to its supporters, it registered a great gain in personal freedom.

In terms of the politics of morality, Annan's generation has much to its credit. In terms of the politics of patriotism, its record is less clear-cut. As young men, they were much affected by the Spanish Civil War and by the Munich settlement. Some of Annan's contemporaries went out to fight (and die) on behalf of the Republic. Many more were indignant at Chamberlain's betrayal of Czechoslovakia. A few turned to Marxism, and it was from their number that the notorious 'Cambridge spies' were recruited: Donald Maclean, Guy Burgess, Kim Philby and Anthony Blunt. Annan is at his best in evoking the bizarre atmosphere in which these traitors were bred among the Apostles during the 1930s, as Marxism, homosexuality and intellectual arrogance together encouraged the belief that Communism and friendship were more important than patriotism and duty. But as Annan points out, these men betrayed their friends as well as their country. They should never have been recruited to the secret service in the first place, and the old boy network was devastated by their treachery. But there was another side to this. For that same old boy network was also responsible for the recruitment of men of genius, like the Cambridge mathematician Alan Turing, without whom the German codes would probably never have been broken at Bletchley.

Many of these people returned to their normal scholarly avocations after the war was over, and Annan devotes a section of his book to telling us what they did once they got back there. He mentions sociologists like Richard Titmuss and Michael Young, whose work on the health service and family life in East London told civil servants and politicians what was going on in the welfare state. He writes appreciatively of such Marxist scholars as Christopher Hill, Eric Hobsbawm and E.P. Thompson, though he dismisses Raymond Williams's work as 'rhetorical, evasive and vacuous'. He explains why A.J.P. Taylor was unhonoured in his own country: he alienated the right by being left-wing, and alienated the left by his too well advertised friendship with Lord Beaverbrook. He praises Isaiah Berlin for his abiding belief in freedom and liberty, but admits that 'he remained marginal to the central issues of any region of national life'. He talks about the generation of economists who had begun as protégés of Maynard Keynes: Richard Khan, Joan Robinson and James Meade. And he explains why C.P. Snow's lecture on 'The Two Cultures' provoked such a savage and devastating response from F.R. Leavis, who in his reply not only destroyed Snow's reputation as a novelist but also dismissed the very idea that there was any such thing as a separate and superior scientific culture.

But many of Annan's generation also went into public life, either as party politicians, or because they were regarded as belonging, like him, to the ranks of 'the great and the good'. Most of them believed in government by consensus: they wanted a truce in the class war. And most of them, having seen the widespread distress of the interwar years, were more concerned about securing full employment than in worrying about inflation. They were strongly committed to the reform and expansion of higher education; but the much-vaunted system of comprehensive schools was never fully implemented, the new universities that were founded were too much in the traditional style, and as a result, Harold Wilson's 'white hot technological revolution' was still-born. In foreign affairs, their record was equally ambiguous. The British Empire was closed down with speed and skill by Iain Macleod, but delusions of great-power grandeur still persisted. Hence Britain's failure to join the Common Market at its inception, a failure which Annan describes as 'the most ruinous diplomatic decision taken by Our Age'. And most of the leaders of the sixties and seventies were equally lacking in vision: Heath and Wilson are awarded low marks; Home and Callaghan barely rate a mention; and Foot and Benn are dismissed as men who effectively made the Labour Party unelectable for a decade.

It is thus scarcely surprising that even in the heyday of Annan's generation, there were some who emphatically rejected its attitudes and values. There was the brilliantly quixotic novelist Evelyn Waugh, who hated the modern world in all its aspects, especially democracy, Parliament, and the middle classes, who became as devoted to the Catholic Church as to the British aristocracy, and who ended his life relishing his bigotry and misanthropy in a manner reminiscent of Hilaire Belloc. There was that most vitriolic of literary critics, F.R. Leavis, who despised the upper middle classes, metropolitan culture, and Bloomsbury and who looked back to a prelapsarian golden age of culture and creativity, which had been destroyed by science, industrialisation, advertising and mindless vulgarity. And there was Michael Oakeshott, who regarded Tory paternalism and

Socialist planning as equally reprehensible, disliked Clement Attlee as much as Harold Macmillan, and dismissed all attempts to build a better world as deluded nonsense. There were others who took equally dissenting views: Kingsley Amis, Malcolm Muggeridge and Enoch Powell. Before the Thatcher years, they found it hard to get an appreciative hearing. But in both the style and the substance of their arguments, Annan believes that they 'taught the successors of Our Age how to rough us up'.

By the late 1970s, Annan suggests, his generation was coming to the end of its period of pre-eminence, and its successors were demanding admission to the public stage. In part, this was the inevitable result of the passing of time: the fiftieth reunion was no longer that far off. But it was also that many of the values which his generation had believed in were being undermined and eroded by the inexorable march of contemporary events. The feminist movement, the demand for gay rights, and the scourge of AIDS portended a new agenda for the politics of morality. The unprecedented industrial unrest, the militancy of the trade unions, and the increasing polarisation in British party politics spelt the end of the postwar consensus. The spiralling rates of inflation suggested that Our Age's traditional preoccupation with unemployment as the greatest social evil was now out of date. Despite the cohorts of internationally renowned economists on which successive governments had been able to draw, the British economy was among the weakest in western Europe, and the comfortable, self-serving belief that Britain was still a great power was simply no longer tenable. In short, by the late 1970s, all of the easy certainties which had been accepted and taken for granted by Annan's generation were very largely discredited.

Then came Thatcher. Although she just qualified as a younger member of Annan's generation, it was she who 'led the hissing as Our Age made their exit from the stage'. Indeed, she did more than that: for it was Thatcher who, in no uncertain terms, gave them their orders to leave. She was the shopkeeper's daughter from Grantham, and she was proud of it. Although she had been to Oxford, she had read chemistry there. She despised the effete amateurishness and the arrogant snobbery of the upper middle classes. She hated academics, the Church of England, the civil service, and the BBC. She regarded royal commissions and committees of inquiry as a waste of time. She thought inflation was a far more serious problem than unemployment. She believed in the importance of wealth creation, and argued that businessmen and entrepreneurs were the people who mattered most. She had no time for consensus, and little sense of humour. And she was determined to turn the country round, to roll back the welfare state, to make Britain great again in the eyes of the world, and to replace the discredited presumptions of Annan's generation with the more wholesome values of the Victorian era, against which they had mistakenly and misguidedly rebelled. In short, her premiership spelt the end of 'Our Age's' vision of life, and signified that a new, and very different group was now in charge.

This is a remarkable account of a remarkable generation by one of its most remarkable ornaments. Although he writes about himself hardly at all in these pages, Lord Annan emerges very well from his book, as a decent, liberal, civilised, tolerant and humane man. The politicians he admires most give the best indication of the sort of person he is: David Eccles, Edward Boyle and Iain Macleod among the Conservatives; Tony Crosland, Denis Healey and (especially) Roy Jenkins on the left. As befits someone who lists his recreation in *Who's Who* as 'writing English prose', he can turn a good phrase or two, as when he says of the Labour politician Richard Crossman that 'the pleasure other men got in seducing women he got in seducing minds'. Just occasionally, Annan's eagerness to sum up a person's life and work in the manner of an end-of-term report gets the better of him, and the self-appointed class president sounds more like a schoolmaster or scout-master. But the book as a whole provides a unique and sweeping panorama of the author's generation, from its formative years at preparatory and public school, via the searing experience of the Second World War, through its period of welfare-state pre-eminence, until its eventual demise in the harsher decade of the 1980s.

Of course, it is still too soon to get their achievements in proper historical perspective, and Lord Annan himself is understandably unsure as to what the final verdict will be. Although he clearly stands by many of the values he learned in his youth, he is too even-handed an observer not to recognise the weaknesses of his contemporaries. His generation made many mistakes: in their flirtations with Communism, in their mishandling of Britain's entry into the Common Market, in their contempt for the process of wealth creation, in their inability to carry through far-reaching domestic reforms, in their failure to adjust to Britain's more circumscribed position in the postwar world, and in the generally low standard of political leadership they provided. Even as intellectuals, their achievements will probably not stand as high as those of their immediate predecessors. Who, of Annan's generation, can be compared with, say, Russell and Wittgenstein, Tawney and Trevelyan, Rutherford and Keynes? As the author remarks, with self-deprecating correctness, 'Our Age played their times in a minor key. We were not original . . . We played variations on our predecessors' themes.' It is difficult to believe that Mrs Thatcher herself could produce a better indictment of Lord Annan's generation than this.

But it is hardly the job of a class president to sell his class-mates and contemporaries down the river of history, and Lord Annan, for all his admirable liberal tolerance, is not inclined to do so. He rebuts the claim that his generation was responsible for Britain's postwar decline: the explanation is, he rightly insists, much more deeply rooted than that. The fact that Harold Wilson's government of 1964–70 was full of former Oxford dons may not be the best argument, or precedent, for letting academics loose on the sordid and practical affairs of the real world: but at least they made less of a hash of things than the Harvard eggheads and Ivy League preppies of the Kennedy and Johnson administrations. And although Annan is prepared to give Thatcher credit for curbing the trade unions, he is surely right to wonder whether she 'turned the country round' in the manner that she promised to do. Inflation and unemployment remain at unacceptably high levels, the nation's manufacturing base continues to contract, and Britain's relations with 'Europe' are still unresolved.

In short, it still remains to be seen whether the newer and younger generation that Thatcher ushered in and pushed to the fore will fare any better or achieve anything more substantial than Annan's did in their own time of power and hope – and disenchantment and disappointment. About them, and about that, it is too soon to know or to tell or to predict. All that can be said for certain is that if the experience of Annan's own cohort and contemporaries is any guide, they will achieve something serious and substantial and significant, but it will also fall seriously and substantially and significantly short of what they hoped or dreamed or intended when they were young men (and, increasingly, young women) poised expectantly on the threshold of fulfilment. In any case, and inevitably, and in their turn, they, too, will one day find themselves dismissed as outmoded, ineffectual and irrelevant by another younger, more striving and more vigorous generation intent on displacing and superseding them, just as they have displaced and superseded those who have gone before. Meanwhile, all that can be said for certain is that Lord Annan and his contemporaries are no longer in charge. They have not yet taken their final curtain call; but after their fiftieth reunion, they have ceased to occupy the centre of the stage. Our Age has become old age.

(1991)

Note

1 Noel Annan, *Our Age: Portrait of a Generation* (London, 1991).

19
Class

When John Major unexpectedly became Britain's Prime Minister in November 1990, he declared that his chief political ambition was to make the country a 'classless society', a commitment which he reiterated even more vigorously in the aftermath of his party's unexpected victory at the recent general election. The fact that Mr Major has apparently turned his back on such eternal Conservative verities as tradition, hierarchy and inequality is only one of the many ironies implicit in this extraordinary remark. The fact that he seems to have committed the Tories to achieving something which Marx eagerly looked forward to as the end-point of the historical process, and which has for most of the twentieth century been the very *raison d'être* of the Labour Party, is yet another. But there is a third irony which for an historian is the most intriguing of them all. In recognising that the classless millennium has not yet been ushered in, Mr Major reminds us just how class-bound a society Britain still is – and, by implication, always has been. Yet in seeing class as so central an element in British life and in British history, he has adopted a position exactly the opposite of that which it has recently become fashionable for social historians to maintain.

It has not always been thus. For thirty years after the Second World War, the social history of modern Britain was written almost exclusively in Marxist – or Marxisant – terms of class development, class consciousness and class conflict. Briefly summarised, the argument ran as follows. The Industrial Revolution transformed not only Britain's economy, but also its social structure, by creating the world's first entrepreneurial middle class and labouring proletariat, who were, inevitably, locked in conflict with each other. By the mid-nineteenth century, the bourgeois industrialists were firmly in control, and their creed of liberal self-help became the prevailing ideology of the nation. By contrast, the working classes fared less well. Their early experience of the industrialising process was disorienting and traumatic, and by the 1830s and 1840s, they were close to insurgent discontent. But their revolutionary ardour was soon blunted, as the prosperous artisans who might have provided the next generation of active leadership, the so-called 'labour aristocracy', were bought off by their employers, and comfortably assimilated into the mid-Victorian 'age of equipoise'. Only during the late nineteenth and early twentieth centuries was the British working class remade, this time seeking to assert its newly discovered identity, and realise its collective potential, through the trade union movement and the Labour Party.

During the last twenty years or so, virtually every aspect of this cogent and still-influential interpretation has come under attack. The Industrial Revolution has been reinterpreted as a gradual, piecemeal phenomenon, which brought with it neither a self-conscious working class nor a homogeneous bourgeoisie. Far from being fully fledged class conflict, the disturbances during the Napoleonic Wars and the 1830s and 1840s were small-scale, localised and ephemeral. Throughout the mid-Victorian period, the middle class remained weak and divided, and there was no such thing as a labour aristocracy. Even in the closing decades of the nineteenth century, the bourgeoisie failed to achieve economic or cultural pre-eminence, while the working class was predominantly conservative and quiescent, and often divided internally against itself. Instead of being a society rent asunder by class antagonisms which were often barely contained, nineteenth-century Britain was a country characterised by a high degree of consensus and consent, in which class divisions were far less clear-cut than it was once fashionable to suppose, where social groupings merged easily and almost imperceptibly one into another, and where national loyalties outweighed sectional interests. Indeed, so great has been this revisionism that recent syntheses of modern British social history have virtually ignored class altogether, something which would have been unthinkable fifteen years ago.

At a deeper level, the appropriateness of class analysis to social history has been further undermined by the growth of interest in theories of language and in the study of gender. As a result of their discovery of what is called 'the linguistic turn', some scholars now argue that the history of class is not, as was once thought, the history of social relations between wage labourers and capitalists: rather it is the history of the language people used, since it was words which provided the essential source of their individual and collective identity. Viewed from this linguistic perspective, class never really existed as a social reality: it was nothing more than a rhetorical construct. Equally subversive has been the work of a new generation of feminist scholars, who have criticised traditional histories of class for having been almost exclusively concerned with men. For they contend that once the history of women is given its due weight, and the underlying tensions between the sexes are recognised and explained, then male class solidarities are powerfully undercut by the competing claims of gender. Women as workers were one thing: women as women were another. Between them, therefore, the social historians of language, and the feminist historians of gender have strongly reinforced that growing disenchantment with traditional class analysis which has characterised recent empirical research.

As is so often the case in the writing and interpretation of modern British history, these latest scholarly developments, away from the old class-based model, have mirrored and coincided with broader changes in the public realm. In Britain, the decline of the traditional working class, the defeat of the trade unions, and the inexorable triumphs of the Conservatives seem to have ushered in a post-socialist society, in which the Labour Party, and the labour historiography of class consciousness and class conflict which was an important adjunct to it, have both become marginalised and outmoded. More broadly, the sudden demise of Communism in eastern Europe has thrown the whole Marxist creed into question, not only as a prescription for the future, but also as an interpretation of the past. Communism is dead, therefore Marxism is dead, therefore class is dead: thus runs the argument. Indeed, this view has recently received a characteristically vigorous articulation at the hands of Mrs Thatcher herself. Class, she recently insisted in the pages of *Newsweek*, was no more than an invention of the Communists, and as such it may now be safely consigned to the trash-can of history, along with the Cold War, the Berlin Wall and the guards outside Lenin's mausoleum.

Even by the much-debased standard of her post-prime ministerial utterances, Mrs Thatcher's remarks seem peculiarly crass, foolish and ignorant. For the substance (and the language) of class evolved in Britain long before Marx came upon the scene. Indeed, recent work on Hanoverian Britain has been much concerned with its essentially tripartite social structure, in which a powerful bourgeoisie has been discerned between the patricians and the plebs. The fact that some British historians have been busy inserting class *into* the eighteenth century casts both logical and chronological doubt on the simultaneous efforts of their colleagues to take class out of the nineteenth. And so, from a different but complementary standpoint, do the words of Mr Major. Assuredly, he is neither an historian nor a sociologist, and there is very little evidence that he has any idea what it would actually take in terms of specific measures of reform to usher in the classless millennium. But in his instinctive feeling that modern Britain remains a class-bound society, he surely does not err. Yet if this is indeed the case, then when and how did this class-bound society come into being? And how can it be reconciled with the recent tendency of many historians to diminish the importance of class during the nineteenth century? It is with these questions in mind that these books – each of them preoccupied with the existence, or non-existence, of class consciousness and class conflict in recent British history – need to be studied and assessed.

In describing the explosive development of Bradford from overgrown village to factory town to industrial city, Theodore Koditschek shows himself well aware of these recent scholarly trends.[1] But in placing class formation and class conflict at the centre of his account, he robustly restates the traditional Marxist view. During the period of which he writes, Bradford became one of the great textile towns of the West Riding of Yorkshire, as production was revolutionised by the application of steam power. Between 1810 and 1850, its population grew sixfold, and its output of worsted woollens increased thirteenfold. For much of this period, it was the fastest growing town in the world, and was appropriately known as 'worstedopolis'. As workers poured in from the countryside, and as new, large, steam-powered factories proliferated, the environment deteriorated alarmingly. There was dreadful overcrowding and pollution, working conditions were often barbaric, local philanthropic efforts were inadequate and ineffectual, there were no Members of Parliament before 1832, and until incorporation in 1847, the provision of services was pitifully inadequate. As one contemporary remarked, Bradford was 'the dirtiest, worst-regulated town in England'.

In such a setting, Koditschek contends, class formation and class antagonism were the dominant social and political developments. From the 1820s, the worsted industry was taken over by a new generation of young immigrant entrepreneurs, most of whom were liberal in their politics, and dissenting in their religion, who sought to make the world in their own image of 'competitive individualism' and self-help. But for the working classes, the impact of such unbridled and unregulated capitalism was terrible. Their customary plebeian culture was destroyed, along with their traditional skills and occupations, which meant they were demoralised, dispossessed and proletarianised. During the severe, uncontrollable economic downturns of the 1830s and 1840s, there was heavy unemployment, unprecedented poverty, and widespread discontent, all of which underlay the Chartist agitation of those years. Here, Koditschek insists, was direct confrontation between the workers and their employers, and violent class war was averted by a hair's breadth. Yet within a decade, this early Victorian crisis was almost completely resolved. The economy improved, and so, in the aftermath of incorporation, did the urban environment. Entrepreneurs became more responsible, and worker militancy declined. The era of 'mid-Victorian stabilization' had been successfully ushered in.

The general contours of this case-study closely resemble the broader account of British history which prevailed in the days when the class interpretation of social change was pre-eminent. But that scarcely does justice to the scope and significance of this book. The research is prodigious, as is the scale of the exposition. The author deals as thoroughly with the bourgeoisie as with the working classes, he is equally at home in economic, urban, social and political history, and he makes important contributions to current debates about the standard of living, the working-class family, and social control. The result is not only the most complete and comprehensive history yet written of an English town during the second half of the eighteenth century and the first half of the nineteenth. It is also salutary, at a time when it is fashionable to minimise the nature and impact of the Industrial Revolution, to be reminded just how disruptive and traumatic an experience it was in certain places. For those who want to know what it was like to be in a frontier town in early nineteenth-century England, here is the answer.

But there are difficulties. Koditschek's prose is often long-winded and contorted: such phrases as 'the arena of exchange where the larger hegemony of capitalism as a system of social relations seemed almost tautologically assured' do not make for ease of reading or comprehension. The book is also frequently overwritten, as words like 'insurgency', 'tyranny', 'extirpation', 'enslavement' and 'catastrophism' seem too extravagant and blood-curdling for the events they actually describe. Nor, despite his heroic efforts, does Koditschek succeeed in demonstrating that class consciousness and class conflict were as pervasive and fundamental as he claims. The middle classes were bitterly divided among themselves on the basis of status, occupation, party politics and religious affiliation, while many members of the working class seem to have been decidedly luke-warm about Chartism. As the author rather wearily admits, 'the historian should not expect to encounter [class] empirically in its pure theoretical form' – even, it seems, in industrialising Bradford. But if the existence of class cannot satisfactorily be demonstrated in a town which furnished one of the most extreme instances of industrial change and social disruption, it certainly raises doubts about the general applicability of that concept to early nineteenth-century Britain as a whole.

As if in corroboration of this point, R.J. Morris's study of Leeds is less dogmatically committed to the traditional canons of Marxist class analysis.[2] In its essential outlines, the story he has to tell is very similar to Koditschek's – not surprisingly, since Leeds and Bradford were scarcely ten miles apart, and both owed their prosperity to the growth of the textile industry. Leeds was always the bigger town, and its economy was more diversified, with large engineering and service sectors, but as in Bradford, it was the uneven yet persistent move from hand to steam power in the woollen industry which provided the essential dynamic to social change and political events. As in Bradford, the old Tory Anglican elite was displaced from its position of economic dominance and civic leadership by a new generation of liberal, nonconformist entrepreneurs from the 1820s onwards. As in Bradford, the combined effects of population growth, technological change and environmental decay were profoundly unsettling for labouring men and women. As in Bradford, there was no parliamentary representation before 1832, and local government was wholly inadequate. And as in Bradford, the fluctuations in the trade cycle during the 1830s and 1840s gave rise to unprecedented popular unrest.

Within this familiar framework, Morris's prime concern is to explore the public and institutional life of the Leeds middle class. They were not the rapacious Bradfordian bourgeoisie depicted by Koditschek, single-mindedly determined to dominate their town in the interests of the entrepreneurial ethic. On the contrary, the Leeds middle class was deeply divided by status and occupation: the merchants and professionals were the class leaders, with most of the businessmen, and the petty bourgeoisie, a long way behind. Religion and party politics were no less divisive, and this meant it was extremely difficult for the Leeds middle class to act in a united way. Only through their voluntary societies were they able to overcome the obstacles to active and coherent class formation, by suspending sectarian and political differences in pursuit of shared aims – cultural self-improvement (e.g. the Leeds Literary and Philosophical Society) and charitable endeavour (e.g. the Society for the Relief of the Poor). Through such efforts, the Leeds middle classes forged a sense of their own identity, and sought to establish a settled relationship with their social inferiors. As such, these voluntary societies were the precarious end-point in a distinctly uncertain process of class formation. For Koditschek, class is the fundamental associational form, and everything else is an aberration. But for Morris, class is what happens only in those rare instances when other, powerfully divisive forces are overcome.

Compared with Koditschek's wide-ranging panorama, Morris's account seems regrettably parochial and claustrophobic. The prose is leaden and pedestrian, the place and the people stubbornly refuse to come alive, and the author seems overwhelmed by the mass of quantitative data which is presented in an excessive abundance of tables and graphs. Although he concentrates on the middle class, he tells us little about their private lives (women hardly rate a mention), or about their broader national and international connections. He claims that party politics were very important, but he scarcely alludes to the campaigns for parliamentary reform or for the repeal of the Corn Laws, and his discussion of general elections is confined to the years 1832 and 1834. The working classes are largely presented as the passive beneficiaries of middle-class philanthropy, and they are never brought to the centre of his account, which means that Chartism – the most explosive and dramatic social convulsion of the nineteenth century – is virtually ignored. Time and again, we are told that voluntary societies were 'the basis of class formation in public life', a 'class project of major importance in the making of the British middle class'. But these substantial claims are asserted rather than proved.

The fundamental problem is that the doctoral dissertation out of which this book has evolved was completed in 1970. Inevitably, this has obliged the author to keep adapting and updating his work, and the result is an unsure and unhappy amalgam of traditional class analysis and more recent approaches. When Morris began his research, Leeds must have offered a splendid opportunity for a detailed study of 'the making of the British middle class'. Since then, he has added on religion and party politics, retreated from approaches and explanations based on class analysis, and tried to assimilate new work stressing the weaknesses and divisions of the bourgeoisie. But this makes it extremely difficult for the author to reach any resounding or distinctive conclusions. As if proclaiming a novel discovery, he tells us that 'British towns of the nineteenth century were the locations and structures within which the middle classes sought, extended, experienced and defended their power.' But who has ever seriously or convincingly maintained that this was not the case? And in search of broader conclusions, he urges the need to see the middle class as 'part of capitalist society, and as part of a complex web of subordination and power relationships'. But this is simply platitudinous: the more fundamental issue, of the relationship between the middle classes in one city, and the broader structures of economic, political and social power in the nation as a whole, is left unaddressed.

Despite their undoubted merits, neither of these books is thus as central as they might have been to the rethinking of modern British social history that has been taking place since the 1970s: Koditschek because of his dogmatic determination to return to the traditional (and outmoded) classbased model of social change and social conflict; Morris because his valiant effort to take on board more recent work merely results in confused analysis and uncertain conclusions. By comparison, Patrick Joyce's concern is to give an extra twist to the 'linguistic turn': by drawing on post-structuralist analysis he seeks to put class firmly in its place – and to move on beyond it.[3] As he sees it, class was only one, and not the most important, of the ways in which the labouring people of industrial England viewed the social order, and their own position within it. After a detailed examination of popular fiction, music hall songs, dialect literature, plebeian histories, working men's almanacs, and seaside postcards, he concludes that class consciousness was much less important than the more inclusive and more traditional notion of 'the people', who thought of themselves and their society in very different terms from those prescribed by Marx. 'Class', Joyce observes, 'did not lurk behind the image of the people. What was there was nothing other than the body of the people itself.'

'Populism' is the name which he gives to this assortment of ideas which, he insists, were the common property and shared assumptions of most nineteenth-century working-class men. They believed in honesty and hard work, in respectability and independence, in fair play and the dignity of labour, in social concord and good fellowship, and in the mutual interests and reciprocal obligations of employers and employed. They took great pride in their craft, in their firm, in their city, in their region and in their nation. They enjoyed entertainments which brought men and women together from varied social backgrounds, and they regarded class antagonisms as alien, divisive and unnatural. Like their eighteenth-century forbears, they disliked the idle and privileged rich, be they aristocrats, businessmen, Members of Parliament, or cabinet ministers. In short, theirs was a robust, patriotic, sentimental, warm-hearted popular culture: nineteenth-century working men did not think of themselves in class terms, and they did not regard Victorian society as a class society. Not surprisingly, these were the attitudes which underlay the popular Liberalism and popular Toryism of the second half of the nineteenth century, and which eventually found their fullest expression in the Labour Party. Only at the time of the First World War were these broader notions of 'the people' superseded by the more narrow and exclusive identities of class, as labour and capital were pitted against each other in an unprecedentedly antagonistic way.

Thus summarised, Joyce's book provides the most sustained assault yet on the idea of class, and the most constructive alternative to it that has so far been offered as a way of seeing and understanding nineteenth-century British society. Or, rather, it *would* do so, if its meaning and its arguments were clearer than, in fact, they are. For this is an exceptionally difficult book to read: the chapters are badly constructed and inadequately signposted, and for a scholar who presumes to write about language, Joyce's prose is abominably opaque, and his tortured sentences frequently defy comprehension. The chronology is also uncertain: he moves too rapidly back and forth through the nineteenth century, and the development of class sometime around 1914 is neither described nor explained in satisfactory detail. The majority of his evidence is drawn from medium-sized factory towns in Lancashire, such as Oldham and Ashton, and it is impossible to know whether they are representative of the British working class as a whole. And for all his claims to be moving 'beyond class', Joyce seems very unsure how far he really wants to go. At the beginning of the book, he tells us he is 'on the verge of denying class'; yet by the end, he informs us that 'when all reservations have been made, it is still of value to retain the concept of class.' Even the most well-disposed reader will find it difficult to make sense of such contradictory signals.

Underlying these complaints are two more fundamental reservations. The first concerns the concept of 'populism'. For most of the book, Joyce seems to be arguing that this is a more appropriate term than class for understanding the mind-set of labouring men, but he never makes clear precisely what he means by it. As used here, 'populism' is a term so elastic and all-inclusive that virtually any expression of working-class opinion

can be incorporated within it, with the result that it lacks historical speci-
ficity, and thus seems devoid of any real analytical purchase or power. The
second reservation concerns Joyce's concentration on language, and on the
recovery of the subjective way in which men – there are very few women
in this book – understood the social order and their place within it. Even
supposing he is correct in his reconstruction of individual perceptions of
society, this does not mean that we know how the social order actually
was, or how it really worked. We are told nothing here about the material circumstances of labouring men, or of their daily relations with their
betters or their inferiors. By privileging language in this way, we are only
given a very small part of the overall picture.

Much more wide-ranging are the essays collected together by Ross
McKibbin, which cover the period from 1880 to 1950, when 75 per cent
of the population of Britain were manual wage earners or people who
depended on them.[4] One of his concerns is to establish the 'social character' of this working class, which he believes was very different from that
ascribed to it by (mainly middle-class) contemporary observers. Of course,
members of the working class gambled: on dogs, horses and football. But
in most cases, this was rational, carefully thought out, and did not drive
the family into penury, despite the conventional wisdom that it did. In the
same way, it was widely believed in the late nineteenth century that the
workers performed sluggishly in the factory because they were more interested in their hobbies at home. But as McKibbin shows, work and leisure
activities were not competing but complementary: those who spent hours
breeding their canaries or tending their allotments were usually the most
alert and energetic at their job. And even when they were unemployed
during the depressed interwar years, as so many of them were, the working classes suffered much less from demoralisation than social commentators were inclined to think. In short, middle-class people knew very little
about working-class life: indeed, the author is cogently sceptical as to how
much any one class can ever really know about another.

McKibbin's second concern is to explore the links between working-
class life and the working-class politics of the fledgling Labour Party. In
fact, these links were often very weak. Before 1914, most working men
were not much interested in politics, and the restricted franchise meant
that only 60 per cent of adult males had the vote. So it was hardly surprising that the Labour Party did not fare well at the polls before the First
World War, and only improved its position after the massive extension of
the franchise in 1918. But even then, McKibbin insists, there remained a

large, anti-working-class majority in the country, which helps explain why the Conservatives were the dominant party during the interwar years. And when Labour *did* obtain a brief spell in government, from 1929 to 1931, it was obliged to cope with a catastrophic slump, for which no obvious remedies were then available, since Keynes's theories of deficit financing had not yet been worked out. Before the Second World War, the Labour Party – and the working class – were thus very much on the margins of British political life, and they only triumphed at Westminster in the very peculiar circumstances afforded by the 1945 general election.

There is a great deal in these essays to savour and delight in. It is important to be reminded how much working-class life changed and improved in Britain during the last quarter of the nineteenth century: the leek-growing, pigeon-racing, football-playing figures depicted here seem a world away from Koditschek's crushed and exploited proletarians of half a century before. In stressing the powerful obstacles to the formation of a radicalised, self-conscious working-class party, McKibbin implicitly endorses Morris's picture of the Leeds bourgeoisie earlier in the century, which was so divided against itself that it could only rarely realise its full class potential. And when he quotes the Labour leader Arthur Henderson as saying that his party was 'in politics, not in the interests of a class, but to further the interests of the community as a whole', we can perhaps detect the authentic voice of working-class 'populism' as described by Patrick Joyce. Even more significant is McKibbin's suggestion that Britain was a nation characterised by a high degree of social cohesion but by a much lower level of social integration. Associational life was rich, but in ways that inhibited, rather than promoted, class conflict. 'Groups and classes', he concludes, 'lived and let live.'

McKibbin writes with uncommon grace and flair, and ventures with remarkable breadth and erudition across an unusually broad terrain. Inevitably, given their brief and self-contained compass, these essays raise more questions than they answer. As with the other authors, the working class of which he writes is almost entirely masculine: the male world of work and hobbies is well treated, but the domestic sphere of the household goes all but unmentioned. The middle classes make only brief appearances, the petty bourgeoisie are conspicuous by their absence, and there is little sign in the book of the 'ideology' referred to in the title. Some aspects of working-class culture are vividly described, as are middle-class prejudice and incomprehension: but in neither case does this amount to an *ideology*. And while it is salutary to be told that social relations cannot be fully understood without taking account of the nature and role of the state, this insight is not followed up in the detail it merits. Nor is the attempt to link social history and political history entirely convincing. The claim that the restricted franchise held back the Labour Party before 1914 has been much criticised. And the account of interwar politics, with an electoral majority powerfully and permanently mobilised against the trade unions and the Labour Party, reads more like a description of the Britain of the 1980s than of the 1920s and 1930s.

It was Karl Marx's belief that 'the history of all hitherto existing society is the history of class struggles', and after the Second World War, a generation of pioneering social historians sought to establish the essential truth of this dictum with reference to nineteenth-century Britain. *Pace* Mrs Thatcher, the fact that Communism has been discredited does not by itself invalidate Marxism as a framework for historical analysis. More devastating has been the growing body of evidence – to which these books, either deliberately or inadvertently, lend their support – that the close and inexorable links which Marx posited between material circumstances, class development and political activity rarely, if ever, existed. The most that can be said is that at certain times, in certain places, a certain number of people did feel a sense of collective identity. But the two opposing armies of fully conscious class warriors were much less in evidence than Marx's theories implied. Instead of using Marx as a way of understanding the nineteenth century, it seems as though historians might be better employed using the nineteenth century as a way of understanding Marx.

But if class can no longer be convincingly universalised as the major explanatory force of historical change in the modern world, where does this leave the social history of the nineteenth century? If the writings of Marx no longer provide a reliable map to the historical landscape, then what are we to put in their place? One answer, favoured by all the authors here except Koditschek, is to stress the associational variety of people's lives – as men or women, husbands or wives, parents or children; as members of trade unions or churches or football teams or political parties; as individuals with loyalties to their firm, their city, their county, their region or their nation – which in turn gave rise to many fluctuating and sometimes contradictory senses of identity and patterns of behaviour. Viewed from this perspective, nineteenth-century social history should be primarily concerned with the recovery of the nuances and subtleties and ambiguities of this associational life – an associational life much more rich and varied than that which took place in the very different societies which Britain was in the eighteenth and the twentieth centuries. Taking the very long view, it may well be that class identities and class divisions were less clear-cut, and less important, during the nineteenth century than in the hundred years before and after.

Yet despite the best efforts of many of today's historians to take class out of the nineteenth century, the fact remains that the Victorians *were* obsessed with it – or at least, with something very like it. Read any contemporary novel, newspaper, or parliamentary debate, and the preoccupation is immediately apparent – not with class in the Marxist sense of collective and conflicting relations to the means of production, but with those finely graded distinctions of prestige ranking to which sociologists give the name status. It is easy to forget (and not one of the books discussed here mentions it) that the changes in social identities wrought by the Industrial Revolution in Britain were imposed on to an elaborate and pre-existing hierarchy of ranks and orders. The result was a society of exceptional complexity, and much of that complexity survives to this day, as it is bound to do in a nation where the head of state is an hereditary monarch, and the formal order of precedence remains little altered since Tudor times. Here, surely, is the origin of the British obsession, not so much with collective class, but with such individual matters as titles, honours, accent, deportment and dress, which does so much to determine how one person is regarded and categorised by another, and which is what Mr Major no doubt has in mind when he talks of making Britain a 'classless' (i.e. status-less) society.

Two quotations may help to make this point more forcefully. For Henry James, it was 'the essentially hierarchical plan of English society' which was 'the great and ever-present fact to the mind of a stranger; there is hardly a detail of life that does not in some degree betray it.' For George Orwell, the matter could be summed up with more brutal brevity: England was, he believed, 'the most class-ridden country under the sun'. Of course, those preoccupied with the 'linguistic turn' will no doubt insist that these remarks only tell us about the rhetorically constructed social vision of James and Orwell. In fact, they also tell us a great deal about the status-conscious nature of British society. What is most urgently needed if we are to understand that nature and that society is neither a history of class nor a history of language, but a history of status – not just for individual towns or regions for fifty years or so, but a comprehensive study of social structure and social attitudes over the last three centuries for Britain as a whole. Thus described, it would be a daunting task. Who, if anyone, is willing to try?

(1992)

NOTES

1 Theodore Koditschek, *Class Formation and Urban Industrial Society: Bradford, 1750–1850* (Cambridge, 1992).
2 R.J. Morris, *Class, Sect and Party: The Making of the British Middle Class, Leeds, 1820–50* (Manchester, 1992).
3 Patrick Joyce, *Visions of the People: Industrial England and the Question of Class, 1840–1914* (Cambridge, 1992).
4 Ross McKibbin, *The Ideologies of Class: Social Relations in Britain, 1880–1950* (Oxford, 1990).

20

Morals

In those far-off days when her power was at its zenith, Margaret Thatcher delighted in celebrating what she called 'Victorian values': the qualities of thrift, independence, sobriety, entrepreneurship and self-reliance which she claimed she had learned at her father's knee at his corner-shop in Grantham; which she believed had made Britain pre-eminent during the long nineteenth century; and which she was certain would make the country great again under her own forceful and formidable leadership. As Lytton Strachey had observed before Thatcher had even been born, and as historians were quick to point out again in the aftermath of her pronouncement, this was a very selective catalogue of Victorian conventional wisdoms, it failed to recognise the complexities and contradictions of nineteenth-century society, and it took no account of the accidental advantages which Britain then enjoyed relative to other nations. And although it was intended to bring about a national rebirth and renewal, this harking back to a semi-mythological era of past greatness and imperial glory was merely one more symptom of that very national decline which Thatcher sought to halt and reverse. In fact, there is very little evidence that she was able to do anything serious or long-lasting to stop the rot, nor did she succeed in persuading the British public to embrace once more the stern, unbending doctrines of Samuel Smiles and Mr Gladstone.

With the fall of Thatcher and the advent of John Major to power in November 1990, these 'Victorian values' went back into hibernation in Britain. They are still sometimes debated by historians, but they are no longer espoused or proclaimed by most front-ranking Conservative politicians. Neither the past nor the future figure as prominently or as precisely in the present Prime Minister's vision of things, as shown by his ill-judged and aborted 'Back to Basics' campaign. For it was never clear just how far back in time the public was being urged to look or to go, and no one had much idea exactly what these basic beliefs were supposed to be or to have been. To be sure, Major's idealised picture of England – of a nation at ease with itself, with warm beer in the pubs, cricket on the village green and ladies bicycling to Holy Communion – might plausibly be derived from the late Victorian era, when penny-farthings and velocipedes first came upon the scene. But it is more likely that his notion of Englishness is an amalgam of Stanley Baldwin's emollient rhetoric of rural decency, George Orwell's wartime celebration of national consensus, and Agatha Christie's depiction of cosy English villages in the early 1950s in her Miss Marple novels. While Thatcher's historical vision was certain and heroic, Major's, as befits his less messianic personality, is merely vague and humdrum.

But while 'Victorian values' have vanished from the political agenda in Britain, except among those far-right Thatcher ideologues who follow Michael Portillo or John Redwood, they have unexpectedly (and implausibly) reappeared on the other side of the Atlantic, where they have been eagerly (and ignorantly) embraced by fundamentalist Republicans, who are determined to roll back the state and to revive and reinvigorate America in the same way that Thatcher sought to revive and reinvigorate Britain. Here is Newt Gingrich, giving the National League of Cities a lesson in nineteenth-century history:

> Queen Victoria's emphasis on morals changed the whole momentum of British society. They didn't do it through a new bureaucracy. They did it by re-establishing values, by moral leadership, and by being willing to look people in the face and say, 'You should be ashamed when you get drunk in public; you ought to be ashamed if you're a drug addict.'

And in his recent book, *To Renew America*, he has further embellished this case, arguing that what the country needs is less government, welfare, regulation and red tape, and more independence, honesty, self-reliance and hard work: in short, a return to the sturdy, wholesome, vigorous virtues of 'classic America', which bear a remarkable – and acknowledged – similarity to those 'Victorian values' which Thatcher had earlier discerned in nineteenth-century Britain.

This recent, far-right, American version of modern British history is suspect in at least two ways. In the first place, it gets many of the facts wrong. There *was* a new bureaucracy established in the 1830s and 1840s, which successfully, expensively and irrevocably extended the reach of the Victorian state: factory inspectors, health inspectors, school inspectors, the police force, local government officials. And such quintessential Victorian statesmen as Lord Palmerston (who fathered several illegitimate children and was cited as co-respondent in a divorce case at the age of eighty) and Benjamin Disraeli (who wrote novels, took drugs and prided himself on being unrespectable) could hardly be said to have provided the nation with serious 'moral leadership'. In the second place, the very idea of 'Victorianism' resonates far less powerfully in twentieth-century America than in twentieth-century Britain. The years from 1837 to 1901, when Queen Victoria was on the throne, have no coherent or monolithic or mythological meaning in the history of the United States. And while for Britain, the nineteenth century was an era of unchallenged supremacy from which it has since rapidly declined, America's rise to global greatness had scarcely then begun.

Although she knew little in detail about it, Thatcher was right in believing that the Victorian era could be presented to a glory-starved British audience as a golden age of domestic peace and international pre-eminence: which is why, for all its superficialities, 'Victorian values' became such a popular phrase. But in historical terms, Gingrich has faced a much harder task making the same slogan take wing in the anxious America of the late 1990s. Or, rather, he has only been able to get it airborne by using it as a proxy for something else which is both historically and geographically much closer to home. For Thatcher and her acolytes, 'Victorian values' really did mean Britain's nineteenth century. For Gingrich and his colleagues, by contrast, it actually means *their* 1950s: that golden era in the history of he United States when (as they see it) Uncle Sam was the unrivalled policeman of the world, when un-American enemies were easy to identify both abroad and at home, when Eisenhower was in the White House and Nixon was Vice-President, when neither civil rights nor affirmative action had yet even been thought of, when women were virgins on their wedding night and stay-at-home mothers thereafter, and when sons ate cherry pie and daughters wore gingham dresses and bobby socks. For all their talk of 'Victorian values', it is the United States of the 'Pax Americana', rather than the United Kingdom of the 'Pax Britannica', which the Republican right ardently wants to see restored.

This has not deterred Gertrude Himmelfarb from producing an impassioned polemic, in which she seems to think she is providing historical validation for the view that nineteenth-century Britain offers the best model for that renewal of late twentieth-century America which she hopes Gingrich and the Republicans are willing and able to undertake.[1] For Victorian England was, she insists, a society in which those virtues subsequently celebrated by Margaret Thatcher (with which and with whom Himmelfarb begins her account) were widely recognised and generally accepted. Thanks to the Bible, nineteenth-century Britons knew what was right and what was wrong: these beliefs were not imposed on one class by another, but pervaded society at all levels. Whatever the shortcomings of their individual behaviour, Victorians did indeed believe in respectability, self-reliance and self-help: in thrift, hard work, cleanliness, discipline, philanthropy and orderliness. And if they failed to live up to this exacting moral code, they were likely to suffer private anguish or public censure – as, in their different ways, did George Eliot, Mr Gladstone, Charles Dickens and Oscar Wilde. 'They tormented themselves', Himmelfarb concludes, 'more than they enjoyed themselves', and she seems to think this was a good thing.

As a direct result of this increasingly powerful and essentially self-regulating morality, Victorian England became the most civilised, successful and stable society of the age: crime fell, violence diminished, drunkenness was reduced, illegitimacy rates went down. All males, of whatever social background, could aspire to become gentlemen – provided they were honest, generous, polite, courageous, gracious and considerate. The family and the home were repositories of both private and public virtues, and women naturally accepted the powers and the responsibilities of their domestic position. Marriage was for life, adultery was frowned upon, and sexual relations between spouses were generally satisfactory. As wives and mothers, most women found their roles satisfying and fulfilling, which is why many of them were not interested in gaining the vote. The New Poor Law of 1834 ensured that the sick and the aged were still appropriately supported, while able-bodied paupers were put in the workhouse but encouraged to look for employment. Thereafter, poverty undoubtedly diminished, partly because individual charitable giving became so high. The Victorians, Himmelfarb argues, were concerned and dutiful philanthropists: witness Toynbee Hall, the Charity Organisation Society, and Charles Booth's survey of life and labour in London in the 1880s. And in the late nineteenth century, the 'new' men and women who rebelled against this moral code – such as H.G. Wells or Eleanor Marx – were very much the exceptions who proved the rule.

Since then, the author insists, things have gone inexorably downhill, as this decent and virtuous civilisation has been subverted and replaced by our increasingly demoralised society. Compared with how the Victorians did things, there is much cause for concern about our contemporary condition: as a result of the permissive legislation of the 1960s, which was the liberal decade when things began to go seriously wrong, crime rates, divorce rates and illegitimacy rates have risen exponentially, both in the United Kingdom and the United States. To these alarming trends must be added the accumulating evidence of welfare dependency, drug abuse, alcoholism, violence, illiteracy and homelessness. To make matters worse, Himmelfarb contends that for a long time, 'social critics and policy makers have found it hard to face up to the realities of our moral condition, in spite of the statistical evidence'. In the 'non-judgemental', politically correct world we now inhabit, where there is no longer any such thing as right or wrong, and where accusations of racisim, sexism and elitism are so easily made and difficult to refute, such antisocial behaviour is more likely to be empathised with rather than condemned. Current notions of self-fulfilment, self-expression and self-realisation, she insists, rest on weak, false and superficial foundations. The result is our narcissistic, solipsistic, relativistic world, which is morally and civically bankrupt, and which is crying out for reform, renewal and regeneration.

By so deftly linking together nineteenth-century Britain and twentieth-century America, in such a broad-ranging, arresting and essentially apocalyptic account, Himmelfarb has produced an historical polemic which has been avidly (and predictably) acclaimed by the right on both sides of the Atlantic. It has been puffed and praised in the Murdoch-owned British press; it has received ecstatic reviews in such conservative American journals as *Commentary*; and in *To Renew America*, Newt Gingrich gave it the ultimate accolade by hailing it as a 'great book'. For many of those, in Britain and America, who think that their nations have gone to the dogs, and that things were much better in the past, this book seems to offer substantial scholarly support. But not everyone has been so impressed. On the one hand, such historians as Stefan Collini, Deborah Epstein Nord and Fritz Stern have complained that Himmelfarb has seriously misrepresented Victorian Britain, and has failed to do justice to the darker side of nineteenth-century life: the poverty, the inequality, the harshnesss, the greed, the hypocrisy, the snobbery, the misery, the intolerance. On the other hand, Anthony Gottlieb and John Gray have argued that she is no less mistaken when writing about our own times. The statistics which Himmelfarb claims prove complete moral degeneration need very careful interpreting. There is ample evidence of strong, rather than 'non-judgemental', feelings about many contemporary moral issues. And most people today, just like their Victorian forbears, still believe in marriage and family life, condemn drugs, crime and violence, and prefer to work than to be unemployed.

Indeed, a close reading of the book suggests that Himmelfarb has made her case far less persuasively than either she, or her conservative admirers, think she has. For there is much in it which supports the alternative, less roseate interpretation of nineteenth-century Britain. 'I am', she coyly admits, 'painfully aware of the difficulties and iniquities of Victorian life.' There was, she concedes, 'a fair amount' of hypocrisy 'in Victorian times'. There is, she recognises, 'a good deal of truth' in the widespread idea that Victorian women were 'lowly creatures, capable of little more than menial tasks in the kitchen and dutiful submission in bed'. The New Poor Law was devised by people who were 'excessively rationalistic, utilitarian, single-minded', and judged by today's standards, it was indeed 'grudging and harsh'. The Charity Organisation Society, for all its good intentions, was often characterised by 'callousness, officiousness and intrusiveness'. Among philanthropists, there were 'self-serving, self-aggrandizing, self-satisfied individuals'. In short, there were enough unpleasant things going on in nineteenth-century Britain 'to give pause to the most ardent Victoriaphile': 'social and sexual discriminations, class rigidities and political inequalities, autocratic men, submissive women and overly disciplined children, constraints, restrictions and abuses of all kinds'. Thus described, Himmelfarb's version of Victorian Britain hardly corresponds to the moral utopia of Thatcher or Gingrich.

But it is not just that nineteenth-century England was in truth a contradictory civilisation, witnessing both the 'good old' and the 'bad old' days (her words again). It is also that the Victorian state played a far greater role than today's anti-government free-marketeers would find palatable. As Himmelfarb reluctantly admits, Parliament had never been busier, passing legislation concerning conditions of work, health, education, housing, sanitation, transport and holidays, while local authorities assumed responsibility for water supply, sewage, public baths, street lighting, libraries, museums and parks. And this legislation also provided the essential moral framework within which ordinary Victorians lived out their lives. 'Victorian values', such as they were, were not invented in a vacuum: they were the product of a specific political culture which was increasingly interventionist. Consider these words of Joseph Chamberlain, self-made Midlands industrialist, radical Mayor of Birmingham, and Colonial Secretary under the Conservative Prime Minister, Lord Salisbury:

> Private charity is powerless, religious organisations can do nothing, to remedy the evils which are so deep-seated in our system . . . I venture to say that it is only the community acting as a whole that can possibly deal with evils so deep-seated as those to which I have referred.

To be sure, this was not the only opinion on offer at the time. But in any account of Victorian England, the attempts to curb the excesses of unbridled capitalism by state intervention deserve greater prominence and more explicit discussion than Himmelfarb gives them here.

It is not easy to get Victorian Britain in a broad and steady perspective, and it is even more difficult to make direct connections with the nineteenth-century United States, something which this book's polemical purposes crucially require. ' "Victorian America" ' (at least she is embarrassed enough by the phrase to put it in quotations), Himmelfarb rather breezily informs us, 'was not at all different, at least in terms of values, from Victorian England.' But this is an exceptionally tendentious remark. To be sure, the two countries had a common language and, up to 1776, a common history. But thereafter, they rapidly diverged. Britain was an insular and imperial power, with a strong state, an established church, and a monarchy and aristocracy. The United States was a continental land mass, with a federal constitution, which went through a civil war. The values of self-help, sturdy independence and moral decency which evolved in both countries were in practice very different, being far more deferentially articulated in England than in America. As Frederick Jackson Turner was surely correct in pointing out towards the end of the nineteenth century, the United States was becoming more and more exceptional, and one of the ways in which this was so was that its prevailing values were forged by and on the frontier – a frontier which no European nation possessed. Turner did not get it completely right. But in seeking to understand and explain the differences between American values and those of the old world, he was on to something important, and he was surely correct in thinking they mattered more than the similarities.

When it comes to moving the story (and the argument) forward to the twentieth century, Himmelfarb's difficulties further increase. The years from 1900 to 1945 are virtually ignored, and it is not clear how developments during this era fit into her interpretation. It is far from helpful for the case she wants to make that Roosevelt's New Deal and Attlee's welfare state, the two most outstanding examples of interventionist government which are now so derided by the new right, were created by men born and brought up in the nineteenth century. The fact that conservatives have occupied both the White House and 10 Downing Street for the majority of the time since 1945, the very period which is deemed to have witnessed the greatest moral decay, is also highly inconvenient. And in any case, since the Second World War, Britain and the United States have become – and are still becoming – even less alike. In their constitutional structure, political culture, geographical dimensions, economic resources, ethnic diversity and world standing, they now have very little in common. Significantly, it is only on the far right that the 'Special Relationship' still survives. Put another way, this means that compared with John Major's Britain, Bill Clinton's America is a much more violent nation, and also a much more religious one. *Pace* Himmelfarb, these two societies are not in the same state of moral degeneracy today, any more than they have fallen from the same state of moral grace one hundred years ago.

As she reaches the end of her polemic, the author finds it difficult to conceal from herself that her arguments have led nowhere. Having admitted that Victorian Britain was both a good and a bad place, and having leaped wildly and implausibly from there to the present-day Anglo-American scene, it is hardly surprising that superficial diagnosis is followed by no less superficial prescription. 'The past', she concludes, and in so doing she differs from both Thatcher and Gingrich, 'cannot – and should not – be replicated': we cannot 'revive Victorianism'. Amen to that. 'The ethos of a society', she goes on, 'cannot be reduced to economic, material, political or other factors.' Quite so: but so what? What is needed, she insists, is 'a thorough-going re-moralization of society'. But since her account has failed to provide any convincing explanation of the complex process whereby the Victorians evolved, contested, developed and changed the values of *their* society, it is hardly surprising that Himmelfarb can offer no guide as to how we should set about changing the values of *ours*. It might be a good idea to 'restore not so much Victorian values as a more abiding sense of moral and civic virtues', but she has no serious suggestions as to how this should be accomplished. As such, her conclusion is all of a piece with the rest of her book: bad history, worse polemic.

The interest of this mistaken exercise in sound-bite scholarship thus derives neither from its intellectual cogency, nor from its prescriptive plausibility. But it *is* a useful place to find out about the mind-set of today's Anglo-American conservative chic. Like them, the book is stridently apocalyptic in tone, celebrating the past, worrying over the present, fearful of the future. Like them, it is deeply hostile to the interventionist welfare state and to 'the evil it has done'. Like them, it is contemptuous of 'liberals', and of the terrible changes they made during the 1960s. Its history may be marginally better than Gingrich's (and Thatcher's), but in its own way, it is as suspicious, discontented, alarmist, overheated, embattled, aggressive, messianic, and full of righteous indignation, as they are. In short, it exhibits many of the hallmarks of what Richard Hofstadter once memorably described as 'the paranoid style' – a style which has long been the special preserve of the American right, and which has recently, under Thatcher, been most effectively taken up by the British right as well. Nor is this Himmelfarb's first venture into the paranoid style. She has been developing it for some time. Her last book bears the apocalyptic title *On Looking into the Abyss: Untimely Thoughts on Culture and Society*.

Of course, it is easy to see why the paranoid style is so appealing to the Anglo-American new right at this time. Notwithstanding victory in the Cold War, Britain's international decline continues apace, and the United States is not the power to be reckoned with that it once was. Communism has been defeated, so there is no longer an external foe to fear or to blame, which means that the only other place to look is under the beds back home. Hence the ferocious onslaught unleashed by the new right in both countries against liberals, intellectuals, feminists, unmarried mothers, cultural elites, chronically dependent underclasses, and anyone else who dares to disagree with them or threaten them. And hence their constant demonisation of the state, as their enemies' all-powerful, overmighty, morally corrupting, fiscally irresponsible instrument of domestic subversion. Yet as befits the practitioners of the paranoid style, there is more fantasy than fact in this formulation. For it is arguable that the real problem in America today is not that the state is too powerful but that the state is *too weak*: too weak to implement necessary gun control laws; too weak to provide adequate healthcare; too weak to raise taxes to pay for essential public services; too weak to regulate Hollywood films, domestic television and the multinational media. Contrary to Thatcher, contrary to Gingrich, and contrary to Himmelfarb, the Victorian value that most urgently needs proclaiming today is not that of incorrigible hostility to intrusive government, but the belief in the moral potential and the regenerative power of the state. Is there anyone left, on either side of the Atlantic, who is prepared to stand up and say so?

(1995)

NOTE

1 Gertrude Himmelfarb, *The De-moralization of Society: From Victorian Virtues to Modern Values* (New York, 1995).

PART THREE
Persons and Personalities

21

Florence Nightingale

The obverse side of the ten pound note depicts one of the most virtuous countenances and heart-warming tableaux in modern British history. The face is that of Florence Nightingale, a lady of high social station, and the very incarnation of modest female virtue, exuding Christian philanthropy and pious humanitarianism from every pore. The scene is a ward in the military hospital at Scutari, near Constantinople, through which Florence glides in the evening, an angel of mercy with a lighted lamp in her hand, bringing hope and encouragement, comfort and reassurance to British soldiers wounded or fallen sick during the Crimean War. In a conflict which saw much death but little glory, Nightingale's legendary nursing achievements soon established her as a popular heroine, a secular (and spinsterly) saint. For the rest of her very long life, her reputation for greatness and goodness, for courage and compassion, was beyond reproach. Peers and cabinet ministers sought her advice, while ordinary soldiers worshipped the very ground she walked upon. To this day, she remains, in the company of those three indomitable sovereigns, Boudicca, Elizabeth I and Victoria, the most famous English woman ever to have lived. (Mrs Thatcher, who in significant ways closely resembles Nightingale, is not yet eligible for membership of this very exclusive ladies' club.)

But as well-informed contemporaries were vividly aware, there was always much more to Florence than the 'Lady with the Lamp' of popular legend and national iconography: she did not achieve all that she did by force of simple goodness alone. Sir Edward Cook's two-volume official life, published in 1913, soon after her death, was tactful and eulogistic in tone, but it was also much more probing and perceptive than the average Victorian hagiography. In chapters with such titles as 'The Ministering Angel', 'The Soldier's Friend', 'The Hospital Reformer' and 'The Popular Heroine', Cook paid ample and appreciative tribute to Nightingale's work, in the Crimea, in India, in the improvement of the sanitary conditions of the British army, and in the creation and establishment of the modern nursing profession. But he also described her lengthy and bitter struggles with her parents and her sister, drew attention to the ambitious and dominating side of her personality, discussed her deliberate and calculated decision not to marry, admitted her unfeeling and cavalier treatment of friends and protégés, and even delicately hinted at the unfulfilled sexual longings which she could only assuage by her public life of ceaseless and restless activity.

Fifteen years later, and heavily (and appreciatively) indebted to Cook's books, Lytton Strachey unfurled his witty, wicked and withering attack on Nightingale in the pages of *Eminent Victorians* (1918). Of course, there were some things about Florence that Lytton genuinely admired: her determination to cut herself free from family ties and make her own way in the world; her active and practical sympathy for the ordinary British soldier; her stamina and her strength, her reforming zeal and her crusading ardour. But in general, he found both the myth and the matron equally unpalatable. The fact that acquisitive, hard-nosed Victorians had chosen to idolise this legendary humanitarian was merely further proof of their own conscience-salving hypocrisy. For all her active goodness, Nightingale herself was far from being the angelic figure of popular adulation: according to Strachey, she was a self-righteous, domineering amazon, who was ruthless in her compassion, merciless in her philanthropy, destructive in her friendships, obsessional in her lust for power, and demonic in her saintliness. Above all, Lytton disliked her because in her frigid indifference to intimate relationships, in her determined suppression of her own erotic impulses, in her lifelong virginity and her unregretted childlessness, she denied her own womanhood, and thus rejected in herself the very humanity which she claimed to be serving in others.

For nearly a generation, Strachey's attack went unanswered, and when a reply was finally made, it was decidedly muted in tone. In 1950, Cecil Woodham-Smith published the first full-length biography since Cook which, she claimed, provided 'a complete picture of Miss Nightingale'. She enjoyed access to an abundance of documentary material which Cook had been denied. She was concerned neither with defence nor with prosecution, but with the re-creation of a personality. And she brought out, as never before, the full extent of Florence's inner conflict with herself and outer conflict with her family. But although the book was widely praised as an outstanding example of literary biography, it failed to answer the criticism that Strachey had made so compellingly, and it was severely attacked for its widespread errors of fact and interpretation. Many of the letters quoted were sloppily transcribed or incorrectly dated. Despite the new material, her biography was excessively – and ungratefully – dependent on Cook's earlier work. And in her analysis of Florence's antagonists – among her own family, in the Crimean War, and in Parliament and Whitehall – Woodham-Smith conspicuously failed to do adequate justice to the characters or the arguments of Nightingale's contemporary critics.

Thirty years later, Professor F.B. Smith launched another assault in *Florence Nightingale: Reputation and Power* (1982), a polemic so forceful and so ferocious that even Strachey's mocking essay seemed almost bland and benevolent by comparison. The essence of his argument was that Florence may have done good deeds (something which he was in fact only very grudgingly prepared to admit), but that did not necessarily mean she was herself a good woman. Instead, he depicted her as a cheat, a liar, a bully, a monster and a confidence trickster. Despite her claims to the contrary, she treated her family far more harshly, ungratefully and unsympathetically than ever they treated her. She was callous and condescending towards the sick, disloyal and dishonest in her friendships, meddlesome and manipulating in her dealings with officialdom, and voracious and vampirish in her drive for power and fame. She wrote letters that were full of lies, threats and half-truths. She deliberately and consistently falsified the historical record to her own glory and advantage. And yet, like Richard Nixon (the comparison is Smith's), she was so self-obsessed that she could not bring herself to destroy the mass of evidence which, sooner or later, was bound to incriminate her.

Clearly, the final verdict is not yet in on Florence Nightingale. Opinions about her remain as varied and diverse as her own many-sided personality, and the full harvest from her voluminous and revealing correspondence has yet to be garnered, let alone interpreted, by a professional historian or biographer. Meanwhile, this selected edition of her letters (fewer than two hundred out of a total of nearly fourteen thousand) is much to be welcomed as an interim exercise in re-evaluation, and a partial attempt at rehabilitation.[1] It lets Florence speak for herself, once again, with all the force and vigour of her superbly assured and magnificently confident prose. It shows how gifted she was as a maker of phrases, as a master of detail, as an advocate and critic. It demonstrates her incomparable abilities as a crusader and reformer: denouncing abuses, assailing officialdom, propounding remedies, enlisting support, defining objectives, carrying the day. It illustrates the perennial conflict that raged within her between the calls of private life and the claims of public duty. And it vividly reveals her ambiguous attitudes to her own sex, and to the liberation of women. At one and the same time, it makes her a more credible, but also a much more complex, historical personality than she has ever been before.

Nightingale was born in 1820, in extremely advantageous circumstances. Her parents were upwardly mobile members of the middle class, by then comfortably established among the landed gentry, and, through an extended circle of family and friends, she was unusually well connected, both with the traditional territorial aristocracy and the Liberal-intellectual bourgeoisie. Thanks to her father, she was also uncommonly well educated: in Greek and Latin, French, German and Italian, history, philosophy and mathematics. As a young lady, her outer life was identical to that of any woman of her class: family visits, social gatherings, foreign travel, and mild flirtations. But inwardly, she craved 'a necessary occupation, something to fill and employ all my faculties'. In 1844, she decided that in order to do God's will, she must devote her whole life to nursing the sick. Her parents and elder sister were appalled, and for nearly ten years, her relations with her family were strained and bitter. Eventually, in 1852, her father capitulated, granted Florence an allowance of £500 a year, and consented to her becoming the Superintendent of the Harley Street Hospital for Gentlewomen. During the next two years, she obtained her only first-hand nursing experience of any length, and also discovered a passion for management and reform, for intrigue and manipulation, that never left her.

It was the Crimean War which unexpectedly provided Nightingale with an arena appropriate to her accomplishments and ambitions. Thanks to her friendship with Sidney Herbert, then Secretary at War, she was allowed to lead a private expedition of nurses to treat and tend the suffering British troops. There was much for her to do. The military administration was chaotic; the hospitals were insanitary and inadequately supplied; and more soldiers were dying from disease than from fighting. For nearly two years, she worked night and day to improve the lot of 'my poor men'. The administration was reformed and the hospitals were cleaned, the food was improved and drunkenness among the patients reduced, the quality of the nursing was immeasurably enhanced, and the death rate fell dramatically. But inevitably, Nightingale made many enemies. She would not acknowledge those nurses who were not directly under her control, there were endless squabbles with military officialdom about jurisdiction and authority, she needlessly antagonised Dr Hall, the Inspector General of Hospitals in the Crimea, and she even subjected Sidney Herbert to frequent scoldings and denunciations by post. As Florence once candidly admitted, 'I am not a lamb – far from it.'

In 1856, she returned to England, exhausted from the accumulated strain and overwork. Her family threatened to engulf her once again, and only by becoming a full-time invalid could she keep them at bay, and devote herself to her duty. For she had been haunted by the spectre of those who had died from preventable diseases rather than war wounds, and now resolved to embark on a career as a sanitary reformer. Her national prestige was unrivalled, and she enjoyed the support of Queen Victoria, the Prince Consort, and the Prime Minister, Lord Palmerston. She bullied the government into setting up a Royal Commission into the Health of the Army, and although she did not sit on it, she was its most influential – if unofficial – member. It was chaired by her friend, Sidney Herbert; she herself provided the most important evidence; and together with Herbert, she wrote the final report. It recommended widespread changes in the administration of the Army Medical Department; it proposed drastic reforms in the construction and superintendence of barracks and military hospitals; and it urged the establishment of an Army Medical School. Nightingale at once set out to ensure these recommendations were accepted, and scarcely noticed that Sidney Herbert was collapsing under the strain. He died in 1861.

By then, she had moved on to bigger and greater things. For it was but a step from reforming the sanitary conditions of the British army at home to reforming the sanitary conditions of the British army in India. And that task could not be undertaken in isolation: the whole of the subcontinent would have to be investigated and improved. The result was a second royal commission, which she again dominated from behind the scenes. Once more, she produced a sweeping programme of recommendations: barracks and hospitals must be rebuilt and reformed; there must be proper supplies of water and adequate drainage; there must be irrigation schemes across the length and breadth of the country; and a comprehensive system of sanitary administration must be established. For the rest of her life, India remained an obsession. She was a tireless collector of information about the country, and she corresponded exhaustively with viceroys, provincial governors, military commanders and sanitary commissioners. But real progress was slow. India was half a world away, and for all her enthusiasm, there was much about it that Nightingale never fully understood. And even she could not overcome the combined inertia of the India Office, the War Office and the government of India itself.

By the 1870s, death had robbed her of her closest official contacts, and only then did she return to nursing. At the time of the Crimean War, a grateful nation had subscribed £45,000 to a Florence Nightingale Fund, and part of it had been used to establish a School of Nursing at St Thomas's Hospital in London. In her declining years, she lavished much interfering attention on it, imperiously telling newly qualified nurses where to take employment, shamelessly promoting her protégées, and then feeling personally affronted if they dared to get married. But she was becoming increasingly isolated and out of touch. She had never accepted the germ theory of disease, nor placed much confidence in vaccination. She was opposed to the professionalisation of nursing, to public examinations and to state registration. But as her memory and her eyesight began to fail, and as she outlived all her contemporaries, including Queen Victoria herself, she eventually became, as Benjamin Jowett described her, 'a legend in her own lifetime'. In 1907, she became the first woman to be admitted to the Order of Merit, and in the following year, she was only the second woman to be granted the Freedom of the City of London. In 1870, she had breezily remarked that 'I am so busy that I have not time to die.' It was to be another forty years before the opportunity finally presented itself.

Such was her life – conveyed here in her own writings, with a directness and an immediacy that outshine all subsequent biographical endeavours. But still the question remains: what are we to make of her? Even among her sternest critics, Florence's achievements have never been in serious doubt: it is over her motives and her methods that the most substantial reservations have been registered. It cannot be said that this book helps us very much in these more complex and controversial areas. The editors have laboured mightily to elucidate their text: they have linked the letters with explanatory passages, they have provided exegetical footnotes and a chronological table, and they have succinctly summarised the contents and viewpoints of all the major biographies. But none of this makes it any easier to evaluate or interpret her correspondence, let alone come to terms with the ambiguities and contradictions of Nightingale herself. As the editors freely admit, she wrote letters for many different purposes: to flatter, to bully, to persuade, to denounce. From reading her words essentially in isolation, it is often not clear what her motives really were, and as F.B. Smith so cogently argued, most of her uncorroborated accounts of events in which she was involved simply cannot be trusted. So how can we know, just by looking at her letters, what to believe and what to disallow?

The reader cannot possibly answer these substantial and significant questions from the evidence which is provided (or not provided) here. Nor, it seems, can the editors. In the end, they settle for the same bifurcated interpretation of Florence's conduct and temperament that has dominated Nightingale studies since Cook first put it forward with such careful discretion in his official biography. On the one hand, they admit, Florence was calculating, ungenerous, vindictive, the self-dramatising creator and jealous guardian of a misleading public image which was itself the key to much of her power. But on the other, they also insist that she was a reformer of genius, endowed with what she herself once described as 'a *must* in her life', from which humanity in general undeniably benefited. So here she is once again: still the unfathomable and familiar mixture of virgin and virago, saint and sinner, invalid and activist, crusader and conspirator, matron and monster, the heroine who was both much less, but also very much more, than the 'Lady with the Lamp'. And as long as studies of Florence persist in being so overwhelmed and so obsessed with her own towering personality, that is where interpretation and analysis are unpromisingly likely to remain.

The real challenge posed by Nightingale – as by most larger-than-life personalities from the past – is that she can only be properly understood by placing her much more fully and perceptively in a broader historical context. One obvious approach would be to see her as belonging to that select coterie of nineteenth-century British civil servants subsequently labelled 'zealots', or 'statesmen [sic] in disguise'. These were contemporaries like Sir Edwin Chadwick, the public health campaigner, Sir Rowland Hill, the inventor of the penny postage, and Sir James Kay Shuttleworth, the educational crusader. All of them (like Nightingale) were impassioned and ardent reformers, in a hurry to get things changed and get things done. All believed (like Nightingale) in the righteousness, the goodness and the greatness of their cause. All were prepared (like Nightingale) to use underhand means to achieve admirable ends – bullying and traducing opponents, lobbying for public and parliamentary support, packing royal commissions and committees of inquiry with their own friends and supporters, and slanting the evidence to justify their own policies and recommendations. In the company of these messianic manipulators, Nightingale seems far less exceptional, in both her virtues and her shortcomings, than she is habitually made to appear by her biographers.

Except, that is, in one particular way. For, to state the obvious, these mandarin zealots were all men, whereas she was a woman. If anything provides the key to understanding Florence, it is surely this: that she was a woman who set out to crusade and to conquer in a man's world. She knew that to get things done in Victorian England, she had to work with men and through men. She loved public business, public life, public fame, regularly referred to herself in the masculine, and proudly admitted to being a 'man of facts' and a 'man of actions'. She regarded most members of her own sex with scarcely concealed scorn: they put private duty before public affairs; they neither relished power nor understood how to use it; and there was too much 'cant about women's rights'. Yet Nightingale was not above exploiting her gender for her own advantage. Her national popularity at the time of the Crimea derived from the fact that she was a woman doing good in what had previously been the all-male world of war and battle: it is impossible to imagine a correspondingly powerful legend developing about a *man* with a lamp. She exploited her illnesses and her physical weaknesses to enhance her moral authority and manipulative power, in precisely the same way that Queen Victoria used her widowhood. And she clearly accomplished more as a string-puller, an operator, and a bully because most Victorian men would have thought it unchivalrous to defy her, to gainsay her, or to call her bluff.

The essential difficulty in understanding Nightingale may thus be succinctly stated: she was (and is) too bossy, too interfering, too governessy for many men; and she was (and is) too uninterested in women's issues and women's rights to be embraced as a feminist role model. But to define the problem is also to suggest a solution. Thus described, she may most helpfully and appropriately be seen as the precursor and soul mate of another very extraordinary British woman: Margaret Thatcher herself. Long before Thatcher, Nightingale both denied and exploited her femininity to gain power in a man's world. Long before Thatcher, Nightingale was possessed of superabundant energy, and was in a righteous rage to get things done. Long before Thatcher, Nightingale hated red tape, loathed bureaucrats, and was determined to sweep away incompetence and inefficiency wherever she found it. Long before Thatcher, Nightingale was congenitally incapable of understanding any point of view which differed from her own. And long before Thatcher, Nightingale took up men, used them for her own ends, and then cast them aside with little regret or remorse. In the age of the Iron Lady, Nightingale seems a much more credible female figure than she has been at any time since her death. In a very real sense, Mrs Thatcher's success is Florence's final vindication. And verification, too.

The Thatcher era is, then, a particularly propitious time for a full-scale re-evaluation of Nightingale's life and work. For she still awaits the biographer and historian who can simultaneously do her justice and take her measure. But what a task he (or she) is going to have! To work through the elephantine mass of relevant archival material will require stamina of positively Florentian dimensions. To decode and interpret her letters correctly and convincingly will demand judgement and intuition of the very highest order. To convey the contradictions of her personality will need the insight of an artist and the expertise of a psychologist. And to do full justice to the astonishing range of her interests and achievements will take a scholar of uncommon versatility and expertise, not just in political history, military history and medical history, but also in women's history, imperial history, administrative history, intellectual history and religious history. Eighty years after her passing, Nightingale remains a daunting and intimidating adversary. But until her biography is properly accomplished, these brilliant yet baffling letters provide the most vivid picture available of this eminent but abidingly enigmatic Victorian. In death, as in life, Florence herself remains emphatically in charge. But not, we must hope, for too much longer . . .

(1990)

NOTE

1 Martha Vicinus and Bea Nergaard (eds), *Ever Yours, Florence Nightingale: Selected Letters* (Cambridge, Mass., 1990).

22
Cecil Rhodes

The British Empire may have been won in a fit of absence of mind, but it was certainly not won in a fit of absence of personality. In the heady and hubristic years of the so-called 'New Imperialism', the men who extended the Empire's boundaries, safeguarded its frontiers, administered its dominions, and evoked its spirit were themselves appropriately larger than life. There were conquering pioneers, like Sir George Taubman Goldie in Nigeria and Sir William Mackinnon in East Africa. There were soldiers of fortune, like Kitchener, Roberts and Wolseley. There were law-givers and proconsuls, like Curzon and Cromer, Lugard and Milner. There were the laureates of Empire, like Kipling, Elgar and Lutyens. And there was Cecil John Rhodes. In an age of imperial titans, he was the most titanic imperialist of all: his ambitions and accomplishments were such that the inevitably punning epithet of 'Colossus' seemed if anything an understatement; while his character was so contradictory, and his achievements were so controversial that it has proved no easier to write his definitive biography than it has been to complete the railway he dreamed of building from the Cape to Cairo.

This is partly because there were four very different versions of Cecil Rhodes, each of which was individually quite extraordinary, and all of which were collectively almost incredible. The first was the archetypal Victorian weakling – a man so unrobust and so unprepossessing that he would never have been awarded one of his own scholarships. He was a delicate child, of uncertain health and indifferent education. In adult life, his voice remained an uncontrollable falsetto, he suffered a series of heart attacks, he soon aged prematurely into a grey and bloated invalid, and he died too young at forty-eight. But the second Rhodes was, by contrast, a self-made Smilesian hero of epic accomplishments. Born in relatively humble circumstances, he left for South Africa knowing almost nothing about the country and with no obvious prospect of fame or riches. Yet before he was thirty, he had made one prodigious fortune in diamond mining and then accumulated another, almost as gigantic, in gold. In his plutocratic prime, Rhodes was one of the wealthiest men in the world; and as P.G. Wodehouse might have said, King Midas himself could usefully have taken his correspondence course.

Yet he was not just a paradoxical compound of wimp and *wunderkind*: he was also a no less astonishing amalgam of dreamer and doer. From a very early age, his private fantasy life was extraordinarily vivid and self-aggrandising, as was made plain in the remarkable series of wills he drew up at regular intervals from the time he was nineteen, which set out in detail his ambitions and agenda. He believed that the British were marked out by God for world-wide dominion; he yearned for the reunification of the Anglo-Saxon races and the recovery of the United States; and he imagined himself as the Man of Destiny who actually brought all this about. For most people, these would have been mere idle and impotent imaginings. But Rhodes's enormous fortune gave him the power, and the Scramble for Africa gave him the opportunity, to convert fantasy into fact. As Prime Minister of Cape Colony, he became the dominant figure in South African politics. As the founder and financier of the British South Africa Company, he added territories to the Queen's dominions which were half the size of Europe itself. And he lavishly endowed the Rhodes Scholarships at Oxford University, in the hope that future generations of ardent young imperialists might continue and complete his work.

Not surprisingly, contemporaries found it impossible to agree about Rhodes. To associates and acolytes like Dr Jameson and Herbert Baker, he was beyond question the greatest man they had ever known, a leader for whom they would gladly have laid down their lives; and in a succession of fervently affectionate reminiscences, they admiringly depicted their revered colossus as an heroic figure of charm and charisma, vision and vigour, grandeur and generosity. For such loyal and devoted followers, belief in Rhodes was truly a substitute for religion. But to his enemies, he was anti-Christ incarnate. From the far right, G.K. Chesterton dismissed him as a cynical, corrupt, unprincipled operator, totally devoid of ideals or morality; and from the left, J.A. Hobson mounted a sustained attack in his book *Imperialism*, first published in 1902, the year of Rhodes's death. For Hobson, Rhodes was little more than an international buccaneer, a ruthless gangster, an unscrupulous villain, an unchecked tyrant, with no respect for law, for life, or for liberty, who used his ill-gotten millions to manipulate politicians, to deceive and exploit the native Africans, and to promote indefensible acts of piracy like the Jameson Raid.

The lengthening perspective of history has only added to these contradictions and confusions. For a time, it did indeed seem as if Rhodes's grandiose imperial designs were gradually coming to full and splendid fruition. In 1903, the first Rhodes Scholars went to Oxford, and in 1929, Rhodes House was opened – an appropriately grandiose monument, designed by Herbert Baker. In the aftermath of the Boer War, the unification of South Africa within the Empire was finally achieved, and many Afrikaners fought loyally by the side of the mother country during the First and Second World Wars. And in 1919, the British obtained a League of Nations Mandate over Tanganyika (the former German East Africa), which meant that Rhodes's dream of an all-red dominion from the Cape to Cairo was finally realised. Against this background of apparently abiding and constructive achievement, successive generations of biographers – from Basil Williams in 1921 to J.G. Lockhart and C.M. Woodhouse in 1963 – continued to depict Rhodes in essentially heroic and favourable terms, as a great man, who may indeed have been tragically flawed, yet who remained a great man none the less.

But in the longer perspective afforded by the late twentieth century, his achievements seem far less significant, admirable and enduring. The reunion of the Anglo-Saxon races never came about, and the British Empire, which once seemed so permanent and so pre-eminent, has completely disintegrated. Instead of producing a succession of outstanding public leaders, the Rhodes Scholarships are essentially a means whereby bright overseas students obtain a second B.A. degree at Oxford to further their careers. In South Africa, the Boers soon wrested power from the British, intensified the policy of apartheid which Rhodes himself had effectively initiated, and in 1961 withdrew from the Commonwealth altogether. Within another decade, Northern Rhodesia had achieved independence from British rule and become the republic of Zambia, and after a longer and more bitter struggle, Southern Rhodesia eventually emerged as the sovereign state of Zimbabwe. From the vantage point of the 1980s, Rhodes's crude and naive dreams have either mouldered into dust or become contemporary nightmares, while in retrospect, the man himself stands condemned – as an imperialist, a racist, and a male chauvinist – for heinous crimes against humanity.

Accordingly, the greatest difficulty in writing a new biography of Rhodes lies in establishing consistent criteria by which to assess the life and evaluate the legacy. To make matters worse, the Rhodes archive itself, although extensive, is not particularly rich in personal material which might illuminate his extraordinary temperament. In addition, it requires outstanding expositional skills to tell a story which moves back and forth from London to the Cape, from Kimberley to Bulawayo, from Pretoria to Johannesburg, and which involves characters as varied as Gladstone and Salisbury, Queen Victoria and the Kaiser, Kruger and Bismark, Olive Schreiner and the Princess Radziwill. Such a life also demands an unusual degree of scholarly versatility: not just a detailed knowledge of British and African history, but of psycho-history, diplomatic history, business history, and economic history as well. Appropriately enough, this latest, most ambitious, and most successful biography has been undertaken by the co-editor of the *Journal of Interdisciplinary History*, himself an expert on the African past and a former Rhodes Scholar.[1]

In its essential outline, the story that Robert Rotberg tells is very familiar. But there are plenty of surprises along the way. Rhodes was born in 1853, the fifth son of a Church of England clergyman who was vicar of Bishop's Stortford. His father seems to have been a distant and unappealing figure, for whom Cecil never had much regard or affection. But during the early years of his life, he enjoyed an unusually close rapport with his mother – which was brutally broken when the next child came along. Here, Rotberg insists, is the key to understanding Rhodes's remarkable adult personality: the brooding, solitary figure, free from shame or guilt, whose confidence in his own powers was unassailable. Here, too, is the explanation for his lack of ease with women, and for his homosexuality, which is explicitly (and very convincingly) discussed in detail for the first time. And Rotberg also maintains that although Rhodes was not a youth of whom great things might have been predicted, he was far from being the delicate weakling of biographical myth, he was not forced to go out to Africa for his health, and in later life, it was his lungs, not his heart, which were his real medical problem.

For whatever precise reason, Rhodes left England at the age of seventeen, and began working in collaboration with his elder brother, Herbert, who was farming cotton and tobacco in Natal. After only a year, he moved to the frontier town of Kimberley, where diamonds had been discovered in 1867. In this rough and brutal environment, Rhodes rapidly discovered his genius for business and for choosing associates – Charles Rudd in mining, and Alfred Beit in financial affairs – and acquired a reputation for cynical and unscrupulous dealing which was to stay with him all his life. Very soon, he was worth over £50,000, and he promptly left the diamond fields for Oxford, where he studied intermittently between 1873 and 1881. In retrospect, it has always been claimed that this was the turning point of Rhodes's life, but Rotberg's interpretation is far less romantic. There was, he insists, no sudden conversion to the cause of public life and British imperialism. On the contrary, Rhodes's time at Oxford was relatively humdrum: he did very little work, acquired few influential friends, made no great impact on his contemporaries, never came under the spell of Ruskin, and only obtained a pass degree.

Nevertheless, during the 1880s, his career in South Africa gathered a seemingly irresistible momentum. Gradually, but inexorably, he bought out most of his competitors in the Kimberley diamond mines, began to dabble in the gold which had been discovered on the Rand, and made a name for himself in London financial circles with men like Lord Rothschild. At the age of twenty-seven, he was elected to the Cape legislature, within three years he was in the Cabinet, and he soon established himself as a formidable figure, successfully urging the annexation of Bechuanaland, so as to forestall the Germans and the Transvaalers, and to keep open the road to the north for future British expansion. At the very end of the decade, when he was still not yet forty, he scored three almost simultaneous triumphs. He overwhelmed Barney Barnarto, his last remaining rival in the Kimberley diamond fields, which meant that Rhodes's company, De Beers, now controlled 90 per cent of world production. He became Prime Minister of Cape Colony and ruled virtually unchallenged. And he obtained a royal charter for his British South Africa Company, which effectively gave him unlimited rights of plunder and annexation from the Limpopo to the Zambezi and far beyond.

The years from 1890 to 1895 saw Rhodes at the zenith of his wealth, power and acquisitiveness: truly he was Caesar, Croesus, colossus and conquistador combined. At the Cape, he lived like an emperor, with a palace for a house, and a mountain for a garden. He surrounded himself with unsavoury and sycophantic collaborators like Grimmer, Silverwright and Rutherfoord Harris. To ensure the support of the Afrikaners in the legislature, he enacted a series of discriminatory measures which deprived the natives of their voting and territorial rights, and which spelt the death-knell of Cape liberalism. North of the Limpopo, King Lobengula was hoodwinked and deceived into signing away his kingdom, and between 1890 and 1893, Rhodes's agents occupied Mashonaland and ruthlessly subdued the Matabele. The inadequate and unsupervised administration of what soon became known as Northern and Southern Rhodesia was one of the most shameful episodes in British imperial history. Most of the white settlers and rulers were callous and self-seeking adventurers; and Rhodes, who regarded the territories as his own personal fief, knew little and cared less. So o'erleaping did his vaulting ambition become that he even planned to topple Kruger's regime and win the Transvaal (and its gold) for Britain, by sponsoring the Jameson Raid at the very end of 1895 – an armed expedition to Johannesburg in support of a hoped-for local uprising against President Kruger.

But the Raid was a fiasco. The uprising fizzled, and Jameson and his followers were easily taken prisoner by the Boers. The British government repudiated the entire enterprise, and the rest of the world condemned it. Thereafter, Rhodes himself never really recovered his power or his position. His health began to give way: indeed, it may have been his increasing awareness that time was running out which had persuaded him to gamble so recklessly. He was obliged to resign as Prime Minister of the Cape, and although he later contemplated making a comeback, it never in fact materialised. In the aftermath of an official inquiry in London into the Raid, he was compelled to quit the board of the British South Africa Company. The Boers never forgave him for his treachery and his piracy, and the Matabele, goaded beyond endurance, rebelled in 1896–97. His house in the Cape was burned down, and he was pursued (and possibly blackmailed) by Princess Radziwill, an unscrupulous and unstable Polish adventuress. The outbreak of the Boer War meant that the political initiative had now passed irretrievably to other hands, and for four months, Rhodes himself was virtually a prisoner while Kimberley was besieged. After obtaining his freedom, he had little more than a year to live, and he was buried in the Rhodesian mountains at a placed called 'The World's View'.

The very least than can be said of this account is that it provides what is undoubtedly the fullest, most detailed and most well-documented survey of Rhodes's life that we are ever likely to get, by comparison with which all previous biographies seem jejeune and superficial. Let cliché have its way and its say: this is an appropriately colossal book about an undeniably colossal man. More precisely, this is the first major effort to accommodate Rhodes to our post-imperial world, to see him primarily from an African rather than a European perspective, and to lay bare the full details of his unscrupulous business methods and his callous treatment of the native populations. Above all, Rotberg has triumphantly succeeded in scraping off the rich accretions of myth and make-believe, which Rhodes so assiduously manufactured, which his acolytes so loyally embellished, and which his previous biographers have so credulously repeated. Only in retrospect did Rhodes live out the whole of his life as an imperialist visionary: in fact, until the late 1880s, he was far less purposeful and more reactive in his doings and his ambitions than it has hitherto been fashionable to suppose.

Inevitably, the massive strengths of this book carry with them their share of corresponding weaknesses. In historical terms, the author is far less surefooted in dealing with the British than with the African context. To give one example. Within little more than a page, we learn that in the 1870s, Oxford 'was undergoing a vigorous intellectual renaissance'; that in the country as a whole, 'a fervour for imperialism was apparent'; and that Rhodes 'would have felt the strength of the positive currents then pulsating through the mother country and its premier university'. One knows what the author means. But this is not history: it is banality. In the same way, the prodigious detail means that on occasions the book is in danger of sinking beneath the weight of its own erudition. It is all very well to show that Rhodes's life in prospect lacked the simple sense of direction it was deemed to possess in retrospect. But it remains an essential part of the biographer's art to give form and focus to his story. Yet all too often, the reader of Rotberg's Rhodes is confronted by an overwhelming mass of unstructured information, which is inadequately signposted, with the result that Rhodes himself sometimes disappears altogether.

The treatment of Rhodes's psychology – which is clearly a subject of central importance – is also disappointingly uneven. The portrayal of his infancy and adolescence (especially his relations with his mother) is altogether too speculative, and it is done in prose that is frequently pretentious and infelicitously jargon-ridden. But when Rhodes becomes an active, assertive (and better documented) adult, the author seems almost to lose interest in his patient. It does not seem very helpful to be told that Rhodes hated Kruger because he reminded him of his own stern and unapproving father, and it is especially regrettable that no effort is made to address the fundamental question which is much more important than that of Rhodes's homosexuality. Was the man actually mad? On more than one occasion, Rotberg rightly refers to Rhodes's persistent delusions of grandeur and to his undoubted, towering megalomania. He presents ample evidence of his astonishing private fantasy world, of his unshakeable belief that he was a man of destiny, and of his unbridled ambition to rule the globe. Yet all this is lightly dismissed, as little more than 'flim flam' and 'hocus pocus'.

So, despite the incomparable erudition of this book, its manifold and fascinating new findings, and its healthily sceptical attitude, the Rhodes who struggles and fights his way out of these eight hundred pages remains a fundamentally unaltered and essentially familiar figure: he is recognisably our old friend (or enemy), the flawed imperial hero. In one guise, he was indeed vain, cynical, corrupt, ruthless, philistine, humourless, overbearing and vindictive – a man who cared little for the rights or feelings of anyone who got in his way, and whose prime legacy has undoubtedly been to make the agony of Africa more bitter. Yet on the other hand, Rotberg repeatedly describes him – apparently quite without irony – as 'the great man', 'the colossus', 'the founder', who did many good works and even enjoyed the occasional 'finest hour'. Like so many previous biographers, his conclusion is the disappointingly even-handed verdict that Rhodes was a Janus-faced giant: he was part genius, part rogue; he was sometimes good, sometimes bad; and his achievements were a mixture of the ephemeral and the enduring. On balance, no doubt, Rotberg's Rhodes is less of a hero than previous versions: but a hero he essentially remains.

So, despite the final chapter, which is promisingly entitled 'enigma and resolution', the conundrum of Rhodes remains essentially unresolved. Indeed, as long as historians continue to see their task as being to construct a balance sheet of his life, this is bound to remain the case. For it will never be possible to reconcile the undoubted contradictions of Rhodes's character, career and contribution simply by examining the man himself in ever greater biographical detail. The only way to obtain a more consistent viewpoint and balanced verdict is to set Rhodes in a much broader historical perspective. For in many ways, he was far from being unique. During the last quarter of the nineteenth century many men made an impact as capitalists and imperialists which was both good-and-bad, ephemeral-and-enduring. Robberbaron plutocrats like Carnegie and Rockefeller were suddenly ten cents a dime, and homosexual egomaniacs like Charles George Gordon and T.E. Lawrence were often able to change the course of history. If we are to understand Rhodes more fully, it is to his time, rather than to his temperament, that we might most usefully direct our attention. We have been given the colossus in close up; we now need the colossus in context.

(1988)

NOTE

1 Robert I. Rotberg, *The Founder: Cecil Rhodes and the Enigma of Power* (Oxford, 1988).

23
Winston Churchill

When Sir Winston Churchill died at the age of ninety in January 1965, he was accorded the most magnificent state funeral that a grateful and grieving Britain could give him. In life, he had received, or refused, every available honour, and his death occasioned a final display of national thanksgiving and global homage which was unique in its intensity and unrivalled in its scope. Setting aside both precedent and precedence, Queen Elizabeth II attended in person to mourn the passing of her greatest commoner and most illustrious subject. Never before, not even for the funeral of President Kennedy, had so many kings and queens, presidents and prime ministers assembled to do honour to one dead man. In Britain itself, and around the world, millions watched, wondered and wept before their television sets. At the end of the same year, the final volume of the *Oxford History of England* set down its authoritative verdict on Churchill's life and achievements. It was written by A.J.P. Taylor, an historian generally renowned for his dissenting opinions and provocative irreverence. But in his eulogistic description of Churchill as 'the saviour of his country', there was not the faintest suggestion of irony or mockery.

Throughout the last decade of his life, Churchill was almost universally esteemed as 'the greatest Englishman of his time'. As a soldier, journalist, biographer, historian, painter, orator, politician, parliamentarian and statesman, he seemed prodigiously endowed with superabundant gifts of mind and spirit, head and heart. Whether predicting history, making history, or writing history, his titanic achievements dwarfed the pigmy ploddings of mere ordinary mortals. As a young Liberal minister, his social reforms had helped to lay the foundations for the modern welfare state. As First Lord of the Admiralty, he had devised the scheme to force the Dardanelles, the only original strategic initiative of the First World War. In the 1920s, and again in the late 1940s, he had been the first western statesman to understand the menacing nature of the Communist threat. During the 1930s, he had fought an almost single-handed campaign to alert the western democracies to the evils of Hitler. In 1940, his 'finest hour', he expressed in unforgettable phrases Britain's resolve never to surrender to Nazi tyranny. And thereafter, his many-sided genius led a united people, a united government, and also – in harmonious collaboration with Roosevelt – the United States, onwards to victory. In Isaiah Berlin's famous words, this Churchill was 'a gigantic historical figure . . . superhumanly bold, strong and imaginative . . . the largest human being of our time'.

Yet in fact, it had taken Churchill almost the whole of his astonishingly long and exceptionally controversial life to persuade his contemporaries to accept him at his own magnificent and magniloquent self-evaluation. During the 1900s, he was hated by the Tories as a turncoat, who put personal advancement before party loyalty, and by the Liberals as an ambitious, unprincipled adventurer, whose commitment to social reform was never more than skin-deep. During the First World War, his career almost collapsed when he was forced to leave the government in the aftermath of the Dardanelles fiasco. During the 1920s, he was, on his own admission, a singularly unsuccessful Chancellor of the Exchequer, who took the controversial decision to restore Britain to the Gold Standard. During the 1930s, he forfeited public confidence by his sustained and belligerent intransigence over Indian constitutional reform. In 1945, his hour of supreme triumph, he was immediately dismissed by the British electorate from all further conduct of their affairs. During his second prime ministership, which was widely felt to have been a mistake, there were constant murmurings in the press and in the Tory Party that he was no longer up to the job. And even during his last years of apotheosis, the publication of the Alanbrooke diaries suggested that his wartime relations with the military high command had been much more acrimonious than his own memoirs had revealed.

So, it was hardly surprising that in the immediate aftermath of Churchill's death, his career and his achievements were once again looked at in a more critical and less flattering light. Robert Rhodes James's 'study in failure', published in 1970, examined Churchill's fluctuating reputation and questionable achievements between 1900 and 1939, and convincingly demonstrated why he was so widely distrusted by so many people for so much of his career. In the same vein, Brian Gardner studied his wartime premiership, and noted that from 1941 onwards, Churchill was constantly subjected to criticism and attack inside Parliament, was on far from cordial terms with certain sections of the press, and was no longer in close touch with the people as a whole. More sensationally, and quite without evidence, Rolf Hochhuth suggested, in his play *Soldiers*, that Churchill had actually connived at the death of the wartime Polish leader General Sikorski in 1943. And the diaries of Churchill's doctor, Lord Moran, vividly depicted his patient as an ageing and infirm old man, burnt out by 1945, and struggling for survival thereafter. With varying degrees of plausibility, these works began the essential process of de-mythologising Churchill, by treating him seriously as a substantive and problematic historical personality, rather than as the legendary and Olympian hero he had only in fact become during his last years of retirement.

As historians have, in their turn, begun to work through the mass of twentieth-century government papers which have become available during the last two decades, this process of revising Churchill has inevitably intensified. Very often, the result has been to show that things were not quite as Churchill or his apologists had later claimed; that his part in events was less significant or less prescient or more mundane or more controversial; and that those who disagreed with him were not necessarily wicked or stupid, but did on occasions have a serious point of view. This is especially so in the case of his record as an opponent of appeasement. We now know that when he was Chancellor of the Exchequer, Churchill's insistence on economy in military expenditure during the twenties cast its dark and baleful shadow forward into the next decade. During the thirties, he was a long-time admirer of Mussolini, he supported Franco in Spain, he was allowed access to government intelligence with the consent of MacDonald, Baldwin and Chamberlain, and his figures about the relative strength of the British and German air forces were sometimes wildly exaggerated. Above all, there *was* a serious case for appeasement: ever since the 1880s, the British had been making concessions to one great power or another, and by the thirties, Britain's empire was overextended while the economy was in deep depression. There *were* compelling reasons for trying to placate Hitler which are seldom considered in the more uncritical celebrations of Churchill's career.

In the same way, Churchill's wartime record was less infallible than it became fashionable to suppose in the aftermath of victory. When Neville Chamberlain appointed him First Lord of the Admiralty after war broke out in September 1939, his performance was more vigorous than well judged, and the disastrous Norway campaign was disquietingly reminiscent of the Dardanelles débâcle. In the summer of 1940, there was a very lengthy debate in Cabinet about the possibility of negotiating a peace settlement with Hitler, and for a time both Halifax and Chamberlain were strongly in favour. Churchill's friendship with Roosevelt was far less cordial than he himself often claimed it was, and he was not as clearsighted about the growing Russian menace as he later implied. His relations with the military were often strained to the point of incoherence, and many of his own pet ventures – in Greece, Crete, Dakar – were over-impetuous. At home, life during the blitz was monotonous or terrifying rather than heroic or sublime, and politically, the country took a decided shift to the left. In the Cabinet, the Labour ministers virtually monopolised all of the domestic appointments, Churchill and Eden did not always see eye to eye, and Robert Menzies, the Australian Prime Minister, became extremely critical of Churchill's conduct during 1941.

Yet while Churchill's own account of his deeds has been substantially modified in many cases, there are other phases of his career where detailed research has vindicated his record and enhanced his reputation. As Colonial Under-Secretary, President of the Board of Trade, and Home Secretary, it is now clear that he played a major part in the imperial and domestic reform programmes of the Liberal governments of Campbell-Bannerman and Asquith. The contemporary criticism that was heaped upon him in the aftermath of the Dardanelles disaster was both excessive and extreme. According to David Moggridge, Churchill's performance as Chancellor of the Exchequer was less inept than was often supposed, since the overwhelming weight of official opinion was in favour of the return to the Gold Standard in 1925. Despite his notorious speech likening Labour politicians to the Gestapo, Churchill was not personally responsible for the defeat of the Conservatives at the general election of 1945: according to Henry Pelling, the reasons were much more deeply rooted than that. And it has recently been argued by Anthony Seldon that his peacetime government was not the flop it was generally supposed to have been, but was actually the most successful postwar Tory administration – until the advent of Mrs Thatcher's.

One result of all this revisionism has been altogether salutary. For by scraping off the rich veneer of Churchillian mythology, it is gradually becoming possible to appreciate his full complexity as an historical personality: instead of being a two-dimensional man of destiny, he becomes a three-dimensional man of flesh and blood. But in other ways, this extended analysis of Churchill's life has been less successful. In part, this is because these detailed pieces of revisionism are often devoid of a broader context, and have not yet been brought together to produce a fundamental reinterpretation of the man and his career. Moreover, they have made absolutely no impact on Churchill's popular image. In Britain – especially Thatcher's Britain – he remains the essential hero. Hundreds of thousands of people each year visit Blenheim Palace, Chartwell Manor, the Cabinet War Rooms and Bladon churchyard. Ships in the Royal Navy are named after him, and so are cigarettes and public houses. His life is the subject of films, television series and even West End musicals. And – as these three vast volumes so weightily but disappointingly demonstrate – he remains irresistible material for the biographer.

William Manchester's book is the second instalment of what promises to be a three-volume life.[1] Although not uncritical, its essentially admiring attitude may be gauged from the tone and content of his acknowledgements, where Manchester records that he has been 'honoured' and 'moved' by the friendship and support of Churchill's relatives and entourage, especially Lady Soames (Churchill's daughter, now the presiding matriarch of the family), Martin Gilbert (Churchill's official biographer, whose monumental labours have just been completed), and the late Sir John Colville (Churchill's former private secretary and most redoubtable champion). He has spoken to almost all of the 'surviving Churchillians': politicians like Lord Boothby, civil servants like Sir David Pitblado, and five of Churchill's secretaries. And he describes one other authority as the 'International Churchill Society's keeper of the flame'. In addition, Manchester has consulted over one hundred private archival collections, as well as the official papers of the British, French, German and US governments. And out of this mass of material, he has fashioned an epic drama couched in messianic prose, of which even Churchill himself might generally – though not completely – have approved.

His concern is to retell (and to reburnish) the familiar story of Churchill's wilderness years, which were, Manchester insists, undoubtedly the greatest and noblest of his career. For most of the 1930s, Churchill was out of office, out of power, out of favour and out of luck. He was spurned, derided and rejected by the lesser men in government; he was regarded as an outcast by the Tory Party managers; and he was banned from speaking on the BBC. He was harried and harassed by creditors, and at one point was even obliged to put Chartwell up for sale. Truly, Churchill was a prophet without honour in his own country. But, undaunted and undismayed, he put together a vast underground intelligence network, which meant he was better informed about German rearmament and territorial ambitions than the Foreign Office. He made a succession of brilliant, unanswerable speeches, in Parliament and throughout the country, damning appeasement as cowardly folly, and struggled to alert the western democracies to the growing menace of Hitler. And so, at the eleventh hour, when all the grievous events that Churchill had so valiantly and vainly foretold had finally come to pass, the people eventually turned to him, as the rejected prophet became the national saviour and gave his country its 'finest hour'.

While Manchester waxes thus fulsome in his eulogistic evocation of Churchill, he shows no mercy to the cynical Judases who were, he believes, the 'betrayers of England's greatness'. His three principal culprits are the prime ministers themselves: Ramsay MacDonald, Stanley Baldwin and Neville Chamberlain. Without exception, Manchester insists, they were weak, shabby, irresolute, provincial mediocrities, who vainly believed that Hitler could be trusted and should be appeased. And they were supported in their ignoble endeavours by such unimaginative and hypocritical politicians as Lord Halifax, Sir John Simon and Sam Hoare, and by such mistaken, foolish, time-serving officials as Sir Horace Wilson (British Ambassador to Berlin) and Sir Neville Henderson (Chamberlain's chief diplomatic adviser). These were the 'guilty men', who believed in peace at virtually any price. Nor, Manchester insists, was this the full extent of their duplicity. For it was not just that they did not want to offend the Führer. Obsessed as they were with the fear of Communist subversion, they actually wanted to support and strengthen Nazi Germany as the most effective European counterpoise to what they saw as the much greater threat of Soviet Russia. And in order to do so, they deliberately misled the British public about the true nature and intentions of the Nazi regime.

As such, Manchester's account adheres very closely to the familiar, majestic interpretation which Churchill himself originally set out in *The Gathering Storm*, the first instalment of his war memoirs, and which Martin Gilbert further elaborated in the fifth volume of the official biography. It was understandable that Churchill should see himself as a man of destiny, and take his revenge on those who had kept him out of power for so long, and Gilbert could hardly fail to adopt a similar view. But in Manchester's hands, this now thrice-told tale seems increasingly threadbare. This is partly because of the way he writes it, as his prose swoops and dips uncontrollably from the hackneyed to the hyperbolic. Hitler is 'freedom's archenemy', Neville Chamberlain is 'the archpriest of appeasement'. Churchill's performances in a hostile House of Commons are likened to 'a bull confronting a matador'. On the other hand, Blenheim Palace is 'splendrous', Chartwell is Churchill's 'great keep', and the chapters of the book are successively entitled 'Shoals', 'Reef', 'Undertow', 'Vortex', 'Surge' and 'Cataclysm'. This is not gourmet biography: it is fast-food journalism.

To make matters worse, these histrionic excesses are accompanied by a disconcerting lack of historical understanding. What does it mean to say that 'the remarkable stability of British society was rooted in a social contract whose origins lay in the medieval relations between lord and serf'? It is wholly unsatisfactory to describe the political elite of interwar Britain in terms of 'the patriciate' or 'the gentry'. It does not inspire confidence to be told that, in the mid-1930s, Stanley Baldwin 'possessed more prestige and political power than any Prime Minister since the death of Queen Victoria'. It is banal to describe Roosevelt in these words: 'After overcoming his appalling paralysis to become the greatest figure in American history, he felt he could do anything.' It may be that Churchill reposed 'absolute faith in democracy', but during the early 1930s, he publicly affirmed his belief that unfettered universal suffrage was ill-advised. Even more disturbingly, the author does not seem to have absorbed any of the recent, revisionist scholarship on appeasement by such scholars as Paul Kennedy, G.C. Peden and C.A. MacDonald. It may overstate the case; but it certainly needs to be considered.

The result is that this book fails completely to set Churchill in the sort of historical perspective which is essential if both his reverses and his triumphs during the thirties are properly to be understood. Manchester gives us a vivid account of Churchill's personality and way of life, including a masterly opening section describing a typical Chartwell day. But evocation is no substitute for analysis, and this Manchester does not provide. He tells us that for much of the thirties, Churchill was 'distrusted, disliked – even hated'. True. But there is no attempt to discuss his long record of mistakes, misfortunes, miscalculations and misjudgements which so plausibly explain why this was so. He tells us that Churchill made some of his greatest speeches against appeasement to a half-empty House of Commons. Also true. But again, what was it about Churchill's record and rhetoric which emptied rather than filled the chamber at this time? To suppose that all people who opposed Churchill were either knaves or fools, men so mediocre that they could not recognise genius, is to ignore the many good reasons why Churchill was disapproved of at that time.

This is all the more regrettable because, despite his generally (indeed, excessively) well-intentioned tone, Manchester does have some surprisingly candid and unexpectedly critical things to say about his hero. Most of Churchill's children turned out unhappily, his marriage to Clementine seems to have been especially strained during the late thirties, and although Manchester discounts rumours of Churchill's drunkenness, he concedes that he possessed a strong 'hedonistic streak'. He was regularly rude to servants, not always loyal to friends, and did not protect his intelligence sources as responsibly as he should have. His attitude to Mussolini and Franco, to the invasion of Manchuria and the plunder of Abyssinia was decidedly equivocal. He behaved very foolishly at the time of the abdication. He underestimated the importance of the submarine and of air power, and habitually overestimated the might and morale of the French army. As First Lord of the Admiralty, he was too easily captivated by dramatic but unsound schemes, deliberately exaggerated the German U-boat losses, and undoubtedly bore the chief responsibility for the follies and failures of the Norwegian campaign in which, following the German invasion of April 1940, British ships landed troops that were soon defeated.

In short, as Manchester correctly admits, while Churchill could sometimes be 'terrifically right', he could also be 'spectacularly wrong', and it is a pity he does not pursue this important (and by now commonplace) point, nor explore its considerable political implications. But he *does* offer one further, startling insight, almost as a casual aside, when he suggests that Churchill and Hitler 'had more in common than either would have acknowledged', especially their charisma, their demagogic skills, their megalomania, their overwhelming sense of personal destiny, their belief in the innate superiority of their own race, and their misplaced confidence in their strategic grasp and military insight. Once again, this is not a novel point: the comparison was actually made by some of Churchill's parliamentary critics in 1942. But it seems odd that a remark which tends to subvert the well-disposed tone of this book should be made so offhandedly, and then be left undeveloped and unexplained.

Nevertheless, to pass on from Manchester's book to Irving's is to move from an impassioned case for the defence to no less determined advocacy for the prosecution.[2] In a succession of previous books, Irving has already sought to unsettle received notions about the aims and conduct of the British and the Germans during the Second World War. In part, he has done this by seeking out archival material which other historians did not use, did not wish to use, or did not know about (something which he does again in this book, drawing extensively on the private papers of many second-ranking wartime figures, and on the government archives in Ottawa, Washington, Canberra and elsewhere). And in part, he has done this by consistently applying an evidential double standard, demanding absolute documentary proof to convict the Germans (as when he sought to show that Hitler was not responsible for the Holocaust), while relying on circumstantial evidence to condemn the British (as in his account of the Allied bombing of Dresden). Coincidentally, he also describes himself as a 'mild fascist', he has spent much more time and money than historians usually do in lawsuits and libel actions, and he has regularly been accused of being anti-Semitic, a charge he has always vehemently denied.

This latest book – the first of a projected two-volume study of Churchill as Britain's warlord – is written from an extremely antagonistic viewpoint. While Manchester made the suggestion, in passing, that Churchill and Hitler were not totally dissimilar men, Irving has been quoted as saying that 'Churchill is frying in Hell with Truman and Stalin and Hitler.' Every Churchillian fault and failure mentioned (or ignored) by Manchester is magnified one thousand fold, while every virtue and victory is disregarded, disparaged or only grudgingly admitted. Indeed, so great is Irving's animosity to Churchill throughout this book that no reputable British publisher would accept it. Both Michael Joseph in London, and Doubleday in New York, to whom it was originally contracted, turned the typescript down; and Macmillan refused it at the behest of Lord Stockton himself. In the end, it has been produced – extremely shoddily – by an Australian publishing house imaginatively called Veritas, Irving himself has been obliged to make his own arrangements for the distribution of the book in Britain, and it has received almost no attention from historians or reviewers. It is easy to see why.

Between 1936 and 1940, Irving insists, Churchill was not the noble prophet celebrated by Manchester, but a drunken, insolvent, embittered failure, a 'busted flush', conducting spiteful, irresponsible personal vendettas against the men who quite correctly kept him out of power. His finances were so precarious that he was effectively the slave of a corrupt syndicate of (mainly Jewish) financiers, to whom he had 'sold his soul', and who essentially dictated his political opinions. His underground intelligence network was peopled by renegades, cranks and fanatics, who lived in a world of 'cloak and dagger fantasies', and produced absurdly exaggerated figures about Nazi rearmament. And he never understood that Chamberlain and

Halifax were not guilty men, but wise men, seeking to sustain and safe-guard Britain's greatness by coming to an accommodation with Hitler – an accommodation which the Führer himself also most ardently wished. Not surprisingly, when Churchill re-entered government as First Lord of the Admiralty, bent only on personal advancement and selfish glory, all decent, sensible, sober men were dismayed. He was excessively belligerent, regu-larly 'half-tight', invariably wrong about military strategy, and constantly sought to undermine Neville Chamberlain, 'despising no covert methods of destroying both the man and his reputation'.

As Prime Minister, Irving insists, Churchill's record was even more lamentable. He knew that his survival in power and hopes for immortality depended on the continuation of the war, so he wilfully refused to coun-tenance peace negotiations with Germany in the summer of 1940, even though the terms would have been 'generous'. Later in the same year, he 'deliberately provoked' Hitler into blitzing London (something the Führer had never intended to do), by cynically sending planes to bomb Berlin. But while Londoners huddled (and died) in their squalid air-raid shelters, Churchill scuttled away to the countryside, thanks to his secret informa-tion from the code-breakers at Bletchley Park, which told him when an air raid on London was imminent. And by begging Roosevelt for aid, and accepting the draconian terms of Lend-Lease, he effectively handed over the British Empire to the hostile and predatory Americans. In short, Churchill's 'finest hour' was nothing of the kind: he was not the architect of Britain's victory, but the harbinger of Britain's ruin. By his obsessive, self-aggrandising determination to thwart Hitler, to win 'victory at all costs', he condemned millions to death, brought about the end of the British Empire, and thereby effectively destroyed Britain as a great power.

Clearly, this is revisionism with a vengeance – in every sense. But much of it is based on ignorance, overstatement and quite inadequate evidence. We are portentously informed that Churchill's understandable unpopu-larity in the thirties is 'an area about which we have hitherto had little information', but this has been an historical commonplace for twenty years. The author's picture of a Churchill enslaved by money-lenders, wire-pullers and Jewish financiers reads like the more lurid pages of a John Buchan novel, and even Irving himself notes that the evidence for this fan-tasy is 'sparse'. He coyly admits that some of Churchill's figures about German military production were accurate, that Chamberlain wanted 'peace at any price', and was callously indifferent to the fate of Czecho-slovakia. His hostile account of Churchill at the Admiralty is largely based on material which, on his own admission, 'should be treated with the reserve that all clandestine writings merit'. But reserve is the last quality on display here. And despite his claims that Churchill was a disloyal colleague of the Prime Minister's, he produces no firm evidence that he actively intrigued to bring Chamberlain down in 1940.

The same excesses, inconsistencies and omissions mar Irving's treatment of Churchill's prime ministership. He may sometimes have left London when there were heavy air raids, but he was also in the capital on many occasions when the bombs fell, and even Irving concedes that 'it was not unreasonable for Winston to wish to preserve himself in the nation's interest.' He quotes extensively from the defeatist diaries of Joseph Kennedy, the American Ambassador in London, but readily admits that they are 'scurrilous'. In describing the controversial decision to fight on in 1940, he seems completely unaware of recent work done on the subject, and quite unable to grasp the essential point that Hitler had never kept his word before, and that there was no reason to think he would have done so in this case. Churchill did not send the bombers to Berlin to provoke an attack on London, but to show the world (and especially America) that Britain's will to fight was undiminished. And Irving's argument that Churchill was the villain who destroyed the British Empire is historically quite naive. Hitler or no Hitler, Churchill or no Churchill, the British Empire was going to be one of the casualties of the twentieth century. The Second World War may have accelerated its demise by perhaps five years, but to most people (although not, it seems, to Irving) that was surely a price well worth paying for the destruction of Hitler.

But it is not merely that the arguments in this book are so perversely tendentious and irresponsibly sensationalist. It is also that it is written in a tone which is at best casually journalistic and at worst quite exceptionally offensive. The text is littered with errors from beginning to end. Churchill is given the wrong government office in 1922, Lord Willingdon's title as Viceroy of India is incorrect, and names like Montgomery-Massingberd, Lord Cranborne and Lord Cork and Orrery are consistently misspelt. De Gaulle is described as 'power hungry' and 'amoral', Roosevelt as 'sly' and 'cynical', Sinclair as 'weak and loathsome', Dalton as 'distasteful', and Brendan Bracken as Winston's 'carrot-topped retainer'. Churchill himself is depicted as a 'pudgy politician', with a 'swelling paunch' and 'soft rolls of flesh', who 'leers', 'gobbles', 'loafs' and 'sponges'. And when we are told that an official followed Churchill after he had visited Paris, 'like a street cleaner after a cavalry parade', with 'bucket and shovel in hand, cleaning up', we have reached the language of the gutter, not just metaphorically, but literally as well.

For Irving to claim that 'this is not a hostile biography' is to demonstrate quite remarkable powers of self-deception, and this is the more unfortunate because he does have some useful things to say. Unlike Manchester or Gilbert, he has looked at the archives of Churchill's defeatist and disappointed critics. Seen through the eyes of Joseph Kennedy, Cecil King, Sir John Reith or Lord Halifax, the great man's encounter with destiny takes on a very different appearance from that to which we are accustomed. For it is clear that he was operating from a very weak base of political support in 1940. In the Commons, it was Chamberlain not Churchill who received most of the cheers. In the Cabinet, the appeasers were still a formidable force. And the fact that Anglo-American relations were officially in the hands of Kennedy in London and Lord Lothian in Washington was hardly encouraging. At this time, Churchill was fighting at home as much as he was fighting abroad, and it was only, as Irving himself grudgingly admits, because of his courage, energy, stamina, resolution and determination that he was able to accomplish what he did. Ironically but appropriately, Churchill emerges from these laboured and hostile pages as an even greater man than before.

To move to Gilbert's book is to leave a project in progress – whether of the Manchester school or the Irving alternative – and to encounter a great work at the very end of the road.[3] Here, eight volumes and nine million words on, is the final instalment of Churchill's official life, which was begun by his son Randolph in 1961, and which was taken over by Martin Gilbert seven years later. These pages deal with Churchill's decisive defeat at the general election of 1945, his years as leader of the opposition, the writing of his war memoirs, his final term as prime minister, and his long, slow, sad decline into enfeebled old age. As such, they bring to a conclusion the greatest biographical enterprise which has been undertaken in Britain in this, or any, century. In the United States, it is still relatively common to entomb past presidents in multivolume vaults, Dumas Malone's life of Jefferson and Arthur Link's biography of Woodrow Wilson being obvious examples. But among English statesmen of the first rank, not even Disraeli (six volumes by Moneypenny and Buckle) or Gladstone (a mere three by John Morley) remotely approaches the colossal dimensions of this particular enterprise – a Churchillian monument on an appropriately Churchillian scale.

As a study in power, politics and statesmanship, the theme of this book may best be described as 'Triumph and Tragedy', the subtitle Churchill himself gave to his last volume of war memoirs. He was deeply distressed to be hurled from office so ungratefully and, despite the disapproval of his wife, was determined to stay on in active politics to 'avenge' his defeat. His performance as leader of the opposition was uneven, his attendance in Parliament was erratic, and his interest in the rethinking of the Conservative programme was minimal. But his position in the party was by now unassailable, and his return to Downing Street in 1951 almost atoned for 1945. He left R.A. Butler to manage the economy, Walter Monckton to keep the trade unions quiet, and Harold Macmillan to build the houses fit for heroes. Predictably, his own concerns were in foreign affairs, where he sought to consolidate the 'special relationship' with the United States, and bring about a summit meeting with the Russians. But Eisenhower was even less amenable to Churchill's fading charms than Roosevelt had been, and both the United States and the British Cabinet were hostile to his hankerings for top-level meetings. Thwarted in his ambitions, and increasingly at odds with his colleagues, there was nothing left for him to do except retire, which he eventually did in April 1955.

But this volume is also a study in fame and fortune. For the last twenty years of his life, Churchill was, beyond any doubt, the greatest celebrity alive. No statesman, before or since, has ever been quite so renowned as he was in his years of apotheosis. He travelled around Europe and the United States to widespread acclaim and adulation, and was loaded with national honours, civic freedoms and university degrees. His speeches at Fulton and at Zurich were those of a private citizen; but they reverberated round the world. His war memoirs sold by the million, brought him financial security at last, and provided the definitive account of that conflict for more than one generation. The parliamentary tribute paid him on his eightieth birthday was completely without precedent in the annals of British public life. He was made an honorary citizen of the United States. He was awarded the Nobel Prize for Literature. He refused a dukedom. And during his last decade, when controversy was all but stilled, and when the stories and the anecdotes gathered around his splendid name in such affectionate abundance, it could truly be said of him (and frequently was) that he had become a legend in his own lifetime.

Inevitably, this book is also a study in old age and infirmity. It is impossible not to be moved by the verve, the courage and the élan with which Churchill attacked this last and ultimately invincible enemy. As in all his campaigns, he assailed his adversary with endless high spirits, expert advice, ample helpings of brandy and champagne, and the loving and long-suffering support of his wife. But he had already endured a mild heart attack in 1941, he was an understandably tired man in 1945, and he was an astonishingly busy man in the years which followed. In 1953 he suffered a stroke, and was not expected to live. In a manner that would be quite impossible today, his condition was kept a secret. Eventually he recovered, and carried on for two more years as prime minister. But his powers were by now visibly fading, and by the time he grudgingly retired, he was generally regarded as being no longer up to the job. The last ten years of his life make truly painful reading, as Churchill became, in words that Lord Rosebery had used of his own father, the 'chief mourner at his own protracted funeral'. In personal terms, the greatest tragedy was that his long-sought and hard-won apotheosis came too late for him to appreciate or even fully understand it.

Given both the subject and the sources (which are mainly Churchill's own papers and the appropriate government files), there is much fascinating material to be found in these pages. There are unforgettable vignettes of Churchill on holiday in Madeira and Marrakesh. The complex and lucrative financial arrangements concerning his war memoirs are expertly described. Even at the very end of his career, his humanity, his versatility, his breadth of vision, his sense of history, his capacity to make phrases were quite astonishing. But as with the previous volumes, it is the reader who has to do all the work. Once again, the format is elementary, pedestrian narrative – a day by day (sometimes hour by hour) catalogue of Churchill's doings, with no attempt to explain, to interpret or to comment. Much of it reads like a briefing document for Manchester's third volume – which is no doubt what it will eventually become. Private family affairs are indiscriminately interleaved with public business in an undifferentiated morass. There is far too much extended quotation from Hansard and from the diaries of Lord Moran and Sir John Colville. The last two hundred and fifty pages contain almost nothing of real importance. In short, there is no interpretation, no judgement, no insight, no artistry.

Even worse, there is no attempt to evaluate the final stages of Churchill's career in the light of recent scholarly discussion. In every previous volume, this self-denying refusal to engage with the proliferating secondary literature has been a glaring omission, and once again, it seems quite inexcusable. We now know a great deal about the record of the Labour governments of 1945–51: how does Churchill's spell as leader of the opposition look in the light of this? We are not told. Much work has recently been done on the reorientation of American foreign policy towards Russia in the aftermath of 1945: but Gilbert's discussion of Churchill's Fulton speech completely ignores this. It is becoming increasingly clear that Churchill's war memoirs need a comprehensive analysis as a work of politics no less than as a work of history: but no such effort is undertaken here. There has been important recent work on the foreign and domestic policies of Churchill's last administration: but it is not even alluded to in these pages. There is no attempt to discuss the growth of the Churchill legend in the last years of his life. And the conclusion to the whole work – a mere two pages reminding us that Churchill was a noble spirit and the champion of liberty – is not just banal, it is infuriating. Is this *all* that the author has learned about his subject after so much work over so many years?

There is a further problem. Although Gilbert clearly – and understandably – thinks well of Churchill, his hero does not emerge from this account with his reputation entirely intact. The unappealing figure who walks through the dark side of Manchester's book, and the power-crazed ogre who is at the very centre of Irving's is also recognisable here. His ill-judged election broadcast, likening the Labour Party to 'some form of Gestapo', and the swingeing attack he made on Sir Stafford Cripps in the aftermath of devaluation rightly diminished his reputation for generosity and magnanimity. His treatment of Anthony Eden was sometimes calculatedly cruel, and he continued to bully colleagues and servants with indiscriminate rudeness. His love of the good things of life, and his delight in the lavish hospitality of the rich remained unabated, and his troubled relations with his children did not improve with age. Some of the letters which passed between Winston and Sarah and Winston and Randolph are truly extraordinary in their rage, bitterness, hurt feelings and mutual incomprehension. At the end of it all, we are still left wondering: what was Churchill really like? The harshest indictment of this massive enterprise is that it makes no pretence at answering that crucial question.

For all their differences of approach and methodology, it should by now be clear that these three books actually have a great deal in common. Taken together, they add up to nearly three thousand pages of text, and utilise an enormous range of archival sources. In each case, the labour of the researches has been prodigious, and the effort of writing immense. As such, they bear abundant – indeed suffocating – witness to the strength and vitality of the Churchill industry. But the Churchill who emerges from their pages is recognisably the same split-personality that most of his contemporaries knew him to be. In one guise, he was (these are Manchester's words) 'brilliant', 'intuitive', 'generous', 'visionary' and 'heroic'. But in another, he was (Manchester's adjectives again) 'domineering', 'inconsiderate', 'self-centred', 'emotional', 'ruthless', 'megalomaniacal'. The one Churchillian persona is immortalised in the famous 'angry lion' photograph taken by Karsh of Ottawa in 1942. The other is (or was: the painting was destroyed on Clementine Churchill's instructions) equally well commemorated in Graham Sutherland's controversial and much less flattering eightieth-birthday portrait.

But it is difficult to suppress feelings of wearied disappointment that so many writers have taken so much space to say what ultimately amounts to so little. And it is easy to see why this is so. For all their archival richness, none of these books makes any pretence at weighing or interpreting their sources properly. Manchester writes from the standpoint of Churchill's admirers, Irving from the perspective of his detractors, and Gilbert from the papers of Churchill himself. But in each case, the evidence is partial, biased and incomplete, and needs the most sensitive, scholarly and sophisticated handling – something which it does not get in any of these books. Moreover, archival richness is no compensation for conceptual poverty. There are hardly any *ideas* in these books: Manchester's are naive and out of date, Irving's are wrong-headed and malevolent, and Gilbert's are simply non-existent. But the greatest weakness of these three writers is that they remain overwhelmed and obsessed with the great man himself. Whether Churchillophile or Churchillophobe, they are all incorrigibly Churchillocentric.

Beyond any question, Churchill was a towering figure, whose achievements still loom large on the horizon of history. But these writers are too preoccupied by this magnificent and monumental edifice to get it in the broad and considered historical perspective without which it cannot be properly understood. What did it mean to be an impoverished aristocratic adventurer in the century of the common man? How does the undulating trajectory of Churchill's public life appear when set against the background of twentieth-century British politics as a whole? How did Britain's position as a world and imperial power alter between 1874 and 1965, the years of Churchill's birth and death? And how should we understand the Second World War, not just from the British standpoint, but in the context of global geopolitics? It is questions such as these which must be posed if Churchill's life and work, triumphs and failures, virtues and limitations, good side and bad side are properly to be understood. They are neither asked, nor answered, by these three writers. Churchill's place in history may be secure. But these books make no attempt to tell us precisely what that place is.

As A.J.P. Taylor remarked, Churchill may well have been the saviour of his country during the Second World War. But it is no longer sufficient to write about the whole of his career in deference to or (in Irving's case) in denial of that extraordinary fact. Instead of asking what the rest of his life looks like in the context of 1940, we need to know what 1940 looks like in the context of the rest of his life. And as the twentieth century moves towards its final decade, a clear answer is beginning to emerge: Churchill spent his career in a vain but heroic attempt to deny and defy the fact that Britain was ceasing to be a great power. In his heart of hearts, he could not conceal this from himself: 'I have achieved so much', he observed towards the close of his life, 'to have achieved in the end NOTHING.' But he was remarkably successful at concealing it from the majority of the British people for much of the time. As long as Churchill lived, Britain still seemed to be a great power. But after he died, the illusion could no longer be sustained. It was not just a man who was mourned in January 1965: it was a nation's sense of its past and its purpose and its power. Like the Count-Duke of Olivares in seventeenth-century Spain, Churchill's true historical identity was that he was a statesman in an age of decline. Until we understand that, we shall never fully understand him.

(1989)

NOTES

1 William Manchester, *The Last Lion: Winston Spencer Churchill*, vol. 2: *Alone, 1932–1940* (Boston, 1989).

2 David Irving, *Churchill's War*, vol. 1: *The Struggle for Power* (Bullsbrook, 1989).

3 Martin Gilbert, *Winston S. Churchill*, vol. 8: *'Never Despair', 1945–1965* (London, 1989).

24
John Buchan

John Buchan, the author of *Prester John*, *The Thirty-Nine Steps*, *Green-mantle* and *Mr Standfast* was raised to the British peerage as Lord Tweedsmuir of Elsfield in 1935. He was the first male novelist this century to be thus ennobled, and there have been only two more since: C.P. Snow in 1964, and Jeffrey Archer in 1992. At first glance, they seem an oddly assorted and incongruous trio. When not writing the adventure yarns for which he was most famous in life, and which are still read more than half a century after his death, Buchan was a lawyer, a colonial administrator, a publisher, an historian, a fisherman, a mountaineer, a biographer and a Member of Parliament, and he ended his career with a proconsular flourish as Governor-General of Canada. As well as being a novelist who specialised in stories set in what he called the 'corridors of power', Snow was a Cambridge scientist, a wartime civil servant, a company director, a public commentator and Parliamentary Secretary to the Ministry of Technology in Harold Wilson's first Labour government. And in addition to producing a string of airport book-store blockbusters, Jeffrey Archer has been a physical education instructor, a fund-raiser for good causes, an incorrigible self-publicist, an accident-prone politician, and a deputy chairman of the Conservative Party. All of which suggests that these men had nothing in common except their versatility, their widely read fiction, and their robes and coronets.

Yet despite the undoubted differences in their careers and their writings, they are in some suggestive ways rather similar figures. All three were born a long way from the heights of the British establishment, to the scaling of which they subsequently devoted much effort and energy: Buchan in the house of a Scottish clergyman, Snow in lower middle-class Leicester, and Archer in the unfashionable seaside resort of Weston-super-Mare. They each married above their social station: Buchan a cousin of the fabulously wealthy Duke of Westminster, Snow the daughter of an (admittedly impoverished) colonial administrator, and Archer a middle-class graduate of Cheltenham Ladies' College and St Anne's College, Oxford. Although the three were best known for their novels, none was ennobled for his services to literature: Buchan never claimed his stories were great art; Snow's fiction was often criticised for its leaden prose and two-dimensional characters; and Archer's books are regularly trashed by the reviewers even as they sell in their millions. Yet they all regretted that their public careers, for which they *did* receive their peerages, were not more successful: Buchan neither reached the British Cabinet nor became Viceroy of India; Snow's reputation never recovered from his brief, unhappy spell at the Ministry of Technology; and Archer has yet to be given even minor government office.

These public disappointments were the more galling because all three enjoyed (and rather flaunted) their friendships with the prime ministers of their day – Buchan with Ramsay MacDonald and Stanley Baldwin, Snow with Harold Macmillan and Harold Wilson, and Archer with Margaret Thatcher and John Major. Yet none was taken as seriously as he wanted to be as a man of affairs, and this may explain why failure is such an important subject in the fiction of all three. Buchan explored it at length in his last novel, *Sick-Heart River* (published in the United States as *Mountain Meadow*), in which the hero, Sir Edward Leithen, gives up his languishing political career, heads for the Arctic to rescue a New York banker, and dies in the attempt. Many of Snow's characters achieve less than they might have hoped, such as Paul Jago in academe and Roger Quaife in politics. And Archer's stories are often built around high-stakes struggles for power or money in which there are always losers. But their novels are also peopled with figures who are much more successful in the world than they were themselves: Buchan's adventures are loaded with heroes who are effortlessly superior and self-assured; Snow's characters include brilliant scientists, masterly administrators and consummate politicians; and many of Archer's cardboard creations wield the sort of power in politics and business that he has craved but never attained.

Humble birth and good marriage, worldly ambition and upward social mobility, bestsellerdom and public fame, career success and disappointment: these are the common themes of their three lives. As befits his position as the senior member of this trinity, Buchan has been the most fully (and the most controversially) investigated. In *Clubland Heroes*, published little more than a decade after his death, when his reputation was at its nadir, Buchan was assessed by Richard Usborne in very hostile terms, as no better a novelist than Sapper and Dornford Yates, and as a snob who was, like his mindlessly philistine characters, obsessed with worldly success. Sometime later, in a justly influential essay, Gertrude Himmelfarb argued, less critically, that Buchan should be understood as the 'last Victorian' with a 'Tory imagination', who was in many ways ill at ease in the twentieth century; but she also drew attention to the anti-Semitism which she believed pervaded his novels. Since these early detractors, Buchan has generally received more favourable treatment. In 1965, Janet Adam Smith, whose father had known Buchan well, and who was herself a friend of Buchan's widow, published a sympathetic biography, based on unrestricted access to his papers, which stressed the range and versatility of his life, and largely acquitted him of the charge of anti-Semitism. Most recently, Jonathan Parry has contended that Buchan was a serious political thinker and public moralist, who stressed the importance of religious belief, proper education and responsible leadership if Britain was to function successfully as the mass democracy which it became after the Fourth Reform Act of 1918.

Now Andrew Lownie has set out to retell the Buchan story, concentrating on his private life and public career rather than on his fiction.[1] The basic outlines are well known; but Lownie is much more sensitive to the ups and downs than previous writers have been. Buchan was born in Perth in 1875, which meant he was a near-contemporary of Winston Churchill's – with whom he never really got on. His father was a dreamy, unworldly Presbyterian minister, his mother was more determined, and she was especially ambitious for John, who was her eldest, favourite and most talented son. The family moved to Fife, and then to Glasgow, where Buchan attended Hutcheson's Grammar School and the local university. He was an uncommonly gifted student, and in 1895 he won a scholarship to Brasenose College, Oxford, where he became something of an undergraduate prodigy. He took a First in Greats, was President of the Union, garnered a glittering array of university prizes, published several books of essays, poetry, history and biography, was given his own entry in *Who's Who*, and was widely spoken of as a future prime minister. Few careers can have begun so triumphantly, and when he went down from Oxford in 1899, Buchan must have felt that the world was at his feet. But compared with this brilliant dawn, the remainder of his life was a long anticlimax, as the heady expectations he had aroused in his golden youth, both in himself and in other people, were disappointed and unfulfilled in his more pedestrian maturity.

From the outset, Buchan found London much harder to take by storm than Oxford had been. He was unsure what he should do, tried too many things, and failed to find his feet. He took up the law, but only passed his exams at the second attempt, and was never an important figure at the bar. He dabbled uncertainly in journalism, his early fiction brought him neither the royalties he needed nor the renown he craved, and his biography of Montrose was severely criticised for being too superficial and biased. He went to South Africa as private secretary to Lord Milner, but he barely stayed two years, acquired a mandarin outlook which would later make him ill-suited to the rough and tumble of partisan politics, and was disappointed in his efforts to obtain a job on Lord Cromer's staff in Egypt. His mother disapproved of his marriage in 1907 to Susan Grosvenor, because she was aristocratic and Anglican, and his father died in 1911, followed one year later by his younger brother William. These family troubles, Lownie perceptively suggests, and the resulting pressure on Buchan to make money and prove himself, may have brought on the duodenal ulcer which was to plague him for the remainder of his life, with serious consequences for his public career. He had already failed to find a seat to contest in the two general elections of 1910, and thereafter, his political ambitions were repeatedly thwarted on account of his suspect health.

But in 1914, having stalled for more than a decade, Buchan's career suddenly moved into higher gear. While convalescing from another bout of illness, he wrote a thriller entitled *The Thirty-Nine Steps*. The book was an instant success, sold twenty-five thousand copies within three months of publication, and became the first of a series of daring adventure stories that were to make his name and fortune, in which clean-living patriots like Richard Hannay and Archie Roylance battled with sinister (and often foreign) villains, and averted the collapse of civilisation in the nick of time. Buchan's second stroke of luck that year was that war broke out. He volunteered, but was declared unfit for active service, which meant that unlike such gilded contemporaries as Raymond Asquith and Lord Basil Blackwood, and his younger brother Alistair, who was killed in 1917, he actually *survived*. He was given a succession of desk jobs in London and in France, was actively involved in publicity and propaganda, and eventually became Director of Information. He also wrote regular reports for *The Times* and the *Daily News*, and between 1915 and 1922 produced *The Nelson History of the War*, initially published in twenty-four parts, and subsequently reissued in four volumes. As a result, Buchan became a household name in official circles and among the general public. But he was often unwell, failed to gain any honours for his work (although Lownie shows how hard he lobbied on his own behalf), and when hostilities ceased, his health collapsed again. Once more, he had to put aside his political ambitions, he did not stand at the 1918 general election, and his career still lacked momentum and direction.

Disillusioned with the intrigue and ingratitude of public service, Buchan left London, and in 1919 set himself up as an English country gentleman, buying Elsfield Manor near Oxford. His books were now bringing him a substantial income, especially from adventure stories like *Huntingtower*, *The Three Hostages* and *The Dancing Floor*, in which he repeated and developed the formula pioneered in *The Thirty-Nine Steps*. But he was also writing biographies, essays and histories, and he was by this time a director of Nelson's the publishers, and deputy chairman of Reuters the news agency. He still hankered after a political career, and in 1927 his health seemed sufficiently restored for him to be elected Conservative MP for the Scottish Universities, an anomalously appropriate constituency, consisting only of alumni, which required minimal work from its representative. Five years later, he was appointed Lord High Commissioner to the General Assembly of the Church of Scotland – a ceremonial position carrying no real power. In 1935, he accepted another largely ornamental office, the governor-generalship of Canada. As Lord Tweedsmuir, he toured the dominion, wore a plumed hat, made speeches, shook hands, cut ribbons and was generally deemed to have done well in representing the crown in Canada. But he really wanted to be British Ambassador in Washington, his health continued to deteriorate, his literary earnings dropped sharply, and he felt cut off from events and people in Britain. It was in this depressed and disappointed mood that he completed *Sick-Heart River* and his autobiography, *Memory Hold-the-Door* (published in the United States as *Pilgrims Way*). By early 1940, he was ready to go home. But while preparing to depart, he died in office in February that year.

Buchan was scarcely sixty-five: what would have happened had he lived another decade or two? Lownie does not discuss this, but it is a tempting and instructive speculation. He would have been neither well enough nor weighty enough to have followed his predecessors, Lords Lansdowne, Minto and Willingdon, from the governor-generalship of Canada to the Indian viceroyalty. He would have returned in September 1940 to a war-torn Britain, governed and galvanised by Churchill, and since their antipathy was mutual, it seems unlikely that further preferment would have come his way – least of all the Washington embassy. At best, Buchan would have been fobbed off with a promotion in the peerage and perhaps the Order of the Thistle, and he would have gone back to his writing and his novels: finery, fiction and frustration once again. It is equally difficult to imagine him living easily or selling well in the postwar world of Attlee's government, Indian independence and the welfare state. The future belonged, not to the old men in clubs, but to the 'new men' (another of C.P. Snow's phrases) in scientific laboratories and government departments. Still less would Buchan have approved of Ian Fleming's reinvention of the thriller in his James Bond novels, which concealed their substantial indebtedness to him by incorporating such un-Buchanesque subjects as sex and violence, unabashed materialism, excessively good living and national decline.

But while Fleming's fiction is now out of fashion, and his life has recently been revealed as having been bleak and bitter, Buchan's reputation is steadily on the rise, and Lownie is eager to contribute to that process of rehabilitation. How far does he succeed in this endeavour? Beyond any doubt, he makes Buchan a more complex and plausible figure than previous writers have depicted. His mind was cultivated and well stocked, and he regarded his public work as much more important than the fiction for which he became best known. Like many an ambitious Scot since the Act of Union with England in 1707, Buchan took the road south, and went out to the Empire, in search of fame and fortune. For someone from his relatively humble background, he achieved both in ample measure. But unlike many of the heroes in his novels, he had to work very hard for his successes, and it is plain from his letters that by the 1920s, he had rather lost his way. Indeed, it is not clear from this biography that Buchan ever satisfactorily worked out who he really was, and Lownie rightly stresses his elusive, chameleon-like capacity for blending in with his surroundings, and his inability to make up his mind whether he was Scottish or English, Glasgow or Oxford, Presbyterian or Anglican, outsider or insider, realist or romantic, progressive or conservative, a man of action or a man of thought, a teller of tall stories or a writer of serious books. Paradoxical though it may seem, he was too versatile and adaptable for his own good – or for his own career.

It also emerges that Buchan's family life was less settled and serene than was previously supposed. His relations with his widowed mother were very close yet also very difficult: she was ambitious for him and dependent on him; he was eager to get away from her narrow-minded views and constant interference, but he knew that was impossible. By the interwar years, she was becoming increasingly irritated at her son's lack of worldly progress and public recognition, which can hardly have been a comfort or help to him. When given his peerage in 1935, he revealingly remarked that it 'may revive mother', and for a time, it did. Notwithstanding the advantages and connections it brought, Lownie also hints at problems in Buchan's marriage: his wife was prone to depression, she had no enthusiasm for the Canadian governor-generalship, she spent much of her time there in bed, and she was disliked by her staff. Buchan was also a distant and domineering father, with predictable results: his daughter rushed into an unhappy marriage; one son went out to Uganda and took to drink; another was sent down from New College, Oxford; the third is quoted inveighing against his father's 'cantankerousness', 'filthy eating' and 'eternal boasting'. Only after his death did his children enjoy the space they needed to develop their own lives and talents and identities, especially William, who became a writer and publisher, and Alistair who was an expert on international relations and an Oxford academic.

What, then, of the public career by which Buchan set so much store? Lownie is surely correct in arguing that it was a success – but not as successful as he (and many others) had hoped and expected. It is easy to see why. Buchan may have believed in the British Empire, and that he had an important part to play in its future: but for a man of his generation, he knew very little of it at first-hand, either as a traveller or as an administrator, and did not visit India, the Antipodes, or Africa north of the Zambezi. That someone of such limited experience should have cherished the belief that he might be Viceroy of India was little short of absurd. His ambitions in British politics were no more realistic. To be sure, many people at Westminster and in Whitehall genuinely seem to have liked and admired him. Yet this did not mean they took him seriously as one of themselves. He may have cheered up MacDonald and Baldwin, drafted speeches for them, and passed on gossip, but they were not prepared to do anything beyond offering him the Lord High Commissionership to the General Assembly of the Church of Scotland. Indeed, when the proconsular Canadian job finally came up, it was at the initiative of the dominion Prime Minister, Mackenzie King, rather than at the suggestion of the British government. Yet Canada was no place for anyone with driving ambitions in British politics. Buchan may have ended his life festooned with honours and caparisoned with grand-sounding offices: but this was not the real thing, not what Oxford had seemed to promise, and in his heart of hearts he knew it.

Although Buchan, like Snow and Archer, wrote with such apparent knowingness about public affairs and men of the world in his fiction, the reality was that he had little grasp of party or Parliament or power. As an MP, he never mastered the House of Commons, was often absent on business or because of recurrent ill-health, and having been elected at the relatively advanced age of fifty-one, he was too old for a junior position but insufficiently experienced for anything more senior. Yet although he was later to deny it in his autobiography, Buchan (to say nothing of his mother) was anxiously and ardently ambitious for cabinet rank (perhaps as Secretary of State for Scotland, or President of the Board of Education) and Lownie quotes some embarrassing letters in which he begged and importuned for office, while affecting to deny that he was actually doing so. Indeed, on several occasions, Buchan seems to have thought that preferment was about to come his way. But this was quite unrealistic. Even in the era of National Governments, he was neither partisan enough nor tough enough to demand or deserve a place. Instead, he was placated with ceremonial and ornamental positions, which further reinforced the view that he was a lightweight, marginal figure, scribbling his stories on the edge of events.

The great irony of Buchan's life (and one which he would certainly not have appreciated) is that he wanted to be recognised and remembered as a man of affairs who wrote novels in his spare time, whereas in fact he was recognised and remembered as a novelist who was a man of affairs in his spare time. To be sure, it was important to him that he wrote on average a thriller a year between 1920 and 1935: but this was primarily to finance his life as an Oxfordshire country gentleman, and to pay his sons' school fees. Buchan never expected these pot-boilers to be critical successes, which was just as well, since they rarely were. But they were great popular successes, selling in their thousands during the interwar years. Why? Lownie is not particularly interested in addressing this question, but he provides some useful clues along the way. When Buchan wrote *The Thirty-Nine Steps*, stories dealing with spies, espionage, great-power rivalries and world-wide conspiracies had already been pioneered and popularised by such writers as William Le Queux, Erskine Childers and Conan Doyle in the era of growing international tensions and 'invasion scares' before 1914. During the First World War and on into the 1920s and 1930s, the public appetite for such thrillers increased still further, as thrones and dynasties tumbled in Europe, irregular warriors like Aubrey Herbert and T.E. Lawrence emerged as national heroes, the Bolshevik 'menace' emanating from Moscow seemed ever more sinister and subversive (as with the 'Zinoviev letter' of 1924), and even the British Empire itself was challenged by the emerging nationalist movements in Ireland, Egypt and India.

Although Buchan was never a spy, his wartime work meant that he knew enough about secret operations and international intrigue to turn out fictional accounts which were simultaneously preposterous yet plausible – and thus exceptionally appealing. They were preposterous because the heroes and villains were at best two-dimensional, and the stories depended excessively on improbable coincidence. But they were plausible because they were set in a seemingly recognisable world of constant danger and uncertainty, because the heroes appeared to resemble the sort of men who had enabled Britain to win the First World War, and because – as befitted an admirer of Sir Walter Scott and Robert Louis Stevenson – Buchan evoked so vividly the landscapes where their adventures took place, whether in the Scottish Highlands, the Greek islands, Latin America, the Near East or Canada. Buchan called these books 'shockers', to distinguish them from his serious writings: but their real attraction was that they were nothing of the sort. They were essentially juvenile fantasies, artfully embellished for adults, which comforted rather than jolted: virtue wins out over evil in the end, the subversive conspiracies (usually of Jewish financiers or anarchists) are thwarted, those who live a healthy, open-air life vanquish effete, town-bred intellectuals or rootless plutocrats, and the natural order of things is safely and successfully reasserted. Thus described, his novels were indeed the products of a 'Tory imagination', and it can hardly be coincidence that the interwar years of Buchan's bestsellerdom coincided with a virtually unbroken period of Conservative dominance in British government and Parliament.

But as befits the 'last Victorian' he in some senses was, Buchan also needs to be understood in a nineteenth-century context. For while he might have been the prototypical novelist-notable of the twentieth century, there had been earlier precedents, most famously exemplified in the person and peerage of Benjamin Disraeli. The comparison between these two is instructive. Like Buchan, Disraeli was an outsider, who married well and wanted to be a figure in the world; and he was no more made

Earl of Beaconsfield because he had written *Sybil* than Buchan was made Lord Tweedsmuir on account of *Greenmantle*. But unlike Buchan, politics was the consuming passion of Disraeli's life, and in his climb to the top of the greasy pole, he deployed a formidable combination of opportunism, artistry and determination which Buchan could neither command nor comprehend. Buchan's strengths were that he was a good man with a good mind; that he was hard-working, self-made, kind-hearted and uncomplaining; that he was uncommonly talented and versatile; and that his novels were (and still are) compelling page-turners. His weaknesses were that he never fulfilled his early Oxford promise, that he was insufficiently single-minded, and that he was out of his depth in the political world. Like Snow and Archer, Buchan wanted to be at the centre of things. His books and his baubles gave the impression that he was. But in reality he was almost always somewhere else.

(1988)

NOTE

1 Andrew Lownie, *John Buchan: The Presbyterian Cavalier* (London, 1995).

25
Lord Beaverbrook

William Maxwell Aitken, first Baron Beaverbrook, wielded a considerable influence on the affairs of Britain and its empire for more than fifty years – an influence which was invariably vigorous, but only intermittently benevolent. He was a self-made millionaire from Canada, with a remarkable flair for business and finance. He became the chief proprietor of Express Newspapers, and thus one of the foremost English press barons of his time. He was a buccaneering politician, who shared with Winston Churchill the unique distinction of having been a member of *both* British War Cabinets. He was a successful, if self-serving, contemporary historian, whose books give a graphic picture of the great events with which he was involved. And the range of his friendships was extraordinarily wide, including Lloyd George and Rudyard Kipling, Aneurin Bevan and Lady Edwina Mountbatten, Brendan Bracken and the Duke of Windsor. Although himself a diminutive figure, he was an outsized personality, who might have stepped out of the pages of a twentieth-century novel. Indeed, such was Beaverbrook's fame, fortune and fascination that on several occasions he did precisely that – as Arnold Bennett's Lord Raingo, as Rebecca West's Francis Pitt, as H.G. Wells's Mr Parham, as William Gerhardie's Lord Ottercove, and as Evelyn Waugh's Lord Copper.

For a man whose long and eventful life regularly blurred the boundaries between fact and fantasy, whose temperament was cross-grained and contradictory to a remarkable degree, and whose reputation was deservedly suspect and controversial, these fictional accounts provided appropriate and revealing portraits. At different times, and by different people, Beaverbrook was loved, admired, envied, feared, despised and hated. In one guise, he was a sincere patriot, generous benefactor, staunch ally and foul-weather friend. In another, he was a scheming monster, incorrigible mischief-maker, vindictive bully and disloyal opportunist. He was a son of the manse, who feared God and feared death; yet he was widely regarded as one of the most sinister and unscrupulous figures of his time. He was a colonial outsider, but stormed every citadel of British establishment exclusiveness – in finance, politics and society. Winston Churchill regarded him as 'one of my oldest and most intimate friends'; but his wife, Clementine, detested and distrusted Beaverbrook as a 'microbe', a 'bottle imp'. Lady Diana Cooper thought him a 'strange attractive gnome, with an odour of genius about him'; yet Clement Attlee remembered him as 'the only evil man I ever met'.

In life, and in death, Beaverbrook has inevitably attracted his share of biographical attention. The first noteworthy effort was by Tom Driberg, a maverick journalist and Labour MP, who enjoyed a typical love-hate relationship with Beaverbrook, and whose biography, *A Study in Power and Frustration*, was published in 1956. As a former client who had become a critic, he was well placed, and well equipped, to present a 'warts and all' portrait. But Beaverbrook exercised so much control over the final product that it was disappointingly bland, and the promise held out in the perceptive title was never redeemed in the text. The second attempt, begun soon after Beaverbrook's death in 1964, and based on an extensive examination of his voluminous papers, was by A.J.P. Taylor, an historian rightly renowned for his coruscating wit and deflating irreverence. But he admitted that he had loved Beaverbrook 'more than any human being I have ever known', and the resulting book, though predictably readable and entertaining, was too discreetly deferential towards its subject. It failed to deal with Beaverbrook's eventful private life, it did not take seriously the widely held view that he was an evil man, and it made no effort to set him in a broader historical context.

Twenty years further on, Anne Chisholm and Michael Davie have made another attempt to retell this twice-told tale.[1] They have worked their way systematically through the Beaverbrook papers, including some files that Taylor ignored, and have interviewed many of the people who had dealings with him. They have benefited from the vast outpouring of biographical and scholarly work on twentieth-century British history during the last two decades. And thanks to a visit which Davie paid to Beaverbrook in the late 1950s, they have had the advantage of acquaintance with their subject, while never having fallen under his spell – or his curse. The result is a biography which, for the first time, provides a rounded and credible portrait – of the man, the financier, the newspaper tycoon, the cabinet minister, and the collector (and manipulator) of the famous and the beautiful. The rich and fanciful veneer of self-aggrandising mythology has been painstakingly scraped away, many of the tracks which he so often covered so carefully have been found and followed, and Beaverbrook stands revealed in most, if not quite all, his irresistible, infuriating and irresponsible complexity.

Aitken (who was always known as 'Max' to his friends) was born in New Brunswick in 1879, the third son of a Scots-Presbyterian minister, in circumstances more modestly comfortable than in later life he was inclined to claim. He did not do well at school, and failed to get into university, but early on discovered that he possessed two unusual and complementary talents: for making money – and for making mischief. He began to sell bonds and insurance, and established himself as a company promoter and broker of mergers and combines. He acquired business interests in the West Indies, became a force on the Montreal stock exchange, and was a dollar millionaire by 1907. Two years later, he formed the Canada Cement Company, by merging several other businesses, and in the process made himself another fortune. But his methods were widely regarded as unethical and unscrupulous, and he acquired an unsavoury reputation in upperclass circles in Canada (and Britain) which lasted for the rest of his life. In 1906, he had married Gladys Henderson, the daughter of a senior Canadian soldier, who became a beautiful, dignified and long-suffering wife. She bore him three children, tolerated his many infidelities, and when she died in 1927 he seems to have been genuinely – if only briefly – guilt-ridden.

In 1910, the Aitkens moved to England – partly to escape the reverberations of the Canada Cement affair, and partly because his imperialist sentiments inevitably impelled him towards London, then the undisputed 'world city'. He soon became friends with another New Brunswick-born Canadian, Andrew Bonar Law, himself a coming man in the Conservative Party, and this important connection facilitated Aitken's entry into British politics. Within a year of his arrival in Britain, he had become a Tory MP and obtained a knighthood, in 1916 he became a baronet, and soon after he was made a peer. This astonishing accumulation of honours – which was much frowned upon in royal and aristocratic circles – was a tribute to his backstairs influence rather than to his public achievements. In 1911, he played a part in propelling Bonar Law to the leadership of the Conservative Party. In 1916, he helped bring down Asquith and install David Lloyd George as wartime leader, later serving in his Cabinet as Minister of Information. And in 1922, he saw his dreams and schemes fulfilled when the Lloyd George coalition fell, and Bonar Law became Conservative Prime Minister. But within two years, Law was dead, and Beaverbrook's longest period of behind-the-scenes influence was effectively over.

By then, he was already set on his third and fourth careers, as a journalist and contemporary chronicler. Between 1916 and 1923, he acquired the *Daily Express*, launched the *Sunday Express*, and took over the *Evening Standard*. He soon established himself as an astonishingly successful newspaper proprietor, dominating his editors and his staff, and rapidly increasing sales and circulation. Between 1928 and 1932, he published *Politicians and the War*, a two-volume account of the fall of Asquith and the rise of Lloyd George, written with characteristic verve and brio, which magnified his own part in the proceedings, and was far from even-handed in its treatment of men and events. But though no longer an insider, Beaverbrook still craved political excitement, and thanks to his newspaper, was able to make considerable mischief, especially during the 1930s. He campaigned for 'Empire Free Trade', and tried – unsuccessfully – to bring down Stanley Baldwin, the Conservative leader. At the time of the abdication, he championed King Edward VIII and Mrs Simpson – once more unsuccessfully. He advocated appeasement, supported Neville Chamberlain, dismissed Churchill as a 'busted flush', had at least one cabinet minister on his payroll, and at the same time patronised left-wing figures like Aneurin Bevan and Michael Foot.

Yet when Churchill came to power in May 1940, he immediately made Beaverbrook Minister of Aircraft Production, entrusting him with the perilous task of supplying the fighters without which the Battle of Britain could not have been fought – and won. Once again, Beaverbrook was at the centre of events, and for a year he was energetically engaged in the war effort. He was ruthless, piratical and indomitable in commandeering men and materials, and his handling of the new ministry was as tempestuous as it was triumphant. Although Beaverbrook and Churchill had had their differences during the 1930s, they were old friends, and 'Max' soon established himself as a member of the Prime Minister's inner circle, comforting and cheering him in the darkest of days. But once the immediate crisis of survival was past, the temptation to make trouble again proved irresistible. He campaigned vociferously for a second front in Europe long before it was a realistic possibility. In the early months of 1942, when disaster was piled on disaster in the Far East and North Africa, he even imagined that he might supplant Churchill as prime minister. And in the general election of 1945, his intransigent attitude towards the Labour Party was seen as a major contribution to the Tories' landslide defeat.

Inevitably, the last twenty years of Beaverbrook's life were something of an anticlimax. He hated the Labour government of Clement Attlee, was never again invited to hold office by the Conservatives, was out of sympathy with the welfare state, and regretted the decline of Britain and its subordination to the United States. His newspapers, though they still sold well, no longer wielded the influence that they were once thought to have had, and his last campaign, against Britain's entry into the Common Market, was ill-judged and ultimately ineffectual. He spent most of his time abroad, in the south of France, the West Indies, the United States and Canada. He was a generous, but predictably demanding, benefactor to the University of New Brunswick. He comforted and entertained Churchill during his declining years. He commissioned biographies of Lloyd George and Bonar Law, which were written out of materials he had collected and controlled. He himself published *Men and Power* and *The Decline and Fall of Lloyd George*. Not long before he died, he married for the second time, and made a memorable valedictory speech at a dinner for his eighty-fifth birthday. He had arranged his affairs so that virtually no death duties were paid on his enormous fortune; he had his ashes interred in Beaverbrook Town Square, Newcastle, New Brunswick; and he vanished from the scene as mysteriously and as ingeniously as he had first come upon it.

Although the outlines of Beaverbrook's extraordinary career have long been well known, Chisholm and Davie provide much new information. They stress the importance of his New Brunswick background in forming his imperialist views. They recount his Canadian business ventures with candour and skill: Beaverbrook clearly sailed far closer to the wind than A.J.P. Taylor was ever prepared to admit. They demonstrate how, in his later histories, he magnified the part he had played in the events of 1911–23. They analyse the methods he used to control his newspapers and to boost their circulations, and show how cavalier he could be with the truth when it suited him. They provide ample evidence of his erratic irresponsibility during the 1930s, when he seems to have taken up causes and individuals, and then dropped them, just for the hell of it. They note how tiresome a colleague he must have been in government between 1941 and 1945, scheming, plotting, intriguing and constantly threatening to resign. And they provide an unforgettable picture of Beaverbrook in old age: as a thwarted and frustrated power broker, who was no longer able to play the influential mischief-maker that he had been in his prime.

But it is in their account of Beaverbrook's private life, and in their evocation of his remarkable personality, that the authors make their most original contribution. They show how difficult – and mutually uncomprehending – his relationships almost invariably were with his parents, his siblings and his children. They admit that the full list of the women with whom he was involved will never be known. But it certainly included Venetia Montagu, Rebecca West, Barbara Cartland, Harriet Cohen, Gwen Ffrangcon Davies and Jean Norton. He treated some well, others abominably, and most somewhere in-between. They note how fascinated he was by gossip, how good he was at exploiting people's weaknesses, and how he alternated between flattery and terrorism in manipulating his friends and his enemies. Above all, they insist that he was fundamentally a lonely man, with a low sense of his own self-worth, who was incapable of forming a stable, loving relationship with anyone. He could charm or he could bully; he could give or he could take; he was glad to see his guests arrive and pleased to see them go: but that was the limit of his social and personal repertoire. Although many people genuinely loved him, he was incapable of believing that this was either possible or true. No wonder he was so restless, so impatient, so vindictive, so quick to lose his temper, so eager to stir things up.

Where this biography is less successful is in placing Beaverbrook's life in the broader context of his times. How significant a figure was he? How much influence did he wield? The authors provide much information, but draw no conclusions. To many contemporaries, he was a malign and unscrupulous operator, combining backstairs intrigue with the propaganda power of his papers, who made and unmade ministries, careers and reputations. But while he interfered a great deal, it is less clear how radically different things would have been if he had not done so. The political convulsions of 1911, 1916 and 1922 would in all probability have taken the course they did, whether Beaverbrook had played a part or not. He failed to carry Empire Free Trade, failed to keep Edward VIII on the throne, and his reputation never really recovered from Stanley Baldwin's memorable retort, that by trying to dictate government policy from Fleet Street, he was seeking 'power without responsibility – the prerogative of the harlot throughout the ages'. And even 'his hour' as Minister of Aircraft Production has recently come under renewed scholarly scrutiny, which suggests that the greatest jump in fighter output occurred *before* Beaverbrook himself took over. Throughout his career, the Max factor was never as substantial or as significant as he himself liked to think.

The most helpful way of seeing Beaverbrook is as a product – though obviously not a typical one – of his late nineteeth-century imperial milieu. Born in a Canadian maritime province, he looked to London more than he looked to Montreal or to New York. His first great hero was the British Colonial Secretary, Joseph Chamberlain, and all his life he believed in some form of close imperial union. Having made his money and his reputation in Canada, he naturally gravitated to Britain, as any successful child of Empire did at that time, in search of greater adventures and opportunities. Yet despite his delight in taking London by storm, he always remained an outsider – suspicious of royalty, scornful of the traditional governing classes, hostile to humbug and 'high-born voices', and proud of his self-made status. He never really understood that the British cared much less about their empire than he did. And in later life, he never ceased to regret its passing, even as he was powerless to do anything to prevent it. Like most old men, he had long since outlived his day and generation. But Father Time was someone whom even William Maxwell Aitken, first Baron Beaverbrook, could not buy, control or manipulate.

(1993)

NOTE

1 Anne Chisholm and Michael Davie, *Lord Beaverbrook: A Life* (London, 1993).

26
Harold Macmillan

Harold Macmillan was Prime Minister of the United Kingdom from 1957 to 1963, and died in 1986 at the age of ninety-two. But his contemporaries were never exactly sure who he really was. To his critics, he was little more than a second-rate actor, implausibly and cynically posturing in a variety of superficial and contradictory parts – crofter's grandson, middle-class publisher, ducal son-in-law, vulgar showman, world leader, stag at bay, elder statesman and poor man's Churchill. Not for nothing was Anthony Sampson's interim biography acutely subtitled *A Study in Ambiguity*. But to his admirers, he was a rich man's Disraeli, a virtuoso performer, who was brilliantly gifted in the arts of political management and party leadership, who recognised the essential importance of gesture and theatricality in playing (and winning) the great game, and who was a past (and present) master at saying one thing while resolutely and effectively doing something completely different. In appearing to be an actor, he was only *pretending* to pretend, and the fact that his critics never noticed this merely demonstrated how completely – and how successfully – they had been beguiled and deceived.

To the end of his very long life, Macmillan's reputation remained as protean as his personality was enigmatic. When he became prime minister of England in the aftermath of the Suez fiasco and Anthony Eden's abrupt resignation, it was widely believed that his administration would last only a matter of weeks. In fact, it became one of the strongest and stablest peacetime governments in twentieth-century Britain, and most of the credit for this belonged to Macmillan himself. He restored the shattered morale of the Conservatives, and led them to a triumphant victory at the 1959 general election. He re-established the Anglo-American 'special relationship' with Eisenhower, paid much-publicised visits to Russia and South Africa, began to dismantle what remained of the British Empire, and played a major part in the negotiation of the Nuclear Test Ban Treaty. And he presided over an unprecedented period of domestic prosperity and affluent consumerism, memorably associated with his famous – if usually misquoted – remark: 'You've never had it so good.'

But halfway through his premiership, it seemed as if 'Supermac' lost his touch, and his final years in office were bedevilled by a series of misjudgements and misfortunes. The economy became overheated, incomes were rising too rapidly, there were recurrent balance of payments crises, and inflation threatened to get out of control. His prestige and authority were gravely weakened when his attempts to get Britain into the Common Market were brutally vetoed by General de Gaulle, and the sordid sensationalism of the Profumo scandal, combined with growing anxieties about national security, further undermined the government's credibility. In the brave new world of John F. Kennedy and Harold Wilson, Macmillan seemed an anachronistic, almost ridiculous figure, out of date and out of touch. In a desperate attempt to re-establish his position, he dismissed seven of his ministers in the 'night of the long knives' of September 1962. But instead of recovering the political initiative, it mortally damaged his much-prized reputation for unflappability. Eventually, ill-health obliged Macmillan to resign the premiership in the autumn of 1963, and his personally chosen successor, Sir Alex Douglas-Home (who was even more of an anachronism than Macmillan himself), led a dismayed and demoralised party to defeat in the general election of 1964.

Yet during his astonishingly long retirement, which lasted twenty-three years, Macmillan almost completely rebuilt his shattered reputation. He produced six volumes of memoirs, which are required reading for any student of recent political history. In the unheroic, unromantic, unstylish years of Edward Heath, Harold Wilson and James Callaghan, his occasional interviews on television, and his public appearances as Chancellor of Oxford University were widely acclaimed as masterly displays of venerable sagacity, sophisticated wit and Edwardian panache. At the age of ninety, he finally accepted a peerage, and returned to Westminster as Earl of Stockton. Sixty years after he had first entered the Commons, he delivered his maiden speech in the upper house – an oration so eloquent, so moving and so generous that only Churchill in his prime could have surpassed it. With that perfect sense of timing for which he had rightly become renowned, the man who in old age was affectionately and admiringly known as 'the old entertainer' had judged his final curtain call to perfection.

But even during these long, mellow, sunset years, Macmillan's detractors were never completely silenced. His multivolume memoirs were widely criticised for being disappointingly prolix and impersonally dull – a self-indulgent exercise in self-serving self-concealment. Sir Anthony Eden never forgave him for his alleged betrayal at the time of Suez, and nor did R.A. Butler for the way in which Macmillan had denied him the prime ministership, not only in 1957, but again in 1963. Towards the very end of his life, it was further alleged that he had callously and deceitfully sanctioned the forced repatriation of thousands of Cossack exiles to Soviet Russia (and thus to certain death) in 1945. And his survival into the 1980s meant that Macmillan was no longer revered as the Grand Old Man of the Conservative Party, but was increasingly dismissed as the discredited embodiment of consensus politics, welfare state idealism and irresponsible government spending – in short of that undoctrinaire middle way which is anathema to Mrs Thatcher's newer and more successful brand of Toryism.

As a publisher no less than as a politician, Macmillan was well aware that the full story of his remarkable life would one day make fascinating reading, and in 1979 he appointed Alistair Horne – himself a Macmillan author – to be his official biographer.[1] On condition that nothing should be published until after his death, Macmillan not only made his entire archive freely available, but also allowed Horne to record his personal impressions in a series of private conversations and probing interviews. The result is an outstanding biography, which combines the authoritative scholarship of detailed research with an unusually intimate and candid knowledge of its subject, and which brilliantly reconciles the apparent contradictions in Macmillan's temperament, career and reputation. This first volume describes his life up to the point at which he became prime minister: as such, it is not the familiar saga of 'Supermac', but the less well-known and much more surprising story of 'Protomac'. For despite the triumphant ending, it is overwhelmingly a study in rejection and disappointment.

Beyond any doubt, Macmillan's early years were unhappy, unpromising and unsuccessful. He was born in 1894, when Queen Victoria still had seven years to reign. His father was a worthy, but rather dull publisher, who was a partner in the family firm. His mother was an ambitious and domineering American from the Mid West. His home life was lonely and joyless, and he was overshadowed by his more brilliant elder brother. He grew up to be physically unprepossessing, excessively shy, subject to fits of depression, and with an excitable, emotional temperament. He dropped out of Eton for reasons which are still not entirely clear, and experienced a major personal crisis when he nearly embraced the Roman Catholic faith. Even at Balliol College, Oxford, where he began to excel in his under-graduate studies, he remained a lonely and unglamorous outsider, who was especially ill at ease in the company of women. His university career was cut short by the First World War, in which he served gallantly in the Grenadiers. But he was wounded three times, did not fully recover for several years, and was left with a shuffling walk and a limp handshake – severe disadvantages for any man who contemplated a career in public life.

Nevertheless, in the aftermath of war, it seemed as if his luck suddenly changed. He joined the family firm, and became a successful and pros-perous publisher. In 1920, he married Lady Dorothy Cavendish, daugh-ter of the ninth Duke of Devonshire, which brought him into intimate contact with one of the greatest political families in the land. Four years later, he was elected as MP for Stockton-on-Tees, and it seemed as if the public life of which his mother had always dreamed was now open to him. But during the next fifteen years, Macmillan made no progress whatso-ever. His wife fell deeply and abidingly in love with the flamboyant Tory adventurer Robert Boothby, and although she remained publicly loyal to her husband and his career, Macmillan was left hurt, rejected, humiliated and lonelier than ever. The Stockton constituency was highly marginal, he was never socially at ease with individual working men and women, and he was out of Parliament between 1929 and 1931. The Cavendishes looked down on him as being middle class, in trade, a publisher's boy; and in the Commons his performances were considered priggish, pompous, boring and dull. In the early 1930s, he seems to have suffered a near-complete nervous breakdown, and it was only his mother's unwavering support which enabled him to survive.

In career terms, Macmillan compounded these personal difficulties by espousing unfashionable and unpopular political opinions. His first-hand experience of interwar unemployment and working-class poverty in Stock-ton moved him deeply (perhaps too deeply?), and he was well acquainted with the writings of John Maynard Keynes, for whom Macmillans acted as publishers. This led him to reject the laissez-faire (and thus deflation-ary) economics of Ramsay MacDonald and Stanley Baldwin, and to urge instead the need for positive government intervention, through state plan-ning, deficit budget financing and a modest degree of public ownership. His arguments were developed most fully in his book *The Middle Way*, published in 1938: but it was a turgid and long-winded volume, which made almost no impact – except to confirm the widespread belief that Macmillan was a maverick, left-of-centre eccentric. At the same time, he also denounced the government's policy of appeasement, supporting Churchill in his advocacy of armed resistance to Hitler, and in his opposition to the Munich settlement. By the late 1930s, Macmillan was regularly voting against his own leadership, and for a time he actually resigned the Tory Party whip. His political career seemed to be no more successful than his marriage, and the outbreak of war brought with it no prospect of preferment or promotion.

Even when Churchill came to power in 1940, Macmillan's reward was decidedly meagre. For two years, he held very junior appointments at the Ministry of Supply and at the Colonial Office. Then in 1942, he was offered the job of Minister Resident in North Africa. It meant exile from Westminster, two more eligible candidates had already refused to go, and Macmillan himself did not immediately appreciate the proconsular potential of the position. But he accepted it, and during the next three years showed unexpected reserves of tactfulness and toughness in dealing with a wide range of problems and personalities. He resolved the internecine struggles between de Gaulle and Giraud for the leadership of the Free French. He won Eisenhower's confidence, and persuaded the Americans to pursue essentially British strategic objectives. In handling the occupation of Italy and Greece, he showed political judgement and administrative ability of a very high order, and he seems to have borne no special blame for the repatriation of the White Russians in the aftermath of the Yalta agreement. By the end of the war, he was truly the undisputed Viceroy of the Mediterranean, and he had won golden opinions from Churchill himself.

Yet even with this undoubted success behind him, he remained a peripheral figure at Westminster and in Whitehall, and his political career had still not yet acquired the necessary momentum. In the 1945 election, he was defeated at Stockton, and although he soon re-entered the Commons, his six years in opposition were dispiriting and unrewarding. He took up the cause of European unity, and played a prominent part in refashioning Tory economic and social policies for the new era of the welfare state. But his parliamentary performances remained unimpressive, and his private life continued lonely and unhappy. When the Conservatives returned to power in 1951, Macmillan was deeply disappointed to be fobbed off with what seemed the insignificant Ministry of Housing. Yet in redeeming the Tory's pledge to build 300,000 homes a year, he became for the first time a national figure and revealed qualities of determination and showmanship which many had hitherto never suspected. But then his career was halted again. For his apparent promotion to be Minister of Defence was nothing of the kind, since Churchill wished to run the department himself. Not surprisingly, by 1955, Macmillan had become the active leader of those ministers who were pressing the visibly ageing Prime Minister to retire.

When Churchill finally departed, and Eden succeeded him, Macmillan became Foreign Secretary, and regarded this as the climax of his career: five years in office, and he could himself retire to his books and his publishing. With Eisenhower installed in the White House, his main concern was to strengthen the special relationship, and he was noticeably less enthusiastic about the cause of European unity than he had been in opposition. But he was too assertive a minister for Eden's liking, and after only eight months, he was abruptly switched to be Chancellor of the Exchequer – a move for which Macmillan never forgave him. His first (and only) Budget was made memorable by his introduction of Premium Savings Bonds – a characteristically daring and slightly vulgar innovation. But even by the middle of 1956, his prime ministerial prospects had hardly improved. He had occupied two senior positions in quick succession – with the result that he had made his mark in neither of them. Above all, Eden himself was two years younger than Macmillan, while R.A. Butler, the generally recognised heir apparent, was a full six years his junior.

Then, in the autumn of 1956, came the Suez crisis, in which Macmillan's part was so maladroit, inglorious and inconsistent that he deserved to have been destroyed by it. Despite (or perhaps because of) his close friendship with Eisenhower, he completely misread the signals emanating from Washington, which made it plain that there would be no American support for armed British intervention. At the outset, he was resolutely in favour of prompt and vigorous military action. Yet it was he who effectively brought the operation to a halt by insisting that, without American financial support, it could no longer be afforded. In Harold Wilson's caustic phrase, Macmillan was 'first in, first out' at Suez, changing almost overnight from being super-hawk to super-dove. But if Macmillan performed badly, the Prime Minister and his heir apparent did even worse. Eden was ravaged by illness, and was soon forced to resign; and Butler, who was afflicted by a viral infection, and still recovering from the death of his adored wife, seemed aloof, detached, indecisive and indiscreet.

Macmillan, by contrast, may have changed his mind; but he never seemed irresolute. And when the prospect of the premiership finally and unexpectedly opened up, he seized the opportunity, and pressed home his claim.

Even summarised thus briefly, this was a truly extraordinary career, only rivalled (as Macmillan himself was sometimes wont to point out) by Disraeli's in its long, hard years of futile disappointment, eventually redeemed by the final triumph that nevertheless came too late. Beyond doubt, Macmillan was courageous and cunning, determined and hard-working. But as Horne makes abundantly plain, the most remarkable thing about him was not that he became prime minister very late in life, but that he ever became prime minister at all. Indeed, until 1945 – or perhaps even 1955 – Macmillan himself does not seem to have believed it was a realistic possibility, and there can be no doubt that he was quite correct in this opinion. His wife's affair with Boothby was widely known, and must have been a great political liability. (In our own less discreet and more censorious era, it would surely have finished both men off completely.) He antagonised most of the leading figures of the Tory Party, from Baldwin and Chamberlain to Eden and Butler. Before 1940 he was easily dismissed as an unorthodox and insignificant rebel, and during the next fifteen years, his ministerial experience was relatively limited. So how did he ever manage to climb to what Disraeli called the top of the greasy pole at all?

Quite correctly, Horne answers this question by stressing two elements which are often so important in political life, but which historians are inclined to underrate: namely willpower and luck. In terms of his own ambition, it seems clear that the more unhappy Macmillan's private life became, the more it strengthened his public resolve to win. Lady Dorothy Cavendish seems to have been the only woman – with the significant exception of his mother – that Macmillan ever really loved. Yet she clearly found him to be sexually inadequate, and it humiliated him deeply that he was thus dishonoured and cuckolded. From the late 1920s, he never seems to have enjoyed physical relations with anyone else. Nor did his children bring him solace or comfort. He was too busy in politics or publishing to have much time for them; his only son became an alcoholic; and his youngest daughter was in fact Boothby's child. It is difficult to resist the conclusion that Macmillan's increasingly resolute determination to seize the political opportunities that came his way was very largely an attempt to atone in his own eyes for his conspicuous failings as a husband and a father.

But in addition, and despite his personal unhappiness and early political failure, Macmillan was in some ways a very lucky man. Or, rather, as events unfolded, he *became* a very lucky man. In the interwar years, his advocacy of government intervention in the economy seemed quixotic: but from the changed perspective of the 1950s he appeared as one of those who had wisely and compassionately foretold the coming of the welfare state. In the same way, his opposition to Nazi Germany had once been a minority opinion: but in the aftermath of the Second World War, an honourable anti-appeasement record was just about the most valuable political asset an ambitious Tory could possess. Likewise, in the forties and early fifties, he may have been disappointed by his second-ranking jobs in North Africa and at the Ministry of Housing: but they gave him unrivalled experience in both domestic and international affairs. And while he was as ill at ease in a working men's club in Stockton as he was amid the treasures and splendours of Chatsworth, this meant he was perfectly equipped to appeal to both the patrician and the proletarian elements in post-1945 Conservatism.

As his firmness of purpose intensified, and as his luck improved, Macmillan gradually caught Butler up in the stakes for the Tory Party leadership. In the interwar years, everything had gone Rab's way: the happy marriage to Sydney Courtauld, the safe seat at Saffron Walden, the early ministerial preferment. Indeed, it may be that the iron entered Macmillan's soul as a result of some woundingly indiscreet remark by Butler at this time about the sad state of his own marriage. In any event, the combination of personal unhappiness and political disappointment meant that Macmillan was obliged, in self-defence, to learn those very arts of showmanship, dissimulation and opportunism without which no politician can reach the very top – arts which Butler so very conspicuously failed to acquire. The result was that by 1956, Rab was increasingly distrusted by the right for being too liberal at home and too accommodating abroad (his stand on appeasement, which had been an asset in the thirties, had by now become a distinct liability), while Macmillan was preferred because he seemed the more robust and assertive figure. Yet on domestic and imperial matters, he was in fact every bit as radical as Butler, if not more so.

Thus does Horne reconcile and explain the apparent contradictions of Macmillan's character and career: the shy and private person who became the consumate public performer; the radical Tory who won the support of the right wing of the party; the lonely, long-distance runner who came from behind to win; the marginal dissident who eventually crossed the threshold of 10 Downing Street. Indeed, so convincing is Horne's portrait that we can already discern the themes that were to characterise his years of supreme power. On the one hand, there would be the cultivated image of studied nonchalance and flippant detachment, the skill in handling Anglo-American relations and in dissolving the British Empire, and the determination to avoid heavy unemployment at almost any cost. But on the other, there would be his isolation from his cabinet colleagues and from the press, his conspicuous failures in European diplomacy, and his inability to recognise inflation as the new economic nightmare. All this, as well as Macmillan's final, hard-won, and not quite certain apotheosis, awaits us in the second volume.

(1989)

NOTE

1 Alistair Horne, *Macmillan: The Official Biography*, vol.1: *1894–1956* (London, 1989).

27
Sir Oswald Mosley

With one conspicuous exception, twentieth-century Britain has not been a promising place for self-appointed men of destiny. In the 1900s, Joseph Chamberlain sought to change the course of history, by resigning from the Conservative government, and by mounting a grass-roots campaign in favour of Imperial Preference and Tariff Reform, which he believed essential for national survival and regeneration. He divided his party, and ruined his health, but accomplished little else. During the 1960s, Enoch Powell trod a more lonely and self-destructive path, having spoken out in lurid language against coloured immigration into Britain. Instead of receiving the gratitude of a country he thought he had alerted to a dire peril, he was disowned by the Conservative Party leadership, and spent the remainder of what had once been a promising political career in embittered and frustrated impotence on the margins of public life. And more recently, there has been Dr David Owen, one of the original founders of the Social Democratic Party, which sought to 'break the mould' of the traditional two-party system. But he was defeated in his efforts to prevent the merger of the SDP and the Liberals, is now almost completely isolated at Westminster, and it seems highly unlikely that he will ever play the prominent part in British politics that was once so confidently prophesied for him.

Yet none of these disappointed messiahs held out so much hope, or betrayed it so completely, as did Sir Oswald Mosley. During the early years of his political career, it seemed as though he was truly destiny's child. His father was a broad-acred baronet, and Mosley, who was born in 1896, grew up rich, privileged and well-connected. He was educated at Winchester and Sandhurst, and served in the Royal Flying Corps and the trenches during the First World War. At the general election of 1918, he was returned as the Conservative Member for Harrow, and became the youngest MP in Parliament, where he soon established a reputation as a brilliant orator. Two years later, he married Lady Cynthia Curzon, the daughter of a former Viceroy of India and Foreign Secretary, and during the 1920s, they led a glittering social life. Meanwhile, Mosley had abandoned the Conservatives, joined the Labour Party, and produced some strikingly original proposals for dealing with unemployment, which demanded a more interventionist role on the part of the government, and anticipated the later writings of John Maynard Keynes. In 1929, he became Chancellor of the Duchy of Lancaster in the second Labour administration, and to many people it only seemed a matter of time before he must become prime minister.

But then it all went abruptly and irredeemably wrong. In 1930, Mosley resigned from the government, because of its refusal to do anything about unemployment, and founded the so-called 'New Party', which fared disastrously in the general election of 1931. Thereupon, he established the British Union of Fascists, and effectively abandoned parliamentary politics for the politics of the streets. In 1933, his first wife died, and three years later he married Diana Guinness (née Mitford) who, along with her sister Unity, was a friend and admirer of Hitler. The BUF became notorious for the violence of its meetings and its political programme; Mosley himself made many vituperative speeches about Jews; and comparisons with Hitler and Mussolini were plausibly and damagingly made. For much of the Second World War, Mosley and his wife were imprisoned – without trial – to widespread public approbation. After their release in 1943, they lived briefly in England and Ireland, but eventually settled in permanent exile in France. During the years 1948–66, Mosley several times tried to make a political comeback in Britain. But it was never to any avail, and by the time of his death in 1980, he was largely a forgotten figure, while among the dwindling few who could still remember him, he was widely regarded as being beyond the pale.

By the generally staid standards of modern British politics, and modern British politicians, Mosley's was an extraordinary career: more meteoric than Chamberlain's, more glamorous than Powell's, and more disruptive than Owen's. But what sort of a man lived this promising, controversial, and ultimately unfulfilled life? And what, if anything, was his historical significance? Thus far, there have been only two serious attempts to answer these questions. Appropriately enough, the first was by Mosley himself, who published his autobiography, *My Life*, in 1968. It was engagingly written, and he emerged from its pages as a person of some charm and substance. But as a whole, the book was an unrepentant and self-deluded apologia, which merely showed how little he had learned, and how much he had forgotten, during the course of his career. He glossed over the most disagreeable episodes in the history of the BUF, denied that he was or had ever been anti-Semitic, described the Second World War as a terrible mistake, denounced the faceless men in authority who had imprisoned him, and offered some pretentious thoughts about the need for European unity. To the end of his life, he remained ready to answer his country's – and destiny's – call, when the ultimate crisis came, as he was sure it would.

The second study was a sympathetic and scholarly biography by Robert Skidelsky, published in 1975, which argued that Mosley should be viewed as a significant historical figure. He admitted that Mosley was a man of unsound judgement, colossal vanity and suicidal impatience. But Skidelsky also stressed his courage, intelligence, originality, eloquence and compassion. He noted the diversity of Mosley's political appeal: to Lord Robert Cecil, Lloyd George and Winston Churchill among the old men; and also to a younger generation which included Harold Nicolson, Robert Boothby, John Strachey, Harold Macmillan and Aneurin Bevan. He argued that Mosley's economic ideas were intelligent and far-sighted; that his Blackshirts were much less violent than popular mythology supposed; that his critique of British foreign policy during the 1930s was well founded; that there was no evidence that he was a Nazi fellow-traveller in 1940; and that his postwar ideas about a united Europe deserved more serious attention than they had received. In short, Skidelsky's Mosley was a sincere and ardent patriot, who vainly tried to halt the economic and political decline of his country, a 'lost leader', under whose vigorous and inspired rule British history might well have been different – and might well have been better.

Now Nicholas Mosley has produced a fascinating memoir of his father and his family.[1] It makes extensive use, for the first time, of Oswald Mosley's private papers, especially his letters to his mother, his wives and his children, and thus depicts him with an immediacy that was lacking in both previous accounts. The fact that his widow, Diana Mosley, was not associated in any way with this enterprise, strongly disagreed with the interpretation it put forward, and disapproved of the publication of her husband's private letters is a further recommendation. And it is particularly appropriate that Nicholas Mosley, himself an accomplished writer, brings the novelist's gifts of insight and imagination to bear on a public man who seems to have spent much of his life inhabiting his own private fantasy world. Put another way, this book represents a serious and sustained attempt by a talented, sensitive son to understand his strange father, whom he found by turns loveable, companionable, amusing, warm-hearted, intriguing, baffling, irritating, disagreeable, infuriating and intolerable. The result is a more subtle and many-sided book than the normal filial biography or self-serving family memoir. Indeed, as an account of a complex relationship between parent and progeny it invites comparison with Edmund Gosse's classic novel, *Father and Son*.

Throughout his life, Mosley was known to family and friends as 'Tom', and it is as a seducer of women that Tom first clearly emerges in Nicholas's account. By the time the First World War ended, he had already established a well-deserved reputation as a philanderer, and soon after his marriage to Cimmie (as Lady Cynthia was known), he returned to the pleasures of the chase, moving from bed to bed with even greater ease than he moved from one political party to another. The only women he pursued were upper class, and they knew the rules of the game as well as he did. By the time he became a Socialist, his priorities were clear: 'Vote Labour; sleep Tory' was his motto. Apparently, Tom felt no guilt about his infidelities, continued to protest his undying love for Cimmie, and by a combination of charm and baby-talk invariably obtained her forgiveness, on the relatively few occasions when she found out. Cimmie suffered agonies of hurt and humiliation as a result, but refused to pay him back, as her friends urged her to do, by having affairs herself. In short, Tom and Cimmie's was a recognisably upper-class inter-war marriage, and Nicholas, who was born in 1923, endured a conventional upper-class childhood, very largely at the hands of Nanny Hyslop, who had previously worked for the Curzons.

But while Tom played the game of philandering uncommonly well, Nicholas suggests that his father was less sure-footed when it came to the game of politics, even during the 1920s when things seemed to be going so much his way. Of course, Mosley was too ambitious, too impatient, too restless, and too tactless in his denunciation of the 'Old Gang': men like Ramsay MacDonald and Stanley Baldwin, whom he despised as middle-aged mediocrities, full of humbug, good intentions and little else. But his son points to a more insidious shortcoming: his father's matchless verbal fluency, in which rational argument and messianic rhetoric were intermingled in an effortless torrent. It never occurred to Tom to ask himself why people were so often impressed, but so rarely persuaded, by his brilliant speeches. And the inevitable result was that the words, instead of being the means by which power was obtained, became all too often an end in themselves, as Tom abandoned himself to a fantasy world of rhetorical excitement and impending crisis which rarely intersected with reality. He never understood the dangers of rhetorical inebriation, which may explain why Nicholas stammered – in unconscious protest against so easy a paternal flow. Perhaps Tom did not really want power at all. He was, Nicholas believes, more interested in becoming a legend than in getting his hands on the reins of government.

Between 1929 and 1933, Mosley broke the rules of both the games he was playing, and paid a heavy price for doing so. After one miscarriage and one Caesarian birth, Cimmie got sadder and older and fatter and frailer, and Tom began an intense and very public affair with Diana Guinness. He hoped he could maintain these two relationships simultaneously, but Cimmie was devastated when she found out, and told Tom he was 'destroying' her. Mosley thought the best solution would be to put this latest affair in perspective by telling his wife the names of all the previous women he had gone to bed with – with the exception of Cimmie's stepmother and sister. Then, in May 1933, Cimmie died, suddenly and unexpectedly, from peritonitis. Nicholas assures us that Tom's grief was genuine. But Cimmie's relatives blamed him for her death, and vainly tried to stop him seeing Diana. In the same year, Diana obtained a divorce from Bryan Guinness, and in 1936 she secretly married Tom at the Goebbels's house in Berlin, in the presence of Adolf Hitler. Whether Tom's philandering then stopped, or whether Nicholas refrains from mentioning it out of deference to his stepmother, is not clear. Either way, it is hard to make out the relationship which Nicholas established with Diana: cordial but never intimate seems the safest verdict.

In personal terms, Mosley reconstructed his life with considerable success. But he failed to reshape the rules of the political game to his own satisfaction. He was extravagantly applauded when he resigned from the Labour government; but his New Party attracted minimal support from the politicians or the public. In the summer of 1931, the economic crisis which Mosley had so often foretold finally happened: but he was on holiday in France, and the 'Old Gang' whom he so zealously despised formed a National Government, and did quite well without him. From the New Party to Fascism was an inevitable – and irreversible – step, which put Mosley for ever beyond the pale of respectable public life. He received financial support from right-wing millionaires like Lord Rothermere and

Lord Nuffield, and between 1933 and 1935, Mussolini was his secretive backer. But as leader of the BUF, Mosley accomplished very little. He predicted another crisis; but it did not come. He attacked the Jews; but this made it easier for people to liken him to Hitler. He waged a vigorous propaganda war; but the Communists got the better of him. He put his men in uniform; but this was promptly banned by the authorities. And he advocated peace with Germany; but this had ceased to be practical politics after Britain's guarantee to Poland. Nevertheless, when war did break out, Mosley urged his followers to prepare themselves to defend Britain, and to do nothing that would help the enemy.

Why, then, was he imprisoned in 1940 for three and a half years, under emergency regulation 18B, which empowered the Home Secretary to detain 'any particular person if satisfied that it is necessary to do so'? The fact that he was held for so long without trial was contrary to all the principles and precedents of British justice, and it seems inexplicable and inexcusable that the relevant Home Office papers are still not available 'on security grounds', after half a century. Part of the answer seems to have been that the Labour ministers in Churchill's wartime Coalition were determined to punish Mosley for his desertion in 1930. And in 1940, when there were still demands in certain quarters for a negotiated peace, it seemed only prudent to put Mosley, who shared that opinion, behind bars. But there were other good reasons for suspicion and concern. It was widely – and rightly – believed that Mosley had been in the pay of Mussolini, and it was known that his wife and her sister Unity were friends of Hitler's. He was thought to be violent, militarist, hostile to democracy, and had said terrible things about the Jews. And he was a brilliant self-publicist, who was bound to make trouble if left at large. His detention may have been vindictive and unjust; but it was easily defensible on the grounds of national security. In war you cannot be too careful.

Yet it was during this very period that Mosley and his son drew as close together as they ever became. While he had been at school, it had clearly embarrassed Nicholas to have a father who was a Fascist leader, and in 1940 Mosley renounced all further responsibility for his three children by his first wife. But in 1942, Nicholas joined up, and as a front-line officer in Italy (he was awarded the Military Cross) he soon came to regard war as a ridiculous amalgam of boredom, absurdity, futility and terror. Since his father held essentially the same view, and since he was now prohibited from making any political statements, this provided unexpected common ground between them. They corresponded extensively, about politics, religion and philosophy; Nicholas described his war experiences as fully as the censor allowed; Tom urged him to read Spinoza, Goethe, Schiller and Nietzsche; and whenever he was on leave, Nicholas went to visit his father and step-mother in jail. He smuggled in food, drink and books; they ate in reasonable comfort; and the conversation ranged widely. Mosley cast himself in the role of a good-humoured oracle, and his son was prepared to play the willing student. Indeed, it was enough to persuade Nicholas that he might study philosophy at university, which he duly did at Oxford, in 1946.

The Second World War marked the high point in the relationship between father and son, and it deteriorated rapidly after the one was released and the other was demobilised. Their contact lessened, as Tom and Diana took up residence first in Ireland, then in France. Nicholas graduated from Oxford, took to writing novels, became convinced of the just-ness of the Second World War, and embraced Christianity. Inevitably, Tom's return to active right-wing politics in 1948, when he established the Union Movement, led first to estrangement and then to a complete break-down in relations. In his election campaign at Kensington in 1959, Mosley spoke out against coloured immigration into Britain in a manner so crude and xenophobic that it could only provoke racial hatred and violence. To his great surprise and disappointment, Tom came bottom of the poll. Nicholas was appalled by the whole episode, and vainly tried to get his father to see that such demagoguery only played into the hands of his ene-mies, who maintained that Mosley had always been a racist at heart. There was a blazing row, in the course of which Nicholas denounced Tom's poli-tics and added for good measure that he had been a lousy father. For many years they did not see each other again, and Tom cut Nicholas out of his will. But eventually, there was a reconciliation, and Tom let Nicholas have his papers, which formed the basis of this memoir.

From them, it should by now be clear, he has fashioned a book which must rank as one of the most perceptive and illuminating studies of a pub-lic figure ever written. For the man who emerges from these remarkable pages is much more credible and much more complex than the two-dimensional hero of his own autobiography, or the lost leader of Skidel-sky's well-disposed public life. By examining both the private and the public figure, Nicholas Mosley has brilliantly teased out the contradictions which riddled his father's temperament, corroded his talents and blighted his career. He was a loving husband and an incorrigible philanderer. He was a benevolent father and a bad-tempered tyrant. He was the best of company and the rudest of friends. He was an orator who inspired and moved multitudes, and a demagogue who plumbed the depths of xenophobic abuse. He was a Fascist but no fanatic, the leader of a violent movement who advocated international peace. He thought he could get away with anything, but in fact he achieved almost nothing. He believed he possessed the divine spark, but most of his career was a damp squib. As Beatrice Webb once remarked, 'with such perfection, there must be rottenness somewhere.' And so, indeed, there was: all through.

If Nicholas Mosley is correct, the fundamental flaw in his father's make-up was a complete lack of human insight – into other people no less than into himself. His judgement of men and events was notoriously bad. His confidence in his own powers was excessive and unjustified – except as a seducer of women. He was totally without any capacity for introspection, and he lacked the imagination to assess the impact of his personality or his politics on other people. He never stopped to consider why so few people accepted him at his own self-evaluation, as a man of destiny. He was as surprised when the Conservatives labelled him a traitor to his class as when the Labour Party turned against him in the 1930s. He did not seem to understand that to denounce Jews laid him open to charges of anti-Semitism, or that his connections with Mussolini and Hitler meant that many doubted his patriotism. And he could not comprehend why so many people were so glad to see him in prison during the Second World War, or why his ideas on Europe were largely ignored in the years that followed. He was so self-absorbed, so arrogant, so impatient that it was easy for men of lesser gifts to out-manoeuvre him, with the result that he not only failed as a constitutional politician, but as an extraparliamentary agitator as well.

So much for Mosley the individual: but what of his place in history? Was he the regretted lost leader, or just a loser for whose defeat we should be thankful? One of the ideas put forward early in Robert Skidelsky's biography, which was insufficiently developed in his pages, was that Mosley should be understood as a displaced and disenchanted aristocrat. He greatly regretted the sale of the family estate just after the First World War, which left him feeling rootless and disoriented, and throughout many changing political allegiances, he was consistent in his hostility to capitalism and democracy, those twin forces which he believed had overturned the old landed order. There is much to be said for this interpretation, not least because during the interwar years, many disappointed and déclassé aristocrats held opinions that were remarkably similar to Mosley's: they regretted and resented the decline of their class; they hated capitalists, especially Jews; they despised democracy and parliamentary government; they were attracted by the authoritarian regimes on the continent; and they wanted peace with Hitler. Viewed against this broader historical background, Mosley may most usefully be seen as the supreme example in his generation of patrician resentment, aristocratic paranoia, and upper-class marginality.

For it cannot be coincidence that two figures in modern British history with whom Mosley may be most instructively compared both came from a similar social stratum, in which privilege was mingled with disenchantment. The first was Mosley's near-contemporary, the Prince of Wales, later King Edward VIII, and subsequently Duke of Windsor. Both were young men of exceptional charm and charisma, for whom great futures were confidently predicted. Both were outraged by the 'old men' in power, but were effectively out-manoeuvred by them. Both believed that 'something must be done' to cure their country's ills, but did not themselves accomplish very much. Both were favourably impressed by Hitler and the Nazis, and regarded the prospect of another war between Britain and Germany with scarcely concealed horror. Both enjoyed a very brief period of power and influence, which they voluntarily and almost self-destructively threw away. Both were pushed to one side during the Second World War – Edward to the Bahamas, Mosley to prison – and were thereafter treated as pariahs by the British establishment. Both settled down as exiles in France, and regularly dined at each other's houses, where they deplored the state of the world, and reminisced about old times. And both died leaving behind a widespread sense of relief, at damage limitation successfully accomplished, mingled with a twinge of regret, at gifts wasted and promise unrealised.

The second comparison is even more revealing: for it is with Mosley's relative-by-marriage, Winston Churchill. It may seem almost heretical to compare one man, widely acclaimed as the saviour of his country, with another, generally regarded as a national embarrassment. But in fact, they had much in common. Like Churchill, Mosley was of aristocratic descent, trained at Sandhurst, and was largely self-educated. Like Churchill, Mosley's rise in politics was meteoric, and he believed himself marked out by providence to save his country when crisis and disaster threatened. Like Churchill, Mosley was a spellbinding orator, who was mesmerised by his own words, and envied by men of lesser gifts. Like Churchill, Mosley was rude, arrogant, unstable in judgement, completely self-absorbed, and utterly uninterested in the lives, feelings and aspirations of ordinary people. Like Churchill, Mosley changed political parties more than once, was disenchanted with democracy by the early 1930s, flirted with authoritarian alternatives, and greatly admired Mussolini. And like Churchill, Mosley was by then dismissed as a man who had once had a brilliant future in front of him, which was now behind him.

But there, fortunately, the similarities ended. For whereas Mosley was another thwarted saviour and disappointed messiah, Churchill's encounter with greatness, which had eluded him for so much of his career, finally took place in 1940. While Mosley languished in jail, Churchill climbed Olympus – from which magnificent heights, incidentally, he showed greater solicitude for Tom's wartime welfare than several other members of his government were inclined to do. As such, Churchill was the exceptional man of destiny in twentieth-century Britain, who successfully became the titanic figure and authentic hero he had always dreamed he might be, and who changed the course of history as a result. Thus regarded, and thus compared, Mosley was the coming man who never arrived, whereas Churchill was the coming man who got there in the end. Thank God he did, and thank God Mosley didn't.

(1991)

NOTE

1 Nicholas Mosley, *Rules of the Game* and *Beyond the Pale: Memoirs of Sir Oswald Mosley and Family* (London, 1991).

28
Robert Boothby

To Evelyn Waugh, who 'never had any esteem for him', one of the most revealing things about Winston Churchill was the way in which he had surrounded himself with a gang of 'crook associates', all of whom, coincidentally, had names which 'began with B'. There was Lord Birkenhead, a self-made lawyer and self-confessed adventurer, endowed with unrivalled powers of repartee and vituperation, who became Lord Chancellor at the end of the First World War, but who spent much of the 1920s drinking himself to death. There was Lord Beaverbrook, an unscrupulous Canadian businessman, who settled in Britain, established himself as a newspaper tycoon and incorrigible mischief-maker, and became a piratical Minister of Aircraft Production in 1940. There was Brendan Bracken, a pushy, headstrong and mysterious Irishman, who was (falsely) rumoured to be Churchill's illegitimate son, and served as his Minister of Information for much of the Second World War. There was Bernard Baruch, a Wall Street speculator and Washington wire-puller, whose business ethics were decidedly suspect, and who was far from being the public-spirited paragon that he liked to pretend he was. And there was Robert Boothby.

Among this highly questionable quintet, Boothby certainly held his own in terms of disreputable behaviour and unsavoury reputation. Although proud of his Scottish blood, he spent most of his life denying and defying what he regarded as the stern, unbending, intolerant injunctions of Calvinist religion. Until late middle age, his finances were chaotically precarious, and he never took money matters as seriously as he should have done. He gambled too much, drank too much, and his private life was by turns reckless, foolish, comic and tragic. His marriage to Diana Cavendish in 1935 ended two years later, and this at a time when divorce in England still spelt social disgrace. His lengthy affair with Lady Dorothy Macmillan, wife of the future Conservative prime minister, led to widespread dis-

approval in the upper echelons of the Tory Party. His failure to declare
his financial involvement in what were called 'Czech assets' meant he was
censured by a House of Commons Select Committee in January 1941, and
was obliged to resign from the government. And in the early 1960s, the
Sunday Mirror alleged that he was a homosexual, and that he had close
contacts with the London underworld. Throughout his life, Boothby
never cared what other people thought of him, and since what they
thought was almost invariably disapproving, it is easy to see why.

But while Boothby could compete on equal terms with Churchill's
swashbuckling B-friends when it came to misdoings and misdemeanours,
he was no match for them in political influence or public achievement. He
was born in 1900, and after Eton and Oxford was elected as Conservative
MP for East Aberdeenshire at the precociously early age of twenty-four.
This was a brilliant dawn to his political career, and he was soon spoken
of as 'the coming man'. In 1926, his prospects were further improved,
when Churchill, who was then Chancellor of the Exchequer, appointed
Boothby his Parliamentary Private Secretary. But with his mentor's eclipse
during the 1930s, no preferment came Boothby's way during that decade,
and even in 1940, as Churchill stormed and speechified his way to immortality, Boothby only wielded power briefly as Parliamentary Secretary to
the Minister of Food. After resigning over the 'Czech assets' affair, he
returned to the back benches, and never held government office again.
Instead, he made a new career for himself as a journalist and television
personality and, in 1958, he was given one of the first life peerages. He
settled down to a useful but marginal retirement in the House of Lords,
occasionally enlivened by adverse publicity and acrimonious exchanges
with old friends and new enemies, which lasted until his death in 1986.

Thus described, it seems that Boothby was little more than a colourful and
controversial footnote to the political history of twentieth-century Britain
– a poor man's Charles James Fox, whose private life ruined his public
prospects, and who infuriated his times when he should have been influ-
encing them. Yet here is Robert Rhodes James, himself a Conservative
MP, and the author of important studies of important figures such as Lord
Rosebery, Sir Anthony Eden and Winston Churchill, lavishing nearly five
hundred pages of affectionate and appreciative prose on a man damningly
dismissed by his *Times* obituarist as a 'political maverick of unfulfilled promise'.[1] Why has Rhodes James bothered? In part, because he was asked to
do so by Boothby himself, and has enjoyed unrestricted access to his

papers as a result. In part because he has set out to establish the truth about a figure who was so often in his day the victim of gossip, rumour and innuendo. And in part because in so doing, he also sheds new light on two of the most important and complex men in twentieth-century British politics: Winston Churchill and Harold Macmillan.

The Boothby who emerges from these pages is certainly a much more appealing and substantial figure than his censorious critics allowed. He was good-looking and good-humoured, possessed a most attractive speaking voice, was a witty, fluent and compelling orator, a marvellous raconteur, and a superb letter writer. He was a hard-working constituency MP, who stalwartly defended the farmers and fishermen of East Aberdeenshire, and they in turn were abidingly loyal to him, despite the vicissitudes of his public and private life. He was extremely well-travelled and well-read for a politician, and served for a time as chairman of the Royal Philharmonic Orchestra. He was an accomplished performer on the wireless and television, and the two programmes with which he was most closely associated, *Any Questions?* and *In the News*, became national institutions. And his range of friendships was unusually wide: Lloyd George, Stanley Baldwin, Oswald Mosley, John Strachey, Harold Nicolson, Duff Cooper, Michael Foot and Richard Crossman among politicians; Somerset Maugham, Thomas Beecham, Compton Mackenzie and Noel Coward from the worlds of the arts and entertainment; and Lord David Cecil, John Maynard Keynes, Maurice Bowra, Lewis Namier and Isaiah Berlin from the more worldly groves of academe. Boothby's fierce loyalty to his friends was unbounded, and this, combined with his 'black velvet voice', meant he became much in demand in his later years as a speaker at their memorial services.

Moreover, as Lord Salter once pointed out, on all the great public issues of the day, Boothby had 'been uniformly right'. He persistently opposed the deflationary policies so rigidly and so heartlessly pursued by a succession of interwar governments. He warned Oswald Mosley against resigning from the Labour Party in 1930, and begged him not to exchange the politics of Parliament for the politics of the streets. He was one of the first MPs to discern the new menace posed by Hitler, consistently campaigned for British rearmament, and vehemently opposed the Munich settlement. He played an essential part in the parliamentary drama and backstage intrigue which brought down Neville Chamberlain in May 1940 and installed Winston Churchill in power in his stead. He was among the earliest in seeing the need for a united Europe in the postwar world, and bitterly regretted the lack of enthusiasm shown by successive Conservative governments during the 1950s. He was an early and influential campaigner for the reform of the laws which made homosexuality a criminal offence. He opposed the disastrous and dishonest policy espoused by Sir Anthony Eden at the time of the Suez crisis. He was a trenchant critic in the House of Lords of the economic policies pursued by the Heath, Wilson and Thatcher governments, and he continued to urge Britain's closer integration with Europe.

This was an honourable and distinguished record: indeed, it was altogether too honourable and too distinguished to bring Boothby the political recognition he deserved. Over the economy, over Hitler, over Europe, and over Suez, he found himself at odds with his own party leadership every time. To have differed from them occasionally and deferentially, and then to have acknowledged the error of his ways, would have done him no harm. But Boothby differed frequently, vociferously, and never doubted that events would prove him right, as they invariably did. This was not the way for a backbencher to get to the top in politics, nor for a Scotsman to win the plaudits of the English. As Rhodes James explains, Boothby never really liked, and never really understood, the English. He was too clever, too independent, too flamboyant for his own good. Unlike most politicians, especially successful ones, he would not dissemble, he hated cant and humbug, and he spoke his mind too forcefully and too freely. Put another way, he was never a safe or reliable party man. Although a Tory, he had more friends on the Labour benches than on his own, and when he entered the House of Lords, he no longer took the Conservative whip, but sat instead as a crossbench peer.

Given the subject, the material and the record, Rhodes James has no difficulty in presenting Boothby as a warm and winning figure. But he also makes it plain why so many people in high places persisted in regarding him as unsound, unreliable and untrustworthy. The 'Good Boothby' was hard-working, high-minded, and public-spirited. But the 'Bad Boothby' was idle, irresponsible and self-indulgent. Between the two, the battle raged, inconclusively, all his life. Although publicly brave, he was often privately weak. His judgement about other people was good, but about himself was notoriously bad. He made a great mistake in not taking up a proper career at the Bar: dabbling and gambling in the City were wholly inappropriate for a man who knew and cared so little about money, and it did his reputation and his career irreparable damage. He was fatally attracted (and attractive) to women: falling in love too often, getting engaged too frequently, and fathering several illegitimate children. The causes he espoused may have been admirable, but his advocacy often did them harm, because his own reputation was so suspect, and because he could not be bothered to do anything about it. And there was also about his temperament something so stubborn, so cross-grained and so counter-suggestible that he invariably fell out with those in authority, especially within his own party. Much of this emerges in Rhodes James's vivid account of Boothby's tempestuous relationship with Winston Churchill.

Boothby knew Churchill for forty years, but his friendship with him was more complex, poignant, uncertain and revealing than the subtitle of this book implies. Churchill appointed Boothby to be his PPS in 1926 because he rightly saw in him a young man of spirit and promise. But Boothby soon turned out to be altogether too spirited: he disapproved of many of the Chancellor's deflationary economic policies, did not see eye to eye with him over Soviet Russia, and on several occasions offered his resignation, only to have it rejected each time. During the early 1930s, when Churchill conducted his ill-judged and ill-starred campaign against the Government of India Bill, Boothby refused to join him in his crusade, and their relations, though still cordial, were no longer close. The fight against appeasement brought them together again, but Churchill's intemperate behaviour at the time of King Edward VIII's abdication so enraged Boothby that he wrote a scathing letter, denouncing Churchill for his inconsiderateness and his lack of judgement, and thereafter the two men were always wary of each other. But this did not prevent Boothby from supporting Churchill for the premiership in 1940, and Churchill in turn rewarded Boothby with junior office at the Ministry of Food – a better appointment than it sounded since the Minister, Lord Woolton, was in the upper house, which meant Boothby had sole responsibility for handling departmental business in the House of Commons.

It was a great opportunity. Boothby clearly enjoyed his brief spell in office, and Woolton came to admire his energy and his skill in handling the Commons. He brought flair and panache to an intrinsically dull subject, was full of bright ideas, and his talks on the wireless and his visits to the provinces were notably successful. But although he recognised the need for it, Churchill soon developed an unreasonable dislike of a ministry concerned with limiting and controlling the intake of food, and several times vented his spleen on Boothby, who staunchly but tactlessly replied in kind. To make matters worse, Boothby did not hide his disappointment with Churchill for keeping so many of the appeasers in his Coalition government (especially Neville Chamberlain and Lord Halifax), and he never understood how weak the Prime Minister's political position was at that time, or how great were the burdens that he bore. Even more foolishly, Boothby campaigned to bring Lloyd George into the government, a terrible error of judgement, since Lloyd George was loathed by the Tory Party, and was noticeably defeatist over Germany. And he compounded this folly by sending Churchill a wild and foolish letter, which even Rhodes James describes as 'insane', presuming to tell him how to set about winning the war. The Prime Minister was understandably incensed by such irresponsible behaviour, and sent Boothby a stinging rebuke: 'If he did not mind his own business, he would perhaps have no business to mind.'

It was in this already overstrained atmosphere that the scandal concerning 'Czech assets' erupted. In the year before war broke out, Boothby became chairman of a committee set up to lobby the British government to meet the claims of those British citizens and Czechs resident in Britain whose assets in Czechoslovakia had been frozen in the aftermath of the German occupation. Boothby's motives were entirely honourable and altruistic: he liked the Czechs, he wanted justice for them, and he would accept no payment for his services. But one Czech businessman with a very large claim was Richard Weininger, who was also a personal friend of Boothby's. At this time, Boothby was heavily in debt, and Weininger offered to help by paying him a percentage of his own claim when and if it was met. Indirectly, therefore, Boothby acquired a personal stake in the resolution of those very claims which he was seeking to persuade the British government to settle. But despite friendly warnings, he failed to see the potential political danger of this. In the autumn of 1940, Weininger was interned as an alien under the infamous Regulation 18B, and when his papers were examined, the relationship with Boothby was discovered. Having failed to declare his own financial interest in Czech assets, either to Parliament or to the Prime Minister, it seemed as though he had been guilty of conduct unbecoming to an MP.

In October 1940, Churchill insisted on a Select Committee of the House of Commons to examine the matter and, unfairly in Rhodes James's view, it censured Boothby for improper behaviour. Early in the following year, he was compelled to resign his ministerial office, though not his parliamentary seat. Churchill had clearly been embarrassed by the whole affair, and at no time had he sent Boothby a private message of support or friendship, and Boothby never forgave him for what he regarded as this betrayal. In Churchill's defence, it must be remembered that he was a titanically busy man at this time; that his power base in the Conservative Party was still very weak; and that he could not afford to have his government tainted by even a hint of scandal concerning someone who was widely known to have been one of his more disreputable associates. But Boothby suspected that Churchill had had enough of him, was determined to break him, and callously threw him to the wolves. This was probably an exaggeration. But it was an episode from which the Great Man emerges with little credit, and Martin Gilbert, his official biographer, is unhelpfully silent on the subject. For his part, Boothby had certainly behaved foolishly, but not dishonourably. The trouble was that given his generally suspect reputation, it was easy to believe the worst of him, and most people did. Thereafter, the 'Czech assets' scandal blighted his political career, and as he brooded on the matter in later life, Boothby became convinced that Churchill had indeed been to blame.

In the postwar years, their relations were never close. They came together again in the late forties in active support of the European movement, and spent time together in Strasbourg. But Churchill offered Boothby no job when he returned to power in 1951, though he did give him a knighthood two years later in the Coronation Honours. In the Commons, Churchill once dismissed Boothby as 'the Member for Television', and Boothby was on one occasion thoughtless enough to walk out of the chamber in the middle of one of the Prime Minister's less successful speeches. As Churchill declined in his retirement into sad and lonely old age, Boothby was one of the few people who continued to visit him. But despite his lingering admiration for Churchill's wartime leadership, he had never been able to give him the total devotion and unquestioning admiration he demanded, and in 1978 he caused a storm by asserting in his memoirs, *Recollections of a Rebel*, that there was in Churchill's nature an 'element of cruelty'. In the ensuing controversy, Boothby more than held his own: he had drawn attention to the ruthless, authoritarian, egotistical side of Churchill's nature, which his admirers were (and are) inclined to ignore or disbelieve, but which undeniably existed. As Boothby in turn succumbed to the ravages of old age, he became increasingly boring and bitter on the subject. But his final verdict, though harsh, is not without an element of truth: 'Winston was a shit; but we needed a shit to beat Hitler.'

Boothby's relationship with Harold Macmillan was of a very different kind. They were both Scotsmen who entered Parliament during the 1920s and soon found themselves at odds with the Conservative leadership – initially over the economy (both admired the writings of John Maynard Keynes), and subsequently over Germany (where Macmillan's record was as honourable as Boothby's). They became political allies and personal friends; but they were very different characters. Macmillan at that time was an exceptionally unattractive man – poorly dressed, with ugly teeth and an untidy moustache. He was also widely regarded as being pompous, boring, more than a touch eccentric, and without serious political prospects. Boothby, by contrast, was captivating and debonair, and seemed to have the social and political world at his feet. In 1929, the affair began between Boothby and Macmillan's wife, Lady Dorothy, a daughter of the Duke of Devonshire, which lasted until Dorothy's death in 1966. Especially in the early years, Boothby and Dorothy were irresponsibly indiscreet, and the relationship was widely talked about in London society – although it never got into the newspapers, which were less prurient and more reticent in those days than they are now. But to many people in the know, this liaison merely confirmed the opinion they had already formed: that Boothby was an unspeakable cad, who had now added to his previous delinquencies by seducing the wife of a parliamentary colleague.

The reality, Rhodes James insists, was very different: for the initiative in this affair came not from Boothby, but from Dorothy. Bored with a husband who seemed unable to satisfy her, she sought excitement and escape, and Boothby provided both in ample and appealing abundance. It was at her instigation, not his, that they became lovers, and Boothby was the father of the daughter, Sarah, whom Dorothy bore in 1930. Even Macmillan was obliged to admit that the lovers were also deeply in love: but he adamantly refused to give Dorothy a divorce so that she might be free to marry Boothby. The resulting situation was both tragic and hopeless, especially for Boothby, who, unlike Harold and Dorothy, had no settled home and no family. He tried to escape, and to re-establish his own life on his own terms: hence his short-lived marriage to Diana Cavendish, Dorothy's cousin; hence many other affairs and abortive engagements. But Dorothy would not let him go – even pursuing him across Europe on one occasion when he threatened to find his freedom and his future with someone else. Once in her clutches, he never succeeded in breaking free, and in later life he described Dorothy as 'the most selfish and most possessive woman' he had ever known. Far from being the bounder who had stolen a colleague's wife, Boothby thus appears to have been more the victim of the affair than the villain.

Whatever the exact nature of this tragic triangle, its political consequences were undeniable and important. Lonely and humiliated, Macmillan turned to politics for consolation and fulfilment, and soon began to display reserves of toughness, ambition and ruthlessness which few had discerned in him before. But while this affair was the making of Macmillan as a politician, it was the ruination of Boothby. To the ignorant, the disapproving and the envious, it only provided further proof of his incorrigible moral degeneracy. By divorcing one Cavendish and sleeping with another, he incurred the abiding enmity of one of the most powerful aristocratic families in Britain. To make matters worse, Dorothy's sister, Rachel Cavendish, married the Hon. James Stuart, Churchill's wartime Chief Whip, and a Tory Party grandee throughout the 1950s, who detested Boothby, and may well have worked to thwart his political career. Above all, Rhodes James believes that the protracted involvement with Dorothy did Boothby serious personal damage, by sapping his will and eroding his self-confidence. Even more than the scandal over 'Czech assets', it effectively destroyed his political career.

One of the greatest ironies of this sensitively told story is that relations between the two men remained relatively cordial throughout. Boothby was generous in making financial provision for the child he fathered by Dorothy, and soon after he became prime minister, Macmillan made Boothby a life peer – not, as some alleged, because he relished the black humour of ennobling his wife's long-time lover with this upstart honour, but rather because Boothby's health was poor (he had recently suffered a heart attack), because Dorothy urged this course of action on her husband, and because he was genuinely eager to comply. 'It is curious but true', Macmillan wrote to Boothby on that occasion, 'that I think we have always agreed in politics.' Thereafter, they continued to correspond, and met each other regularly. When Dorothy died, suddenly and unexpectedly, both men were devastated. Boothby took to the bottle with self-destructive determination, and was only rescued by his second, and very happy marriage, to Wanda Senna in 1967. Macmillan destroyed Boothby's letters to Dorothy unread; Boothby burned her letters to him. Thus ended one of the most extraordinary and protracted emotional entanglements in British political history, the full details of which will never be known, and the like of which could not happen again with the intrusive media of today.

For many readers, and certainly for many historians, the accounts of Boothby's relations with Churchill and Macmillan will be the most important and fascinating things in this book, and they certainly give it a wider significance than at first glance it might seem to possess. By seeing these two men through Boothby's eyes, we gain new perspectives on them, which add greatly to our understanding of their very complex characters. But Boothby could only have enjoyed – and endured – such extraordinary relations with Churchill and Macmillan because he was himself such a resilient and remarkable man, and it is that figure, by turns weak and wise, foolish and fearless, infuriating and irresistible, that Robert Rhodes James brings so vividly and sympathetically alive in one of his best and most satisfying books. That Boothby was no paragon, he himself was always the first to admit. That he was more serious, more sensitive and more sombre than his buccaneering image implied seems equally certain. Boothby's ultimate tragedy was that he could not resolve the contradictions of his own nature. Perhaps it was, as he himself suspected, because of some fundamental character flaw: an inner sense of emptiness, futility and despair. Or perhaps, as Evelyn Waugh had spotted, it had something to do with the fact that his name began with B.

(1992)

NOTE

1 Robert Rhodes James, *Robert Boothby: A Portrait of Churchill's Ally* (New York, 1992).

29
A.J.P. Taylor

A.J.P. Taylor was an historian of extremes. His career contained everything except moderation, and during the course of it, he changed his views with infuriating and irresponsible frequency. His hatred of the Germans was deep and abiding, but he admired Bismarck, and wrote a book exonerating Hitler from having caused the Second World War. He saw himself as the 'people's historian', yet he knew little of the lives of ordinary men and women, and spent most of his time writing about the ruling elite. He thought politicians were self-important and corrupt, but he was bewitched by Lord Beaverbrook, one of the most self-important and corrupt politicians of his time. In one guise, Taylor was so clever, so productive and so famous as to be in a class by himself; in another, he was so bitter, so unhappy, and so disappointed as to be scarcely fit to live. Both characterisations are true; neither is the whole truth. A northerner by birth, a southerner by adoption, he never found his real identity, a middle way of life. Of course, he was one of the troublemakers. Not for nothing was that the title of his own favourite book. He made trouble for everyone, himself included. But no one knew when or where or with whom he would be making trouble next. The only thing that was predictable about Taylor was his total unpredictability.

Except in his writing style – which was at once inimitable, and yet a parodist's dream. Indeed, as anyone familiar with Taylor's *oeuvre* might recognise, the opening sentences of this essay pastiche the beginning of *The Course of German History*, one of the most famous – and notorious – first paragraphs yet written by a twentieth-century historian. That beginning was quintessentially Taylorian. It was a bravura display of showmanship and pyrotechnics. The judgements were crisp, clear and supremely self-confident. There was a riveting blend of scholarship and polemic, history and politics. But as his critics hastened to point out, the argument was tendentious and vulgar, the issues were distorted and oversimplified, and historical verisimilitude was easily sacrificed to cheap rhetorical effect. The trouble with Taylor, it was commonly remarked, was that he was not only the master of his scintillating style: he was also the slave. It was at once his greatest strength and his besetting weakness. He revelled in short one-verb sentences. He was cheeky, flippant, perverse and epigrammatic. He never could resist a joke or a jibe. He loved showing off. He coruscated on very thin ice. But as Adam Sisman's pioneering biography makes clear, the prose provides a key to understanding the person.[1]

At one level, Taylor's career was as glittering as any of his finely fashioned phrases. He knew he was a star, and he made sure everyone else knew it too. He was widely and rightly acclaimed as the greatest and most popular narrative historian of his day. He was prodigiously creative, pouring out eighteen books, dozens of essays and scores of reviews. His live television lectures were virtuoso performances, delivered directly to the camera without notes or autocue, which no one since his time has come remotely close to equalling. The *Journal of Modern History* devoted an entire issue to his work, and he was honoured with three *Festschriften*. And he was as well connected as he was widely known. At Oriel College, Oxford, his undergraduate contemporaries were James Meade and Ronald Syme. He had powerful patrons among the professoriate: Sir Lewis Namier, Sir Llewellyn Woodward and Sir George Clark. His pupils included not only Michael Howard, Martin Gilbert, Roger Louis and Paul Addison among historians, but also Kenneth Baker, William Rogers, David Marquand and Maurice Oldfield. His second wife was Anthony Crosland's sister. And in addition to Lord Beaverbrook, he was friendly with Michael Foot, Malcolm Muggeridge, John Betjeman, Robert Boothby and Nicholas Henderson.

But at another level, Taylor's life was as paradoxical as one of those balanced, antithetical sentences in which he so delighted. The more famous he became, the less appreciated he seemed to be. Official recognition never came his way. Oxford University declined to make him a professor, and he was denied the Regius Chair of Modern History in 1957. The state did not deign to offer him even a knighthood, let alone a peerage or the OM. At the same time as his public career blossomed, his private life shrivelled. He was thrice married and twice divorced. This did him no good in strait-laced circles. To make matters worse, he could not let go of Margaret, his first wife, and soon went back to living with her. This effectively ruined his second marriage, to Eve Crosland, and it came close to sabotaging his third, to Eva Haraszti. And although Taylor's public persona was incorrigibly cocksure and insufferably opinionated, the private man was very different: uncertain of himself, often indecisive, easily hurt, insecure, self-pitying, resentful, vainglorious and embittered. Towards the end of his life, he seems genuinely to have concluded that he had been a failure. Professionally speaking, this was nonsense. But in personal terms, it was much closer to the mark. He was always a very troubled troublemaker.

Nor is this the only contradiction which Sisman brings out so well. One persona that Taylor liked to cultivate was that of the no-nonsense, down-to-earth, pipe-smoking Lancastrian. There was some truth in this, but not all that much. For the Lancashire he knew was not that of clogs and cloth caps, but of privilege and plutocracy. He was born in 1906, the only surviving child of rich parents who were unhappily married. His father was a member of the Manchester cottonocracy, a dissenter in religion and a radical in politics. Taylor grew up in material comfort, and inherited and amplified his father's scepticism. He was sent to Bootham School in York, the most famous Quaker academy in the country. He then went up to Oxford, and affected surprise that in the south there existed towns where there were no smoking factory chimneys. After graduation and two parentally subsidised years as a research student in Vienna, he returned to Lancashire in 1930 as a history lecturer at Manchester University. He subsequently claimed that this was the happiest period of his life, and it brought him two important friendships: with Lewis Namier, who became head of Taylor's department soon after; and with C.P. Scott, the editor of the *Manchester Guardian*, for whom, thanks to Namier's efforts, Taylor soon began to write.

But by then, Oxford already held him in thrall. As an undergraduate, he had claimed to despise the place: 'blow it up, after I have gone down,' he once observed. But the qualification is revealing. From the moment Taylor began lecturing at Manchester, he was determined to get back to the dreaming spires, and after two unsuccessful attempts, he returned to a Fellowship at Magdalen in 1938. There he stayed. He was offered chairs elsewhere, including Namier's at Manchester; but he refused to budge. For all his claims to be a loyal son of the north, the only place he wished to be was in the south, and the only recognition he wanted was Oxford's. Nor did he do that badly. He was invited by Oxford University Press to write *The Struggle for Mastery in Europe*, and this brought him early election as a Fellow of the British Academy. He was Ford Lecturer and

Romanes Lecturer, and produced the final volume of the *Oxford History of England*. He was Vice-President of his college; he was elected an Honorary Fellow on his retirement; and his portrait hangs in Magdalen to this day. But none of this atoned for the great disappointment of his life. Oxford University refused to give him a chair, let alone make him Regius Professor. How could the place he loved so ardently fail to reciprocate, denying him the recognition he sought so much?

The answer was that Taylor was largely the victim of his own contrariness. As with the north and the south, Manchester and Oxford, he wanted everything both ways, the best of both worlds. He was foolish enough to think that he could get it, and when he failed to do so, he became obsessively unhappy. He flaunted his cleverness, his irresponsibility, his worldly fame; but he expected the safe, grey, dull men in mortarboards to cheer him on and to reward him for doing so. He liked to play the outsider, the latter-day Cobbett, the scourge of the establishment (a term he is credited with inventing); but he also wanted it to clutch him to its stately bosom. As Sisman shows, while Taylor affected not to care about the Regius Chair, in fact, he craved it very much indeed. In the same way, he claimed to despise honours: yet he was deeply disappointed that none was ever offered him. And although he resigned from the British Academy over the Blunt affair, he was soon putting out feelers to see whether he could be re-elected. Taylor's trouble was that he wanted to have his cake and eat it, to be both *enfant terrible* and grand old man, to rock the boat yet be promoted Admiral of the Fleet, to be the traitor within the gates who also rode in triumph – if not through Persepolis, then at least through Oxford and London.

In fact, and as Lord Annan explained in *Our Age*, there was never any realistic chance that this would happen. Taylor's failure to obtain the Regius Professorship in Oxford may have been the result of academic intrigue, but there were very good reasons why he received no national honour. Or, rather, there were reasons that were good in that they were cogent, even if they were not so good in the sense of being admirable. The trouble with Taylor was that he alienated both the mainstream left and the mainstream right. Although he had friends in the Conservative and the Labour Parties, they were mavericks like himself, on the edge of events, who were unlikely or unable to do much for him. Meanwhile, Taylor offended the men in grey suits as surely as he enraged the grey men in gowns. As an opponent of Suez, a founder-member of CND, and a severe critic of the Macmillan government's policy towards the Common Market, there was less than zero likelihood of him receiving an honour from a Tory government. And although Tony Crosland and Michael Foot tried to get something for him, Taylor's standing in Labour circles was irretrievably damaged because of his connection with Beaverbrook. In any case, Harold Wilson preferred Arthur Bryant.

Significantly, the two closest friendships of Taylor's life were with both men who came from the margins, and Sisman explores them extremely thoroughly. One was with Lewis Namier. At first glance, they seem an unlikely duo. What did Taylor, the most fluent narrative historian of his generation, admire in Namier, one of the most constipated writers who ever lived? Although they came from totally different worlds, they had much in common. Both were outsiders, eager to climb to the top of the greasy pole. Both adored Oxford, and were bitter that their love was unrequited. Both hated the Germans and opposed appeasement. Namier put newspaper work Taylor's way, and introduced him to publishers. Taylor dedicated *The Habsburg Monarchy* to Namier, named his first-born son after him, and co-edited Namier's *Festschrift*. In 1947, he lobbied unsuccessfully for Namier to be given the Oxford Regius Chair. Ten years later, Namier (by then in retirement) seems to have supported Taylor for the same post. But Taylor was convinced – for no apparent reason – that Namier had 'betrayed' him, refused to speak to him thereafter, and even spurned his offer of a death-bed reconciliation. It is not a story from which Taylor emerges with very much credit.

His second close friendship – with Lord Beaverbrook – was no less surprising. Taylor was renowned for his iconoclasm and irreverence, especially towards those in authority, and he had once observed that 'though Lord Beaverbrook has often made news, it has not been news of any significance.' This was surely right. But in the late 1950s, he fell under Beaverbrook's spell. Both saw themselves as radical nonconformists, fighting the establishment, and after the debacle of the Regius Chair, Beaverbrook cheered Taylor up, reinforced his prejudices, and encouraged his innate tendency to recklessness. He accepted gifts, wrote for Express Newspapers, and praised Beaverbrook's works of history with toadying excess. On his master's death, he became Beaverbrook Librarian and Beaverbrook's biographer. Predictably, his book was full of scintillating narrative and memorable anecdote. But it was conceptually impoverished, lacked a broad historical perspective, was far too idolatrous, and portrayed Beaverbrook as Mr Pickwick rather than as Citizen Kane. 'I loved him more than any human being I have ever known,' Taylor once claimed. Which merely prompts the thought that Taylor cannot have loved many people or, alternatively, that he did not know what love meant. As Sisman shows, he hadn't, and he didn't.

Interestingly enough, both Taylor's closest friends were not only outsiders but also social misfits: Namier because he was Jewish, joyless, arrogant and the prince of bores; Beaverbrook because he was Canadian, self-made, and obsessed with manipulating people, turning them on and off like a tap. Perhaps Taylor was drawn to them since he, too, was essentially a loner, who found close personal relationships very difficult to sustain or even to understand. He was brought up an only child, and was clearly deeply affected by the collapse of his parents' marriage. He never seems to have been on intimate terms with his first or his second wife, and was more than a touch dismayed when his third wife insisted that they share the same bed. Not surprisingly, he had very little awareness of human beings as interactive individuals. He never really learned how to handle those who were senior or superior to himself; he often rowed unforgivably and unforgivingly with friends and contemporaries; and he only seems to have got on well with younger people by whom he did not feel threatened. As Sisman candidly admits, Taylor was selfish and self-centred. Neither as a man nor as an historian did he try to get beneath the skins of other people, to project himself imaginatively and empathetically into their hearts or minds. It was a great limitation: both personally and professionally.

Sisman's admirable biography is well-written, fair-minded and fully documented. It strikes a judicious balance between the man, the career and the writings. It uses the limited archival sources with skill and imagination. It takes us behind Taylor's sad and self-serving autobiography, which it renders more credible even as it questions so much of its contents. And it shows us how much money mattered to him. Thanks to his upbringing, he was used to it, and once he started producing books that sold, writing for the newspapers, and appearing on television, he was soon able to earn considerable amounts by himself. But like many rich men, he was also very mean. When he lent money to friends, he charged them interest; and when he had people to dinner, he refilled his wine glass, but not theirs. For much of his life, and especially in his sad old age, he seems to have been worried about money. These fears were exaggerated, but not groundless. His marriages and divorces were clearly expensive, and there seems little doubt that sheer financial need was one reason why he felt driven to write so prolifically. During the late forties, fifties and sixties, he was publishing a book every year or so, and a review once a week. Even for someone as fluent as Taylor, this was too much. Small wonder that his critics said he was often glib, journalistic and superficial. Of course, they were envious. They were also right.

They were also right in their accusation that Taylor liked stirring things up. Indeed, he seems to have invented, almost single-handedly, the job of the historian as mischief-maker, a function which would have been abhorrent to the generation before his, which included such high-minded paragons as H.A.L. Fisher and G.M. Trevelyan. To be sure, there had been dissenting, radical historians such as Arnold Toynbee, the Hammonds and the Webbs. But they were never frivolous: quite the opposite. Taylor, by contrast, was a self-appointed and self-styled subversive in the Lytton Strachey mould. But unlike Strachey, he was a wide-ranging iconoclast. He was sceptical of complex explanations, and stressed the importance of accident and contingency in the historical process. He thought most men in authority were neither admirable nor exemplary: instead, they were knaves or fools, fudging and blundering their way through events. He could not take his fellow-historians seriously, and liked upsetting and provoking them (though he was always upset and provoked when they paid him back in his own coin). And he even mocked his own cleverness, insisting that he never knew what he was going to write (or say) until he wrote (or said) it.

Taylor's wish to make money and to make mischief inevitably influenced the kind of historian he became, and the sort of history he wrote. He preferred narrative to analysis, not only because it was more colourful, but also because it was in some ways easier (and quicker) to do. With the exception of his earliest books, and the Beaverbrook biography, he rarely went in for time-consuming archival research, relying instead on printed documents and secondary sources. He concentrated almost exclusively on diplomatic and political history, and showed little interest in religious issues, economic development, social structure or ideology. He had no time for those who were impressed by the subtleties of the historical process, by the challenges of the primary evidence, or by the tragedy of the human condition. The next deadline was always in prospect, and it was high time for him to be getting back to his typewriter. Not surprisingly, the resulting history was more prolific than profound, more entertaining than empathetic. Short sentences, polished antitheses and verbal flourishes were not the best way to convey the bewildering and humbling complexity of the past. But for Taylor, there was no other method. Given his temperament and his circumstances, it is easy to see how this came to be.

That said, his writings deserved more admiration than they usually evoked, and more analysis than they have thus far received. Whatever his weaknesses as an historian, he *was* an uncommonly gifted stylist. No one else since Macaulay has driven a narrative forward with such brio, such vigour, such elan and such irrepressible high spirits. At his best, Taylor is still impossible to put down. He once described Macaulay's prose as being like tank warfare: 'mobility, velocity, momentum, and the flash of deadly fire'. Much the same can be said of his. And the range of emotional effects which he could produce was remarkably varied. Compare the much-criticised first paragraph of *The Course of German History* with the much-admired final paragraph of *English History, 1914–1945*. Both deploy the standard Taylorian stylistic devices. Yet they do so for diametrically opposed purposes. The one is Germanophobe, scornful and dismissive; the other is Anglophile, lachrymose and triumphant. It is Taylor celebrating the English as he believed them to be: 'a peaceful and civilised people, tolerant, patient and generous'. It was not the whole truth even then, and it certainly isn't now. But it is impossible not to be moved by sentiments expressed with such consummate literary artifice.

Nevertheless, by writing history the way he did, Taylor ensured that he was as much a loner in his profession as he was in his life. During the fifties and sixties, when he was at the peak of his powers, his work already seemed to many to be old-fashioned and out of date, and it only became more so in his declining years. Here, indeed, was ample ammunition for those who wished to do him down and keep him out. His dissenting patriotism and radical populism were anathema to the Marxist left, be it old or new. He stayed with political and diplomatic history, but social and economic history were increasingly all the rage. He stuck stubbornly to narrative at a time when analysis was *de rigueur*. He ranged across the whole of modern European history in an era when specialisation became ever more intense. He wrote readable books and sparkling reviews, when arid monographs and arcane articles were the best guarantee of obtaining a university post. He had graduate students, protégés and admirers: but he founded no school of historians in his own image. Perhaps he had never wanted to. He preferred admiration to emulation. With due acknowledgement to that famous last paragraph of *English History, 1914–1945*, this piece concludes by trying to do both.

Despite his long and productive career, A.J.P. Taylor never fully came of age. He was wonderful but impossible, precocious yet never properly grown up. He only considered his own needs, and he very much wanted to win. From beginning to end, he waged his war of words in pursuit of that objective. But he did not attain it to his own satisfaction. Future biographers may see him as an old-style historian and man of letters. They will be right to do so. That was how he saw himself. He set out to tell stories, to make mischief, to raise the temperature – entertainment at all costs. He succeeded. No one reading his books, his essays and his reviews can doubt that they were a dazzling firework display. Yet they were produced in vain defiance of the scholarly trends of the time. Traditional approaches lost much of their force; other approaches took their place. Old-fashioned history was on the way out. The 'new' history was on the way in. Academic history became less popular. Popular history became less academic. Few now wrote great narrative surveys. Fewer still did so with style, assurance and success. Taylor had written them, all the same.

(1994)

NOTE

1 Adam Sisman, *A.J.P. Taylor: A Biography* (London, 1994).

30

Margaret Thatcher

During the last one hundred and fifty years, Britain has been ruled by only four prime ministers who might properly be described as authentic outsiders. The first was Benjamin Disraeli, an indebted novelist and Jewish adventurer, with unconventional tastes in clothes, who nevertheless became leader of the Conservative Party, was prime minister in 1868 and again from 1874 to 1880, and finished his life as Earl of Beaconsfield and as a Buckinghamshire country gentleman. The second was David Lloyd George, a small-town, petty bourgeois Welsh attorney, who supported the Afrikaners against the British at the time of the Boer War, hated the traditional governing classes in all their snobbish guises, and yet became prime minister in 1916, when he led a grateful nation to victory in the First World War. The third was James Ramsay MacDonald, an illegitimate Scotsman born in humble circumstances, who (like Disraeli and Lloyd George) went neither to public school nor to university, threw in his lot with the fledgling Labour Party at a time when its prospects of power seemed remote, was prime minister in 1924 and from 1929 to 1935, and ended his career despised and rejected by most of his erstwhile supporters.

The fourth of these atypical interlopers into the restricted world of Westminster and Whitehall is Margaret Hilda Thatcher, who has led the Conservative Party since February 1975, and been Prime Minister of Britain since May 1979. Unlike the other three, her name alone is enough to explain why she is in one significant respect the most distant and disqualified outsider of them all. It is true that she is sprung from the petty bourgeoisie, yet dominates a party traditionally renowned for its aristocratic pretensions and enjoyment of inherited wealth. It is also a fact that she studied chemistry at Oxford University, when most would-be prime ministers read history or the classics. And it cannot be denied that her cabinet experience was very limited before she became party leader: a mere four unremarkable years as Minister of Education in Edward Heath's ill-fated administration. But all this pales into insignificance beside the simple and sensational fact of her gender. *For she is a woman* – a woman leading a party which is notoriously male chauvinist in its social attitudes; a woman governing a nation which has never been in the forefront of the struggle for female emancipation; and a woman who has even surpassed her own quite limited expectations as to what, in her lifetime, someone of her gender might realistically hope to achieve in British politics.

Still, for all her unprecedented outsiderliness, Thatcher has time and again beaten the insiders at their own game. Indeed, her triumphs have been so complete and so continuous that they are unrivalled in British history since the passing of the Great Reform Act in 1832. Ten unbroken years in power, and three consecutive victories at general elections put her far ahead of such textbook titans as Sir Robert Peel, Lord Palmerston, Mr Gladstone, Lord Salisbury, H.H. Asquith or Winston Churchill. Not until we reach back to the pale and shadowy figure of Lord Liverpool, who was prime minister from 1812 to 1827, do we find her equal. But he was the last survivor of the undemocratic and corrupt world of eighteenth-century politics, when the electorate formed less than 5 per cent of the total population, and when governments were made and unmade in Parliament, not by the voters. Nor is this the full measure of Mrs Thatcher's political dominance. She has brought her country military triumph unknown since the Second World War; she has survived a carefully plotted assassination attempt; she has been likened to Winston Churchill for her invincible courage; and she has given her name to a political style and a political philosophy, a distinction she shares with no other twentieth-century British politician.

Hugo Young's detailed, compulsive and rightly acclaimed biography was published in Britain at the time of Mrs Thatcher's tenth anniversary as prime minister.[1] As anyone knows who has tried their hand at it, contemporary history is a notoriously difficult genre to get right or do well. How is it possible to be wise after the event when the events themselves are still taking place, when the participants are very much alive, when the archives are closed, and when the problems have not yet come clearly into focus? And to write contemporary biography of an active and highly controversial political figure is even more difficult. It is very hard to avoid the pitfalls of polemic – excessive criticism or sycophantic praise. There are things that cannot be known and, because of the law of libel, there are things that cannot be said. And in Thatcher's case, the fact that she is still in power means that this interim biography is not even a complete account of her official life. The magnitude of her achievement means that she is already part of history: but it will be the second decade of the twenty-first century before we can hope to get her full measure as an historical personality.

Nevertheless, Hugo Young has produced a quite outstanding book, which brilliantly transcends the ephemeralities of instant journalism, and will remain required reading for as long as Mrs Thatcher continues to fascinate contemporaries and intrigue posterity – which means for a very long time indeed. Although he is a journalist with left-of-centre opinions (he writes regularly for *The Guardian*), Young is neither grinding axes nor paying off scores in this book. He is clearly unsympathetic to many of the things that Thatcher believes in and stands for, but he is fascinated by her personality, and very well aware that someone who has been in power for so long must be taken seriously – not just out of politeness, but because the record will permit no other treatment. He has read almost everything that has been written about her, he has talked extensively to the politicians, civil servants and other advisers who have worked closely with her at all stages of her career, and he sets her life in as broad an historical perspective as contemporary circumstances allow. The result is not only a perceptive study of the most powerful and remarkable woman in the world today: it is also the most rivetingly readable account of what Disraeli once called 'the vicissitudes of politics', by comparison with which even the novels of Jeffrey Archer seem unconvincingly lack-lustre.

The essential details of her pre-prime ministerial life are well known. She was born in 1925 in Grantham, a small and unfashionable town in the north of England, where her father owned a local grocery store, taught his daughter the Victorian virtues of thrift, self-help, hard work, ambition and independence, and played a prominent part in municipal affairs. Inspired by his example, the young Margaret made her way to Oxford University, where she studied chemistry, and became president of the Conservative Association. She married Denis Thatcher in 1951, produced twins and qualified as a lawyer two years later, and was elected Tory MP for Finchley in 1959. She held junior office under Harold Macmillan and Sir Alec Douglas-Home between 1961 and 1963, and became Minister of Education under Edward Heath in 1970. But she soon came to abhor his infirmity of purpose, and his irresponsible belief in big-spending government, and when he led the Tory Party to two humiliating defeats in 1974, she was the only candidate with the determination to challenge him. Having conquered the Conservatives with her new brand of free-market, conviction politics, it was only a matter of time before she conquered the country as well, and in 1979 she duly won the general election with a sure majority of forty-three seats.

But while the facts cannot be contested, it is clear to Young that the Thatcherite interpretation of them is not always reliable. Her family home in Grantham was less deprived than she is wont to admit, and her father's belief in big-spending local government is something she has conveniently forgotten. From the late 1940s to the mid-1970s, she made little impact on the nation at large, and shared the prevailing Tory commitment to the welfare state and co-operation with the trade unions. As Minister of Education, she played very little part in the overall formulation of government policy, was herself in charge of a big-spending department, and was far less repressed in office than, in retrospect, she has claimed. Her subsequent conversion to the virtues of the free market owed more to the example of Sir Keith Joseph than to her own very limited efforts at political philosophy. When the Conservatives elected her as leader in 1975, it was not so much because she was a right-wing ideologue, but because she was so obviously not Edward Heath. And her victory in 1979 was more a protest against the Labour government and the crippling strikes of the previous winter than it was a positive endorsement for her or her policies. She may already have had the courage of her convictions, but as her party manifesto showed, it was not yet clear precisely what those convictions were.

Not surprisingly, then, her first term in government began inauspiciously, and with every prospect that it would be her last. Indeed, Young argues convincingly that she was genuinely unsure of herself when she began the job of prime minister: she knew little about foreign affairs, was regarded as a jarring and untried extremist by many in her own party, and was surrounded by a Cabinet full of Heathite Tories, men like Jim Prior, Sir Ian Gilmour, Christopher Soames and Lord Carrington, who did not share her belief in the free market. Since she was committed to cutting taxes, to balancing the budget, to reducing public spending, and thus to raising interest rates, the initial effect of the government's fiscal policies was only to depress still further an economy already in the powerful grip of stagflation. By 1981, industrial production had fallen, and unemployment risen, to levels reminiscent of the worst years of the interwar depression, yet at the same time inflation soared to 20 per cent. There were riots in Toxteth and Brixton, several ministers wondered whether the country – or the Tory Party – could possibly survive such unprecedented strain on the social fabric, and by December 1981 the opinion polls reported that

Thatcher was the most unpopular prime minister since such records had been kept.

Then, in the spring of 1982, came the Falklands War, the successful outcome of which transformed her political position, not just in Britain, but throughout the world. Yet it was in many ways a close-run thing, not just because the government would have been destroyed if the military gamble had failed, but also because Thatcher's record was neither as clean nor as honourable as she liked to suppose. Ironically, the Argentinians only invaded in the first place because Britain's naval presence in the South Atlantic had been weakened as a result of cuts in the defence budget on which the Prime Minister herself had insisted. The two ministers most closely concerned with handling the diplomatic and military aspects of the crisis – Francis Pym at the Foreign Office and the Defence Secretary John Nott – were both men whom she disliked, distrusted and later dismissed. And it seems possible that there was some sort of cover-up over the controversial sinking of the Argentinian cruiser, the *General Belgrano*. But all this was of little account in the euphoria of a military victory which atoned for the failures at home, established Thatcher as a conquering heroine in the eyes of Britain and of the world, and brought her, in June 1983, a landslide victory at the general election.

But although she took the opportunity to create a Cabinet much more to her liking, by dismissing most of the remaining Tory dissidents, and by promoting protégés like Nigel Lawson and Leon Brittan, her second administration was even less purposeful than her first. In the immediate aftermath of victory, Cecil Parkinson was forced to resign because of his relationship with Sarah Keays, and the American 'invasion' of Grenada – which was still a British colony – was an embarrassment and a humiliation. The administration's legislative record was unimpressive, the decision to ban trade unions at the Government Communications Headquarters at Cheltenham was exceptionally controversial, and the sustained attempt to ban the publication of Peter Wright's bestseller *Spycatcher* was, by turns, vindictive, ludicrous, pathetic – and totally unsuccessful. In early 1986, the Westland affair erupted, and the government's inept handling of a bankrupt helicopter company meant that two senior ministers were forced to resign, and that for a brief moment the Prime Minister herself feared for her future. Later that year, the American bombing of Libya from US air-force bases in Britain was extraordinarily unpopular, and it was widely rumoured that the Queen was worried by Thatcher's 'uncaring' image, and by her contempt for most Commonwealth leaders. By the end of 1986, many Tories believed the government would lose the next election, and that a hung parliament would be the most likely outcome.

Once again, however, the Prime Minister confounded her critics. The coal miners' strike, which began in March 1984, was exceptionally bitter and protracted, and the government's victory was far less unequivocal than it had been over the Argentinians. But to a nation long since fed up with industrial action and trade union militancy, it was a timely triumph, and for the Conservatives in particular it finally avenged the humiliating defeat of Edward Heath at the hands of the miners in 1974. The privatisation of British Telecom, British Airways and British Gas was an outstanding success, created a new breed of small-scale shareholders, and coincided with a sustained stock exchange boom. The burgeoning revenue from North Sea oil made possible a succession of hitherto unthinkable tax cuts, inflation was brought under control, and the fact that unemployment remained high somehow ceased to matter. Meanwhile, the Prime Minister cut a positively regal figure on the world stage, not only as the close friend of President Reagan, but also as the first western leader to take Mikhail Gorbachev seriously. Indeed, her triumphant visit to Moscow in March 1987 was effectively the start of her next election campaign, and three months later she duly won another resounding victory at the polls, which gave her the still-unshakeable parliamentary majority she enjoys today.

How far is this extraordinary success to be explained – as Thatcher herself would have us believe – in essentially personal terms? Quite rightly, Young has no doubt that she has been the beneficiary of much deeper historical forces, of which she herself is not always fully aware. The recession of the late 1970s and early 1980s was clearly a global phenomenon, which led to a widespread turn to the right, not just in Britain, but also in the United States, West Germany, Canada, Denmark, Norway and elsewhere. In all these countries, the desire to cut public spending, to balance the budget, and to allow market forces free play has become the stated (if not always realised) objective of government policy. Moreover, for most of her premiership, Thatcher has enjoyed the wholly adventitious blessing of a divided opposition. The Labour Party has abandoned itself to internecine quarrels, and in Michael Foot and Neil Kinnock has produced two leaders who are incapable of bettering her in the House of Commons, and who are generally regarded as lightweight windbags. And the creation of the Social Democratic Party in January 1981 merely guaranteed that at the next two general elections the opposition vote would be fatally split.

But it is not just that Thatcher has frequently been the beneficiary of forces beyond her control: it is also that she has achieved much less than her self-congratulatory rhetoric might lead us to suppose. In the nation at large, there is no recognisable pro-Thatcher majority: at the general election of 1987, only 32 per cent of the electorate voted for her; public opinion as a whole remains unshakeably wedded to the welfare state and collectivist government; and although she herself is admired, feared and respected, she is certainly not widely loved. On the contrary, she is that extraordinary paradox, a populist who is not popular. At the same time, the 'economic miracle' over which she claims to have presided looks much less robust on closer inspection: the improvement in output since 1981 has only just cancelled out the catastrophic fall in production during the first two years of her administration; the decline in inflation owed much to the world-wide fall in commodity prices during the early 1980s; only the windfall gains from the revenue of North Sea oil have made widespread tax cuts possible; and the overall rate of economic growth has been no greater than in the period 1968–73, years viewed by Thatcherite devotees as the apogee of collectivist mismanagement.

Nor are her claims to have rolled back the British state at home, while reasserting it abroad, entirely convincing. As a percentage of GNP, government spending has not been reduced at all during her decade of dominance. The powers and funds of local authorities have been much eroded, while central government has become more intrusive than ever. She may have won back the Falklands in the short term, but in the long term, their return to Argentina seems inevitable, and in the case of Hong Kong, she has not even attempted to stem the tide of history. Despite her close friendship with President Reagan, and her unassailable popularity in America, this does not mean that the old 'special relationship' with the United States has been re-established. As the Falklands War emphatically demonstrated, Britain can only act as a military power on the sufferance of the White House, and as America's attention is increasingly drawn to the Pacific rim, the old transatlantic ties seem bound to lessen and loosen. And notwithstanding her loathing of the Common Market and general dislike of Europeans, it seems clear that the forces of integration must draw Britain ever closer to the continent in the years ahead. For all her oft-expressed desire to halt Britain's decline as a great power, she has in practice done little to avert it.

There is one final charge which Young levels against Mrs Thatcher, and that concerns her very mode of governing. She dominates her so-called ministerial colleagues to a degree that is both unprecedented and unhealthy. In cabinet meetings, she harangues and bullies, and often seems quite impervious to rational argument. She has sacked more ministers than any previous premier, and that is not just to be explained in terms of her record tenure of the highest office. She has created protégés, like John Biffen and Leon Brittan, and then easily cut them down and cast them aside. She has used the most devious means to undermine ministers with whose policies she disagrees, such as Jim Prior over trade union reform, and Michael Heseltine over the Westland affair. Instead of taking responsibility for her actions and her mistakes, she has thrust forward civil servants – especially the previous Cabinet Secretary, Sir Robert Armstrong – to take the blame and the flack on her behalf. Despite her claim to be honest, truthful and straightforward, her record over the miners' strike, the *Belgrano* sinking and the Westland debacle is far from spotless. In the conduct of foreign affairs, she is often abrasive and offensive to a quite extraordinary degree, and repeatedly sacrifices long-term objectives for short-term gains. Above all, she remains temperamentally incapable of taking in any view but her own, and regards those who disagree with her as traitors, quislings and Marxists.

Still, as Young himself recognises, this lengthy catalogue of caveats and complaints in no sense undermines the extraordinary position that she has created for herself in British public life. For what she has managed to do – partly by a prodigious capacity for hard work, partly by sheer force of personality, partly by quite astonishing good fortune, and partly by the cumulative effect of so many years in power – is to capture and keep the political initiative in a way that is quite without precedent in modern British history. She has outlasted two American presidents, three Soviet leaders and four French prime ministers. She has seen off Harold Wilson, James Callaghan and Michael Foot, to say nothing of her enemies in the Tory Party itself. She has remade both the Cabinet and the civil service in her own image. She has broken the power of the trade unions, and put the BBC, the universities and the Church of England on the defensive. She has halted, and irrevocably reversed, the trend towards the increased nationalisation of industry. She has elevated the private virtues of good housekeeping into the public canons of government policy. She is the visible embodiment of petty bourgeois triumphalism. Although the long-term perspective of history will undoubtedly diminish her stature, there can be no contesting the degree to which her contemporaries believe that she has dominated her own times.

But there remains one final question, to which even Young cannot provide a fully satisfactory answer. Is Mrs Thatcher's gender important, and if so, then how? One view is that she is, in essence, an honorary man: tough, combative, determined and aggressive, she conspicuously displays many masculine qualities, and has deliberately taken lessons to lower the pitch of her voice. Another is that she may be a woman, but is essentially de-eroticised: in one guise an amazonian warrior, a latter-day Boudicca, leading her troops into battle; or alternatively a sort of national nanny, always saying no to the slightest hint of waywardness or self-indulgence. But there is clearly more to her femininity than that. She has obviously benefited from residual male chauvinist chivalry, which means that in the Cabinet and the Commons, her opponents do not stand up to her as they would to other men. She is much concerned with what she wears, and apparently displays a housewifely concern for her own immediate entourage. She has a weakness for well-groomed, middle-aged men, with a touch of the buccaneer about them, like Cecil Parkinson. And it is also clear that many politicians and international statesmen find her very sexy indeed. Perhaps President Mitterrand summed her up best when he remarked that she had the eyes of Caligula but the mouth of Marilyn Monroe. (It is, incidentally, not known by which he was the more captivated.)

If, as Harold Wilson once averred, a week is a long time in British politics, then Mrs Thatcher's uninterrupted years in Downing Street are more than just a decade: they border on an eternity which shows no discernible signs of coming to an end. Like its predecessors, her third administration has run into the mid-term doldrums. Her most recent cabinet reshuffle this summer was characteristically brutal but uncharacteristically maladroit. The new poll tax has enraged many of her supporters, as well as her by now traditional opponents. The balance of payments deficit seems out of control, inflation is once more on the increase, and interest rates have again been pushed to alarming levels. And with the Social Democrats in what might be terminal disarray, it may no longer be possible for her to count on the luxury of a divided opposition vote. Nevertheless, if past precedent is any guide, none of this will prevent Mrs Thatcher from winning the next election or, as she herself once put it, from 'going on and on and on and on'. It is just possible to imagine her in serene old age and venerable retirement, ennobled and apotheosised as the Countess of Grantham or the Duchess of Dulwich. But barring accidents, this unwanted transformation will not happen until she herself decides that it should. For Margaret Thatcher almost invariably gets her way.

(1989)

NOTE

1 Hugo Young, *One of Us: A Biography of Margaret Thatcher* (London, 1989).

Acknowledgements

These essays reprinted here originally appeared in the following publications:

Chapter 1   *London Review of Books*, 16 October 1997
Chapter 2   *London Review of Books*, 13 February 1992
Chapter 3   *Times Literary Supplement*, 3 November 1995
Chapter 4   *London Review of Books*, 5 October 1995
Chapter 5   *London Review of Books*, 20 October 1994
Chapter 6   *London Review of Books*, 16 August 1990
Chapter 7   *The New Yorker*, 4 March 1991
Chapter 8   *The New Yorker*, 13 August 1990
Chapter 9   *London Review of Books*, 8 December 1994
Chapter 10   *The Guardian*, 6 September 1997
Chapter 11   *Times Literary Supplement*, 22 December 1989
Chapter 12   *New York Review of Books*, 21 November 1991
Chapter 13   *New Republic*, 24 December 1990
Chapter 14   *New York Review of Books*, 16 June 1988
Chapter 15   *New York Review of Books*, 15 February 1990
Chapter 16   *Past & Present*, no. 147, May 1995
Chapter 17   *Times Literary Supplement*, 7 September 1990
Chapter 18   *New Republic*, 19 August 1991
Chapter 19   *New York Review of Books*, 17 December 1992
Chapter 20   *Prospect*, December 1995
Chapter 21   *New Republic*, 13 August 1990
Chapter 22   *New Republic*, 19 December 1988
Chapter 23   *New York Review of Books*, 15 June 1989
Chapter 24   *The American Scholar*, Summer 1998
Chapter 25   *New Republic*, 10 May 1993
Chapter 26   *New York Review of Books*, 27 April 1989

ACKNOWLEDGEMENTS

Chapter 27   *The New Yorker*, 5 August 1991
Chapter 28   *The New Yorker*, 22 June 1992
Chapter 29   *Times Literary Supplement*, 4 February 1994
Chapter 30   *New Republic*, 11 December 1989

Index

Prochaska, F.K. – *cont.*
Making of a Welfare Monarchy, 25–32,
162
Profumo, John, 251
proportional representation, effect on the
monarchy, 22
Punch (magazine), 93

Radziwill, Princess, 211, 213
Reagan, Nancy, 6
Reagan, Ronald, 293, 294
Redwood, John, 189
Rees-Mogg, Lord, 75
Reform Act (1918), 135
Reform Act (1867), 131, 134
Reformation, the, 109, 114
Reith, Sir John, 227
Rhodes, Cecil, 208–15
Rhodes, Herbert, 211
Rhodes James, Robert, 217; *Robert
Boothby: A Portrait of Churchill's Ally*,
269–78
Rhodesia *see under* Zambia; Zimbabwe
Ridley, Nicholas, 110
Rivere, Pierre, 104
Roberts, Frederick Sleigh, first Earl, 208
Robinson, Joan, 169
Robinson, Ronald, 144
Rockefeller, John D., 215
Roebuck, J.A., 131
Rogers, William, 280
Romania, 64
Rome, 121
Romilly, Esmond, 167
Romney, George, 33, 37
Romsey, Lord, 73
Roosevelt, Theodore, 194, 219, 222, 225
Rose, Kenneth, 29, 40
Rosebery, Lord, 229, 270
Rotberg, Robert I.: *The Founder: Cecil
Rhodes and the Enigma of Power*, 208–15
Rothermere, Harold Sidney Harmsworth,
first Viscount, 263
Rothschild, Nathan, first Baron, 15, 28, 212
Rowe, D.J., 160
Rowlandson, Thomas, 33

Rowntree, Seebohm, 137
Rowse, A.L., 155
Royal Hospital Fund, 28
Royal Marriages Act (1772), 23, 35
Rudd, Charles, 211
Russell, Bertrand, 172
Russell, John, 34
Russia, 47, 92, 221, 250, 252, 273
Rutherford, Ernest, first Baron, 172

Salisbury, Lord, 14, 193, 211, 289
Salter, Lord, 271
Salvation Army, 125
Samuel, Raphael: (ed.) *Patriotism: The
Making and Unmaking of British National
Identity*, 89–95
Sandringham (royal residence), 5, 12, 63
Sapper (ps. of Herman Cyrial McNeile),
167, 235
Saxe-Coburg-Gotha, House of, 6
Scandinavia, 22
Schama, Simon, 104
Schiller, Johann Christoph Friedrich von,
265
Schreiner, Olive, 211
Schumpeter, Joseph, 144
Scotland, 151, 159, 160, 163
Scott, C.P., 281
Scott, Sir Walter, 92, 241
Seldon, Anthony, 219
Seeley, Sir John, 143–4
Senna, Wanda *see* Boothby, Lady Wanda
Shakespeare, William, 119; *As You Like It*,
37; *Henry V*, 72
Sharpe, Tom, 7
Sheridan, Richard Brinsley, 34; *The School
for Scandal*, 37
Shuttleworth, Sir James Kay, 205
Siddons, Sarah, 34, 35
Sikorski, Vladyslav, General, 218
Silverweight, 212
Simon, Sir John, 221
Simpson, Mrs Wallis, *see* Windsor,
Duchess of
Sinatra, Frank, 6
Singapore, 145

Thompson F.M.L. – *cont.*
159–64; *The Rise of Respectable Society*,
134–7, 162
Titmuss, Richard, 168
Tolpuddle Martyrs, the, 93
Tomalin, Claire: *Mrs Jordan's Profession:
The Story of a Great Actress and a Future
King*, 33–8
Townsend, Peter, 6, 109
Toynbee, Arnold, 157, 286
Trevelyan, George Otto, 18; *What Does She
Do with It?*, 11
Trevelyan, G.M., 155–6, 157–8, 160,
163–4, 166, 285
Trollope, Anthony, 123
Truman, Harry S., 224
Turing, Alan, 168
Turner, Frederick Jackson, 194
Tweedsmuir, Lord *see under* Buchan, John

Ulster *see under* Ireland
United States of America: Edward VIII
fears communism in, 55; reaction to
death of George VI in, 59; royal visit to,
63; reaction to death of Diana, Princess of
Wales, in, 76–8; and 'special
relationship', 89; racism in, 92; influence
of, 97; divorce rate in, 110; economic
competition with British Empire, 148;
Britain in debt to, 149; investment in
Canada and Australia, 150; Britain
responds to pressure from, 153; and
'moral leadership', 190; and notion of
'Victorian America', 194; Rhodes and,
209; and effects of Lend-Lease, 225;
Britain subordinate to, 247; recession in,
293; and Pacific rim, 294
Usborne, Richard, 235

Van Gogh, Vincent, 119
Vasso, Madam, 7
Vaughan Williams, Ralph, 93
Vicinus, Martha, and Bea Nergaard: (eds),
*Ever Yours, Florence Nightingale: Selected
Letters*, 199–207
Victoria, Queen: and concept of royal

family, 3; death of, 4; and typhoid, 5; and
evolution of royal regime, 8; expenditure
questioned, 10; aristocratic attitude to,
12; and civil list, 13; wealth of, 14, 31; in
seclusion, 20; Bogdanor on, 21; and
charitable donations, 27, 28; Dorothy
Thompson on, 39–47; and birth of future
George VI, 61; not interested in defeat,
89; Tory patriotism during her reign, 91;
in public life, 100; and Diamond Jubilee
celebrations, 132, 153; and empire, 148;
and 'moral leadership', 190; as a famous
Englishwoman, 199; supports Florence
Nightingale, 203–4; makes use of
widowhood, 206; Rhodes and, 211; prime
ministerial power since her death, 222;
Macmillan during reign of, 252
Victorian Society, 130
Victorians, 129–42; *see also* Victoria, Queen
Vietnam War, 156
Villiers, Elizabeth, 33

Wade, John: *The Black Book*, 30–31
Wales, 151, 159–60, 163
Walpole, Sir Robert, 155
Walton, J.K., 160
Ward, Freda Dudley, 49, 52, 55
Warwick, Countess of, 33
Watt, James, 132
Waugh, Evelyn, 7, 169, 243, 269
Webb, Matthew (Captain), 132
Wedgwood family, 167
Wedgwood, C.V., 155
Weininger, Richard, 274
Wellington, Arthur Wellesley, first Duke
of, 35
Wells, H.G., 191, 243
West Indies, 145, 150, 245, 247
West, Rebecca, 243, 248
Westminster, Palace of, *see under*
Commons, House of; Lords, House of
Wheeler–Bennett, Sir John, 50, 56, 60–61
Whitehouse, Mary, 94
Whitlam, Gough, 72
wife-sales, 112–13
Wilde, Oscar, 191